WHERE THE BOYS ARE

WHERE THE BOYS ARE

Cinemas of Masculinity and Youth

Edited by
Murray Pomerance
and Frances Gateward

WAYNE STATE UNIVERSITY PRESS   DETROIT

Contemporary Approaches to Film and Television Series

*A complete listing of the books in this series
can be found online at http://wsupress.wayne.edu*

General Editor
Barry Keith Grant
Brock University

Advisory Editors

Patricia B. Erens
Dominican University

Robert J. Burgoyne
Wayne State University

Lucy Fischer
University of Pittsburgh

Tom Gunning
University of Chicago

Peter Lehman
Arizona State University

Anna McCarthy
New York University

Caren J. Deming
University of Arizona

Peter X. Feng
University of Delaware

Library of Congress Cataloging-in-Publication Data

Where the boys are : cinemas of masculinity and youth / edited by
Murray Pomerance and Frances Gateward.
p. cm. — (Contemporary approaches to film and television series)
Includes bibliographical references and index.
ISBN 0-8143-3115-7 (pbk. : alk. paper) 1. Boys in motion pictures.
2. Masculinity in motion pictures. I. Pomerance, Murray, 1946–
II. Gateward, Frances K. III. Series.
PN1995.9.B7W54 2005
2004013598

∞ The paper used in this publication meets the minimum requirements
of the American National Standard for Information Sciences—
Permanence of Paper for Printed Library Materials, ANSI Z39.48-1984.

I get bored sometimes
when people tell me to act my age.
Sometimes I act a lot older than I am—
I really do—
but people never notice it.

J. D. SALINGER, *The Catcher in the Rye*

Contents

vii

Part 2. Bonds and Beatifications

Part 3. Struggles and Redefinitions

Acknowledgments

Most people who read and cherish anthologies have little idea of the strange and taxing difficulties that beset those who edit them. This is a book we are particularly happy to see completed, since although it was conceived a long time ago, a number of arcane and pesky difficulties found their way into our path, not the least of which was the problem of collaborating with authors around the world. We are particularly grateful to all of the authors who have joined us here, especially for their forbearance in the face of our many demands and for their extraordinary grace under pressure. In addition we'd like to name a number of people who worked very hard to assist us, especially Rene Bastian (Belladonna Productions, New York), David Desser (Champaign and Hong Kong), Celia Fallon (Notre Dame, Indiana), Nathan Holmes (Toronto), Robert Lang (Marseille and Tunis), Robin MacDonald (Cinémathèque Ontario Library, Toronto), Terry Mallory (Spokane), Euzhan Palcy (Paris), Nellie Perret (Toronto), Ariel Pomerance (Toronto), John Sakeris (Toronto and Santa Barbara), Jessie Walker (Apple Canada, Toronto), and Greg Williams (Lot 47 Productions, New York).

Curtis Maloley has been a patient, devout, and careful assistant in all stages of the production of this book.

And we are happy to be in the happy and astute company of our friends in the Contemporary Approaches to Film and Television Series at Wayne State University Press, notably Barry Keith Grant (St. Catharines) and Jane Hoehner (Detroit). Our thanks go as well to the Wayne State University Press staff—Kristin Harpster Lawrence, Adela Garcia, and Danielle De Lucia Burgess—and to copy-editor Dawn Hall for their help in fashioning this book.

To all the contributors whose work is contained in these pages we offer a special thank you. To our many demands they have responded with unfailing grace, speed, wit, and insight. And they have remained loyal through the very long process in which this book has accomplished its own coming of age.

INTRODUCTION

Murray Pomerance and Frances Gateward

It is remarkable how infrequently one finds an actual definition of "boys" in the literature of boyhood. To be sure, "boys" are males who have not yet reached adulthood, but what exactly, in our society and our world, is meant by this word? It is as though nothing needs to be said about what boys are, or about what makes the category of boys distinct and discrete. Stories in print and onscreen have presented boyhood to us in the guise of an obvious and natural, perduring, matter-of-fact, and taken-for-granted reality. Boys, it seems, are simply there.

More and more as studies of gender find the light of publication, their authors interrogate girls and women, often, and quite sensibly so, on the basis of longstanding and insufficiently explored social inequality. Yet a truly progressive agenda, which is implied in some way or made explicit in most studies of gender and cinema, surely requires attention to boys—not only in terms of the pathways by which they come into adult male agency, the transformations by which their vulnerabilities become empowerments, or the way gender role expectations restrict, reshape, and corrupt masculinities but also in terms of how boys' power affects girls. Even in the critical study of gender and representation, however, male power goes largely uninspected and unseen, an invisible background that "innocently" speaks to the way things are. And to the extent that masculinity has been studied, attention has been focused on grown-up males. What are males *before* they mature? What is the foundation upon which masculinities are built?

Typical of the presentation of boys in narrative texts, and also seminal in its way, is this description by Rudyard Kipling in *The Jungle Book* ([1894] 1987): "When he was not learning, he sat out in the sun and slept, and ate and went to sleep again. . . . And he grew and grew strong as a boy must grow who does not know that he is learning any lessons, and who has nothing in the world to think of

1

except things to eat" (20–21). Clearly intimated here is the presence
of another sort of boy, the one who knows that he *is* learning lessons, but this boy is given no space in Kipling or in most other narratives. The boy we meet in cultural narrative is typically brash and
dirty, covered with oil or grease or burrs or straw, freckled and
wide-eyed, innocent in a way the most innocent girl can never be,
physically agile, fond of the outdoors or at least comfortable there,
a follower of snakes, snails, and puppy-dog tails—which is to say,
curious about the animal world and empowered to relate easily
with it and therefore, somehow, animal himself. And as Kipling
shows, the boy is quintessentially lazy, by which we mean existential. He would prefer to do nothing but exist in the sunlight. Learning is not his cup of tea, nor, if a mountain spring is nearby, is tea.
At the conclusion of William Golding's *Lord of the Flies* we hear
from a naval officer that British boys are expected to "give a good
show," but no boy, British or otherwise, in the land of narrative at
least, *wants* to be performing if instead he can be running wildly
with the wind, climbing the trees for nuts, or dreaming of the
exquisite form of a cloud.

Missing from this romanticization, of course, is the boy's
place in the social order as inheritor of privilege and command and
the specific discourses through which this place comes to be understood and appropriated, its rules and tricks taken in and naturalized. If literary discursions can avoid filling in this gap, since textual narrative being pointed can also point away, film treatments
of boyhood must inevitably show the boy in his surround. In films
of boyhood we have reason to search for more than descriptions,
romantic or otherwise, of boyhood pleasure, and perhaps reason to
expect we might find the links that reveal the details of socialization, the mechanism of the transfer of power, the roots of the pre-
sumption of gender superiority, the foundations of "boys' nature."
As cinema scholarship has come more and more deftly to explore
the relationship between screen images and social propaganda,
surely it may now be possible to examine screen images of boyhood
for clues about the wider social world, its gendered social structure, and the process of building masculinity in the modern world.

While boyhood was defined with relative clarity in feudal
society as the phase of the male lifecycle before the assumption of
full social responsibility, a phase of explicit dependency, indeed,
that led directly into adulthood in the middle of what we would
now call the teenage years (marriage at thirteen, fourteen, fifteen

years of age), the development of capitalism changed all that. In mass technological society, thanks to the extreme rapidity of social change and the benefits to the owning class of maintaining a large dependent work force, adult men have less and less relevant knowledge and social power to pass on to their sons. Consequently, adolescent boyhood is extended, in a kind of unending consumer dream state, with a vast population of physically mature males being denied the full responsibilities of adult citizenship in order that their activities might be made the more predictable, the more controllable, and the more exploitable. Although popular culture, fashion, and mass media have emphasized the theme of mature women taking boys as lovers by actually narrating "remarkable" tales in which adolescents are cast (Larry Clark's *Ken Park* [2002] is but an extreme example), in a sociological sense most adult heterosexual relations in consumer capitalism are between mature women and men who are living out an extended adolescence in one way or another. As masculine youth is extended, and the moratorium on adulthood put back further and further, it becomes increasingly difficult to find the line where boyhood actually ends.

Accordingly, in this book, there is a fairly rough definition of what it means to be a boy. Murray Pomerance's essay on the man-boys of Steven Spielberg only begins to sketch the depths of the problematization implied here, and other essays range in subject from preteenagers, through traditional adolescents (males younger than twenty), through extended adolescents who are equally denied the privileges of full adulthood in a society that holds back from the mass distribution of adult rewards. In *My Own Private Idaho* (1991), for example, as discussed by Matthew Tinkcom, the protagonists are in their late teens. When Scotty (Keanu Reeves) comes into his inheritance he dresses as a grown-up but continues to behave with the petulance and impulsiveness of youth. As Paul Goodman put it in 1959, our society is one in which boys "grow up absurd." What has changed, if anything, since the middle of the twentieth century is only the speed at which change happens, and therefore the now exponentially increased unlikelihood that one generation can hand the world over successfully to the next. Males are floundering in every direction, hapless boys, while at the same time they struggle to display a masculine prowess their social circumstances do not permit them fully to experience.

In film, boyhood has long held a central place. Since the earliest days of cinema—what Tom Gunning has called the "cinema of attractions"—people have been watching the capers of the mischievous boy onscreen. In the Lumières' *L'Arroseur arossé* (*Watering the Gardener*, or *The Bad Boy and the Gardener* [1896]), for example, this character occupies the crux of the narrative as he steps on the gardener's hose and sets up the self-watering that is the punch of the film. This kind of teasing, half-mocking irresponsibility in the name of pure delight—that quite early became a hallmark of the cinematic boy—made, according to Charles Musser, "a formative contribution to the popular bad-boy genre of early film comedy" (1994, 141). Musser describes a number of bad-boy films. From Biograph there was *The Bad Boy and Poor Old Grandpa* (1897) "in which a naughty boy creeps up behind an old man reading the newspaper and sets it on fire" (231). A little later, audiences might see *Foxy Grandpa* (1902), with "two actors playing mischievous boys" (308), or *A Shocking Incident* (1903), in which a bad boy attaches the wires of a battery to a turkey the heroine is preparing for dinner "with disastrous results" (340), or even *The Story the Biograph Told* (1903), where a "naughty office boy surreptitiously uses his new talents to grind away with the camera" at a moment when the boss thinks himself alone with his secretary (355). In *Tom, Tom, the Piper's Son* (1905), Tom is "pursued, caught, and chastised for his transgression" (383), and in *Terrible Ted* (1907) a boy "imagines he is an invincible gunslinger" (455). Musser also cites bad-boy films from Edison: in *The Terrible Kids* (1906), boys are captured by police after disrupting a community, but they "escape punishment with the aid of their faithful dog" (460). *Young Americans* (1907) was available from Filmograph, with "mischievous boys playing pranks on a variety of adults" (486). Bad boys, argues Musser, soon enough found their way into westerns.

In the silent films of the 1920s, we find a smattering of boys, although in general the silent screen tended to be populated with dramatic, indeed hyperdramatic, adults. But George D. Baker's *The Lion's Den* (1919) and Robert F. McGowan's *Our Gang* bring boys' attitudes, postures, and responses to the fore. More boys populate the screen after the birth of sound, in the "Our Gang" sequels, for example (1935 and 1937), in Jean Vigo's provocative *Zero for Conduct* (*Zéro de conduite* [1933]), which chronicles life troubles in a run-down boarding school for boys, and in "Dead End Kids" films such as *Little Tough Guy* (Harold Young, 1938), *Call a Messenger* (Arthur Lubin, 1939), and *Angels Wash Their Faces* (Ray Enright, 1939).

Even from the beginning of narrative film, then, boys have been seen onscreen as unruly tikes, agents of aggression, symbols of the collapse of the civilized forces of nature as contradistinguished from refined products of socialization and control. Inherent in screen boyishness has been a disregard for limitation, a spontaneous expression of freedom, a mocking wit, in general a stylishly choreographed antisocial impulse. And the end product of screen boyhood, the screened man, is either a grown-up continuity of what he always was—blithe rogue, tongue-in-cheek and lovable criminal, awkward adventurer, all of these adamantly presexual and Panic— or a cop-out, a prisoner of the culture he had once fought in the mud puddles but could at some crucial point of transference and surrender resist no longer. Jeff Goldblum has very frequently typified the former onscreen, as did Jimmy Cagney and as do Bruce Willis and Robin Williams. Paul Newman, after *Butch Cassidy and the Sundance Kid* (1969), is the man who has forgotten his boyhood, like Tom Cruise in virtually every role after *All the Right Moves* (1983), like John Malkovich, like Clint Eastwood.

The presexuality, or asexuality, of screen boys is an important characteristic in that it can function to free them from one whole field of narrative requirements or to imprison them in another. It is vital to our understanding of Luke Skywalker, for example, that he should be, instead of sexually precocious like Ferris Bueller, awkward and uninformed. If he is no mature choice for Princess Leia, neither is the slightly older, but equally rambunctious, Han Solo. Bueller, for his part, is trapped by his own horniness, and the film in which he plays is worked out as a coming-of-age narrative. In *Rebel Without a Cause* (1955), Jim Stark's sustained and withheld sexuality is one of the forces "tearing him apart." Further, the lack of sexual commitment makes boys seem appropriate in performing borderline asocial activity, so that the boy prankster, the scofflaw, or the criminal tike is commonplace. In the 1930s this was especially true, as in the case of William Wyler's *Dead End* (1937), Norman Taurog's *Boys Town* (1938), or Michael Curtiz's *Angels with Dirty Faces* (1938), where Frankie Burke and William Tracy struggle in Hell's Kitchen to grow up into James Cagney and Pat O'Brien; and in the case of the Andy Hardy films, which sold audiences a grinning, brashly mischievous, irrepressible—yet thoroughly well-behaved—boyhood through the agency of Mickey Rooney: *A Family Affair* (George B. Seitz, 1937), *Love Finds Andy Hardy* (George B. Seitz, 1938), *You're Only Young Once* (George B. Seitz, 1938),

Judge Hardy's Children (George B. Seitz, 1938), *Andy Hardy Gets Spring Fever* (W. S. Van Dyke, 1939) and *Babes in Arms* (Busby Berkeley, 1939). *The Healer* (Reginald Barker, 1935), and *Hoosier Schoolboy* (William Nigh, 1937), two early Mickey Rooney B-features, were re-released after the success of the Andy Hardy films.

Historically, boys onscreen are as often as not associated with traditional genres. Douglas Croft is stunningly energetic and self-possessed as the youthful George M. Cohan in Michael Curtiz's *Yankee Doodle Dandy* (1942), especially in the sequence where he performs *Peck's Bad Boy* onstage with a little too much ego and must be reprimanded later in the dressing room by his father (Walter Huston). Melodramas display the callow (and typically abandoned) boy—one who comes immediately to mind is Darryl Hickman as the crippled Danny Harland in John M. Stahl's *Leave Her to Heaven* (1945); another is Lew Ayres as Ned Seton in George Cukor's *Holiday* (1938). In Hitchcock (a genre unto himself) there are numerous important boys, typically understudied in criticism: the boy with the bomb in *Sabotage* (1936), the younger brother in *Shadow of a Doubt* (1943), the prankster boys of *Rope* too perverse to acknowledge their own immorality (1949), "poor Reggie" in *Suspicion* (1941), J. B.'s unfortunate brother, a mere invocation and yet the center of the story in *Spellbound* (1945), Hank McKenna in *The Man Who Knew Too Much* (1956), and so on. Hitchcock is the creator of what may be the most famous screen boy, the boy who can never leave his mother, Norman Bates (1960), the boy who will never be born. In these pages, Nicole Marie Keating invokes the mamma's boy in more contemporary, and equally disturbing, films.

In the western, the young or very young man learning how to handle a gun, how to look other men in the eye, how to aim with his own eye, and how to be with women at the side of a lone morally upright hero was made archetypal by Jack Beutel as Billy the Kid learning the ropes by trying to outfox his mentor and friend Doc Holliday (Walter Huston) in Howard Hughes's *The Outlaw* (1943). Soon, Howard Hawks began a chain of boy-developing-into-man-in-the-west sagas with *Red River* (1948), where Montgomery Clift and John Ireland struggle with each other under the tutelage of John Wayne; to be followed by such other pupils of Wayne as Rick Nelson in *Rio Bravo* (1959) and James Caan in *El Dorado* (1967). Jeffrey Hunter apprentices with Wayne in Ford's *The Searchers* (1956), showing himself to be clumsy in love with Vera Miles and somewhat clumsy in loyalty to Natalie Wood; Harry

Carey Jr. is a different kind of boy in this film, robust, taciturn, eager, devoted, and totally out of his league. The Horst Buchholz more or less takes off on Nelson in John Sturges's *The Magnificent Seven* (1960) and, of course, in 1953, Brandon de Wilde is archetypal against Alan Ladd as the hero-struck Joey in George Stevens's *Shane* (1953). All of these cow-boys are boisterous, energetic, awkward though well-intentioned, uncivilized yet magnetic, presexual or at least sexually unknown, and beautiful to look at.

In sci-fi and fantasy we have the aforementioned Luke Skywalker (Mark Hamill), the ultimate space-boy, confronting the father, learning love, racing across the universe for pursuits noble and death-defying, and studying life at the side of a little green tutor to end all tutors (is he not?). Other boys of sci-fi include the computer genius-nerd David Lightman (Matthew Broderick) in *WarGames* (1983), the videogaming Alex Rogan (Lance Guest) in *The Last Starfighter* (1984), the romantic and princely Jack (Tom Cruise) in *Legend* (1985), the centrally important John Connor (Edward Furlong) in *Terminator 2: Judgment Day* (1991), Casper Van Dien, Jake Busey, and Neil Patrick Harris in *Starship Troopers* (1997), the heroic Leo Beiderman (Elijah Wood) in *Deep Impact* (1998), not to mention Elijah Wood portraying Frodo Baggins's continuing trauma in the *Lord of the Rings* cycle or Daniel Radcliffe's portraying Harry Potter's.

In horror film, the tender (and often beautiful) boy is an ideal victim, actual or threatened, and an equally ideal source of horror: Michael Landon in *I Was a Teenage Werewolf* (1957), Steve McQueen in *The Blob* (1958), Harvey Stephens as a boy antichrist in *The Omen* (1976), Johnny Depp as the archetypal boy who'd rather not get out of bed in *A Nightmare on Elm Street* (1984), vampirish Kiefer Sutherland and crowd in *The Lost Boys* (1987), or Haley Joel Osment as the boy everyone's dying to get close to in *The Sixth Sense* (1999). In action film, we can find Patrick Swayze, C. Thomas Howell, and Charlie Sheen in *Red Dawn* (1984), Jason Gedrick in *Iron Eagle* (1986), Sean Astin, Wil Wheaton, and friends in *Toy Soldiers* (1991), and Tobey Maguire and James Franco in *Spider-Man* (2002).

If boy heroes are legion in the history of cinema they have come to hold a central place in blockbuster cinema of the 1980s and beyond, originally, perhaps, because of the boyishness of the directors who framed them. Spielberg, Lucas, Milius, Avildsen, Cameron—all these had learned cinema as boys, apprenticing at the side of the masters much as contemporary Montgomery Clifts watching the every move of some contemporary directorial "John Wayne." What has emerged is the boy blockbuster—from *Home Alone* (1990–97) and *The Sixth Sense* to *Titanic* (1997), *Spider-Man* (2002), and *Lord of the Rings* (2001–2003). And rampant in cinema, too, are boy box office kings, or at least consistent attractions who came to fame playing boys: Ben or Casey Affleck, Sean Astin, Christian Bale, Orlando Bloom, Matthew Broderick, Rob Brown, Tom Cruise, Ice Cube, John Cusack, Matt Damon, Jeremy Davies, Johnny Depp, Leonardo DiCaprio, Vin Diesel, Emilio Estevez, Laurence Fishburne, Michael J. Fox, Brendan Fraser, Leif Garrett, Crispin Glover, Cuba Gooding Jr., Topher Grace, Seth Green, Jake Gyllenhaal, Anthony Michael Hall, Josh Hartnett, Cole Hauser, Ethan Hawke, C. Thomas Howell, Joshua Jackson, Ashton Kutcher, Jean-Pierre Léaud, Heath Ledger, Robert Sean Leonard, Rob Lowe, Ralph Macchio, Tobey Maguire, Andrew McCarthy, Matthew McConaughey, Ewan McGregor, Judd Nelson, Edward Norton, Ryan Phillippe, Joaquin or River Phoenix, Keanu Reeves, Mickey Roarke, Tupac Shakur, Kerr Smith, Will Smith, Patrick Swayze, Eric Thal, John Travolta, James Van Der Beek, Forest Whitaker, Elijah Wood; not to mention Kieran, Macaulay, or Rory Culkin, Charlie Korsmo, Jonathan Lipnicki, Jake Lloyd, Haley Joel Osment, or the ubiquitous Bart Simpson. About the last, indeed, the *National Post* prints a story on January 23, 2003, by Julie Smyth to report that teachers "should allow boys . . . to relate school texts to television shows such as the *Simpsons*" since, apparently, "boys do read, they just don't read books" (A1).

Considerable scholarship has focused on gender studies in general and there is a notable body of recent literature on masculinities. However, virtually no material has appeared in print in an organized and schematic way to discuss aspects of boyhood itself, especially boyhood onscreen. Paul Smith's *Boys*, a broad and interesting collection to be sure, is not focused on cinema. In particular, the process whereby masculinities are socially, historically, economically, aesthetically, and psychologically created in male coming-of-age as depicted onscreen has not been the subject of a multivocal treatment such as is found in these pages, where a range of boys is studied from a range of interesting perspectives. The development of young masculine sexuality is still a cultural taboo of sorts, and for the most part filmic investigations of boyhood are restricted to narrativizing boys as agents of violence, aggression, or withdrawal (*Basketball Diaries* [1995], *Menace II Society* [1993], *Kids* [1995], *Cruel Intentions* [1999]) or as routinely glossed agents of screen romance (*Titanic* [1997], *She's All That* [1999]) or as the butts of ridicule in coming-of-age comedies (*American Pie* [1999], *Porky's* [1982], *Cooley High* [1975]).

At a time when youth dominates all forms of popular culture, and when Western society is structured through an extended adolescence—in which decision-making more and more comes into the province of males who have not achieved maturity, and in which the baby boomer generation has parented a generation of boys now coming of age and watching their prototypes come of age onscreen—this seems an extremely rich territory for investigation. In an era when people are eager to watch films such as *Dead Poets Society* (1989), *The Cider House Rules* (1999), or *Lord of the Rings*—merely to suggest some of the many titles of boy films on the market—a close examination of screen boyhood is needed more than ever. The intersections of boys and class, boys and race, boys and gender identity, boys and social power all merit the kind of attention they receive in the essays in this book.

As dudes and daredevils and delinquents, as masturbators and mamma's boys and masqueraders, as homophobic and homophilic, as paragons of Englishness and Frenchness, Japaneseness, Chineseness, Jewishness, or Hindiness, as truant and traumatized, as colonized, exploited, feminized, and confounded, boys have populated our screens, and screens around the world, as icons of movement, potentiality, desire, achievement, and never-ending progress. But they have also typified, now so frequently as to normalize and naturalize it, what Leslie A. Fiedler in 1972 called "a radical metamorphosis of the Western male—utterly unforeseen in the decades before us, but visible now in every high school and college classroom, as well as on the paperback racks in airports and supermarkets," and, he might well have added, onscreen: "All around us, young males are beginning to retrieve for themselves the cavalier role once piously and class-consciously surrendered to women: *that of being beautiful and being loved*" (1972, 202). The boy in our culture, then, has become the beautiful boy. And the boy who loves has transformed himself into the boy who is the object of our love.

In this book we have divided the essays into three sections, organized by their treatments of three great themes. The first subdivision, Archetypes and Façades, examines well-recognized, historically central typifications of boyhood, the most accessible categories for seeing and understanding boy characters. Certainly in contemporary society, thanks to the pervasive influence of media in general, it is through such categories that young males are perceived and subjected to situational and institutional treatment. Discussions in this section focus on conventional cinematic constructions, a useful way of critiquing cultures' constraining expectations based on narrowly defined gender and age ideals. This is an especially relevant area of study, for the films frequently consider coming of age, defining for viewers both the boundaries of masculinity and the roles and behaviors expected of adult males. The cinematic boy, who takes shape either as a peculiar and clearly marked character, or as the central figure in a clearly formulated narrative, is shown here to be considerably more than meets the eye.

We begin then, with Hollywood's fascination for the juvenile delinquent, perhaps *the* ubiquitous archetype in the construction of cinematic boys. Timothy Shary traces the development of the male juvenile delinquent, revealing how the rebellion has moved through a range of thematic discourses while revising, and often reviving, past notions of masculine behavior through depictions of deviance and violence. His essay, discussing scores of films from *Wild Boys of the Road* (1973) to *We Were Soldiers* (2002), immediately raises questions of the social identification of boys in a moral spectrum, their existence as objects of valuation, and how they become defined as "bad." The American film industry's specific sensationalizing of boys' behavior in particular is seen by Shary to be a result of the readiness of culture to vilify boys in general, a suspicion that has grown since World War II in a steadily increasing way. Prior to World War II, "bad boys" were seen as redeemable; after the war, they were depicted as "hopelessly trapped by their fate" and then as objects of an "outright cultural obsession," culminating in the more "explicitly evil" behavior of boys onscreen in the 1980s and the "pointless savage brutality" of films like *187* (1997). The delinquent as caricature, then, has not been a stable Hollywood icon, but has evolved in tune with cultural developments. By the 1980s, there had grown a "new generation of teen cinema in general, with slasher pics and sex comedies yielding appealing profits for a film industry that had been worried about declining revenues."

Certainly when conducting examinations of boyhood, it is imperative that an interrogation of how boys are commonly defined, according to the binary opposition of sex and related gender expectations, is required. Cordula Quint provides such an inquiry in her analysis of the Belgian film *Ma Vie en rose*, a film concerned with gender norms challenged by a boy in his struggle to create and maintain a transgender identity in a climate of what Monique Wittig has called "compulsory heterosexuality." At a time when "coming out as queer was often a high-profile, 'hip,' and even satirized media event," *Ma Vie en rose*, Quint shows, openly confronts the violation of a boy's innocence through both community and family pressures. Quint's analysis of this fascinating film reveals the importance for any serious consideration of boyhood onscreen of attention to the emergence of queer agency. The problems of the boy here ultimately constitute a "crisis of masculinity."

This intersection of construction, classification, and social control is continued in a study of the fat boy and his function in ensemble films. Jerry Mosher's study reveals the changing medical and cultural attitudes toward obesity, and how the fat boy's presence onscreen as both comic figure and provider of nurturance is central to a number of boy ensemble films. Included in his wide-ranging discussion are such films as *The Bad News Bears, Our Gang, Little Men, Stand by Me, The Goonies*, and *Lord of the Flies*. If the fat boy "has traditionally been the object of scorn," Mosher shows that he has "also been a reliable and occasionally charismatic character in American cinema," since for well over a hundred years the fat body "was valued as a marker of health, prosperity, and authority" as well as a marker of deviance. Inspired by the fact that the fat boy onscreen is as scarcely studied as he is enjoyed by distanced viewers, Mosher concludes that "his embodied deviance and perceived femininity represent a troubling future for American masculinity."

Recalling Huck Finn and Tom Sawyer, the southern boy of American film is an archetype that calls up historical memory, cultural schism, and nostalgia. Mary O'Shea's chapter, which examines the coming of age of Southern boys in films such as *The Client, Rambling Rose, The War, Frailty*, and *Crazy in Alabama*, focuses attention on the Southern boy as an often idealized icon of cultural nostalgia. The intersection of race, gender, age, and myths of the American South in narratives of wide variation, reveals similar trajectories in their depictions not only of boys but also of older women and their role as a principal means of boys' maturation. If in "southern boy" films, the present is reinvented "through a freshly idealized past," ultimately, still, the new worlds shaped by and for southern boys are patriarchal in the extreme, with females relegated to their margins. The nostalgia evoked by the Southern boy is a reactionary impulse, and O'Shea's analysis suggests that a culture eager to accept such nostalgic narratives looks backward as it moves toward the future. The agency of this regard is the central boy character, "bearer of nostalgic impulses."

No book on boys and the cinema would be complete without an examination of the filmmaker whose work is perhaps the most controversial depiction of boys in the contemporary cinema, Larry Clark. In his study of *Kids, Bully,* and *Another Day in Paradise,* Sudhir Mahadevan draws from themes consistent in Clark's work as a photographer to raise the critical question of the true nature of the eroticism casually depicted by this director onscreen. To what extent can the boys of Larry Clark—archetypes in their own right, given the notoriety and idiosyncrasy of the artist who screens them—be understood as erotic creatures, as homoerotic ones, or as mere straight foils for a treatment of youthful male sexuality that pretends to reveal boys' erotic links to one another but remains commercially and superficially heterosexist in focus? Mahadevan queries the exploitativeness of Clark and implies that even critical responses to these films may be tinged with the "ingenious" and the "disingenuous" qualities the films display.

The next essay, on the "beautiful English boy," is an in-depth analysis of a type familiar and often idealized, yet rarely considered in print. Dianne Brooks's case study of *Oliver!* analyzes the film as adaptation, genre film, and coming-of-age film with particular focus on the image of English manhood and the problem of staging this in a musical context. Comparing the central characters of *Oliver!* and *Harry Potter,* Brooks suggests that the former is "a throwback to the ways of the old English gentleman" while Harry, admittedly a public school wizard-boy, seems to embody more the contemporary bourgeois pretense of classlessness than the ideals of Old World aristocracy. As "English gentleman," Oliver is in many ways dominated by social forces, but his "extensive experiences of abuse and suffering" are curtailed for the musical film, which renders him "blank and silent." This screen idealization of English boyhood, writes Brooks, "has all but disappeared, the closest contemporary reference being Prince William." Ultimately, then, Sir Carol Reed's *Oliver!* can be seen as a metaphor for the end of the British Empire.

The section closes with Murray Pomerance's "The Man-Boys of Steven Spielberg," a study of the enormously popular, but often unexamined, American director's oeuvre with a focus on *E.T. the Extra-Terrestrial, Hook, Empire of the Sun,* and *Close Encounters of the Third Kind.* The author demonstrates how Spielberg's "innocent masculinity" serves as a gender model tied to the postcapitalist age of technological change and the social forces of historical displacement and intergenerational conflict. Pomerance reveals that in many of Spielberg's films we find the paramount example of unending boyhood—reaching its apotheosis in Roy Neary of *Close Encounters*—a condition in which male children of the modern age find it difficult, if not impossible, to achieve adulthood. The masculinity of the man-boy is seen here as paradoxical: if every male has to be either a boy or a man, "this creature is nothing but a man who is getting away with *pretending to be a boy.*" The method of unlocking the paradox is an examination of the functions the man-boy character can serve in Spielberg's films, among them the ability to move a complex and philosophically sophisticated plot while retaining a certain characteristic chastity, and the ability to reflect the condition of adult viewers who lack control over what they do and influence over its outcomes in a global economy.

In the second section, Bonds and Beatifications, our authors remind us that boyhood exists onscreen in relations, not independently. It is through friendships, partnerships, emotional attachments, and interpersonal conflicts that we find screen boys defining themselves. Essays in this section consider the way cinematic boys reveal themselves through particular key relationships; with friends, mothers, lovers, teachers, and larger political forces.

Frances Gateward explores the depiction of interracial romance in coming-of-age narratives, with a focus on boyhood sexuality and its relation to issues of class, race, and ethnicity. Studying *Liberty Heights, A Bronx Tale, Foreign Student, Crazy/Beautiful, Save the Last Dance, Fakin' da Funk,* and *Zebrahead* in the context of numerous titles dealing with boys, romance, and race, Gateward offers a penetrating interrogation of the racist conventions of conventional Hollywood cinematic representation, showing that the interracial teen romance onscreen operates "to reveal and work through contemporary racial anxieties."

Using Mikhail Bakhtin's theory of the chronotope, Peter Clandfield and Christian Lloyd provide a perceptive, close analysis of Gillies and Billy MacKinnon's often overlooked *Small Faces,* an

intriguing film that links coming of age with Glasgow's urban redevelopment and wider issues of nationalism and identity. The "wee
men" of Glasgow are understood as metaphors for the wee neighborhoods in which they grow up; and coming of age is linked to the
politics of urban renewal. The boys of *Small Faces* are shown to
play out their roles in the context of a heritage film and a gang film
at once, the plot representing not just a realization on film of contemporary sociological conditions in Glasgow but a metaphor for
Scottish life.

Next we have an essay on Euzhan Palcy's *Sugar Cane Alley*,
an important yet understudied film. In this adaptation of the
famous novel, *La Rue cases-nègres*, the young protagonist seeks a
future beyond the harsh labor of the sugar cane fields. His transition to manhood, complicated by race and the postcolonial condition, as Tarshia Stanley shows us, is not without cost, requiring collective effort as well as collective sacrifice. In this bildungsroman
film, it is precisely that transition to manhood that centralizes the
filmmaker's effort: dominated by the perspective of others, the boys
in this film must achieve a form of political and cultural independence in order to grow into men.

Patrick White takes a fresh look at a much-discussed film,
François Truffaut's *The 400 Blows* along with another important
work, *The Wild Child*. Working out of art history and the psychology of perception, recognition, and memory, his essay positions
self-portraiture as both method and subject, offering significant
new ways of thinking about personal cinema and boyhood in film.
For White, Truffaut's famous cinematic boys are artists in the making; and the confrontations of their childhoods, narrated with a
scathing and unadorned directness, invoke our attention because
they threaten to stifle the artistic impulse wedded to the boyish
perception of the world.

The rarity of queer adolescence in widely distributed popular
culture makes Matthew Tinkcom's study of *My Own Private Idaho*
critical to any analysis of boys and varying masculinities. The discussion makes use of psychoanalytic approaches, not only in the
focus on queer desire, but also in the focus on the role of the maternal. For Tinkcom, it is centrally important that the "problem" of
the queer child or adolescent—here, River Phoenix's protagonist in
Idaho—is that "he or she fails to inhabit one of the more powerful
cultural teleologies of sex/gender, namely that queers simply
appear fully formed as adults on the social landscape. In point of

fact such children and teens grow and develop as queers throughout the early parts of their lives." The significance of this film is its positioning homosexuality in a biographical and familial context, and in its showing the adolescent development of homosexual identity.

The portrayal of mothers in mainstream American cinema has historically been fraught with troublesome contradictory ideologies. Nicole Marie Keating further explores the relationship between mothers and sons, looking at this primary dyad in recent American films such as *Heavy, You Can Count on Me, Smoke Signals,* and *Finding Forrester.* Her essay reveals that upon closer inspection, many films that seemingly value mother-son relations are more concerned with the missing fathers. Keating is interested in considering the mother-son bond as a principal one, against the backdrop of a popular cultural assumption that the boy-father (male-bonding) relationship is of dominant significance for boys.

The section closes with John Troyer and Chani Marchiselli's investigation of masculine bonding in the "dude genre," films that demonstrate homosocial behaviors that both produce and negate same-sex desire. Examined here are a wide ranging group of "dude" films, including *Bill and Ted's Excellent Adventure* and *Dude, Where's My Car?* For Troyer and Marchiselli, the dude is a "liminal subject, simultaneously at ease and out of place in the New World," and his adventures onscreen may be thought of as "allegorical imaginings of America's awkward adolescence." Underpinning the boys of dude films, then, is a national boy figure, the nation itself.

Drawing on films from outside as well as inside the mainstream canon, the last section of the book, Struggles and Redefinitions, provides examples of boys who attempt to resist the constraining definitions of young manhood imposed by social structures—religious, ethnic, racial, and economic. The essays remind us that "alternative" films offer alternative perspectives on youth and gender expectations, while re-examinations of successful commercial features provide inspired studies of overlooked issues and constructions.

Gina Marchetti's detailed study analyzes the compelling autobiographical experimental narratives of independent filmmaker Kip Fulbeck. Marchetti provides an in-depth, detailed study of several of his key works, which make use of home movies, commercial media forms, and newly created footage to chronicle his maturation as a "hapa" (meaning half non-Hawaiian). Fulbeck's boyhood is seen by him in retrospect and, as Marchetti notes, "distance makes some aspects of boyhood seem less significant and others move more sharply into focus." Indeed, "stepping back" is a central element of Fulbeck's visual style, and Marchetti concludes that the boy of his memory and imagination must "step back from the agony of living in a racist society to accept himself and his place within his family."

Christopher Ames interrogates the ways cultural anxieties concerning the continuing rise of juvenile crime are manifested in Japanese cinema, offering fantasy solutions to a social problem that denies simple remedies. His focus is *futoko*, a form of truancy especially endemic among Japanese boys. Their dissociation in such films as *Battle Royale* and *Hope beyond the Crimson Skies* reveals tensions between traditional Japanese societal structure and modern youth culture that threatens not only the safety and security of the public, but the future of Japan as a nation.

One of the most significant and difficult processes boys experience in adolescence is identity construction. Steven Alan Carr looks at two very controversial films that problematize notions of fixed identities. The image of the Jewish boy in *L.I.E.* highlights the relationship between ethnicity and sexuality, while *The Believer* questions the fixity of ethnicity. But beyond problematizing fixed identities, writes Carr, these two films are remarkable in that they "find commonalities between closeted or camouflaged ones." The films become radical precisely in their "insistence on ambiguity."

Charlene Regester's study of *Cooley High, Cornbread, Earl and Me,* and *Boyz N the Hood* addresses issues of the feminization of black athletic boys. Concentrating on three cinematic killings that are remarkably similar to one another, she reveals the fraught implications of life in the 'hood as well as the systematic reduction of dignified and strong young black males to passive and victimized status.

Corey Creekmur examines a much overlooked aspect of an often discussed subject—the angry young man of 1970s Hindi cinema. Focusing on the technique of the "maturation dissolve," a temporal leap in which boys are transformed onscreen into men, Creekmur traces the dramatization of childhood in Hindi cinema. The suffering of boy characters there is analyzed as a cultural trauma viewed in a personal and historical sense, with the "maturation dissolve" figuring onscreen as a method for expressing the nature and effects of this. Notable in Hindi cinema is the "angry young man" character frequently portrayed by Amitabh Bachchan.

In a long line of films, Bachchan's character is traumatized as a boy, leading Creekmur to observe the importance of the "continuity his films maintain with earlier Hindi cinema."

Finally, Steven Jay Schneider looks carefully at a central trope in cinematic representation of boyhood, the masturbation scene, as a way of identifying cinema's penchant for reproducing a site of boyhood vulnerability and powerlessness. From *Fast Times at Ridgemont High* to *Y tu mamá también,* the problem of the boy desiring private access to his own embodied sexuality has been accorded little attention, although, as Schneider shows, it is analytically central to many films. What makes the films he studies here significant, writes Schneider, is that "they operate so as to reinforce the negative feelings surrounding sexual self-satisfaction while nevertheless responding to our collective need (especially on the part of those adolescent males just getting used to the act) to bring jerking off out of the closet."

Although this collection contains twenty essays, we can hope to make no assertion that it is utterly comprehensive of the many possible points of view one could take on boys in film, or that it finds all of the most important cinematic moments and spaces *where the boys are.* It does, however, discover fascinating tropes, characters, constructions, relationships, and images from the voluminous record of the adventures of the cinematic boy. Historically boys have been pivotal cinematic figures, and as major film industries around the world increasingly produce product specifically for younger demographics, there are more boys in cinema than one book could possibly contain. We attempt here to address an area of film and gender studies that has gone unexamined for too long, in the hope our effort will inspire others to help fill the gap, interrogating those areas we have not been able to include. As the companion volume to *Sugar, Spice, and Everything Nice: Cinemas of Girlhood* (Wayne State University Press, 2002) this anthology offers to readers the other side of the coin, so that together the books will perhaps provide a comparative examination of gender, children, and cinema.

Works Cited and Recommended

Cohan, Steven. 1997. *Masked Men: Masculinity and the Movies in the Fifties.* Bloomington: Indiana University Press.

Cohan, Steven, and Ina Rae Hark, eds. 1993. *Screening the Male: Exploring Masculinities in Hollywood Cinema.* London: Routledge.

Creekmur, Corey, and Alexander Doty, eds. 1995. *Out in Culture: Gay, Lesbian, and Queer Essays on Popular Culture.* Durham: Duke University Press.

DeAngelis, Michael. 2001. *Gay Fandom and Crossover Stardom: James Dean, Mel Gibson, and Keanu Reeves.* Durham: Duke University Press.

Fiedler, Leslie A. 1972. *Unfinished Business.* New York: Stein and Day.

Gateward, Frances, and Murray Pomerance, eds. 2002. *Sugar, Spice, and Everything Nice: Cinemas of Girlhood.* Detroit: Wayne State University Press.

Golding, William. 1954. *Lord of the Flies.* London: Faber & Faber.

Goodman, Paul. 1960. *Growing Up Absurd: Problems of Youth in the Organized Society.* New York: Vintage.

Gunning, Tom. 1990. "The Cinema of Attractions: Early Film, its Spectator and the Avant-Garde." In *Early Cinema: Space, Frame, Narrative,* ed. Thomas Elsaesser, 56–67. London: British Film Institute.

Kaplan, E. Ann, ed. 1999. *Women in Film Noir.* London: BFI.

Kipling, Rudyard. [1894] 1987. *The Jungle Book.* New York: Viking.

Lehman, Peter, ed. 2001. *Masculinity: Bodies, Movies, Culture.* New York: Routledge.

Musser, Charles. 1994. *The Emergence of Cinema: The American Screen to 1907.* Berkeley: University of California Press.

Penley, Constance, and Sharon Willis, eds. 1993. *Male Trouble.* Minneapolis: University of Minnesota Press.

Pomerance, Murray, ed. 2001. *Ladies and Gentlemen, Boys and Girls: Gender in Film at the End of the Twentieth Century.* Albany: State University of New York Press.

Smith, Paul, ed. 1996. *Boys: Masculinities in Contemporary Culture.* Boulder, CO: Westview Press.

Smyth, Julie. 2003. "Study Says Boys Do Read, They Just Don't Read Books," *National Post,* January 23, A1+.

Tasker, Yvonne. 1993. *Spectacular Bodies: Gender, Genre and the Action Cinema.* New York: Routledge.

ARCHETYPES AND FAÇADES

1

BAD BOYS AND HOLLYWOOD HYPE

Gendered Conflict in Juvenile Delinquency Films

Timothy Shary

Over the course of Hollywood history, movie studios have reveled in a crafty fascination with juvenile delinquency, which has been traditionally founded on a certain masculine mythology. There has recently been new attention given to how the media have represented delinquent girls (Kearney 1996; Orenstein 1996; Shary 2000), yet the historical dominance of boys' delinquency in movies is primarily due to how "JD" films depict the ripe conflict of boys becoming men within a supposedly progressing society. This essay traces the development of the male juvenile delinquent in teen movies, showing how rebellion has moved through a range of thematic discourses while revising (and often reviving) past notions of masculine behavior in cinematic depictions of teenage deviance and violence. The analysis reveals that despite the constant struggle of young men dealing with their conflicted gender roles, Hollywood has changed its methods of generating sympathy for the plight of delinquents while nonetheless remaining consistent in showcasing the rousing thrills of delinquency itself.

Juvenile delinquency has evolved through the generations, and young people find that their acts of deviance must be more extreme than those of their predecessors in order to gain attention. Such behaviors as swearing, stealing, vandalism, and fighting have been somewhat common among youth for centuries, while the sophistication of these particular acts develops within their social contexts. Swearing, for instance, can only be determined by what terms adult authorities deem problematic, and vandalism also changes its nature with its surroundings, since young people need to be told what objects are of most value (schools, churches, cars) in order to select their targets. Class is thus an integral issue to youth movie delinquency, with working-class characters often stereotyped as "typical" delinquents struggling to rise above their lowly status while wealthy brats turn to delinquency out of boredom and in

21

retaliation for their privilege. In both cases, teens must find ways to break free of their class expectations, and this parallels boys' efforts to both disrupt and conform to their gender expectations, as they resist following the cultural order and yet long to prove their prowess through traditional customs.

In recent years juvenile delinquency has taken on more life-and-death consequences, with youth gaining greater access to guns (which allow them to be more cowardly in their attacks by enacting violence at a distance), engaging in more recreational drug use (which may distort their sense of reason), and being more sexualized by capitalist culture (which objectifies their bodies and thereby makes them easier targets for abuse). Other trends have also been factors. With the sharp rise in divorce rates since World War II, many children have grown up in divided households with competing sets of moral views. Not long after the open rebellion of youth in the 1960s, the children of those rebels more aggressively questioned moral standards. And the proliferation of the Internet since the 1990s has given youth entry into a world of sensitive information and potentially dangerous covert activity, although movies have generally ignored this development.

One of the primary reasons why the American film industry has specifically sensationalized boys' behavior is that boys are quite readily vilified by the culture at large. Hollywood has become steadily more suspicious of young men since the post–World War II era, and until recently was portraying deviant boys in ever more threatening ways, as in the progression from stylized gang conflict in *West Side Story* (1961) to drug-driven felonies in *Bad Boys* (1983) to pointless savage brutality in *187* (1997). In most films before World War II, the opposite was true, when the few delinquents onscreen were often shown as redeemable on some level and were usually reformed in the end (e.g., *Wild Boys of the Road* [1933], *Boys Town* [1938]). After the war, as David Considine (1985) points out, Hollywood began producing films in which society became a larger culprit in generating delinquency, and thus troubled youth were hopelessly trapped by their fate (e.g., *City Across the River* or *Knock on Any Door* [both 1949]). In the 1950s, delinquency became an outright cultural obsession as "teenagers" emerged, disenchanted by postwar prosperity and filled with existential angst, most famously in *Rebel Without a Cause* and *Blackboard Jungle* (both 1955). While the sensational focus on teen deviance somewhat subsided over the next generation, by the 1980s delinquent boys were becoming more inexplicably evil, committing apparently random crimes for glee, and Hollywood expanded its exploitative options by pushing delinquency into a variety of teen subgenres, such as slasher films, science fantasies, sex comedies, and even war dramas. Nonetheless, everything about depictions of "bad boys" would change by the end of the 1990s, after the series of high-profile school killings—particularly the massacre at Columbine High School in Colorado—would make any fictional depictions of delinquents not only precarious but also less harrowing than the truth. After Columbine, the possibility that boys' deviance may actually be worse in reality than in the movies has resulted in Hollywood ignoring delinquents, which has stunted social interest in juvenile delinquency overall.

STUDYING THE DELINQUENT

While the infamous Payne Fund studies of the 1930s examined the supposedly deleterious effects of movies on children (Jowett, Jarvie, and Fuller 1996), little serious attention was paid to actual depictions of children until half a century later. The first study of teen delinquency in movies did not appear until 1982 when Mark Thomas McGee and R. J. Robertson published *The J.D. Films: Juvenile Delinquency in the Movies,* in which they considered the social contexts of American films about youth delinquency, drawing out a bifurcation in youth representation that characterized teen films through much of the post–World War II era. JDs are divided into two film groups: "thoroughly reprehensible 'bad' teenagers and the basically decent if often misunderstood 'good' teenagers" (1982, viii), a distinction that allows for both moral idealization (the good kids) and fanciful indulgence in deviant thrills (the bad kids). This is a distinction that had worked rather consistently in the years before McGee and Robertson conducted their study, and it would persist until the mid-1980s, when the moral status of delinquency became complicated to the point of ambiguity. Indeed, this is what makes such a study of current youth delinquency particularly difficult, since the identification of morality has become increasingly judgmental and inexact.

Evidence of this dilemma began to appear in subsequent examinations of teen movie delinquency, most notably in the first comprehensive study of youth films, Considine's *Cinema of Adolescence.* The contemporary 1970s films that Considine examined had moved away from the 1950s images of teenage crime waves invading the suburbs and had started to present more sensitive and personal portraits of troubled youth, such as Sonny Crawford (Timothy Bottoms) in *The Last Picture Show* (1971), Matilda (Nell Potts) in *The Effect of Gamma Rays on Man-in-the-Moon Marigolds* (1972), Deborah (Kathleen Quinlan) in *I Never Promised You a Rose Garden* (1977), and Ben Meechum (Michael O'Keefe) in *The Great Santini* (1979). Yet at the same time, youth "invaders" were taking on more diverse generic forms, like the telekinetic prom queen *Carrie* (1976), the orphaned murderess introduced as *The Little Girl Who Lives Down the Lane* (1976), the deviant victims of *Halloween* (1978), and the working-class hellions in *Animal House* (1978).

None of the early research explored the gendered status of delinquency for teen characters, primarily because the vast majority of JDs until the 1990s were boys. In fact, more tellingly, the distinction between "bad" and "good" often fell *between* genders rather than within them, and thus studying delinquents as a group did not engage this cross-gender conflict. In most JD films, girls had often played the role of reformer, usually for just one boy, and within a context suggesting that female domesticity was a salvation for men's problems yet also a threat to masculine progress. The politics of feminist liberation began to finally change that notion in films about adults during the 1970s, but the inherent sexism of this equation remained strong in youth films until the 1990s. This further weakened the linkage of delinquency with gender rebellion, since the former was always viewed as an aberration, and thus any potential empowerment that could arise from youth deviance was vitiated through cautionary warnings about violating norms. In the case of gender politics, these were norms that often needed to be violated in order to bring further equality (and less tension) between the sexes.

The most specific (if clinical) research on teen film delinquency in the 1990s was in three articles by Scott Snyder (1991, 1995a, 1995b), who illustrated the ramifications of Hollywood's ambivalent tendency to hype JD violence, arguing that youth may be too influenced by the dramatically thrilling aspects of delinquency films to appreciate their moral messages. Thus, even when positive and negative options are presented, the lingering impact on youth remains the excitement of delinquency itself. This argument would gain further credence with studies such as Charles Acland's *Youth, Murder, Spectacle: The Cultural Politics of "Youth in Cri-*

sis" (1995), which argued that not only do youth movies such as *River's Edge* (1987) and even *The Breakfast Club* (1985) serve *adult* authority, worse yet, they delude youth with a false sense of power. In more blatant terms, youth are sold the entertainment of their deviance, which arises from the defamation of their images and the degradation of their own authority. In depicting delinquency onscreen in dynamic and dramatic ways, most teen films are artificially providing rebellion for youth who are told that what they do outside the theater will be of little consequence.

Concerns over youth power and progress were the focus of another major study of teen films, *The Road to Romance + Ruin* by Jon Lewis. Despite some methodological problems in his analysis, Lewis does make the very good point that "the failure of the young identifies the failure of the generation in power to coerce youth into their way of thinking (e.g., the failure of institutionalized, public education to enforce, or at least re-inforce, the authority of the ruling class)" (1992, 54). While I view youth as having more of their own authority in reality than Lewis allows (Shary 2002), I think he is accurate in locating the social tension of youth delinquency in the power struggle between forces of adult ideological control and teens' resistance to that control. And, I would add, the prevailing issue in that matrix of control is gender expectations. Some teen films by the early 1990s began to demonstrate this struggle through conspicuously transferring the power of delinquency from male to female youth, with typically disturbing results: *Heathers* (1989), *Lisa* (1990), *No Secrets* (1991), *Brutal Fury* (1992), *Poison Ivy* (1992), *The Crush* (1993), *Guncrazy* (1993), *Fun* (1994), and *Mi Vida Loca* (1994).

In fact, a sure sign that Hollywood was beginning to change its previous traditions of depicting youth delinquency emerged after the industry began examining the role of race for delinquent boys during the brief swell of African American crime films in the early 1990s (beginning in 1991 with *Straight Out of Brooklyn* and ending in 1995 with *Clockers*). This sparked a surge of film scholarship that examined the racial etiology of teen delinquency (Jones 1991; Guerrero 1993; Wiegman 1993; Forman 1996; Watkins 1998), but just as the new film trend began to fade, the increasing presence of girl delinquents onscreen became unmistakable, and ironically seemed to indicate the ultimate neutralizing of boys' deviance in U.S. films. Films like *Freeway* (1995), *Foxfire* (1996), *Girls Town* (1996), *Wild Things* (1997), *The Opposite of Sex* (1998), and *The*

Rage: Carrie 2 (1999) showcased a new generation of girls strategically using their pent-up irritations to redress their gender inequality. Meanwhile, studies like *Tough Girls* by Sherrie Inness (1999) appeared, which examined the broader question of female empowerment through violence. Authors such as feminist film critic Molly Haskell (1999) began to question the very notion of teen power, which strategically marketed films have been selling to youth as a concept while deceptively exploiting teens' insecurities by showing them gleefully surrendering to consumption and ignorance.

Another indicator of the recent dea(r)th of JD films, and films addressing teen aggression in general, was the publication of Wheeler Winston Dixon's essay "'Fighting and Violence and Everything, That's Always Cool': Teen Films in the 1990s" (2000). Despite his title, Dixon does not actually deal with fighting or violence in 1990s teen films, presumably because the incidences of such had become so infrequent. Save glancing references to *Scream* (1996) and *Starship Troopers* (1998)—with no mention at all of the African American teen crime films earlier in the decade—Dixon does not cite any 1990s films that actually address youth delinquency. Dixon's omissions parallel the omission at work in the film industry, wherein previously profound issues of the contemporary angry young man have been all but forgotten, or, at best, displaced into the recent boom of war fantasies, for example, *Saving Private Ryan* (1998), *Three Kings* (1999), *The Patriot* (2000), *Behind Enemy Lines* (2001), *Black Hawk Down* (2001), *Pearl Harbor* (2001), and *We Were Soldiers* (2002). Delinquent boys remain prominent in our culture, and I would argue they are still dormant in our society and in our cinema, waiting for the next outlet in which their primal anger will be unleashed.[1]

DELINQUENT TRENDS

Since the earliest days of American cinema, films about JD boys have become increasingly confrontational about the sources of their protagonists' rebellion, whether they are an unsatisfying domestic surroundings fostered by inadequate parents and/or the more complex operations of social conditions, such as class status. The earliest series of bad boy films—for instance those featuring the "Dead End Kids" of the late 1930s and the "East Side Kids" of the early 1940s—examined these sources as well, as they further questioned the supposedly traditional moral values under which these boys were raised. The questioning of teen rebellion in films after World War II became comparatively explicit and informed (Perlman 1993), often siding with the youth who ultimately want to achieve success and independence but have simply chosen impractical—not necessarily "wrong"—ways to proceed. Nonetheless, the rise of post–World War II moral panics around wayward youth originally led Hollywood to begin celebrating and capitalizing on the image of juvenile delinquency (Barson and Heller 1998), leading to a new exploitation—American ephebiphobia, the fear of teenagers. Teen movie delinquents soon found their archetypes in the Marlon Brando and James Dean roles of the 1950s, which introduced the tough-but-tender young man of the time.

James Dean's performance in *Rebel Without a Cause* is certainly the most influential of any juvenile delinquency depiction in American cinema. Dean's Jim Stark struggles mightily to make his upwardly mobile middle-class parents understand his inarticulate needs, expressing himself through alcohol, petty fights, and family tantrums. A crucial aspect of Jim's pathology is the weakness of his own father, who is so browbeaten by Mom that he's effectively emasculated (a domestic crisis born from postwar fears of women's liberation). Jim tenuously hangs on to what he perceives as masculine obligations: he abhors being seen as cowardly, and reluctantly gets into fights and drag races to show his virility, while he quickly acquiesces to a paternal role with Plato (Sal Mineo) and a spousal role with Judy (Natalie Wood). The fact that both Judy and Plato have crushes on Jim further complicates his gender role. He is a love object for girls *and* boys and he awkwardly accepts his own desirability to both, this leaving him in an anxious and ambiguous epicene state. Jim bears all the hallmarks of teen angst that would be filtered through angry young male roles of the following generations, and since he displayed a spectrum of emotions from explosive to subtle Dean was able to portray Jim as far more complex than sinister students like Artie West (Vic Morrow) in *Blackboard Jungle* or depraved delinquents like Mike Denton (Tommy Cook) in *Teenage Crime Wave* (both of which also appeared in 1955).

Fringe film studios like American International and distributors like Republic Pictures then began to exploit the burgeoning teenage market through an increasing number of rock fables (excited kinetics in *Shake, Rattle and Rock* [1956] and *Rock All Night* [1957]), gang dramas (overwrought menace in *Motorcycle*

Gang [1957] and *Juvenile Jungle* [1958]), and beach romps (teasing sexuality in *Beach Party* [1963] and *Beach Blanket Bingo* [1965]). Thomas Doherty (1988) accurately argued that these films led to a "juvenilization" of American cinema, the effects of which are felt ever more acutely today.[2] Such movies as *West Side Story* were exceptions to these more sensational films in two ways. First, they were produced by larger studios that were more concerned about "proper" public relations and were thus more cautious about outright exploitation films. And secondly, they tapped into the teen tensions of the time—in this case between different ethnic groups—within fanciful formats like song-and-dance musicals, and thereby made the implicit danger of their scenarios less realistic to young audiences.

By the time of the visible political upheavals among youth of the late 1960s, which made teens an even more suspect segment of the population, movie studios were no longer using youth aggression in its previously melodramatic or genre-bound forms. Rather, films like *Wild in the Streets* (1968) and *R.P.M.* (1970) tapped into extremist anxieties about a comprehensively dominant youth culture. Max Frost (Christopher Jones), the twentysomething rebel-singer-stoner hero of *Wild*, rises to the presidency after the U.S. voting age is lowered to fourteen, and he soon orders all the over-thirty types to be interred in concentration camps and kept on acid. Of course, after Max achieves his absolute power, his rebellion is quashed similar to that of all who had come before, but in this case he faces contrition not in front of the law or parents but rather at the feet of younger children, who plan "to put everyone over ten out of business." Such images were no longer based on the actual case studies that had inspired films in the vein of *Rebel* or *Splendor in the Grass* (1961), but were instead extrapolated from fantastic musings about the fate of late 1960s youth.

In a cycle that has recently repeated itself in the teen genre, movie studios in the late 1960s and early 1970s seemed to dodge many of the truly relevant issues facing teens (and the country), and the demise of the teen exploitation film by the end of the 1960s ironically signaled Hollywood's general disinterest in youth culture for the next decade (Betrock 1986). The few notable depictions of teenage boys by the late 1970s—the conflicted title character played by Robby Benson in *Ode to Billy Joe* (1976), the dancing stud Tony Manero (John Travolta) in *Saturday Night Fever* (1977), the marginalized working-class kids in *Breaking Away* (1979), the endangered band of brothers in *The Warriors* (1979)—showed them as confused, intimidated, and insecure, with the implicit fallout of Vietnam and Watergate weighing on them heavily. However, these films did deal with boys' deviance in one form or another, and suggested an increasingly complex set of reasons for why they rebelled. The secret to Billy Joe's *Ode* turned out to be his painfully repressed homosexuality; Tony in *Fever* sublimated the doubts of his family into his bravado on the dance floor; the boys in *Breaking Away* were shamed by the fate of their laboring fathers; and the gang in *Warriors* was literally running for their lives because dozens of other gangs erroneously perceived them as responsible for thwarting gang unity.

Perhaps the most notorious bad boy film of the 1970s, *Over the Edge* (1979), was so provocative that its release was delayed by Warner Bros. (Bernstein 1997, 158). The highly publicized but relatively small skirmishes that had erupted earlier in the year at screenings of *The Warriors* put the film industry on alert that, in fact, young men were bringing much anger to their theater experience (McGee and Robertson 1982, 153–54), even as the studios offered more popularly mollifying fantasies to youth at the time such as *Superman* (1978), *Grease* (1978), *Star Trek* (1979), *The Black Stallion* (1979), and *The Blue Lagoon* (1980). *Over the Edge* blatantly pointed to the brewing unrest among suburban youth, here a group grown monstrous within an adult-oriented civic system dominated by self-absorbed disco-era parents who were distracted by faddish signifiers of class ascension (a theme that would be dramatically revisited in *The Ice Storm* some eighteen years later). The shiftless teens of the "model" community become increasingly hostile and violent, in part because the town planners have not provided adequate youth recreational facilities. Faced with a lack of fun and safe outlets, Carl (Michael Eric Cramer), Richie (Matt Dillon), and Mark (Vincent Spano) learn to take drugs and deal them, and commit vandalistic crimes that lead to the police killing Richie. This results in an orgiastic youth fantasy of the time that now rings rather prescient, when Richie's friends lock their parents and teachers inside their school and threaten to kill them all.

The 1980s spawned a new generation of teen cinema in general, with slasher pics and sex comedies yielding appealing profits for a film industry that had been worried about declining revenues. When Ronald Reagan assertively took over the presidency in 1981 from the mildly agreeable Jimmy Carter, Americans seemed eager for a refreshed sense of patriarchal ambition (Traube 1992). At that time, the long-delayed examination of men's trauma in Vietnam was just about to change from the primarily shell-shocked Carter-era images of *The Deer Hunter* (1978), *Coming Home* (1978), and *Apocalypse Now* (1979) to the Reagan-era revenge rides of *First Blood* (1982), *Uncommon Valor,* (1983), and *Missing in Action* (1984). Boys in teen films similarly encountered—and often enjoyed—a new sense of aggression that renewed their ideals of masculine potency (Whatley 1988), an aggression manifested by the lecherous longings of sex-starved lotharios (goofy Artie [Dan Waldman] in *Goin' All the Way* [1981], hapless Gary [Lawrence Monoson] in *The Last American Virgin* [1982], cocky Woody [Tom Cruise] in *Losin' It* [1982], ambitious Joel [Cruise] in *Risky Business* [1983], and excitable Barry [Michael Zorek] in *Hot Moves* [1984]), and by the angered, often ambivalent violence wrought by displaced delinquents. In the latter case, some films attempted to "organize" the violence of boys around fighting competitions, with *The Karate Kid* trilogy (1984–89) being the most popular example. Yet more often, fighting took the form of tense gang violence, as in *Class of 1984* (1982), *Bad Boys* (1983), *The New Kids* (1985), and *Tuff Turf* (1985).

By the 1980s, many JD films had begun minimizing much of the pathos and sympathy that had marked depictions of previous hoodlums—most of these films portrayed the juvenile offender as vindictive, uncaring, or at best gullible, thus producing an image of teen crime that was generally lacking in sentimentality. This is clearly the case in the above gang films, and became more apparent in films including *Dangerously Close* (1986), where a secret school society weeds out the "undesirable" students; *At Close Range* (1986), in which a teen inherits his father's criminal legacy; *Three O'Clock High* (1987), with its parodic yet vicious playground showdown; and *The Principal* (1987), a portrait of barbarous youth crime met with absurdly tyrannical adult authority. Nonetheless, these films continued to exhibit a stylized violence and romantic luster that made them appealing to youth, both boys and girls (which was most evident in the two 1983 films Francis Ford Coppola made about JDs, *The Outsiders* and *Rumble Fish*). Two distinct types of bad boys had emerged, indicating a shift from the past practices identified by McGee and Robertson in 1982. Boys heading into a downward spiral of corruption and danger, who had almost always been antagonists in films until the 1980s, were now taking on protagonist roles, and even though they were often doomed they effectively drew the audience's attention. The other type of Hollywood bad boy, who tries to rise up, reform, and renounce his criminal past—a staple character in many post-*Rebel* films—was now becoming less popular and less appealing, indicated by the low output of, and low returns on, quality fare like *Tex* (1982). In a decade when multiplex theaters began depending on ever-larger crowds of youth for revenue, and started relaxing barriers on minors seeing R-rated violence, many JD films displayed their characters' deviant acts in detail, structuring their narratives into a crime spree and/or a flight from being caught. Thus followed *Reckless* (1984), with its motorcycle rebel stealing his girl right out of school; *Out of Bounds* (1986), where a churlish boy finds himself the prey of murderous drug thugs; and *Dudes* (1988), in which a pair of punks terrorizes a group of rednecks in a protracted rampage of revenge. Few films actually addressed the long-term consequences of youth crime; when *The Beat* (1988) and *Lost Angels* (1989) did, audiences were nowhere to be found. The consequences of being bad are always implied in JD films, but by leaving such likely possibilities at a distance, the films were able to frolic in the intensity of violence and danger, whether or not they glorified the criminality of their characters.

A rare film of this time that featured a JD protagonist navigating the poles between incorrigible and redeemable was the aptly named *Bad Boys*, one of the more serious portraits of a delinquent character who is actually sent to prison. Here Mick (Sean Penn), a drug-dealing hood, lands in a juvenile detention facility where he soon learns a new set of brutal rules to establish himself as the "barn boss." The film hinges on a patriarchal order of power, with Mick overpowering his competitors inside the prison and then his rival from without, thereby gaining the respect of both his fellow inmates and his superiors. Curiously, his girlfriend is used as a pawn in the narrative's construction of masculine exchange: when she is raped by Mick's rival, Mick affirms his own sense of humanity while she is virtually destroyed in the process. Yet the film presents the conservative view that Mick is responsible for his criminality, since there is no attempt by him or the narrative to shift the blame to cultural surroundings or family background. It is as if "the filmmakers know that an old-fashioned environmental critique is not going to wash with a modern audience," as Tom Doherty observed (1983, 27), even if such a critique may be incidentally rendered by the film's depiction of all the young characters' impoverished and corruptive milieux. After Mick is sent to prison, his deviance is generally revealed to be defensive rather than malicious, and the film's ending—in which Mick spares the life of his rival—suggests a certain nobility, since he comes to realize that he can indeed walk away from his violent impulses. This is a nobility that few movie men achieve, and which few subsequent teen films of the 1980s would endorse.

By far the most critically discussed JD film of the 1980s was *River's Edge* (1987),[3] in which a group of teenage friends learn that one of them, John (Daniel Roebuck), has killed his girlfriend and for some time keep the murder a secret among themselves. Matt (Keanu Reeves) becomes the conscience of the group, eventually and reluctantly leading police to the site of the murder, leaving John little time to enjoy his adulation as the killer since he is himself soon killed by a local sociopath. Perhaps more than any other youth film of the 1980s, *River's Edge* ironically screams out the apathy that many disenchanted youth have felt.[4] The film was certainly working off of the real-life fascination that the media had with these teenagers who could keep a murder of one of their own to themselves. In fact, John's murder is intercut with Matt having sex with his own girlfriend for the first time, making a certain link between death and sex, but more so juxtaposing the lack of emotion all of these characters feel toward two such extreme experiences. Attention must also be paid to the teenage character who is at once over- and under-represented here, the dead girl. A veritable matrix of 1980s youth film representations runs through the image of her naked, stiff body next to the river. She is the final result of all the abuse inflicted upon prematurely sexualized young women in the exploitative sex romps from earlier in the decade (cf. *Goin' All the Way, The Last American Virgin, Hot Moves*); she is the victim of ultimate teen anomie without an identity; and she is the spectacle of a male sadistic fantasy in which boys truly fail to comprehend the significance of their actions. In the impassive cold body of this dead girl, which the film employs as its signifying index to adolescent nihilism and depravity, the most comprehensively articulate statement on young male delinquency in the 1980s is achieved.

Numerous JD movies continued to the made in the years after *River's Edge*, but a significant number of them were small productions that have faded into obscurity, among them *3:15—Moment of*

Truth (1986), *China Girl, Summer Camp Nightmare* (both 1987), *The Beat, Lost Angels, Sing* (all 1989), and *Class of 1999* (1990). Curiously, five years after *Bad Boys*, Sean Penn played a cop in *Colors* (1988) investigating a series of crimes among the Latino and African American gangs of Los Angeles. While the film focused on the cops, one message that the film offered about youth criminality is that the youngest members of each gang are recruited and "trained" to rise up in competence within the gang—replacing the dying and imprisoned members who drop out in their twenties and thirties—thereby maintaining a futile cycle of generational delinquency.

This theme, as well as a clearer attention to the influence of racial issues on crime, became most prominent in the African American teen crime films of the early 1990s. These films represented a departure for American cinema in general, since they addressed contemporary racial conditions from a sensitive, youthful perspective (unlike the "blaxploitation" films of the early 1970s). Yet, like similar trends in JD films, these films gained much of their notoriety from their intensified violence, as evident in the cycle's biggest hit, *Boyz N the Hood* (1991), which features a rousing revenge killing by one of the story's protagonists. To be fair, usually the main character in each film—other examples included *Juice* (1992), *Menace II Society* (1993), *Fresh* (1994), and *New Jersey Drive* (1995)—attempted to resist his violent impulses, even as all of the films suggested that young black men needed to negotiate their angry urges. This presented a set of tricky issues in the films that portrayed urban African American youth, for many filmmakers wanted to reveal the long-suppressed conditions of their characters' real-life equivalents, but many also appealed to a notion of criminality as a way of life, despite all of these films' explicit messages that crime does not pay.

The complications of this condition may help explain the gradual, and now certain, demise of the African American youth crime film by 1995. More diverse and less ghettoized representations of African Americans began reaching the screen by the mid-1990s, and the repetitive themes—and problematics—of the youth crime film had become apparent. Audiences and critics had begun to question the films' linkage of black youth with crime, as the films' typing of African American boys seemed to fuel the very racist stereotypes that the films had been trying to challenge. The films' messages about the morals of masculinity—being a good son,

Tre (Cuba Gooding Jr.) in *Boyz in the Hood* was a popular paradigm for conflicted but sensitive 1990s teens dealing with their own potential delinquency. By the end of the decade, the images of such "bad boys" in American teen films had become curiously disregarded.

becoming a responsible father, representing yourself among your peers—had become rote by the mid-1990s, resulting in a spate of parodies that implicitly criticized these heavy-handed themes. Yet one aspect should be emphasized: the African American crime film was the dominant style of youth film through the early 1990s, and it had a definite cross-generic influence on future youth films, which appeared unable to reasonably address delinquent youth concerns in ways that were as effective.

Case in point: the other JD films of the 1990s without racial themes devolved into a smattering of odd tales, few of which gained much recognition, despite star power (e.g., Brad Pitt and Rick Schroder in *Across the Tracks* [1991]), novel titles (e.g.,

Teenage Bonnie and Klepto Clyde [1993]), or bizarre concepts (e.g., *Powder* [1995], with its quasi-alien albino teen theurgist). These films still revealed curious aspects of young male gender identification, especially two 1995 films, *The Basketball Diaries*, in which a drug-addled teen succumbs to turning tricks for heroin, and *To Die For*, which featured an adolescent boy lured into murder by a sexually assertive (if not sexually ambiguous) older woman. While the former film with teen heartthrob Leonardo DiCaprio was passed over by audiences uninterested in its dour downward spiral, the latter film's success was no doubt due in part to the casting of adult stars Nicole Kidman and Matt Dillon (erstwhile JD himself), and the fact that they were the primary characters. However, films that dealt with delinquent boys as protagonists generally remained off the public's radar, especially the choice few that strove for sympathetic character development, for example *Hurricane Streets* (1997), in which a boy tries to save his girlfriend from her abusive father; *Squeeze* (1997), with its group of naive youngsters tempted by the lure of local hoods; and *Light It Up* (1999), where angry students take over their school to demand better educational conditions.

Shining examples of why movie studios no longer felt comfortable dealing with young male delinquency began to emerge in such mortifying features as *Kids* (1995), *The Doom Generation* (1996), and *187*. These three films were indicative of how the industry now viewed bad boys: in all three cases the kids are akin to hedonist savages, running on rampages of crime, drugs, and sexual manipulation, with no sense of direction and no final deliverance. The fact that all three films had sensational marketing campaigns and featured some of the most extreme scenes of gratuitous violence in any youth films further called attention to the vapid state of JD representation. (In *Kids* a boy is apparently grossly beaten to death in a crowded public park by skateboard-wielding teens; in *Doom Generation*, skinheads castrate a boy with garden shears while they rape his girlfriend with a small statue; in *187* the students are so wicked they're kept in classrooms retrofitted to appear as if they are cages.[5]) By the late 1990s, the handful of JD films that surfaced had clearly become warped by ambitions of violent appeal, especially in studio productions, such as with the terrorizing boyfriend in *Fear* (1996), the vigilante avenger of *The Substitute* (1996), the maniacal parents in *Disturbing Behavior* (1998), and the hate-mongering racists of *American History X* (1998).

Then, not unlike the turn of events with Vietnam in the late 1960s, Hollywood retreated from the battle lines of juvenile delinquency in 1999. Undoubtedly the surest sign of the industry's sudden discomfort with the bad boy concept was the delayed release of *O*, which was slated to appear in 1999 and then delayed until late 2001, despite the rising star status of its young cast. This contemporary high school updating of *Othello* was in production during the peak of the late 1990s school killings, which culminated in the Columbine massacre. Miramax feared that the film's violence would be ill-timed to recent events, and yet upon its eventual release, critics uniformly noted the irony of the studio's self-censorship: the film was a rare example of involved and informed youth criminality, rather than the emotionally empty experiences represented by recent JD films.

This sense of repression and/or displacement has been evident for the past few years, both in terms of Hollywood's output of JD films and their reception by audiences. In 1999, two films went so far as to explain their boys' delinquency with hokey supernatural gags—*Deal of a Lifetime*, with its Faustian tale of a kid selling his soul for a hot date, and *Idle Hands*, wherein the demon force is focused on the fingers of the wayward teen—while an increasing amount of responsibility for juvenile offenses continued to fall on girls, as in *Teaching Mrs. Tingle* (1999), *Crime and Punishment in Suburbia* (2000), and *Traffic* (2000). And even though the latter film became quite a success (with its central focus on adult characters), further films with arguably JD characters continued to draw virtually no interest. *The Joyriders* (1999), *Pups* (1999), *Black and White* (2000), and *Cheaters* (2001) were all met with indifference upon release, despite a huge marketing push for the last two films. Large audiences now appear willing to engage in JD themes only when the topic is a minor part of a more complex drama, as in *Traffic* or *Save the Last Dance* (2001), not when it is the focus of a film, such as *Bully* (2001). The failure of *Bully* is a telling statement on the state of JD representation. Although Larry Clark was able to actually *increase* his contemptible debasement of youth beyond what he had rendered in *Kids* six years earlier, audiences, and even many critics, were no longer interested. *Bully* was more revealing in its inability to illuminate the insane behavior of its bad boys, who exhibit an extreme range of angry behavior (fighting, drug abuse, rape, murder) reduced to outrageous displays that no longer shock their audience but rather numb it.

After the suppression of *O* and the folly of *Bully*, Hollywood made it clear that it no longer knew how to handle or how to hype juvenile delinquency. Now it seemed that Hollywood and the rest of America would rather avoid the topic of boys' badness altogether than take the chance of being responsible for changing it.[6]

We are at a point where the media industry that so relies upon and influences youth has chosen to ignore the very vital issues of boys' delinquency and their causes. Hollywood has in many ways regressed to its own adolescent state before World War II, electing to place a slaphappy spin on teen troubles in films like *American Pie* (1999), *She's All That* (1999), *Bring It On* (2000), *Not Another Teen Movie* (2001), and *Josie and the Pussycats* (2001), which have a more modern appeal in their sexual titillation and often scatological humor (Zacharek 1999; Dickinson 2001). The very pressing issue of young men's anger and confusion has not subsided, despite the decline in school shootings and the ebbing of extremist delinquency depictions. In fact, in the wake of 9/11, the nation should be more concerned than ever that its boys (and girls) have deep-seated anxiety that will soon manifest itself in retaliatory expressions. Our media industry is obligated to explore these kinds of concerns, yet since it is based on such a delicate foundation of maintaining profits and placating the public we are likely to see an effect inverse to what happened in the 1950s. Back then the movie studios fanned the flames of a gestating youth revolution, capitalizing on adults' fears more than teens' realities. Now we could soon see teens themselves slowly enacting the next wave of delinquent behavior long before Hollywood knows how to exploit it.

NOTES

1. Curiously, other than the McGee and Robertson study in 1982, the only other book-length evaluations of juvenile delinquency in movies have both appeared outside the United States in the past few years. See Fantoni Minnella 2000 and Spotorno 2001. For a compelling polemic on the possible future of our youth, see Schneider and Stevenson 2000.
2. Evidence of Doherty's argument can still be found in the blockbusters of each year, which are kid-friendly movies about adults: *Armageddon* (1998), *The Mummy* (1999), *Charlie's Angels* (2000), *Pearl Harbor*, *Goldmember* (2002).
3. David Edelstein gives an illuminating account of the production history of *River's Edge* and prophetically describes how it will generate

critical attention (1987, 43–44). His article appeared weeks before the film's national theatrical release.

4. Worth noting is the connection between *River's Edge* and its rough equivalent (in theme and name) from the late 1970s, *Over the Edge:* Tim Hunter directed *River* and cowrote *Over.*

5. For more complete criticisms of the problematic *Kids,* see hooks 1996 and Shary 2004.

6. For more on *Bully* see Cynthia Fuchs 2004.

WORKS CITED

Acland, Charles. 1995. *Youth, Murder, Spectacle: The Cultural Politics of "Youth in Crisis."* Boulder, CO: Westview Press.

Barson, Michael, and Steven Heller. 1998. *Teenage Confidential: An Illustrated History of the American Teen.* San Francisco: Chronicle.

Bernstein, Jonathan. 1997. *Pretty in Pink: The Golden Age of Teenage Movies.* New York: St. Martin's Griffin.

Betrock, Alan. 1986. *The I Was a Teenage Juvenile Delinquent Rock 'n' Roll Horror Beach Party Movie Book: A Complete Guide to the Teen Exploitation Film, 1954–1969.* New York: St. Martin's Press.

Considine, David M. 1985. *The Cinema of Adolescence.* Jefferson, NC: McFarland.

Dickinson, Kay. 2001. "Pop, Speed and the 'MTV Aesthetic' in Recent Teen Films." *Scope.* Online at http://www.nottingham.ac.uk/film/journal/articles/pop-speed-and-mtv/htm.

Dixon, Wheeler Winston. 2000. "'Fighting and Violence and Everything, That's Always Cool': Teen Films in the 1990s." In *Film Genre 2000: New Critical Essays,* 125–42. Albany: State University of New York Press.

Doherty, Thomas. 1983. Review of *Bad Boys. Film Quarterly* (Fall), 27.

———. 1988. *Teenagers and Teenpics: The Juvenilization of American Movies in the 1950s.* Boston: Unwin Hyman.

Edelstein, David. 1987. "Some Kind of Horrible," *Rolling Stone,* April 23, 43–44.

Fantoni Minnella, Maurizio. 2000. *Bad Boys: Dizionario critico del cinema della ribellione giovanile.* Milan: B. Mondadori.

Forman, Murray. 1996. "The 'Hood Took Me Under: Urban Geographies of Danger in New Black Cinema." In *Pictures of a Generation on Hold: Selected Papers,* ed. Murray Pomerance and John Sakeris, 45–55. Toronto: Media Studies Working Group.

Fuchs, Cynthia. 2004. "'The Whole Fucking World Warped around Me': Bad Kids and Worse Contexts." In *BAD: Infamy, Darkness, Evil, and Slime on Screen,* ed. Murray Pomerance, 273–85. Albany: State University of New York Press.

Guerrero, Ed. 1993. *Framing Blackness: The African American Image in*

Film. Philadelphia: Temple University Press.

Haskell, Molly. 1999. "Teen Power." *Scenario* 5, no. 2, 8–9.

hooks, bell. 1996. "White Light." *Sight and Sound* (May), 9–12.

Inness, Sherrie. 1999. *Tough Girls: Women Warriors and Wonder Women in Popular Culture.* Philadelphia: University of Pennsylvania Press.

Jones, Jacquie. 1991. "The New Ghetto Aesthetic." *Wide Angle* 13, no. 3/4, 32–43.

Jowett, Garth S., Ian C. Jarvie, and Kathryn H. Fuller, eds. 1996. *Children and the Movies: Media Influence and the Payne Fund Controversy.* New York: Cambridge University Press.

Kearney, Mary. 1996. "Girls Just Wanna Have *Fun!* Female Avengers in '90s Teenpics." In *Pictures of a Generation on Hold: Selected Papers,* ed. Murray Pomerance and John Sakeris, 97–105. Toronto: Media Studies Working Group.

Lewis, Jon. 1992. *The Road to Romance + Ruin: Teen Films and Youth Culture.* New York: Routledge.

McGee, Mark Thomas, and R. J. Robertson. 1982. *The J.D. Films: Juvenile Delinquency in the Movies.* Jefferson, NC: McFarland.

Orenstein, Peggy. 1996. "The Movies Discover the Teen-Age Girl," *New York Times,* August 11, sec. 2, 1.

Perlman, Marc. 1993. *Youth Rebellion Movies.* Minneapolis: Lerner.

Schneider, Barbara, and David Stevenson. 2000. *The Ambitious Generation: America's Teenagers, Motivated but Directionless.* New Haven: Yale University Press.

Shary, Timothy. 2000. "Angry Young Women: The Emergence of the 'Tough Girl' Image in American Teen Films." *Post Script* 19, no. 2: 49–61.

———. 2002. *Generation Multiplex: The Image of Youth in Contemporary American Cinema.* Austin: University of Texas Press.

———. 2004. "The Only Place to Go Is Inside: Confusions of Sexuality and Class in *Clueless* and *Kids.*" In *Popping Culture,* ed. Murray Pomerance and John Sakeris, 223–31. Boston: Pearson Education.

Snyder, Scott. 1991. "Movies and Juvenile Delinquency: An Overview." *Adolescence* 26, no. 101, 121–32.

———. 1995a. "Movie Portrayals of Juvenile Delinquency: Part 1—Epidemiology and Criminology." *Adolescence* 30, no. 117, 53–64.

———. 1995b. "Movie Portrayals of Juvenile Delinquency: Part 2—Sociology and Psychology." *Adolescence* 30, no. 118, 325–37.

Spotorno, Radomiro. 2001. *50 años de soledad: De Los olvidados (1950) a La virgen de los sicarios (2000): Infancia y juventud marginales en el cine iberoamericano.* Ocho y Medio, Libros de Cine: Festival de Cine Iberoamericano de Huelva.

Traube, Elizabeth. 1992. *Dreaming Identities: Class, Gender, and Generation in 1980s Hollywood Movies.* Boulder, CO: Westview Press.

Watkins, S. Craig. 1998. *Representing: Hip-Hop Culture and the Produc-*

tion of Black Cinema. Chicago: University of Chicago Press.

Whatley, Marianne H. 1988. "Raging Hormones and Powerful Cars: The Construction of Men's Sexuality in School Sex Education and Popular Adolescent Films." *Journal of Education* 170, no. 3, 100–121.

Wiegman, Robyn. 1993. "Feminism, 'The Boyz,' and Other Matters Regarding the Male." In *Screening the Male: Exploring Masculinities in Hollywood Cinema,* ed. Steven Cohan and Ina Rae Hark, 173–93. New York: Routledge.

Zacharek, Stephanie. 1999. "There's Something about Teenage Comedy." *Sight and Sound* 9, no. 12, 20–22.

2

BOYS WON'T BE BOYS

Cross-Gender Masquerade and Queer Agency in *Ma Vie en rose*

Cordula Quint

> The cause of the origin of a thing and its eventual utility, its actual employment and place in a system of purposes, lie worlds apart.
>
> Friedrich Nietzsche, *On the Genealogy of Morals*

As a mass medium, the silver screen is likely one of the most productive cultural sites on which identities are performed and incorporated through representation and reception into an elaborate, albeit fictional, system of sociopolitical, economic, and kinship relations. It is part of a dense network of discursive practices in which patriarchal power over the definitions of gender, sex, and sexuality has been and still is, by and large, manifested. Coming-of-age scenarios tend to show how boys learn to confront life's challenges with an ideologically "appropriate" set of actions and reactions. In this sense, boy protagonists undergo rites of passage into adult male subjectivity by tackling very particular challenges that are always already defined as "masculine" by the hegemonic culture into which these maturing subjects are assimilated and socialized.

Such scenarios bolster what Monique Wittig has referred to as "compulsory heterosexuality." For Wittig, as queer theorist Judith Butler points out, the terms "'male' and 'female' exist only within the heterosexual matrix; indeed, they are the naturalized terms that keep that matrix concealed and, hence, protected from a radical critique" (Butler 1990, 111). Wittig, according to Butler, also demonstrates to what degree heterosexist imperatives become manifest "in the discourses of the human sciences . . . [which] 'take for granted that what founded society, any society, is heterosexuality'" (115–16).

At the foundation of the coming-of-age narratives—the characters, their adolescent concerns, and their problems and conflicts with adulthood—is a nexus of ideas Butler refers to as "heterosexual coherence." Causal links are erroneously assumed between three distinct dimensions of selfhood: the anatomical sex, the performances of gender in social life, and sexuality. In other words, a male anatomy is assumed to be coextensive with performance of masculine gender and with heterosexual desire for women. Easily overlooked, then, are the widespread discontinuities between the discrete dimensions of selfhood among heterosexuals, bisexuals, gays, lesbians, and transgendered and transsexual peoples. Culturally marginal forms of sexuality falling outside the heterosexualist continuum are effectively rendered unintelligible by mainstream narratives, including (and especially) those focused on boyhood and emergent masculinity.

In the 1990s, coming out as queer was often a high-profile, "hip," and even satirized media event. As the closet door was forcefully opened, the previously "unnatural" and "aberrant" even ran up against the danger of co-optation and assimilation. It was the decade during which the narrative conventions of the celluloid closet began to be scrutinized for the heterosexist imperatives they fulfill and during which emancipatory progress was made regarding the representation of queer subjectivities. In this sense, films focused on gay, lesbian, bisexual, transgendered, and transsexual characters remedy a symbolic absence eloquently described by Eve Kosofsky Sedgwick as "that long Babylonian exile known as queer childhood," marked as it is by "the terrifying powerlessness of gender-dissonan[ce]" and other stigmas (Sedgwick 1993, 4).[1] As Butler observes in her reading of his *Three Essays on the Theory of Sexuality*, Freud suggests that

> it is the exception, the strange, that gives us a clue to how the mundane and taken-for-granted world of sexual meanings is constituted. The presuppositions that we make about sexed bodies, about them being one or the other, about the meanings that are said to inhere in them or to follow from being sexed in such a way are suddenly and significantly upset by those examples that fail to comply with the categories that naturalize and stabilize the field of bodies for us within the terms of cultural conventions. Hence, the strange, the incoherent, that which falls "outside," gives us a way of understanding the taken-for-granted world of sexual categorization as a constructed one, indeed, as one that might well be constructed differently. (1990, 110)

In this essay I hope to address the strange, the incoherent, and that which falls "outside," in order to throw light on that which is embraced as the norm and to bring into relief the cultural agency that the "abnormal, aberrant, and incoherent" fulfills for the contingent redefinition of such norms.

MA VIE EN ROSE

Ma Vie en rose (1997), the critically acclaimed first feature of Belgian director Alain Berliner, is of interest here because the film's seven-year-old protagonist is at a comparatively early stage in his socialization toward masculinity. Ludovic Fabre (Georges du Fresne) finds himself increasingly at odds with his family and the wider community because he loves to dress up in girls' clothing and fantasizes about his future marriage to his best friend Jérôme (Julien Rivière). The narrative explores his maturation and the complications that arise when homosexual desires surface and Ludovic embarks on an existential quest for self-understanding and an affirmation of his desire. Transgender and transsexual concerns are also addressed in the obstacles he encounters, since his initial innocence is progressively violated by the punitive measures with which the community and his family attempt to bring his transgressions under control. Although the film's seemingly childlike naiveté invites its classification as a "film for children," its analysis of social processes poignantly cuts right to the core of compulsory heterosexuality and the epistemological fallacies on which it is based.

The story also illustrates how the queer imagination is constrained within the universe of heterosexual fantasy even in its earliest, most innocent expressions, and how, in turn, the queer appropriation of straight narratives undoes the assumptions that underpin them. In this sense, the film carefully lays bare how a breach of gender and sexual norms unsettles the myths on which the stability of the sexed and gendered self, of the entire neighborhood, indeed of straight society at large, are erroneously founded. In *Ma Vie en rose,* the socially conservative equilibrium of middle-class suburban life is deeply disturbed by Ludovic's presence, a development that far exceeds his own and his community's comprehension. The film depicts the escalating violence of a neighborhood's ostracism, a family's shame and helplessness, and the psychic resilience of a young "girlboy" who finds him/herself caught up in the process of a social and discursive reformation.

At the outset of the film, the Fabres have just returned to their hometown because the father, Pierre (Jean-Philippe Écoffey), has been offered a lucrative new job. They are eager to settle in and to establish friendly ties with their new neighbors. The subsequent interaction among three traditional families—the Bruns, the Lemieux, and the Fabres—will make them representative of the social processes the film seeks to illuminate. Neighborhood events, parties, and backyard barbecues reveal how moral and ideological values are negotiated among these agents to assure communal integrity. While the film's charm and power reside in its telling of this complex story from the perspective of a seven-year-old boy, the seamless integration of his fantasy life into the visual narrative is used to show when and why he agrees or disagrees with the reality lived and negotiated by the adults. The film's seamless shifts between fantasy and "reality" also bring into focus the constitution and bolstering of domestic and communal life by public and private fictions.

During the opening shots, the camera pans slowly through a plastic dollhouse interior of many shades of red, pink, and orange in an excerpt from Ludovic's favorite TV show, "Pam's World." The visual narrative then segues to "real life" and the portrayal of the three families' preparations for the Fabres' housewarming party. In this manner, the film plays cleverly on the expectations and associations of the viewers. As the adults are seen dressing up for the occasion, the viewers are drawn into an ambiguous world between fantasy and reality, a fusion of children's rooms and dollhouse interiors. Here a young child participates in the same ritual of preparation but remains largely hidden and out of sight. Shots of lipstick being applied to the child's mouth are interspersed with shots of jewelry, accessories, and Barbie dolls with big blond hair, while outside, adults and children are seen enthusiastically pouring into the neighborhood streets on their way to the Fabres' party.

As seen through the naive eyes of the boy hero, the community is a world brimming with exuberant bourgeois optimism. The families are eager to support one another, the children make friends easily, and the adults are confident that their work and communal ties are well integrated to assure a future of the same. As the neighborhood gathers in the Fabres' backyard and as the first introductions are made, the camera follows a pair of red shoes descending down the stairs. Then a white curtain is pulled aside, and the crowd is heard cheering the entrance of an alluring young girl in a pink princess dress. Whispers of "Isn't she pretty!" fill the air as the child, visibly moved by the reception, basks in the neighbors' applause with great pride and self-assurance.[2] It turns out, however, that the girl is not Zoé (Cristina Barget), the Fabres' only girl, as was expected, but Ludovic, their youngest son. Mild bewilderment sets in among the crowd as the confounded father awkwardly continues the introduction of "his tribe" by describing his youngest son as somewhat of "a farceur." This mild public reprimand is followed by the fretful "unmasking" of Ludovic in the kitchen: surrounded by his parents and his grandmother Elisabeth (Hélène Vincent), the boy finds himself the center of adverse attention.

While the adults initially display a limited tolerance on the assumption that eventually the boy will honor the imperatives of heterosexual reproduction, tensions arise when his behavior can no longer be dismissed as a playful exploration of identity ("a joke," "a farce," "natural until the age of seven") but must be recognized as an enduring psychosexual disposition. Early in the story, indeed, the boy is totally unaware of biological limits and cultural prohibitions. Ludovic at first firmly believes that one day he will be a girl, and his cross-dressing is devoid of the irony and self-consciousness that distinguish the adult performance of camp. His coming of age, on the other hand, is in part the story of his losing precisely that innocence. Soon, he comes to recognize his predilections as taboo. While much of the film's analysis of the inculcation of gender and sexual norms in all aspects of everyday life is somewhat simplistic, the portrayal of the boy's development of forms of "queer resistance" is inspirational and far from culturally naive. In defiance of the censorship and repression he suffers, the boy invents cultural tactics that allow him to assert his emerging sense of self and to acquire meaning within the symbolic universe into which he is being socialized. Indeed, he proves remarkably creative and intelligent, and progressively enhances the scale and reach of his interventions.

On one occasion, for example, Ludovic appears at the breakfast table wearing his underpants backward as if the absence of the buttons down the front of the garment could somehow change or camouflage his "real" sex. This playful if naive queering of the gendered dress code convinces the parents to take him to a psychologist (Marie Brunel). The boy also repeatedly inserts himself into narratives of heterosexual romance assuming female subject positions—certainly one counterhegemonic avenue for expressing desire. "Pam's World" here fulfills a number of complex psychic and cultural functions. The main characters of the series, Ben (Michael Cordera) and Pam (Delphine Cadet)—the Belgian equivalents of Ken and Barbie—initially play the same role for Ludovic as they do for the heterosexual imagination.[3] Their hyperbolic gender constitutes the "psychic ideals" of masculinity and femininity as defined by a patriarchal economy of desire on which our relatively imperfect quotidian citations of gender are modeled. More importantly, however, Pam's dominance in the boy's fantasy life—her vibrant red dresses and blonde bombshell appeal (Dolly Parton–style drag)—calls up in him an awareness of male desire and his own desire to oblige it. In one scene, he is even seen singing and dancing along: "I read all the books about romance and roses / I mark all the parts where the boyfriend proposes / I long to be happy, it's like a neurosis."

Not surprisingly, then, Ludovic's attempts at "being a girl" strictly fit the conventional narrative model established by Pam, according to which female happiness and success mean being sexually attractive, chosen, proposed to, and finally married—in short, being passive and desired. Whenever real life fails to accommodate him "as a girl," the boy escapes into his primary-colored fantasy world where Pam, a mixture of fairy and sex symbol, comes to his rescue with her magic sparkles. Hers is a world where the boy is able to cast her/himself in the role of a young bride, where s/he can spend whole days combing her hair, gazing into mirrors, or gaping at the city park with its wedding pavilion and heart-shaped duck pond. The TV program caters perfectly to the boy's need for to understand his same-sex desire, regardless of how culturally antiquated the portrayed gender norms are. Evidently, the *tank-girl* revolution has left this world perfectly intact in both its real and fantasy dimensions. If Ludovic's sincerity engaging in his cross-gender daydreams adds much charm to the story, later he comes to learn that he has violated behavioral norms merely by liking a TV program that belongs to the "girl genres" of popular culture. During a "show-and-tell" at school, he and the neighbor's daughter, Sophie (Morgane Bruna), both bring along their doll versions of the series characters. The teacher (Anne Coesens) praises the girl for being "very romantic," while Ludovic is teased by his classmates and finds out the specific constraints under which his "preference" is acceptable. The teacher speculates, "You want to be like Ben, right? You and Sophie would make a pretty couple." Predictably, the boy suffers multiple anxieties and trauma at the hands of the community. In school, Jérôme soon refuses to sit next to him in the fear that he will "go to hell," and in the psychologist's office Ludovic stands in silent terror and breaks out in panic sweats while overhearing the discussion between his parents and the expert.

The film's interest in portraying the emergence of queer agency is more clearly emphasized when Ludovic coaxes Jérôme into play-acting the marriage vows in front of a fat brown teddy bear cast as the vicar. Ludovic provides "his boyfriend" with detailed instructions for his performance as the groom, while he himself plays the bride (dressed in Jérôme's sister's pink princess dress) and supplies the voiceover for the "cleric" under whose auspices the ritual is to acquire public legitimacy. While Ludovic demonstrates inventiveness, willfulness, and persistence as a *metteur-en-scène* his ultimate aspiration, ironically enough, is to be valued as a "traditional girl," passive, desired, and beautiful ("We walk down the aisle. I look gorgeous. . . . *Tout le monde me trouve belle*").

Indeed, this scene blatantly cites J. L. Austin's definition of performative utterance in *How to Do Things with Words*. Here the marriage vows are used as exemplary for a category of first person singular present indicative active statements about which "it seems clear that to utter the sentence (in, of course, the appropriate circumstances) is not to describe my doing [a thing] . . . or to state that I am doing it: it is to do it" (Austin 1975, 6). Indeed, Ludovic is engaging Jérôme in a queered "doing" of the "I do," but his staged citation of the marriage vows fails to be performative because it takes place in the absence of witnesses and so the "ceremony" can bear no legitimacy in the public eye. Because the boy's action takes place in the wrong circumstances the queer agency manifest in it is no more than provisional; it fails to engage socially with the community.

Later on, in a school production of *Snow White and the Seven Dwarfs*, Ludovic has an opportunity to remedy these limitations. He steps decidedly beyond the sphere of private play and asserts his needs as a social being by seeking witnesses for his performative appropriations. Locking the girl who has been cast in the role of Snow White into the school's washroom, Ludovic takes her place in the glass coffin. Jérôme, cast as the heroic prince, dutifully comes along to rescue her, and at this moment the queered fairy tale deploys its truly unsettling cultural potential. The scene illustrates what can happen when witnesses find themselves addressed by queer appropriations of straight discourse. The audience, by now well acquainted with Ludovic's "disposition," reacts with outrage, shock, and incomprehension. Shortly afterward, the Fabres are seen leaving the schoolyard while the other parents and pupils stand by in silent hostility. This incident will lead to Ludovic's dismissal from the school.

Clearly, the boy's repeated citation of heterosexual narrative and ritual signals the initial entrapment of his imagination within the straight symbolic universe and also the degree to which queer desire is "a love that cannot speak its name" outside the "vocabulary" that is already intelligible to the surrounding culture (see Butler 1990, 116). For Judith Butler, language—the language Ludovic might conceivably use to express himself—is not merely utterance itself but a "history of discourse and power" that fashions and limits the way a "queer and queering agency is forged and reworked" (1993, 228). That one's gender and one's sexual desires and practices may not be continuous with anatomically sexed bodies in the way that compulsory heterosexuality prescribes can be communicated only by means of performative cultural tactics that stress discontinuity: for example, a male body citing the gender prescriptions for the female and vice versa.[4] In so doing, the queer subject addresses its citations directly to homophobic presumptions and attempts to subvert them. The danger is that the performance might be misread by a homophobia that, as Butler points out, "often operates through the attribution of a damaged, failed, or otherwise abject gender to homosexuals, that is, calling gay men 'feminine' or calling lesbians 'masculine.'" Butler concludes that homophobic terror is often "a terror over losing proper gender" (1993, 238). Drag performance and camp are in this sense playful interventions that foreground the performative status of gender and dispel the notion of a damaged, failed, or otherwise incomplete gender. They "speak" the liminal position of the queer subject. It is important to note that although Ludovic's performances are consistently brilliant and engaging his emergence through performance as a sexual being in *Ma Vie en rose* is only somewhat autonomous.[5]

However, Ludovic's queering agency also targets more weighty and authoritarian discourses. Despite the mounting aggression and setbacks, he eventually comes around to defy precisely those ideologies that most immediately get in the way of his "becoming himself," that is, religion and biology. He takes on both their discursive constraints, merges them and invents a story of how he erroneously came to be a boy against all the odds of divine and biological determinism. In a virtuoso spiel ranging from science and Christmas folklore to theology, he reasons that in God's plan he was meant to be a "girlboy" and that God originally tossed two X's and one Y down to earth to make up his identity. As one of the X's accidentally fell into the trashcan instead of through the chimney, he ended up a girlboy trapped inside a boy's body. Against all the warnings, but in the hope of confirming the validity of his liminality, the boy tells everyone of this "scientific error" and of God's authority being intercepted by chance and accident. Incidentally, when he later explains to Jérôme that in due course "God will fix it. He'll send me my X and we can get married, okay?," the "boyfriend" grabs the chance to enforce the economy of desire into which he has been socialized, flippantly rejoining, "Depends what kind of girl you are!"

Ludovic's siblings (Gregory Diallo and Erik Cazals de Fabel) are unsure of the ideological and moral depth of their brother's transgressions: "He didn't kill the pope" . . . "Is it like putting the cat in the dishwasher?" . . . "Worse, you moron!" The psychologist concedes defeat and terminates Ludovic's therapy. And the conservative contingent in the neighborhood begins to use stronger measures against his courage and determination—ostracism. In response to the boy's queer performances, the straight community responds with its own discursive defense: "Shame on you" (see Sedgwick 1993, 4). The shaming performed by straight culture engages in what Butler identifies as a constitutive concealment of diversity; for her, "[t]he construction of coherence conceals the gender discontinuities that run rampant within the heterosexual, bisexual, gay and lesbian contexts in which gender does not necessarily follow from sex, and desire, or sexuality generally" (1990, 135–36).

Shame finds its witnesses and continuities are imposed as the father loses his job and the garage door is covered with hate messages: "Bent Boys Out!" Thus, the community purges what it perceives erroneously as a threat against its cohesion, against its meaningfulness, against its primary ideological foundation, masculinity. It is the father who appears most seriously crushed and defeated. His sense of dishonor and humiliation is unmatched. Ludovic, in turn, undergoes the most painful and violent castigation when his mother, Hanna (Michèle Laroque), sits down to cut his hair and brands her son for the first time directly with homophobic slurs: "'Bent' means a boy who likes boys, like you do." What was repressed as unspeakable and taboo up until this point (Ludovic's potential queerness) is now forced into the open, and the hair clipper is turned into a suitable tool for ritual punishment. Earlier in the film, the mother had defended her son against the father's proposition that Ludovic's hair be cut by saying, "Yes, darling. We could also crucify him." Now she is turned into the main enforcer of a code of external gender differentiation while the rest of the family stands by and watches.

The Crisis of Masculinity

The haircut not only marks the climax of communal tension but also clearly indicates the extent to which "the problem" is truly a crisis of masculinity. In fact, for the father, Ludovic's "long hair" had repeatedly been one of the most symbolic manifestations of his son's unsettling liminality, and during a soccer practice, at an advanced stage in the course of events, he identifies it as getting in the way of competitiveness ("Don't worry, you'll get the hang of it. You look hot in all that hair. We'll cut it . . . Go, Go!"). Interestingly, the reasons of the male and female characters for exerting pressure on the boy are consistently poles apart. For the men, masculinity, indeed patriarchy, itself is at issue, while for the women practical concerns and the equilibrium and stability of family life are the primary causes for intervention. These "gendered differences" are directly informed by the agents' position and function in society. For a film made at the turn of the twenty-first century, *Ma Vie en rose* depicts rather traditionally gendered families, and possibly deliberately so. For most of the couples, the division of labor casts the women as dedicated homemakers and mothers, and the men as breadwinners. When women are professional, they work predictably in vocations related to childcare, such as teaching and child psychology. The film particularly brings to light the impact of the boy's behavior on the men and on their function within the public sphere since norms are inherently dependent on collective reaffirmation. As Steve Neale points out, "[h]eterosexual masculinity has been identified as a structuring norm in relation both to images of women and gay men" and "current ideologies of masculinity involve so centrally notions and attitudes to do with

aggression, power, and control" (1993, 9, 11). Ludovic's mere presence among the men of the community is a catalyst for an epistemological and ideological crisis, and thus the stability of the entire
community begins to unravel. Heated exchanges and fistfights
come very close to breaking out among the men over the rumors
circulating about them or their families.

Ludovic's consistent identification with femininity has direct
bearing on the degree to which the other men can hold onto the
authorizations patriarchy has inscribed into its constructions of
masculinity. Male authority figures (the father, the father's boss,
the school principal) and eventually even the boy's peers overtly
carry out the function of maintaining the existing patriarchal
order, and their punitive measures progressively escalate in the
"aggression, power, and control" they exert over Ludovic. Beginning with mild reprimands and censorship by the father, this
collective exercise of masculine control over the definition of gender and sexuality—the psychic structures that ensure patriarchal
stability—manifests itself subsequently in more explicit prohibitions, punishments, humiliations, and eventually downright
ostracism. The project of disciplining Ludovic aims to produce
another affirmation of the ontological myth through him and his
corrected performance of masculinity, the very ground on which
patriarchal authorizations are validated. Most revelatory, in this
vein, is the boss's claim that the actual cause for Ludovic's
demeanor can be found with the mother. In his conversations with
the boy's father, Albert (Daniel Hanssens) argues that Ludovic
"doesn't need a shrink. Don't take offense, but Hanna has too
much control over your boys."

It will not come as a surprise, then, that Albert's wife, Lisette
(Laurence Bibot), functions as little more than an ideological
mouthpiece for his own social vision. As a critique of the Fabres'
taking their son to therapy, she reasons at one of their barbecues
that "if society wasn't so sick, there wouldn't be any loony bins."
Also for Thierry (Jean-François Gallotte), the Fabres' other neighbor, the soft approach of child therapy is easily dismissible as
"Baloney! Like drinking to stay sober!" Both Thierry and Albert
champion a harder, more disciplinarian, and more masculine remedy poignantly captured in Thierry's advice, "Stick to sports, I say!"
The men's "collective" disapproval of therapy defines what
Ludovic's dad does next in his reaction to peer pressure. After his
wife's "alarming" control over their son has been pointed out by

the boss, he initially defends his family politics but later makes a bargain with Ludovic that appears as tender and forgiving ("You are right. I've been working too much. Let's be together more."). However, his rapprochement turns out to be somewhat of a Trojan horse for the boy, as the offer translates into going to soccer practice together. In fact, the father's decisions are frequently based directly on social considerations—when the principal informs the Fabres of Ludovic's dismissal from school, the father does not protest in the name of injustice or discrimination as his wife does but first and foremost ascertains whether the Bruns and the Lemieux were supporters of the petition. For him, his and his family's respect in the public eye has priority over more abstract issues such as the putative legal foundation that underpins this communal action.

Throughout the film, boys are repeatedly shown in physical combat, be it their wrestling matches in the schoolyard, their games of cowboys and Indians in the backyard, or their scuffles on the soccer field. In one climactic incident Ludovic becomes intimately acquainted with this culture of bonding. The scene begins with a large group of boys crowding into the school's locker room after a victorious game. While the boys prepare for the showers, shouting, "We are the champions!" Ludovic's shyness and introversion, his inhibition about changing in front of the others, is turned into a cause for intimidation and bullying. The scene ends in a violent beating and hazing ritual, during which he is called "Fancy Pants" and accused of trying to hide his tits. Finally, as the tribal energies unleashed by the team leader intensify, the entire group swarms upon him with the threat of castrating him. "Do we pull it off? Make you a *real* girl?" Clearly, it is reality at stake here for the boys, and Ludovic's provocative "bending" of the illusory stability of heterosexual coherence has to be put right. Neither his friend (Jérôme) nor his two older brothers dare to interfere and defend him. The episode culminates with the boy's attempted suicide. For Ludovic, however, none of these coercive measures have any lasting effect. When the father offers him the fulfillment of a wish after the desperate boy is found in the family freezer, the first thing that comes to his mind is being granted permission to attend Sophie's birthday party wearing a skirt.

However, the communal defense of masculinity and its concomitant underbelly of athletic competition also have an economic dimension. Albert, as the father's employer, leads the way in the systematic ostracism, exactly as Ludovic's father earlier predicted he might: "Jérôme is Albert's son. Albert is Daddy's boss, so don't wear girl's clothes with Jérôme or anyone else." Positioned to define what values become more dominant among his neighbors, Albert is directly involved in the firing of Ludovic's dad. This assault on the father is clearly meant to jeopardize the Fabres' survival within the community and also to ensure that the economic order survives in its current form. The purging of the feminine in the male aims at achieving the highest competitive potential for the community at large, as though the community were a kind of sports team. In this sense, Albert's prohibition reveals a socioeconomic, indeed a distinctly capitalist, underbelly. Moreover, those who are most aggressive, most competitive, and therefore most able to enforce control over the group also ensure their own continued dominion. Homophobia is thus a variant of misogyny, a strategy geared to foster the hegemony of patriarchal control. In Albert's universe, socioeconomic competitiveness and the health of society are both tied to the defense of masculinity, while effeminacy/femininity is a symptom of their degeneration.

Sedgwick has mapped the "interimplication of homophobia and paranoia," observing that "it is the paranoid insistence with which the definitional barriers between 'the homosexual' (minority) and 'the heterosexual' (majority) are charged up, in this century, by nonhomosexuals, and especially by men against men, that most saps one's ability to believe in 'the homosexual' as an unproblematically discrete category of persons" (quoted in Edelman 1994, 7). Sedgwick has identified these "definitional barriers" as sites of a "brutally anxious will to power over the interpretation of selfhood" (7).

The women's position is quite different. For much of the time, the grandmother, the mother, the older sister, the psychologist, and the homeroom teacher place an emphasis on tolerance to nurture Ludovic's "natural" finding of an identity: "It's natural," says the mother, "until the age of seven, we search for our identity. I read it in *Marie-Claire*." This attitude drastically changes, however, when the father's dismissal threatens the material stability of domestic life. The mother's "ritualized crucifixion" of her son (the haircut) indicates her anguish for her family's well-being. While earlier she had voiced a protest that the community had legally no right to discriminate, she now blames Ludovic instead of the community for the ostracism they all suffer. In fact, at this point, she displays as much aggression as the father—"It's all your fault. Everything, . . .

You really mess up our lives." While her homophobia is less a defense of masculinity than an anxiety over survival and sustenance, she fails, like all the others, to identify its actual causes. In fact, none of the characters can envision that Ludovic might simply be all right, wearing the clothes he wants and expressing his desire. At the height of the crisis, when the increasingly confused and traumatized boy conveys his profound alienation from his family, and in particular from his mother, only the grandmother's home is a safe haven for him. The granny is the only person who frames the crisis differently: "It's not such a big deal. Don't over-react like all those idiots!" She, too, can be understood as misapprehending the situation, however. At least as important as over-reacting is naming the origin of the terror and dread gathered under the names *homophobia* and *homosexual panic*. That origin is the protection of patriarchal hegemony, the assumption of heterosexual coherence and the ontological fictions underwriting it.

Inversions and New Horizons

Ma Vie en rose ends with a number of inspiring inversions. Ludovic's last dream, before the family leaves their present neighborhood, involves another wedding to Jérôme, another white bridal dress-cum-veil, but this time in a virtual ceremony not staged in Albert's house but set inside the precincts of *Pam's World*. Indeed, the boy's imagination concocts a complete narrative turnaround, as all of the agents of his earlier ostracism are present to cheer him on—"The Bride! The Bride!"—dancing along with the procession down a pink carpet. Distinctly patriarchal aspects of the ceremony are queered: *not* the bride but the *groom* is handed over by his parent, and *not* Albert but *Jérôme's mother* leads her son with his pink bow tie to the bride. Clearly, Ludovic's mind has pegged Albert for the bully he really is, and his queering of the ceremony implicitly proposes that a matrilinear society might accommodate him and his desire more fully. The ritual ends with the two children on top of the wedding pavilion next to the heart-shaped duck pond, waving like a royal couple to the community below, while Albert, as the fat patriarchal villain, is seen pounding a "For Sale" sign into the lawn in front of the Fabres' former home. The need for communal and public validation of queer desire is possibly not captured elsewhere with as much charm and childlike naiveté as in *Ma Vie en rose*.

Ludovic inside "Pam's World."

A second turnaround takes place when the father lands another job and the Fabres move to another town. This time it is their new neighbors who initiate the family's integration, and here the cyclical structure of the narrative opens up horizons of change, if ever so tentatively. At first, Ludovic is filled with apprehension and worry, preoccupied with what the future might hold for him. Perhaps nothing will really change; nothing has been resolved. He is seen hanging out beside a nearby freeway to escape his family and their pressures, gazing at a billboard advertising "Pam's World," still a sanctuary to nurture his psychic needs. Ironically enough, the girl next door, Christine (Raphaelle Santini), is a rambunctious girlboy whose haircut is as choppy as Ludovic's and who appears to care little about her appearance and dress, preferring instead to shoot stones with her slingshot. In fact, many viewers will at first mistake her for a boy since she is dressed in clothes nearly identical to Ludovic's and since she displays rather aggressive and controlling behavior when the boy at first refuses to play with her.

In this neighborhood as in the last, get-togethers weave the life of the community. Shortly after the Fabres arrive, Ludovic is invited to Christine's birthday/costume party. Visibly ill at ease, the boy arrives in the masquerade of a musketeer. Surely, a new beginning, a totally fresh new start is attempted here. However, Christine looks equally uncomfortable in her light blue princess dress, and while the children play in the backyard the young hostess turns out to be quite a bully and forces Ludovic to switch costumes entirely against his will. The film introduces here a female inverse image of its boy protagonist. In fact, at the end the physical appearance of the two children collapses the hyperbolic gender dyad so deeply encrypted in the public imagination. The performativity brought into relief here is far less threatening to everyone except the Fabres. When the exchange of costumes is discovered, Ludovic's nearly hysterical mother confronts her child. However, before the boy is once again violently attacked, Christine reveals the true circumstances.

Important for the teleological aim of the film is that no one teases the girl for being "bent" (see Butler 1993, 104). No one advocates visits to a sewing circle or beauty school; she is simply treated as acceptable the way she is. Indeed, the absence of censorship and shaming in Christine's life suggests that the specters of ideal gender performance and their perceived perversion and deformation in queer performance is superseded. Heterosexual coherence is replaced by a concept of fluid and mutable identifications that have no bearing on communal stability and apparently threaten no existing way of life. If, as Butler argues, conventional gender performance "conceals the gender discontinuities that run rampant within the heterosexual, bisexual, gay and lesbian contexts" (1990, 135–36), then the two children at the end of *Ma Vie en rose* reveal and foreground those discontinuities.

Most importantly, the narrative now continues its inversion of itself and presents a provocative collapse of fantasy and realism, possibly in order to signal self-consciously that its purpose is more to envision a near-utopian alternative than to depict a lived reality. The film ends with a complete reconciliation between parents and child and an unconditional acceptance of Ludovic's behavior. The mother, after hearing that Ludovic did not instigate the costume exchange, is seen chasing after her boy in a sequence that revisits a number of key scenes with which we are already familiar, among them a visit to the family freezer to rescue him. In her panic, she then races along the freeway, sees the billboard advertising "Pam's

World," and climbs a ladder leading up to the spot where a partly open door is included in the layout. But she is able to open it. Inside, she sees Ludovic pleading with Pam to take him away with her and turning on his mother in anger and protest: "I won't ruin your life. I'm giving you a break." When Ludovic then pulls Pam with him along a bright yellow road to escape more deeply into the doll's world, the mother attempts to follow suit but her large real-life body drops through the floor and we find her back at home, lying on a couch. Whose fantasy are we watching? Is it the mother's dream-attempt to heal the rift between her and her child by connecting with her son's fantasy life where she confronts her guilt and her fear of losing him? Or, is it Ludovic's daydream in which he projects a happy ending to their collective trauma? In the real-life conversation that follows, both parents and Ludovic share references to the recent events as if they had been a shared reality. Ludovic then offers to take off Christine's robe, but the father tells him to "do whatever feels best," and the mother assures her son that "whatever happens, [he'll] always be [her] child." Champagne bottles are opened in the backyard, and the Fabres celebrate yet another housewarming.

In this, the film projects a queering of the preceding narrative as a whole, presenting a new paradigm for social cohesion not based on the stark gender polarity that previously endorsed the system of kinship relations. The narrative concludes by affirming the idea that the shift from an ontologically founded concept of heterosexual coherence on one hand to performativity and the acceptability of the (queer) dis-continuum on the other does not automatically entail a radical undoing of the "straight way of life" but merely repositions it in terms of its truth-claims. Ultimately, homophobia and the psychic injuries it inflicts can only be remedied if and when the entire community experiences a discursive reformation, one that replaces ontology with performativity. This reformation is implicitly grasped by the psychologist early on when she advises Ludovic that, "There may be things your parents never understand. You may have to wait till you are older to say them out loud." When she terminates her prescriptive intervention with the insight that, "Emptiness is scary but it can help us to know ourselves better," what she refers to as "emptiness" is in fact that loss of ontological grounding, an experience at the heart of postmodern culture, that has often been vilified as a form of cultural hollowness that leads to the dissolution of values. It is a profound menace to those who prefer conceiving of cultural life as governed by immutable and universally valid axioms about which truths can be told.

Given the deep-seated anxieties over masculinity surfacing in contemporary culture, Berliner's *Ma Vie en rose* offers insights that reveal the origins of the fear and nervousness at the heart of the matter. The narrative not only exposes what specific ideological forces discipline a boy's entry into male adulthood but also offers a penetrating look at the political and philosophical reasons why an entire community rises up to constrain him. Socially acceptable boyhood centers in ideas about how human beings are positioned in the world, that extend out and affect the equilibrium of communal life and the entire socioeconomic system in which Ludovic must reinvent himself.

The last images of the film present Pam, floating above the real neighborhood adrift through the film characters' and our imagination with her flamboyant red dress and blond hair. Her hyperbolic femininity and her golden magic sparkles may now, and only now, strike the viewer as self-consciously ironic, as "camped up." Most suggestive is her last secretive wink at the viewers, which might be read as a sign of secret amusement or a private signal of some kind, as though a drag queen were signaling a certain knowingness about her performance and involving the audience in the fun. In this, she brings to closure the film's discourse on gender imperatives and on the initial innocence with which children are acculturated into this regime and come to think of it as real. If the last images of Christine and Ludovic confound conventional heterosexual gender norms, then Pam can from now on be seen only as a chimera, a psychic hallucination, against which our real-life gender performances will never truly measure up. However alluring she is in all her perfection, she has no more claims to validity and truth than the two children do, in their musketeer and princess outfits, their short choppy hair, and their sensible shoes.

NOTES

1. See, for example, *Victor/Victoria* (1982), *Privates on Parade* (1982), *Lianna* (1983), *Silkwood* (1983), *Another Country* (1984), *Buddies* (1985), *Kiss of the Spider Woman* (1985), *Dona Herlinda and Her Son* (1985), *Desert Hearts* (1985), *Parting Glances* (1986), *My Beautiful Laundrette* (1985), *Prick Up Your Ears* (1987), *Philadelphia* (1993), *The Crying Game* (1992), *Better Than Chocolate* (1999), *When Night*

Is Falling (1995), *Salmonberries* (1991), and *Boys Don't Cry* (1995).

2. Here, and throughout this essay, the English translations of the original French are by Nigel Palmer.

3. Although the series uses live actors, who reappear in the boy's fantasies, the television program is also marketed via other commercial vehicles such as doll versions of the two actor/characters.

4. This is not the case for all gay male or lesbian subjects. In fact, in heterosexual, bisexual, gay, lesbian, transgender, and transsexual communities there is a great range of different combinations of genders, sexes, and sexual desires/practices. Queered performances of heterosexual coherence are nevertheless psychic staples of the subculture.

5. In *Bodies That Matter*, Judith Butler writes that "the conceit of autonomy implied by self-naming is the paradigmatically presentist conceit, that is, the belief that there is a one who arrives in the world, in discourse, without a history, that this one makes oneself in and through the magic of the name, that language expresses a 'will' or a 'choice' rather than a complex and constitutive history of discourse and power which compose the invariably ambivalent resources through which a queer and queering agency is forged and reworked. To recast queer agency in this chain of historicity is thus to avow a set of constraints on the past and future that mark at once the limits of agency and its most *enabling conditions*" (1993, 228).

Works Cited

Austin, J. L. 1975. *How to Do Things with Words.* Ed. J. O. Urmson and Marina Sbisà. 2nd ed. Cambridge: Harvard University Press.

Butler, Judith. 1990. *Gender Trouble: Feminism and the Subversion of Identity.* New York: Routledge.

———. 1993. *Bodies That Matter: On the Discursive Limits of "Sex."* New York: Routledge.

Edelman, Lee. 1994. *Homographies: Essays in Gay Literary and Cultural Theory.* New York: Routledge.

Grosz, Elizabeth. 1994. *Volatile Bodies: Toward a Corporeal Feminism.* Bloomington: Indiana University Press.

———. 1995. *Space, Time, and Perversion: Essays on the Politics of Bodies.* New York: Routledge.

Neale, Steve. 1993. "Masculinity as Spectacle: Reflections on Men and Mainstream Cinema." In *Screening the Male: Exploring Masculinities in Hollywood Cinema*, ed. Steven Cohan and Ina Rae Hark, 9–20. New York: Routledge.

Owen, Craig. 1987. "Outlaws: Gay Men in Feminism." In *Men in Feminism*, ed. Alice Jardine and Paul Smith, 219–32. London: Methuen.

Sedgwick, Eve Kosofsky. 1986. "Comments on Swann," *Berkshire Review* 21, 104–9.

———. 1988. "The Epistemology of the Closet (I)." *Raritan* 7, no. 4, 39–69.

———. 1993. "Queer Performativity: Henry James's *The Art of the Novel.*" *GLQ: A Journal of Lesbian and Gay Studies* 1, 1–16.

Segal, Lynne. 1990. *Slow Motion: Changing Masculinities, Changing Men.* London: Virago Press.

Wittig, Monique. 1980. "The Straight Mind." *Feminist Issues* 1, no. 1, 103–11.

3

SURVIVAL OF THE FATTEST

Contending with the Fat Boy in Children's Ensemble Films

Jerry Mosher

> George Cole had been spoilt by an overindulgent mother, who
> stuffed him with sweetmeats till he was sick, and then thought
> him too delicate to study, so that at twelve years old, he was a
> pale, puffy boy, dull, fretful, and lazy.
>
> Louisa May Alcott, *Little Men: Life at Plumfield with Jo's Boys,* 1871

> "Listen, Mr. Buttermaker, quit buggin' me about my food.
> People are always buggin' me about it. My shrink says that's why
> I'm so fat. So you're not doin' me any good—so just quit it!"
>
> Mike Engelberg, fat catcher in *The Bad News Bears*

These quotations—one from a classic of children's literature, the
other from a widely imitated children's ensemble film—span more
than a century, but they share a common purpose: to explain the
causes of a boy's obesity. Because the fat body is such a visible display of corporeal deviance, it is subjected to intense scrutiny and
regulation, which often takes the form of a *narrative*—the need to
explain how a fat person "got that way." The modern medical use
of the case history has shaped the way popular narratives circulate
about bodies and behavior, perpetuating the belief that character is
evident in the materiality of the body. When these narratives are
repeated over and over again, they enforce corporeal norms and naturalize any variation as symptomatic of behavioral deviance. Thus
George Cole in *Little Men* is not just fat, he is also "dull, fretful,
and lazy," traits that have become virtually synonymous with fat
in media characterizations of obesity. Similarly, Mike Engelberg in
The Bad News Bears (1976) displays stereotypical qualities such as
irritability and an obsession with food. Because these fat boys are
supporting characters who receive limited narrative attention, their
physical deviance and stereotypical behavior serve as a kind of
shorthand, enabling the audience to easily recognize them as familiar stock characters.

The stereotype, however, is "a complex, ambivalent, contradictory mode of representation, as anxious as it is assertive" (Bhabha 1994, 70). The fat boy has traditionally been the object of scorn, but he has also been a reliable and occasionally charismatic character in American cinema. When an American film features an ensemble of child actors there is almost invariably a fat boy, who seldom gets a date but often gets the best lines. Fat girls rarely are seen—reflecting the widespread marginalization of fat women in American media—but the fat boy role has maintained steady popularity throughout cinema's sound era. Whereas the fat girl has few adult role models, the fat boy's sheer size makes him a potential Babe Ruth—or, at least, a William "Refrigerator" Perry. It is thus not surprising that the fat boy has been a comic staple of children's sports films, as witnessed in *The Bad News Bears* and its many "band of misfits" imitators. In adventure films like *Lord of the Flies* (1963; 1990) and *The Goonies* (1985), he often plays a caretaking role in addition to providing comic relief. These ensemble films may suggest the presence of parents and authority figures, but more often than not they portray boys among their peers with little context of family. In the competitive world of the playground and the primitive setting of the camping trip, the boys often feel compelled to mimic adult masculinity and adopt a "survival of the fittest" mentality that punishes the fat boy or forces him into a subservient role. That the fat boy usually survives these demeaning trials with humility and a sense of humor is a testament to his resiliency.

Since the nineteenth century, childhood has been privileged as a time of presexual innocence and wide-eyed curiosity, but the popular narratives created to explain the fat boy's obesity usually suggest there is nothing innocent about him: he is greedy, corrupt, lazy, and dull. However, these narratives are complicated by the attribution of responsibility. Are fat children to blame for their obesity, or are their parents? Is childhood obesity a result of heredity, or environment? Stereotypical characterizations of fat children are too fleeting to convey the complexity of these issues, but they are nevertheless historically and culturally specific, dependent on the swift recognition of accepted wisdom and popular medical opinion. Medical experts currently estimate that at least 25 percent of American children are overweight or obese, a figure that has doubled in the last thirty years.[1] If this trend continues, they expect that virtually every American adult will be overweight within a few generations (Hill and Peters 1998, 1371). Because popular narratives of childhood obesity are expected to have a concomitant increase in cultural significance, it is vital that critics and producers of children's media begin to understand how these narratives have historically been constructed and utilized.

In this essay I will examine the fat boy in American cinema as a historically specific representation, focusing on the ways that popular narratives of "how they got that way" have reflected changing medical and cultural attitudes regarding childhood obesity. I will additionally draw upon examples from juvenile fiction, which constitutes many children's earliest encounter with these narratives and is often the literary source for children's films. By examining the norms and narratives that have figured the fat boy in American cinema, I am attempting to reveal this beleaguered, seemingly one-dimensional character as a voice of social articulation—a voice that has seldom been heard in accounts of children's media and culture.

HISTORICAL PRECEDENTS: PERFORMING THE "LITTLE FAT MAN"

Through most of the nineteenth century the fat body was valued as a marker of health, prosperity, and authority. Physicians and insurance companies had begun to associate adult obesity with early mortality, but a fat baby was considered a healthy baby and prominent gourmands like "Diamond Jim" Brady (1856–1917) promoted the idea that fat men had fat bank accounts. By the 1890s, however, popular notions of embodied deviance—specifically, the association of fat with material excess and moral weakness—were contributing to the widespread condemnation of fat. Historian Peter N. Stearns maintains that the increased desire for a thin body at this time was largely *compensatory* (1997, 56–65). The rise of public opinion and consensus, facilitated by urbanism and communications technologies, created growing awareness and guilt about rapidly changing social mores. Stricter discipline of the body, therefore, was viewed as spiritual compensation for excessive consumerism, declining religious practice, and greater social freedoms. Diet and fitness regimes began to be adopted in middle-class households, based on the belief that obesity was metabolic and required individual adjustments of diet and activity.

Childhood obesity did not receive serious medical attention until the 1940s. Undernourishment, a longstanding pediatric concern, was still prevalent during the Great Depression, and many parents welcomed having an overweight child, believing its "baby fat" to be only temporary. Dieting, when considered at all, tended to be focused on urban adolescent girls. Attention to boys' bodies usually focused on building them up, not slimming them down, evidenced in bodybuilder Charles Atlas's extensive advertising in comic books from the late 1920s through the 1940s. Atlas's muscularity program intended to help boys avoid becoming a "ninety-eight pound weakling" (Stearns 1997, 76). Medical research had not yet conclusively made the correlation between childhood overweight and adult obesity, but Atlas's advertising made it clear that a boy needed to start developing a man's body as soon as possible. This tendency to view boys as "little men" in the process of becoming "real men" had been evident for some time in juvenile literature such as *Little Men* and the tales of Horatio Alger.[2] It would have a significant impact on cinematic representations of fat boys. Their fatness might have been attributable to glandular conditions out of their control, but as "little fat men" they would be implicated in the turn against fat that associated adult obesity with behavioral deviance.

The commercial potential of exhibiting excessively fat bodies, well established in nineteenth-century carnivals and circuses, had been realized in early cinema. Actualities (documentary shorts) such as the Edison Company's *Largest Fat Boy in the World* (1905) established the fat boy as a cinematic site of spectacle. For child actors playing fat boys in narrative feature films, the experience has continued to be regarded as a novelty; few find steady work as adolescents unless they lose weight. Because the most important requirements for playing a fat child are youth and obesity, viewers understandably believe that fat children are merely playing themselves.[3] When fat actors are asked to play typically limited, stock characters, this conflation of actor and role only contributes to the perception that fat stereotypes are indeed true. Fat boy actors are thus perceived in real life to be like the stock characters they play onscreen.

The only fat boys to enjoy a high-profile career in classical Hollywood cinema appeared in children's ensemble serials. Dozens of children's series were produced between the wars but the best known was *Our Gang*, which was seen in 221 shorts between 1922 and 1944 (the series would later be re-released on television as "The Little Rascals" [1954]). *Our Gang* featured a mix of mostly lower-middle-class boys and girls who represented distinct "types" in a

In the first half of the twentieth century, attention to boys' bodies usually focused on building them up, not slimming them down, evidenced in bodybuilder Charles Atlas's extensive advertising in comic books from the late 1920s through the 1940s. Atlas's muscularity program intended to help boys avoid becoming a "ninety-eight pound weakling."

comedic microcosm of American life: in addition to the fat boy, there were the clubhouse leader, the troublemaker, the flirt, the snobby girl, and racial stereotypes such as the pickaninny. The serial's most famous fat boy, Joe Cobb, debuted in *Our Gang* in 1923 at age five and appeared in eighty-six silent and talkie shorts through 1929 when he was replaced by the equally robust but less charismatic Norman "Chubby" Chaney.[4] *Our Gang* creator Hal Roach looked for a worthy successor until the serial's conclusion, but he never found another fat boy who could match Cobb's talent and likeability (Maltin and Bann 1992, 249).

Roach later claimed the secret of his success was finding "some clever street kids to just play themselves in films and show life from a kid's angle" (Maltin and Bann 1992, 9), but it was

Our Gang's original fat boy Joe Cobb (top left) and his successor Norman "Chubby" Chaney (top right) worked together in four episodes of the children's serial in 1929. Other Gang members are (l to r) Allen "Farina" Hoskins, Mary Ann Jackson, Bobby "Wheezer" Hutchins, Jean Darling, and Harry Spears. Pete the Pup looks on.

obvious that these kids frequently were mocking adult customs and affectations. In particular, their undermining of aristocratic pretensions established a working-class perspective that pervaded the series. In the episode "Stage Fright" (1923), the kids act in a play about ancient Rome in which Cobb plays Emperor Nero, parodying the tragic hero of William Fox's 1922 feature film *Nero*. In *Our Gang*'s parodies of cultural icons and its lampooning of office politics and society manners, these little men and women unmasked the thin veil of artifice that maintained adult distinctions of class and authority.

Cobb, who ostensibly played himself onscreen, took advantage of the seriality of *Our Gang* to perform a variety of fat boy personae, such as an overweight jockey in *Derby Day* (1923) and a heavyweight boxer in *Boxing Gloves* (1929). He frequently displayed the childish obsession with food expected from a fat boy, but his parodies of fat historical figures and his sheer bulk contributed to his status as a "little fat man." By playing so many variations on fat stereotypes, Cobb often met and confounded audience expectations in the same episode. Cobb is one of the few fat boys in American cinema to appear onscreen with a girlfriend or in pursuit of one, acknowledging the often-overlooked fact that fat boys have libidos too. And unlike the typical fat boy who is begrudgingly admitted to the gang only to be the butt of jokes, Cobb was considered an equal member of *Our Gang.*

The appearance of a likeable fat boy on U.S. movie screens in 1923 was particularly timely since Hollywood was still reeling from the murder charges leveled at film comedian Roscoe "Fatty" Arbuckle. Arbuckle was acquitted in April 1922, after three highly publicized trials, but the sordid rumors about Virginia Rappe's death in his San Francisco hotel room ruined Arbuckle's career and branded fat men as sexual deviants with monstrous appetites. Sensing the need for "something fresh and wholesome" (Maltin and Bann 1992, 9), Roach created *Our Gang* as an antidote to Hollywood scandal. Cobb, along with his Roach studio colleague Oliver Hardy, was thus given the task of recuperating the popular narrative of the infantilized fat male as comic innocent. Such an undertaking revealed the complex relationship between sweetened screen depictions of children and the expectations placed upon them by world-weary grown-ups. In these children, film historian Vivian Sobchack notes, "what seems a looking forward toward the possibilities of the future is a longing backward toward the promise once possessed by the past" (1996, 149). Indeed, the lovable Cobb does not seem to represent a fat man of the future so much as the promising, pretrial young man of Arbuckle's past.

Like all cinematic fat boys, Cobb embodied ambivalent American attitudes about fat. He may have been a good-natured lad, but in American culture the fat boy represented the antithesis of Horatio Alger's lean, industrious newsboys—the hungry urchins who worked their way out of the streets into middle-class respectability. In the early twentieth century Alger's boys would be embraced as "rags to riches" embodiments of the American dream. The fat boy violated this myth of the self-made man by prematurely acquiring the corporeal surplus afforded only to successful older "fat cats." Like the gangster who rises too quickly from the under-class to the leisure class and must be punished, the fat boy's accu-mulative tendencies made him a lamentable case of "too much, too soon." The analogy was made explicit in the 1932 short film *Little Geezer*, Theodore Huff's hilarious parody of *Little Caesar* (1930), in which an ensemble of children plays gangsters and their molls.[5] Not surprisingly, a fat boy plays the titular mob boss who is inevitably gunned down. Little Geezer's fate would prove to be prophetic; with the demise of *Our Gang* and the appearance of vio-lent children's ensemble films in the postwar era, obese boys would repeatedly be reminded that "fat does not pay."

Lord of the Flies: Working-Class Fat

After decades of worrying about underweight children, in the 1940s medical experts began to express the belief that overweight children would likely grow up to be obese adults. This opinion, historian Hillel Schwartz notes, was related to the 1940s "mental hygiene" movement that associated childhood obesity with inadequate socialization and with the polio epidemic that left many children disabled and prone to weight gain (Schwartz 1986, 287–90). Polio and obesity became linked to the point that the obese child, like the polio-stricken child, was expected to become a disabled adult. Diet consciousness among Americans of all ages exploded in the 1950s, facilitated by an expanding postwar economy and television adver-tising that promoted the consumption of dieting aids, especially for women. Dieting became big business and *failure* became the foun-dation of this industry. When obesity had been considered a meta-bolic ailment, diet fads during the 1920s aimed to reduce the fat *body;* after the Second World War, however, doctors and psycholo-gists suggested that the fat *person* needed help. Fat had lost any ves-tiges of its leisure-class signification; it now indicated a failure to "measure up" in an increasingly corporate society. The image of the fat cat monopolist that had sustained so many Depression-era movies was all but forgotten, replaced by one of the lean, college-educated corporate managers who in 1956 would be the subject of sociologist William H. Whyte's bestseller *The Organization Man* and portrayed by Gregory Peck in *The Man in the Gray Flannel Suit.*[6] The most iconic representations of fat men in the 1950s showed them as working-class and undereducated: Ralph Kramden (Jackie Gleason), the loudmouthed bus driver in the "The Honeymooners" television series (1952–57); and Marty, the lonely butcher from the Bronx in *Marty* (played by Rod Steiger in the 1953 teleplay and by Ernest Borgnine in the 1955 feature film). Like these disenfranchised men, fat boys in postwar films such as *Lord of the Flies* (1963) would be marginalized for their obesity and especially the working-class culture it represented. *Lord of the Flies* and subsequent films like *Stand by Me* (1986) contested the myth of the self-made man, suggesting that class and heredity indelibly marked boys' bodies and their fate in the world.

British novelist William Golding's *Lord of the Flies*, published in 1954, depicts a group of proper English schoolboys who descend into savagery when they are stranded without adult supervision on a deserted island. Provoked by the horrors of the Second World War, Golding's novel suggested that evil was not limited to the adult world, for original sin lurked within even the most civilized young men. Despite the novel's British origins, its widespread adoption in American secondary school curricula throughout the late twentieth century would make its fat boy, "Piggy," one of the most influential representations of boyhood obesity for several generations of American adolescents. Reflecting its appeal in the United States, British director Peter Brook's faithful film adaptation, which used nonprofessional actors, premiered in New York before it premiered in London. (An inferior U.S. remake that changed the boys to American military school students was released in 1990.) In its tragic depiction of a fat working-class boy isolated among lean upper-class males, Brook's adaptation confirmed fat's shifting class signification in postwar cinema.

Lord of the Flies has three main characters: Ralph (James Aubrey), the commonsensical leader who attempts to organize the boys' survival efforts; Jack (Tom Chapin), the rebellious leader of the "hunters" camp who wrests control of the majority; and Piggy (Hugh Edwards), the most vocal proponent of civilization whose obesity, asthma, spectacles, and social inferiority render him incapable of initiating action. Among these boys from better schools, Piggy's accent and poor English reveal his working-class status. Literary critic Patrick Reilly notes, "Neither Ralph nor Jack would ever have met Piggy back in England except as their employee, for while they are so obviously, in their respective ways, officer material, Piggy is just as obviously born to be an underling all his days" (1998, 173). When Piggy and Ralph stumble upon each other in the film's first scene, Ralph is cool to the fat boy's insistent questions, implying that he doesn't usually talk to boys who look and talk like Piggy. After Ralph states that his father is a military officer, Piggy reveals his lack of credentials and the causes of his obesity: his parents are dead and his aunt won't let him swim or run because of his asthma. It is Piggy, however, who gives Ralph the idea to blow on a conch shell to summon the boys. Ralph realizes that Piggy's intellect might be an asset to his leadership, and Piggy is happy to make Ralph his mouthpiece because he cannot gain the other boys' respect on his own. While the privileged boys argue among themselves over petty grievances, the working-class fat boy prepares for the worst because he does not take his survival for granted. Only Piggy—whose glasses provide their means of making fire—has the foresight to suggest that the boys might have to coexist on the island for the rest of their lives.

Piggy's caretaking and domestic concerns reveal a maternal side that has long characterized fat boys in children's series fiction. The most famous of these is Chet Morton, the fat sidekick in the hugely successful *Hardy Boys* mysteries, published in more than one hundred volumes since 1927 by the Stratemeyer Syndicate. The publishing dynasty's vast number of children's series were ghost written by multiple authors and followed strict narrative formulas. The leading characters, Stratemeyer historian Carol Billman notes, are physically fit and "indisputedly extraordinary adolescents . . . skilled at everything that comes their way" (1986, 29). An amiable fat friend, whose incompetency and limited intelligence serve to highlight the protagonists' superior talents, appears in many series.[7] In *The Hardy Boys*, girls have very minor roles and "more often than not, Chet replaces the fair sex as the object of a daring rescue" (Billman 1986, 86). Like Piggy, Chet is often accused of talking too much, and his eagerness to cook for the boys or tend to their injuries further mark him as their feminine companion. In *The Clue of the Screeching Owl* (1962), Joe Hardy is rescued from a frozen stream and Chet applies treatment, rubbing "Joe's body briskly with his big woolen shirt" (quoted in Wedwick 1998, 26).

The sexual tension between the subservient fat boy and his lean, athletic cohorts, occasionally intimated in the Stratemeyer stories depicting "boys without girls," is underplayed in Brook's cerebral adaptation of *Lord of the Flies*. It is more pronounced, however, in the updated, "Americanized" 1990 version. Jack (Chris Furrh) menacingly calls the fat boy (Danuel Pipoly) "tits" and "Miss Piggy" (obviously referencing the frumpy Muppet), and taunts him, "I want you, Piggy." Jack's threats evoke the well-known scene in

In *Lord of the Flies* (1963), the sensitive, intelligent Piggy (Hugh Edwards, right) cannot gain the other boys' respect, so he is happy to make Ralph (James Aubrey, left) the mouthpiece of his ideas.

Deliverance (1972), in which mountain men rape the fat member of a river rafting expedition while he is forced to squeal like a pig. Like the adult group of river rafters, the little men in *Lord of the Flies* must designate the weakest member who cannot "pull his weight" as subservient or feminine to validate their own anxious masculinity.[8] Piggy will indeed be sacrificed, killed with a boulder while making a desperate plea for order. Upon being rescued, Ralph will weep for "the end of innocence" and this tragic fat boy, "the true, wise friend called Piggy" (Golding [1954] 1997, 235).

The Bad News Bears: Fat and Unhappy

By the 1970s two generations of Americans had grown up in a culture of slimming, and parents' internalization of diet consciousness was being projected onto their children. Medical attention to childhood obesity, which had focused primarily on adolescents in the 1950s and grade-schoolers in the 1960s, was now concerning itself with the health risks of fat among toddlers and even fetuses. Weight-loss programs and fitness centers no longer courted a predominantly female customer base and targeted middle-class men and boys concerned about heart disease. Magazine advertisements for Fleischmann's liquid corn oil margarine asked, "Should an 8-year-old worry about cholesterol?" and "Is there a heart attack in his future?" (Schwartz 1986, 295) In addition to these worries, beleaguered fat boys like Mike Engelberg in *The Bad News Bears* had to contend with shrinks who applied psychoanalytic methods to weight control and to children who overwhelmingly declared in grade-school surveys that fat bodies were "obnoxious, sloppy, ugly, lonely, lazy and even stupid" (295).

The Bad News Bears comically utilized children's myriad prejudices, transferring the rule of "survival of the fittest" from *Lord of the Flies'* deserted island to America's baseball diamonds. Its savvy commentary on how adults' competitive urges are inscribed in their children scored a hit at the box office, earning the seventh-highest grosses of 1976. The film took a "band of misfits" approach straight out of *Our Gang*, presenting a ragtag group of distinct types from lower-middle-class suburbia: the fat kid, the know-it-all, the bad boy, the black kid, the Mexican brothers, and the girl who's a better athlete than any of them. (The overconfident opposing players, in contrast, are exclusively white males.) What distinguishes *The Bad News Bears* from its sequels and imitators are its crude language and unflinching look at the narcotized ennui of suburbia, where frustrated parents bully their children, and bored children bully each other. In what film historian James Monaco calls "the ultimate anti-Disney movie" (1979, 365), children swear, use racial epithets, smoke, drink beer, and mix martinis for their alcoholic coach (Walter Matthau), who passes out while pitching batting practice. Because the kids are not seen at home or in school, their frustrations and flaws are magnified within the competitive, rule-driven boundaries of the playing field.

In this world of organized dysfunction, the fat catcher Mike Engelberg (Gary Lee Cavagnaro) does not provide the cuteness of a Joe Cobb or the civilized intelligence of a Piggy. His bulk enables him to hit home runs but he is frequently angry and dirty, his ill-fitting uniform smeared with food stains. The fat boy's surliness and references to his shrink suggest that his obesity is the result of

In *The Bad News Bears* (1976), the fat catcher Mike Engelberg (Gary Lee Cavagnaro, right) does not provide the cuteness of a Joe Cobb or the civilized intelligence of a Piggy. He is frequently angry and dirty, his ill-fitting uniform smeared with food stains.

individual neurosis, reflecting the psychological explanations of obesity that gained acceptance in the postwar decades. No longer viewed as metabolically challenged victims of heredity, fat people were now characterized—for instance, in a widely publicized 1947 *Time* magazine article titled "Fat and Unhappy"—as forlorn and tormented by inner conflicts. Psychoanalytic therapies sought to uncover the sources of fat people's unhappiness, and a growing recognition of addictive behaviors led to group therapy approaches to dieting such as TOPS (Taking Off Pounds Sensibly, founded 1948); Overeaters Anonymous (1960); and Weight Watchers (1961). Given the unbridled consumerism of suburbia, it was only a matter of time before food became an object of substance abuse requiring regulation and medical scrutiny. Unlike cigarettes and alcohol, however, obesity-inducing fast food was marketed and sold to children in their schools and sports leagues (in *The Bad News Bears*,

two teams are sponsored by Denny's and Pizza Hut, respectively).
The mixed messages children receive are cruelly apparent in the
film's depiction of a popular postgame ritual: after exerting themselves on the playing field, the kids celebrate by gorging themselves
at McDonald's. Within two decades, America would have millions
of Mike Engelbergs to contend with.

The Goonies and Stand by Me: Kinder, Gentler Fat

Psychological theories of overeating and dieting often characterize
them as nostalgic acts in which fat people hope to return to an idyllic past when food was comforting and good. In the dysfunctional
culture depicted in The Bad News Bears, it is not surprising that
many Americans resort to overeating and dieting in an attempt to
recapture "a time when one could be satisfied, when one was thin-
ner, when the range of choices in the world neither bewildered nor
intimidated" (Schwartz 1986, 307). In the 1980s, the Reagan and
Bush administrations responded to the post-Vietnam malaise with
their nostalgic vision of America as a nation of humble people and
family values. Like Ronald Reagan, two of the decade's most influential filmmakers—George Lucas and Steven Spielberg—based
their mythic, Manichean narratives on the movie serials and comic
books of their youth. The adult yearning for childlike innocence
and escape from a fragmenting culture was evident in The Goonies
(1985) and Stand by Me, two children's ensemble films structured
as episodic adventure stories. Their fat boys resembled Our Gang's
affable Joe Cobb more than the surly Mike Engelberg, revealing the
desire for an idealized past when fat boys were jolly and obesity was
less understood and therefore less complicated.

The Goonies, produced by Spielberg and modeled on his
Indiana Jones films and The Hardy Boys, depicts a typically ragtag
bunch of kids in the Pacific Northwest who hunt for buried treasure in a murky labyrinth of caves, fend off a gang of criminals, and
ultimately save their town from demolition by developers. The fat
boy, called Chunk (Jeff Cohen), is a gregarious clown whose obsession with junk food becomes acute whenever he's in danger. His
search for the healing powers of ice cream lands him in a cell with
Sloth (John Matuszak), an enslaved human "monster," whom he
feeds and nurtures. After sharing a candy bar Chunk and Sloth pro-
fess their "love" for each other, which encourages the monster to
help the children escape from the criminals. Playing the jovial

companion and feminized caretaker, Chunk is a throwback to Chet Morton of *The Hardy Boys*. His perpetual grin and jiggling baby fat recall the prewar image of the little fat man as infantile comic innocent.

Stand by Me, based on Stephen King's short story "The Body," laments the loss of innocence in American boyhood that was felt so acutely in the post-Vietnam era, nostalgically depicting a simpler, rural America at the end of the Eisenhower years. In the summer of 1959 a quartet of twelve-year-old boys embarks on an overnight camping trip to search for a dead body rumored to be in the forest outside Castle Rock, Oregon. As in most children's ensemble films, the four boys represent distinct personality types: there is the tough kid, Chris (River Phoenix); the fat and dumb kid, Vern (Jerry O'Connell); the crazy kid, Teddy (Corey Feldman); and the sensitive kid, Gordie (Wil Wheaton), who narrates the story in flashback as an adult. The fat boy is typically buffoonish, but the film's overt class consciousness enriches his limited characterization by suggesting that for all of these boys their fate in the world is already sealed. Each boy is emotionally wounded in some way, but only Gordie has the advantages of a middle-class background. The tough-but-wise Chris realizes how their class difference will determine the courses they take when they begin junior high school in the fall: "You'll be taking your college courses, and me, Teddy, and Vern will be in shop courses with the retards making ashtrays and birdhouses."

The boys go through a journey of trials and hardships that reveals their varying levels of physical and mental competency. The film suggests that middle-class Gordie and tough Chris have the skills to succeed in the modern world, but fat Vern and crazy Teddy will be severely limited by their handicaps. Proving the point, at film's end we learn that Gordie is a writer and Chris became an attorney before his untimely death. Vern, on the other hand, is a forklift operator at a lumberyard, and Teddy does odd jobs and has spent time in jail. *Stand by Me* closes on a cheerful note, but the film cannot conceal a painful truth: the end of a boy's innocence is marked by the realization that his prospects have rapidly begun to narrow. In the postwar era, working-class fat boys like Vern and Piggy in *Lord of the Flies* learned at an early age that their medical and economic prognoses were not good.

Often overlooked in critical analyses of *Stand by Me* is the extraordinary depiction of its other fat boy. While the boys sit

In *Stand By Me* (1986), Gordie's campfire story, "The Revenge of Lard Ass Hogan," accentuates the carnivalesque aspects of the titular fat boy's body (performed by Andy Lindberg), turning it literally inside out in a "complete and total barfarama."

around a campfire, Gordie tells a story, "The Revenge of Lard Ass Hogan." Lard Ass is a morbidly obese boy who is the laughingstock of his town. Before participating in the county pie-eating contest, Lard Ass prepares his revenge by swallowing a raw egg and castor oil. The fat boy then devours numerous blueberry pies and vomits on another contestant; the act sets off a chain reaction of vomiting among the townspeople in "a complete and total barfarama." Harkening back to the simple days when obesity was neither a disease nor a civil rights issue, the story is terribly crude and does little to confirm Gordie's writing talents. The other boys' questions, criticisms, and embellishments of the story, however, contribute to the film's thematic concern with "the way in which stories are told and give rise to other stories" (Wojcik-Andrews 2000, 12). In this sense, Gordie's fictional creation demonstrates how popular narratives of obesity are constructed, revised, and repeated. "The Revenge of Lard Ass Hogan," one of the most grotesque depictions of obesity in cinema history, exploits the carnivalesque spectacle of the fat body, turning it literally inside out in an exaggeration of its orality and vulgarity. Yet Gordie feels the need to make his grotesque protagonist sympathetic by explaining that his obesity is "not his fault—it's his glands." Lard Ass's revenge, Gordie implies, is justified because his obesity is not a character defect and thus does not warrant the townspeople's insults. This desire to have it both ways—to grossly exploit the fat boy's physical deviance and show understanding for him—would pervade cinematic representations of fat boys in the late twentieth century as childhood obesity reached epidemic proportions and the social problem of size discrimination entered public awareness.

THE FAT BOY FRANCHISED

After billions of dollars had been spent on medical research, therapy, and diet and fitness regimens, American adults and their children were only getting fatter in the 1990s. Blame was usually attributed to two factors: technology and sedentary jobs making it possible to avoid exercise, and fast food culture beginning to dominate American eating habits. At the end of the century, when 90 percent of American children between three and nine years old were visiting a McDonald's once a month, fast food culture was becoming synonymous with children's culture (Schlosser 2001, 47–49). Conglomeration and corporate synergy made fast food companies major players in the production of children's toys and entertainment, facilitating product placement and cross-promotion. After McDonald's and the Walt Disney Company signed a ten-year global marketing agreement in 1996, a *Newsday* headline asked, "You Want First-Run Features with Those Fries?" (Bates 1997). The popular children's narratives produced by these corporate conglomerates were market-driven vehicles for the hawking of food, toys, clothing, and related products.

The industry predictably seized upon Paramount's *Bad News Bears* formula, softening its vulgarity in a series of meek and forgettable children's sports films: ice hockey in *The Mighty Ducks* (1992–96); football in *Little Giants* (1994); and soccer in *The Big Green* (1995). The films preached that winning isn't everything, but the underdogs' ultimate victories were never in doubt. This winning attitude was undoubtedly necessary to market products, since the Walt Disney Company made the unprecedented move of buying a National Hockey League franchise and calling it the Mighty Ducks, a stunning example of cross-promotion run amok. Ironically, *The Mighty Ducks* films depicted the misfit team defeating heartless corporate interests.

With rampant childhood obesity constituting a public health crisis, studio conglomerates could hardly afford to offend their corporate partners and rapidly fattening target audience with the pointed humor displayed in *The Bad News Bears* series (as, for example, when Mike Engelberg noshes from a bucket of Kentucky Fried Chicken while sitting on the toilet). Their cinematic representations of fat boys in the 1990s offered easily recognizable, bland stereotypes, much like the Stratemeyer Syndicate's mass-produced fictional characters. Fat boys are always given the "squatting" position—catcher in baseball, goalie in ice hockey and soccer, center in football—which enables them to eat (and fart) during games. The films made no attempt to comprehend the boys' experience of obesity or how they got that way; fat boys were just expected to be there because the formula dictated it. Engelberg's angry eating and need for a psychiatrist were considered bad for business in the 1990s. The new market-driven children's sports films presented amiable, dim-witted fat boys who were, first and foremost, ideal consumers.[9]

Acknowledging obesity's impact on American boys and the jokes (and profits) it could generate, in 1995 Disney and *Mighty Ducks* writer Steven Brill cannibalized the misfit children's summer camp formula made popular by the four *Meatballs* films (1979–1992) to create *Heavyweights,* an ensemble film set in a boys' summer fat camp. Ostensibly a diet program, "Camp Hope" is actually a refuge for middle-class fat boys where their size is accepted and they can smuggle in snacks—until an overzealous fitness guru (Ben Stiller) purchases the camp. After being submitted to a harsh diet and exercise regimen, the boys predictably rebel and hold the "fitness nazi" hostage until their summer haven is restored. Recognizing the burgeoning size-acceptance movement in America, *Heavyweights* comically demonstrated that constant dieting was a curse worse than being fat.[10] Its dependence on fat jokes for its humor, however, provoked many critics to accuse the film's producers of "having their cake and eating it too" (Mosher 2001, 238). The film was awash in mixed messages, encouraging and condemning the boys' self-destructive eating habits, and advocating their resistance to the fitness guru's Anthony Robbins–style motivational techniques while implying that they would never measure up in an image-conscious corporate world. Despite its ambivalence and predictability, *Heavyweights* capably depicted one of the most overlooked causes of childhood obesity: the vengeful rebelliousness of secret eating, which sociologist Mildred Klingman calls "the secret to staying fat. It is one of the ways in which fat people can go on a diet and still succeed in not losing any weight" (1981, 8). Additionally, its inclusion of fat African American boys was an overdue acknowledgement of childhood obesity's severity in the black community.[11]

The most memorable moment of social critique in *Heavyweights* occurs when a bus loaded with obese boys on their way to fat camp passes through a stretch of highway lined with fast-food restaurants. The scene poignantly illustrates obesity researchers James O. Hill and James C. Peters's argument that "within any environment, an individual's becoming obese is not a certainty, but an event that occurs with a certain probability." For many Americans, Hill and Peters note, obesity is merely a "natural response to the environment" (1998, 1371). The fact that two of the major shapers of that environment—Disney and McDonald's—would sign their marketing pact only a year after *Heavyweights* was released reveals the shallowness of the film's critique and confirms the powerful ability of hegemonic institutions to subsume resistance. Disney's hypocrisy is nothing new, for it merely echoes Americans' conflicting attitudes toward fat and an economy of abundance. A majority of Americans is overweight, yet when fat appears we insist that it be hidden or eradicated. The fat boy—who might wish to hide but must attend school and obey his elders—is a too-visible reminder that children are vulnerable to the same daily hungers and excesses that tempt adults. For succumbing so soon, the fat boy must be punished: if he is white and affluent, he is characterized as a greedy, corrupt descendant of the Capitalist Fat Cat; if he is of color or working-class, he is characterized as a slow-witted prole with little hope of success in an image-conscious culture. Either way, his embodied deviance and perceived femininity represent a troubling future for American masculinity—a future that many males would rather not contemplate. Attempts to shame the fat boy out of existence, however, only serve to guarantee his continued presence in American cultural discourse. This longstanding ambivalence has made the fat boy a popular, yet stigmatized, cinematic role, one that is sure to endure as a generation of "little fat men" grows into adulthood.

NOTES

1. Statistical analyses of childhood obesity often encompass both children (ages 6–11) and adolescents (ages 12–17). Obesity is generally defined as 20 percent above the maximum healthy body weight. Overweight is defined as any weight above the maximum healthy weight.
2. Feature film adaptations of *Little Men* have appeared in 1934, 1940, and 1998. The novel's fat boy, George "Stuffy" Cole, receives very limited screen time. Surprisingly, there have been no film adaptations of Alger's novels.
3. Jerry O'Connell, now a thin professional actor, described playing the fat boy Vern in *Stand by Me:* "It wasn't much of an acting stretch for me. I was an 11-year-old fat kid playing an 11-year-old fat kid" (Hobson 2000).
4. After leaving *Our Gang* in 1931, Chaney would reach three hundred pounds in his teens and die in 1936 at age eighteen (Maltin and Bann 1992, 255). Cobb died in 2002 at age eighty-five. The cherubic clubhouse leader George "Spanky" McFarland, who became *Our Gang's* best-known member during his tenure from 1932 to 1942, might be considered fat by today's standards, but he was not read as "fat" at the time, nor was he expected to play the fat boy role.
5. Director Alan Parker would take a similar approach in his ambitious 1976 gangster musical *Bugsy Malone,* in which a cast of children plays molls and gangsters who tote machine guns that shoot whipped cream. A fat boy plays the mob boss who operates "Fat Sam's Grand Slam Speakeasy."
6. Nostalgic throwbacks to the era of the Capitalist Fat Cat occasionally appeared in postwar children's ensemble films. In *Willy Wonka and the Chocolate Factory* (1971), based on Roald Dahl's popular 1964 children's novel *Charlie and the Chocolate Factory,* the gluttonous German fat boy Augustus Gloop (Michael Bollner) repeatedly displays the cold-blooded avarice associated with Gilded Age fat cats. As a consequence he is the first child to be eliminated in the contest to win a lifetime supply of Wonka's chocolate.
7. In addition to Chet Morton, other Stratemeyer Syndicate fat boys include Bob Baker, called "Chunky" in The *Motor Boys* series (1906–24); Fenn Masterson, called "Stumpy" in *The Darewell Chums* series (1908–11); and Jimmy Plummer, nicknamed "Doughnuts" in *The Radio Boys* series (1922–30) (Pickrell 1996, 12–13).

8. Video artist Rene Broussard's *The Fatboy Chronicles* (1994–2001), a three-part "appropriated video diary," uses clips from dozens of feature films to explore how fat boys are sexualized at the hands of sadistic teachers and school bullies.

9. Like Mike Engelberg, the fat boys in *The Mighty Ducks* series (Goldberg [Shaun Weiss]) and *The Goonies* (Chunk) are Jewish. (Chunk often mentions his religious affiliation, even reciting the blessing "Baruch atah Adonai . . ." when he's in trouble.) Are these merely lazy appropriations of *The Bad News Bears* formula, or are these little fat men, who used to evoke greedy turn-of-the-century robber barons, now embodying similar stereotypes about Jews?

10. The National Association to Advance Fat Acceptance (established 1969) combats size prejudice and advocates use of the word "fat," arguing that "obesity" is a pathologized term of the medical industry.

11. Secret eating and the compound socioeconomic liabilities of being a fat and black male in America are also addressed in *Monster's Ball* (2001), in which an African American single parent (Halle Berry) cannot control her young obese son's clandestine food binges. Wracked with guilt, she laments, "I didn't want him to be fat like that, because I know a black man in America, you can't be like that."

WORKS CITED

Bates, James. 1997. "You Want First-Run Features with Those Fries?" *Newsday*, May 11.

Bhabha, Homi K. 1994. *The Location of Culture.* London: Routledge.

Billman, Carol. 1986. *The Secret of the Stratemeyer Syndicate: Nancy Drew, the Hardy Boys and the Million Dollar Fiction Factory.* New York: Ungar.

"Fat and Unhappy." 1947. *Time,* October 20, 61.

Golding, William. 1997, ©1954. *Lord of the Flies.* New York: Riverhead.

Hill, James O., and James C. Peters. 1998. "Environmental Contributions to the Obesity Epidemic." *Science,* May 29, 1371–74.

Hobson, Louis B. 2000. "Playboy in Space." *Calgary Sun,* March 6.

Klingman, Mildred. 1981. *The Secret Lives of Fat People.* Boston: Houghton Mifflin.

Maltin, Leonard, and Richard W. Bann. 1992. *The Little Rascals: The Life and Times of Our Gang.* Rev. ed. New York: Three Rivers Press/ Crown.

Monaco, James. 1979. *American Film Now.* New York: Oxford University Press.

Mosher, Jerry. 2001. "Having Their Cake and Eating It Too: Fat Acceptance Films and the Production of Meaning." In *The End of Cinema as We Know It: American Film in the Nineties,* ed. Jon Lewis, 237–49. New York: New York University Press.

Pickrell, H. Alan. 1996. "All the World Loves a Fat Boy, Doesn't It?" *Newsboy* 34, no. 5, 11–15.

Reilly, Patrick. 1998. "*Lord of the Flies:* Beelzebub's Boys." In *Lord of the Flies, Modern Critical Interpretations,* ed. Harold Bloom, 169–90. Philadelphia: Chelsea House.

Schlosser, Eric. 2001. *Fast Food Nation: The Dark Side of the All-American Meal.* Boston: Houghton Mifflin.

Schwartz, Hillel. 1986. *Never Satisfied: A Cultural History of Diets, Fantasies and Fat.* New York: Free Press.

Sobchack, Vivian. 1996. "Bringing It All Back Home: Family Economy and Generic Exchange." In *The Dread of Difference: Gender and the Horror Film,* ed. Barry Keith Grant, 143–63. Austin: University of Texas Press.

Stearns, Peter N. 1997. *Fat History: Bodies and Beauty in the Modern West.* New York: New York University Press.

Wedwick, Linda. 1998. "The Last Accepted Prejudice: Fat Characters in Children's Series Fiction." *Studies in Popular Culture* 20, no. 3, 19–31.

Wojcik-Andrews, Ian. 2000. *Children's Films: History, Ideology, Pedagogy, Theory.* New York: Garland.

4

CRAZY FROM THE HEAT
Southern Boys and Coming of Age

Mary B. O'Shea

The South that is a "magnolia-scented memory piece" (Travers 1991), in which no tree is without its garland of Spanish moss, is a landscape every moviegoer finds hauntingly familiar in a way that has no necessary connection to lived experience. Like the American West, it is less a real place than a cultural simulacrum built from a particular combination of climate, geography, history, narrative, stereotype, and conflict, existing whole in no single text but accessible through and referred to by many. In fact, the South of American myth is anything but monolithic. As John Shelton Reed points out in his typology of Southern characters, "[t]he moonlight and magnolias South is not really consistent with the moonshine and motor speedway South, and neither goes well with sado-historical epics like *Mandingo, Slaves,* or [. . .] *Uncle Tom's Cabin.* Hillbilly comedies of the Lum and Abner variety present still another South, as does the Tennessee Williams–Erskine Caldwell school of degeneracy" (1986, 9). This fragmentation, however, is overridden by a consensus: the South is, in almost any representation, haunted by the past. The West is the clean new slate where a man is free to reinvent himself; the urbanized North is continually pushing toward a more prosperous future; but the South remains defined by its inescapable heritage of class, gender, and especially racial disharmony. The South is America's great landscape of nostalgia. Indeed, most southern texts are doubly nostalgic, evoking our own sense of the past while presenting us with characters who are themselves continually conscious of theirs.

As Fred Davis recognizes, the actual material of nostalgia is always secondary to the feeling itself—that is, "nostalgia tells us more about present moods than about past realities" (1979, 10). Nostalgia, whether individual or collective, enables and encourages a positive and coherent view of the present as stable and consistent. It is a means of using the (idealized or simplified) past to redeem the (complicated and painful) present. But the impulse to reverse or deny change, implicit in nostalgia, often has troubling, reactionary implications: even the most benign memories of the past are inextricably bound up with scenes of oppression and violence. Indeed, we might ask if the South can truly be the object of "nostalgia" as such. Paul Monaco's definition of nostalgia as "recollection sweetened, mystified, or mythified," as "memory without pain" (1987, 100), is difficult to reconcile with the musings of the central character in Martha Coolidge's *Rambling Rose* (1991) who, revisiting his childhood home, finds that "a painful nostalgia gripped me for the South itself."

The South of our collective nostalgia does not exist only as a landscape. It is also, and perhaps more importantly, "America's most fecund seedbed for regional social types" (Reed 1986, 5). Many of these types—particularly black types—have been rendered considerably less common by changes in the national discourse that have made us uncomfortable with explicit degradation: rarely seen in their classic forms are, for example, the "Mammy figure, 'mother' to the white plantation family which relies on her as a mainstay" (O'Donnell 1981, 159); or the happy old slave, Uncle Remus, who gratefully and gracefully accepts his own degradation at Master's hands; or Jim, the capable and intelligent black man who willingly settles into his place as the white's sidekick. While versions of such figures may appear in recent films such as *Driving Miss Daisy* (1989) or *The Legend of Bagger Vance* (2000), they must now be idealized to the point where their only function is to highlight and solve the problems of the whites who learn from them. Whatever trace of the nostalgic impulse adheres to such figures is overridden by their dehumanized function as simplistic representatives of social progress. Still directly available for the redemptive work of nostalgia, however, are any number of familiar white types who evoke various versions of the South: the strong-willed belle (Scarlett O'Hara), the aging gentleman farmer (Big Daddy), the quixotic lawyer struggling for justice (Atticus Finch), the cheerfully corrupt politician (Willie Stark), the slow-witted but sadistic hillbilly (the unnamed villains of *Deliverance* [1972]). To their number we can add a particular type of southern boy: intelligent if unschooled, mischievous but not malicious, largely self-reliant, more at home in the country than the town, unlikely to have many strong family connections, more likely to be lower than upper class, fundamentally marginalized by his society—in short, and to give him his most familiar name, Huck Finn.

The Finn figure has elements of both the innocent ("whose simplicity recalls the rusticity and naiveté of our forefathers" [House 1993, 68]) and the trickster ("who fights authority through wit, deception and trickery" [66]). This character's marginalization, enabling his critical vision of society and thus his antiauthoritarian impulses, is exemplified in Mark Twain's novel, which positions "the simple domain of children" against "a world that was becoming increasingly technological and complex" and thus uses "the child's innocent perspective and keen perception to bring to the surface social ills" (Jackson 1986, 21). Particularly when positioned as the central figure in the almost invariably nostalgic mode of the coming-of-age story, the Finn archetype carries the nostalgic weight of adolescence itself.

Jon Lewis identifies as one of the characteristics of recent American culture—expressed in and given currency to recurrent waves of teen films since at least the 1950s—"the celebration of youth as the *sine qua non* of contemporary happiness," resulting in a "pervasive nostalgia for one's own youth that seems to elide just how difficult it is being young" (Lewis 1992, 34). If nostalgia is understood as a denial of the tensions and complications of the present, then identification with the adolescent carries obvious nostalgic potential for the adult. Nostalgia's potential for reinvention of the present self is most directly realized in the coming-of-age story, which typically documents the integration of the initially marginalized self into normative and available roles and relationships. It is thus the narrative of the self joining our collective fantasy of how society should be organized, and as such focuses on the individual's acceptance of the social order. The Finn figure complicates this. Founded not only in youth but also in his social class and his fundamental isolation, his alienation allows a critical vision and therefore a shifting of the coming-of-age narrative, making it about not only the molding of the individual but also the remaking of the world. He is thus a vehicle for both collective and individual redemption through nostalgia, an archetypal outsider whose clear vision of the society he is entering allows for it to be reordered and healed.

This nostalgic potential for societal revision resides in the Finn figure even when he is inserted into contemporary narratives, such as Joel Schumacher's thriller *The Client* (1994). The central character and Finn figure here is Mark Sway (Brad Renfro), an eleven-year-old Memphis trailer park resident with a single mother, bitter memories of an abusive father, and a thick southern accent. Despite his intelligence and resourcefulness, Mark is treated as a delinquent by nearly every adult he encounters, and his frequently sullen behavior indicates that he has largely internalized an identity of exclusion and marginalization. Sneaking into the woods one day to teach his younger brother Ricky (David Speck) the pleasures of illicit smoking, Mark witnesses the suicide of a mob lawyer, who reveals to him the location of an incriminating body before dying. As his brother slips into a shock-induced coma and his mother Dianne (Mary-Louise Parker) is reduced to hysteria, it falls to Mark to protect himself and his family from the mob (which wants to kill him) and the forces of law enforcement (which want him to testify). He is helped by Reggie Love (Susan Sarandon), an attorney who finds in Mark an opportunity to redeem herself for her failures with her own children. The climax comes when Mark and Reggie journey to New Orleans, uncover the body, elude the killers, and trade Mark's information to the cops for entry into the Witness Protection Program.

Mark's refusal throughout the story to trust any official is justified less by the mob's threats of reprisal than by ludicrously incompetent, gleefully malevolent, or ruthlessly ambitious law enforcement officers. The primary representative of law and order in the film is Roy Foltrigg (Tommy Lee Jones), a federal prosecutor who sees Mark as his stepping-stone to the governorship of Louisiana. Although not corrupt, for much of the film he is treated as a villain because of his willingness to threaten, endanger, and even imprison Mark in pursuit of his evidence. Assertive, arrogant, and utterly assured of his own dominance, Foltrigg is a vision of excessive power, an alpha male with no obstacles to his desires.

One of Mark's primary functions as the bearer of nostalgic impulses in the film is to correct Foltrigg's version of masculinity, which resembles nothing so much as the "hard body" hero of the 1980s as described by Susan Jeffords. In tracing representations of American masculinity in popular culture over the last quarter century, Jeffords has argued that masculine authority, while never wholly displaced from its dominance, was significantly challenged by the perceived failures of Vietnam coupled with "the advent of women's rights, civil rights, the 'generation gap,' and other alter-

Mark (Brad Renfro) under the maternal protection of Reggie (Susan Sarandon) in *The Client* (1994).

ations in social relations" in roughly the same time frame (1989, xii). The 1980s response, not only in popular texts but also in the carefully crafted public image of President Reagan, was what Jeffords dubs "hard body" masculinity, embodied in such cinematic heroes as Rambo and the Terminator. This model might well be called hypermasculinity, bordering at moments on parody. While Foltrigg is not an action hero, he is presented as an impermeable and invulnerable expression of the phallic masculine ego. However, he is out of step with his time; Jeffords argues that in the 1990s the hard body hero is displaced by "a body in which strength is defined internally rather than externally, as a matter of moral rather than muscle fiber" (1994, 136). These new heroes remain central to social function, but replace unfeeling toughness and aggression with sensitivity, emotional connections to their societies and families, and, above all, a reclamation of fatherhood.

Mark's repeated refusal to consent to Foltrigg's authority is licensed by the autonomy and self-reliance that are his by virtue of his type. In finally forcing Foltrigg to accept his and Reggie's help and demands, Mark creates a kind of temporary family structure that tempers Foltrigg's absolute power and transforms him into a more appropriate 1990s man. This symbolic restoration of the nuclear family, however fleeting, is one of the ways the film's nostalgic content elides the anxieties of the present. Of course, it is still Roy Foltrigg alone—although his information comes from Mark and his tie is straightened by Reggie—who announces the successful resolution of the investigation on camera at the end of the film; he will be likely to obtain the governmental power that is his final goal.

That masculine privilege is ultimately not challenged by the narrative is hardly surprising—nor is it surprising that *The Client* is much more concerned with restoring its female characters to their properly maternal roles. This is most apparent in the film's central relationship between Mark and Reggie. Initially suspicious of a "woman lawyer," he refuses to tell her the full extent of what he knows, and his suspicions seem justified when he learns that Reggie has a history of alcohol and drug abuse. But she regains his trust by taking him to the suburban home she shares with her mother, Momma Love (Micole Mercurio). For the remainder of the film Reggie will be more associated with this domestic space than with the office and courtrooms where she initially appeared. There, Reggie reveals to Mark that her husband had her declared an unfit mother, and that she rescued herself from her subsequent substance abuse by putting herself through law school in order to prevent other such miscarriages of justice. Her children, however, still want nothing to do with her.

Significantly, Mark's promise that he will reveal his own secrets in exchange for Reggie's disclosures is not completely fulfilled. Instead, the film cuts to the villains setting fire to Mark's trailer, destroying the space he had shared with his own family. The loss hardly seems to matter, however, because Reggie's shift into the space of Momma Love and her confession that she is motivated by unsatisfied maternal feelings have effectively given Mark a new, and rather more reliable, family. In a later scene, when Mark needs her help, we see Reggie frantically searching Momma Love's garage for her notes from law school, but she is diverted from her search by the discovery of tokens of her children. The scene neatly summarizes Reggie's transformation from a competent professional and "icon made from every 'progressive' slogan of the last quarter century" (Geary) to a subservient, flustered woman who offers little more than emotional support. Her reward is to be assured, by both Mark and his mother, Dianne, that she would be a good mother, which the film clearly regards as better than being a good lawyer.

Reggie's transformation is mirrored by and in some respects enables the restoration of Dianne Sway to a properly maternal character. Confined to Ricky's hospital room for the bulk of the film, Dianne's character arc is determined by her increasing acceptance of Mark's ability and authority to act in the interests of the family. Her own inadequacy as a caregiver is evident from the first scene of the film, where Mark must remind her of everything she needs to take with her to her sweatshop job. In most of her early scenes, Dianne is little more than a stereotype of "white trash" behavior; her trailer park home is matched by her series of terrible jobs, her teen motherhood, her history of being abused and abandoned, her blank incomprehension concerning much of what is happening around her, her frequently slovenly appearance, and her hysterically hostile responses to authority. She is redeemed by Mark, who by the end of the film has arranged not only for better care for Ricky but also for his mother to get both a better job and the "white house with a walk-in closet" she always dreamed of. Mark has become the homemaker, the patriarchal head of the family if not the actual patriarch. At the end of the film it is he, not Dianne, who hovers over Ricky's sickbed. When Dianne arrives in New Orleans to be informed of Mark's accomplishments, the dirty jeans and flimsy blouses she has worn throughout the film have been replaced by a modest dress and subdued behavior; she muses about joining the PTA.

The boy's coming of age in *The Client* depends as much on his complicity in the renewed repression of the feminine as on his assumption of normative adult roles—indeed, in this film the two are indivisible. Understanding how this boy comes to terms with his society is impossible without consideration of the women around him, his relation to their gender roles, and the film's conventional gender alignment. Mark's ability to reorder society, to restore proper—that is, conventional—gender and power relationships, is founded in his role as a figure of nostalgia. His self-reliance is obvious; again and again his decisions to rely on his own instincts and abilities are rewarded. So, too, is his skill as a trickster. At one point he uses the credit card he steals from a hostile cop to order $250 worth of pizza; later he mimics the symptoms of Ricky's post-traumatic coma to escape from prison.

Most vitally, however, Mark is an innocent, which I take here to mean one whose fresh vision of society and the world around him offers an alternative to predetermined social truths. Ultimately it is Mark's status as a witness, his clarity of vision, that enables him to reorder the world—just as Huck Finn's child's-eye view of slavery was the vehicle for a reexamination of race. Consider Mark's insistence, as the film nears its climax, that it is not enough to tell Foltrigg where the body is. He and Reggie must drive to New Orleans (along Huck's river) and verify that it is actually there, going so far as to rip open the plastic it is wrapped in and see the maggots. As a plot device, this absurdity is necessary to expose Mark and Reggie to danger from the killers. But it makes considerably more sense in the context of Mark's need to bear witness to the reality of what is happening, including the reality of death. It is his status as witness, after all, that motivates the entire plot; his willingness to take this to its logical extreme completes his occupation of his role.

The central importance of this witnessing function to the Finn figure is no less visible in films that are set in the South of the past, and that consciously evoke nostalgia for it. In Jon Avnet's *The War* (1994), set in Mississippi in the summer of 1970, the central relationship is between the Finn figure, Stu (Elijah Wood), and his father Stephen (Kevin Costner), a good man who has returned from Vietnam suffering from nightmares and unable to hold a job, haunted by his failure to save a friend during a firefight—a story, significantly, told only to his son. Stu sees how Stephen's experience has marginalized him from a society based in expressions of aggression, self-assertion, and violence. No longer quite a man by the standards of his community, Stephen tries to show his son the costs of fighting and the moral value of peace. While Stephen ultimately redeems himself by saving a co-worker during a mine cave-in at the cost of his own life, the central drama of *The War* is Stu's struggle to understand and use what Stephen has taught him. Driven nearly wild by Stephen's death, Stu initially responds by declaring "war" himself over the elaborate tree house he, his sister, and their friends have built, and which has been taken from them by the nearly feral, bullying children of the Lipnicki family. Their war is fought with fireworks and smoke grenades, tractors and fists, and quickly turns savage and dangerous. At its height, Stu looks around him, his vision privileged and marked by slow motion, and witnesses the cruelty being practiced by both sides, seeing as well that the tree house itself is being destroyed. From his position in the crumbling tree house, Stu is able to see that the youngest Lipnicki boy is risking his life by climbing a rickety water tower perched at the edge of an abandoned quarry. The things Stu has seen coalesce, and he ends the fighting and risks his own life to save the boy who had been his enemy, symbolically healing the rifts that have divided the children of the town. The damage done to masculinity by Vietnam—described by Jeffords and embodied by Stephen—is thus repaired by Stu, and specifically by his ability both to witness the world around him and to act upon what he sees.

Rambling Rose demonstrates what happens when the Finn figure fails to translate witnessing into action. Like Mark and Stu, thirteen-year-old Buddy Hillyer (Lukas Haas) is forever listening at windows and peeking through doorways. The things he witnesses revolve around Rose (Laura Dern), an alluring young woman who has come to work for his family in Georgia in the 1930s. As Buddy sees, the male authority figures who dominate his society—including his father (Robert Duvall)—alternately indulge, exploit, and condemn Rose's freely expressed sexual appetites, ultimately projecting their own transgressions onto her. Indeed, Buddy himself engages in this behavior, pushing Rose into a sexual encounter for which he then allows her to tearfully take the blame. Buddy professes to love Rose and clearly understands how she is being mistreated, but he never finds a way to articulate or act upon what he has seen in order to save her, as Mark saves his family and Stu saves the Lipnicki boy. When Rose is exiled into a clearly inappropriate marriage near the end of the film, Buddy can only sob inarticulately. In the film's coda we see that Buddy has become a middle-aged man with no apparent connections other than his elderly father, who tells him Rose has died. Thus, Buddy's failure to save Rose is ultimately a failure to heal or regenerate his society—a failure to come of age and join a social realm that can sustain and perpetuate itself. Buddy remains helplessly mired in the past, left as part of a crippled society, doomed by the loss of the feminine that he could not act to preserve.

On the extreme far end of the spectrum from Buddy's utter failure as a witness is Adam Meeks, the central figure of Bill Paxton's *Frailty* (2001), whose ability to cleanse society through what he witnesses is actually given divine sanction. In flashbacks set in rural Texas in 1979, which constitute the bulk of *Frailty*'s complex plot, Adam (Jeremy Sumpter) and his older brother Fenton (Matt O'Leary) are forced to help their widowed father (Bill Paxton) in a mission he says was given them by an angel of the Lord: to destroy the demons around them, disguised as human beings. The sins of these demons, their father tells them, will be revealed when he lays his hands upon them, immediately before dismembering them with his axe. While Adam enthusiastically embraces this divine mission, Fenton believes their father has gone insane. Frustrated in his attempts to escape or inform the authorities, Fenton eventually kills the father after feigning acceptance of their mission. Years later, a man claiming to be the adult Fenton (Matthew McConaughey) tells FBI agent Wesley Doyle (Powers Boothe) that Adam is now continuing his father's work, as the serial killer called God's Hands. In the movie's climactic twist, however, the McConaughey character is revealed to be Adam, who has already killed Fenton and has now come to Doyle, a matricide and therefore himself a demon, only in order to lure him to his own destruction. It is further revealed that, like Doyle, all of the other victims really were guilty of horrible crimes, and that Adam was sincere in claiming to see these sins revealed under his father's hands. The Finn archetype is thus refigured here as divine avenger, sanctioned in his violence precisely by his ability to witness what others cannot see.

When, for example, the young Adam asks what superpowers the "family of superheroes" will have to aid them, his father's first reply is, "We can see the demons, while other people can't." In addition, the fact that other people, particularly authority figures, are blind compared to Adam is repeatedly emphasized in the closing segments of the film; another FBI agent who saw Adam with Doyle fails to recognize him when they meet again. Even the camera system at FBI headquarters shows only static in the place of Adam's face, its abilities presumably frustrated by the same divinity that has given Adam clear vision and avenging power. As if to complete the contrast with *Rambling Rose*'s ineffectual and essentially neutered Buddy, we learn at the end of the film that Adam has a pregnant wife who shares in his mission. In Buddy and Adam, then, we see the possibilities of the Finn figure taken to its most excessive extremes, one to the limits of helplessness, the other to the limits of the righteous correction of societal ills.

In all of recent film, Peejoe (Lucas Black), the thirteen-year-old central figure of Antonio Banderas's *Crazy in Alabama* (1999), may well be the character who most precisely fits the traditional Finn model, a self-sufficient country boy whose social connections are minimal at best. In the film's opening moments we see him and his brother (who manages, despite being conscious throughout the narrative, to be as inconsequential as comatose Ricky in *The Client*), dressed in overalls, running playfully through a field. Peejoe informs us in a voiceover that they are orphans who have lived on their grandmother's farm for as long as he can remember. Indeed, he claims they have "hardly ever been off it." Forced by the mechanics of the plot to move into Industry and live with his Uncle Dove (David Morse), a mortician, Peejoe finds himself in the middle of a potentially violent civil rights conflict. The blacks of Industry are demonstrating for the right to vote and other considerations, but are opposed by John Doggett (Meat Loaf Aday), the corpulent, thick-headed, virulently racist sheriff whose type is every bit as familiar as Peejoe's. Dove, an essentially good but ineffectual man, has been unable to have Doggett removed. Ultimately it is only Peejoe's marginalized vision that can effect any real change.

On Peejoe's first day in town, as he and Dove drive past a demonstration at the town courthouse, Peejoe scrambles into the back of Dove's hearse, parting the curtain over the windows to prolong his view. The curtains effectively frame what is happening as performance, transforming the demonstration into a spectacle staged in order to be witnessed by the boy. This arrangement of the world around Peejoe's vision occurs repeatedly throughout the film. At the town's segregated swimming pool, we share Peejoe's point of view as he floats underwater, watching the dangling legs of the people around him, legs that suddenly begin to move to the edge and leave the water. Turning, Peejoe sees that a black body has entered the pool behind him, and surfaces to find himself face to face with Taylor Jackson (Louis Miller), a boy his age who had also been at the earlier demonstration. After Taylor is expelled from the pool, it is Peejoe who first sees him returning with a number of other black children to stage a sit-in. Crucially, after this protest is violently disrupted it is Peejoe alone who sees Sheriff Doggett pull Taylor backward off a fence, killing him. Later, only Peejoe can confirm Doggett was also among those who violently disrupted Taylor's funeral. Underlining the significance of his vision, Peejoe suffers an accident with a lawnmower early in the film and spends the bulk of the narrative wearing an eye patch. The message is clear: even with one eye, Peejoe sees more clearly than those around him. The crucial test for Peejoe in this film will be how he decides to use what he has witnessed.

If Peejoe is the most accurate recent articulation of the Finn legacy and tradition, it is not least because the things he sees revolve around race. Frequently sharing his view, *Crazy in Alabama* constructs its black characters as idealized paragons of righteousness and patience. This treatment reaches its peak in the film's representation of Martin Luther King Jr., who comes to preach in Industry when Taylor's death attracts national attention. King's face never appears in the film; even when he shakes the hand of Peejoe (introduced to him as "the boy who stood up for Taylor Jackson"), the camera, sharing Peejoe's view, registers only a burst of sunlight, suggesting that King cannot be directly looked upon. The actor who plays King is not even identified in the credits, as though to sustain the impression that an otherworldly being has descended into the world of the film. While the avoidance of a direct presentation of King's face might be understandable simply from a practical point of view, the film's other black characters are also regularly accorded sanctified representation. At Taylor's funeral, for example, the blacks of Industry—accompanied, naturally, by Peejoe—honor him by swimming in the pool where he died, and are there set upon by a violent mob led by Doggett. As the violence rages around him, Taylor's younger brother David (Carl Le Blanc III) carefully removes his jacket and climbs into the pool, where he floats on his back, his arms stretched out, a vision of Christian suffering and virtue. Despite their unblemished natures, of course, the blacks of *Crazy in Alabama* must be delivered from their trials by the testimony of a white boy, a construction of race relations no less reductive than the repeated implication that racism itself is located only in Doggett (no other character being identified as sharing his views). The dilemma of race in America is thus refigured as an opposition between two white characters. Similarly, Peejoe's inevitable victory over the corrupt sheriff is motivated less by his desire for social justice than by his concern for his aunt—a concern that the film represents as more dramatically compelling than any mere treatment of civil rights.

Peejoe's Aunt Lucille (Melanie Griffith), with her angular sunglasses, stylish clothes, and aggressively flirtatious and playful manner, is severely out of step with the other citizens of Industry. A mother of seven who has decided to take a shot at film stardom, as the film opens she has killed and decapitated the abusive husband who would keep her barefoot and pregnant in Alabama. She sets off on a cross-country jaunt to Hollywood, highlighted by car theft, gambling, and sexual escapades, and within days of her arrival joins the cast of "Bewitched" as a sultry southern belle. Only Peejoe, who adores his aunt and is awed by her courage, is entrusted with Lucille's exact destination, and only he knows that she is taking her husband's head with her in a Tupperware container to further punish the dead man with her triumph. When Lucille is captured and returned to Industry for trial, Dove arranges for a lenient verdict of insanity in exchange for Peejoe's silence about the murder Doggett has committed.

Like Mark in *The Client*, however, Peejoe insists upon his right to decide for himself how to use what he has witnessed. His courtroom proclamation of Doggett's guilt frees Lucille to pursue the verdict she prefers—"not guilty by reason of sanity"—and sets up her own speech, in which she details her husband's years of abuse and defends her actions as self-defense. Although the jury finds her guilty, the sympathetic judge suspends the sentence and sets her free. Peejoe's testimony thus frees his aunt, but not to the life of self-determination and liberation she enjoyed during her trip. Instead, we see her outside the courthouse ecstatically gathering her children around her and reuniting with Norman (Richard Schiff), the good man she met on her travels who has become devoted to her. Even if she resumes her acting career, it is clear that Lucille's future will be dominated by this Norma(n)tive heterosexual relationship, and by her renewed dedication to the children she had previously left behind. We are clearly meant to see this as a satisfying ending, just as we are meant to see the removal of Doggett as effectively ending the racism of the community. The final scene of the film—in which Peejoe, his brother, and Taylor's brother watch workmen fill in the pool with cement rather than allow it to be integrated—does acknowledge that the basic structure of discrimination remains in place. In showing the two white boys and the black one playing together—something that has not occurred throughout the rest of the film—while Peejoe's final voiceover assures us that "freedom goes on forever," however, it also suggests that such discrimination has essentially ceased to matter.

In the end, what is achieved by the fully realized Finn figure as he comes of age is the establishment of not only a new self but also a new community, a society in which the troubling aspects inherent in both the old one and our contemporary world are simply and effectively eliminated. Nothing could more perfectly illustrate the wish-fulfillment aspect of the nostalgic impulse—the reinvention of the present through a freshly idealized past—than the pure vision of a child innocent of sins that must be cleansed. This linking of a collective, communal renewal with an individual boy's entry into adulthood expresses a fundamental desire for rebirth, a wish that the arrival of the new man can also be the occasion for the generation of a properly organized society, a return to the kind of golden age that nostalgia can allow us to believe in. Further, the boy's transformation, which is also the community's, is facilitated principally by his ability to witness and name all of what must change. His coming of age no longer an individual experience, the Finn figure's unique vision licenses him to remake the social realm in his own image, creating a new order that seems as natural and correct as his own new manhood. While *Rambling Rose* and *Frailty* illustrate what happens when this dual transformation cannot be enacted (either because the boy cannot act on what he has seen or because his transformative vision is so powerful that it exists above, rather than within, the social realm), *Crazy in Alabama, The Client,* and *The War* demonstrate how the Finn figure's unique perception of societal ill enables him—and him alone—to correct and reform society, and precisely in order that he may enter fully into it. The new worlds that the boys in these films construct around their healing visions may be idealized, but they are also, perhaps inevitably, deeply patriarchal. For the heroic boy to open up room at the center of these worlds requires moving strong-willed and autonomous females back to the margins, where they can function only through their relationships with dominant men. The nostalgic impulse, we are reminded, is ultimately a reactionary one.

The Finn figure may be benevolent, but he is also represented as solely responsible for the shape the new world takes, and thus as its dominant male. His vision, after all, has remade the new communal reality, and it is a vision that depends upon weakened femininity. Just as society cannot come to justice without the boy's transformative witnessing and corrective vision, a boy seems unable to come to completeness without keeping normative femininity in the background.

WORKS CITED

Davis, Fred. 1979. *Yearning for Yesterday: A Sociology of Nostalgia.* New York: Free Press.

Fitzsimmons, Lorna. 1999. "Respecting Difference: An Interview with

Martha Coolidge." *Literature Film Quarterly* 27, no. 2 (March 1). Online. Academic Search Premier, March 1, 2002.

Geary, Robert F. 1993. "A Fading Formula." *World & I* 8, no. 9. Online. MasterFILE Premier, March 1, 2002.

House, Jeff. 1993. "Sweeney among the Archetypes: The Literary Hero in American Culture." *Journal of American Culture* 16, no. 4, 65–71.

Jackson, Kathy Merlock. 1986. *Images of Children in American Film: A Sociocultural Analysis.* Metuchen, NJ: Scarecrow Press.

Jeffords, Susan. 1994. *Hard Bodies: Hollywood Masculinity in the Reagan Era.* New Brunswick, NJ: Rutgers University Press.

———. 1989. *The Remasculinization of America: Gender and the Vietnam War.* Bloomington: Indiana University Press.

Lewis, Jon. 1992. *The Road to Romance and Ruin: Teen Films and Youth Culture.* New York: Routledge.

Monaco, Paul. 1987. "Memory without Pain." In *Ribbons in Time: Movies and Society since 1945,* 93–125. Bloomington: Indiana University Press.

O'Donnell, Victoria. 1981. "The Southern Woman as Time-Binder in Film." *Southern Quarterly* 19, no. 3–4, 156–62.

Reed, John Shelton. 1986. *Southern Folk, Plain and Fancy: Native White Social Types.* Athens: University of Georgia Press.

Travers, P. 1991. "Why She's Gotta Have It." *Rolling Stone,* October 3. Online. Academic Search Premier, March 1, 2002.

5

"PERFECT CHILDHOODS"

Larry Clark Puts Boys Onscreen

Sudhir Mahadevan

Larry Clark has made three feature films that have been released commercially, *Kids* (1995), *Another Day in Paradise* (1998), and *Bully* (2001). Since *Bully*, he has directed a made-for-cable remake of one of Samuel Z. Arkoff's B-movie monster flicks from the 1950s, *Teenage Caveman* (2002), and *Ken Park* (2002), which, although it screened at the 2002 Toronto International Film Festival, has yet to open commercially in the United States. Clark's films are presentations of boyhood that offer up unprecedented visions of bodily and social utopias and horrors. They mark a recurrent grim investment in the male teenaged body, whether it be threatened by AIDS in *Kids,* threatened by paternally motivated murder in *Another Day in Paradise,* actually knifed to death by its own peers in *Bully,* or finally, annihilated by suicide in *Ken Park.*

Clark's central aim is to confer the stamp of veracity and documentary authenticity on his representations of teenage life through the use of particular prepubescent and pubescent body types (his actors often have little or no prior acting experience). Marked by a continuity with his photographic work—the books *Tulsa* (1971), *Teenage Lust* (1983), and *The Perfect Childhood* (1995, banned in the United States)—and combining teenage bodies with unprecedented (full frontal male) nudity, sex, violence, and the near-complete absence or thematic impotence of parental figures, Clark's films seem to depart from the genre of the teenpic and move toward sexploitation and the pornographic. Often labeled "controversial," the films gain a distinct advantage in marketing.

Clark's aging sentient body, naked or otherwise, is central to his project to reclaim and live teenage life. At the end of *Teenage Lust,* he makes clear that he was acutely aware of the growth of his own body as a teenager. He refers to himself as "bug-eyed," "fucked up" and "real skinny," "stammering" and wanting to "crawl in a hole." With astonishing detail, he chronicles the development of his body in this monologue, from the skinny, stammering kid with "the big fucking nose . . . 'cause the nose grows first, right? And your body grows into it, right?" who was used to "shooting smack" and "speeding my fucking brains out," to the kid who "shot up towards six feet" with a "super-fuckin healthy" sense of being (Clark 1983, n.p.). It is as if Clark were always seeing with an acute awareness of how his body could relive the teenage life through the bodies that he captures in his photographs. Clark's authorial persona confessing to a cathartic relationship of the teenage life and body and the personalized responses of many of his reviewers suggest that his images are visceral and gripping. The only response possible to them is confession, yet to some viewers his images of teenage life may ring false, contrived, and even campy. The aesthetic of his movies is haunted by the photographs of *Teenage Lust*, in such a way that the teenagers in his films vacillate between being secular icons of cool pubescent beauty and palpable bodies with unbridled sexual urges. The two modes, iconographic and documentary, coexist in his filmic representation of the teenaged body.

KIDS

Kids (1995), Clark's first film, narrativizes preoccupations with death and sex. It is also the sparsest film to date by him, both affectively and narratively, presuming to offer a stoic ethnographic bildungsroman of teenagers and their urban lives. The central teenager in question in *Kids* is Telly (Leo Fitzpatrick), whose single-minded quest for virgins drives him and his perpetually drugged-out friend Casper (Justin Pierce) up and down the island of Manhattan, through Washington Square Park where they viciously beat a black man to near death with their skateboards, through his mom's house where he steals some money, through a Korean deli where Casper steals a bottle of beer, dropping it through his fly so it settles at the ankle of his baggy pants, and through multiple spaces where teenagers (mostly boys) accumulate to shoot drugs, watch skateboarder movies, and talk and do sex. Telly's seemingly uneventful day is interspersed with desperate attempts by the sexually inexperienced Jenny (Chloë Sevigny) to find him after she learns that she is HIV-positive and realizes, even as he plots to "deflower" his next virgin, that only Telly could have passed the virus on to her. In the final scene Telly accomplishes his goal, spreading the virus more widely; Jenny collapses in exhaustion

Roaming the streets in Larry Clark's *Kids* (1995).

after she finds him already having sex with another girl, and the drunken Casper undresses her unconscious body and proceeds to have nonconsensual sex.

In a swimming-pool scene in this film, it is evident that Clark achieves with many pictures what he cannot, quite as effectively, achieve with the still photograph. Having illegally climbed across the fence of a city swimming pool on a hot summer evening, Telly, Casper, and the other boys and girls in their group undress before diving in, and the camera frames each one of them in single shots, edited to eye-line matches as they appraise each other at the moment of undressing. The presence of the girls incites the black kid in the group to swing his dick around like a lasso as he asks them if they've seen a "nigger's dick" before. He is shown mostly up to his waist but at two moments Clark's camera makes a dash for the crotch shot (that we *barely* see) and comes back up, attempting therefore to replicate the frank nudity of his photographs. While in the photographs genitalia function somewhat as the punctum that shocks us into recognition of teenage bodies, in the films, aimed at a wider and more censorious audience, Clark is forced to achieve such punctuation surreptitiously. That desperate dash by Clark's camera often relies on the persistence of vision to convey nudity to us. Clark builds moving pictures on the metaphysical foundation of his still nudie-pics of teenagers; their faces and bodies are transformed into icons and tableaux that we animate while inspecting. As Claire Vassé put it, in *Kids,* "the cinema does not participate any longer in the domestication of the photograph" (1995, 16).

But there's also the frame of the narrative that literally mobilizes the images by opening them up to a social space. Laura Mulvey writes eloquently of the role of narrative: "The cinema's articulation of its own [visual] space carries with it a momentum that is subsumed into the linear pattern of narrative and overflows onto the narrative's dramatic figurations. And these linear patterns of narrative space, transmuted into characters in the drama on the screen, are inevitably themselves informed by the ideologies and aesthetics of gendered place" (1992, 56). As Clark's films move their narratives forward, we are treated to a succession of images that institute what Marie-José Mondzain calls an "iconocracy" (2000, 59). *Kids,* is a perverse quest for the grail, after all: what is most interesting is the way that quest is for a certain kind of body. Here the HIV virus rests not in the body of an *adult* gay male, or—more recently—in the pandemics of Africa and Asia, but in the body of a sixteen-year-old white teenage boy and in the contagion spread by that body. The first shot of Telly and the virgin he sweet-talks into a fuck-fest is exactly graphically matched in a reverse-shot of Telly and another girl at the end of the film (a replica of another photograph from *Teenage Lust* of a boy and girl in a tub, the girl clutching at the boy's penis with dedication). The search for the source of the virus not only results in the same person, Telly, but also stops at the same originary moment of his sweet-talking a girl into sex (Jenny, in this respect, belongs to Telly's and the film's timeless prehistory).

As Jenny engages in her desperate flânerie, searching for Telly, the city of New York is littered with spaces that contain teenage bodies performing sex acts and teenage faces talking sex talk. The narrative focus and duration that the film covers—one day in the life of a bunch of teenagers and Jenny's quest through the course of that day—allow us to witness various "little scenarios" of "previously hidden further truths" about teenage life (Williams 1989, 45).

What are these hitherto invisible, hidden truths? Scrawny, sweaty, smelly, horny teenage boys with their fingers plunged into vaginas and retracted to be smelt with rapture (there's a scene where Leo holds his fingers up to Casper's nose after his sex with a virgin) parade before us and leave us with the vestigial feeling of watching the mating habits of animals in a wildlife documentary on the Discovery channel. Sometimes, the sense of embodiment is verbally accomplished, as in the scene where Ruby (Rosario Dawson) tells Jenny and other girls, during a conversation entirely about boys, their cum, and their dicks, that she doesn't like swallowing because sperm sticks between her teeth. Clark seems to want us to believe that we are witness to a grand bio-pic of some enigmatic species now suddenly removed from its invisibility.

By having actual teenagers play the roles of teenagers, Clark might like us to think that he is exposing the traditional conceits of the documentary and fiction film modes for what they are: merely conceits. The documentary is never as precise as it claims to be, the fiction never as displaced from everyday life. To paraphrase William Rothman, every revelation made by Clark's camera about the fictional *Kids* is also about the real kids who incarnate them; the revelations emerge through—express and thus reveal—the relationship between the camera and the kids. The only thing that matters is that the subject be allowed to reveal itself (Rothman 1997, 4).

BULLY

What kind of a subject is revealed to us by Clark's films as they vacillate between the beatific and the hyperembodied, between the iconic presentation of kids in a vision of childhood and the iconoclastic undermining of such a vision in the tactility and palpability of Clark's embodiment of teenagers?

Kids abounds in iconicity, moments where, as Amy Taubin puts it, "as if they were Botticelli angels . . . the kids look lit up from within" (1995, 19). As Jenny sits in the cab, riding uptown to the party where she hopes to find Telly, and looks out the window at the passing city, her tear-stained face is side-lit by available light. The shot of Jenny is a direct allusion to a shot in Hector Babenco's *Pixote* (1981), a film that has influenced Clark (Cieutat and Rouyer 1995, 20), where in the opening scene, *Pixote,* with a face as feral as Jenny's, looks out of a van at the passing city on his way to a home for street children. At the party in *Kids* again, four boys, frontally framed and barely more than ten years old, shirtless, crushed against each other, and their bodies suffused in golden light, smoke weed and watch the rest of the older teenagers making out with each other. Presented thus as a beatific tableau, the image is no longer a neutral conveyance of information: the kids become emblematic icons of their childhoods, an idealized vision of childhood itself.

Such moments come as Buñuelesque interruptions even in *Bully* (2001), Clark's third film, which has the most classical, psychologically driven narrative of all of his films thus far. *Bully*, a Senecan rewriting of "Macbeth"/"Julius Caesar," traces the conspiracy and inevitable murder of Bobby Kent (Nick Stahl) by his "best friend" Marty Puccio (Brad Renfro), Marty's girlfriend Lisa (Rachel Miner), her friend Ali (Bijou Phillips) and a bunch of other teenage friends (including Leo Fitzpatrick, from *Kids*, playing a local ex-pimp/hit man/car stereo thief). The murder is motivated by Lisa's resentment of the long-entrenched sense of domination over Marty by Bobby.

Set in the suburbs of coastal Florida with its identical homes, strip malls, and swampy wastelands, *Bully* opens with a shot of Marty looking into the camera, talking into the phone as he says, "I want you to suck my dick." The postcredit sequences start off as a sunny teenpic, following the pair of Marty and Bobby as they work at a fast food joint and spend their free time driving around, until they meet the horny twosome Lisa and Ali (a much-remarked shot in the film is a close-up of Ali's crotch as she sits with her legs spread apart in her tiny cut-off denim shorts). As each girl makes her choice (the more uncertain and introverted Lisa goaded by her friend to flirt with Marty), the movie plunges us into familiar Clark territory as the four have sex in Bobby's car, a scene to which I will return. What marks the close friendship between Marty and Bobby, however, is Bobby's relentless ear-twisting physical and verbal abuse of Marty. In one scene, as Marty and Lisa hang out at the beach, Marty confesses, crying and drooling like a regressed baby without any defenses, that his friendship with Bobby has been marked by domination since childhood—this, notwithstanding a brand of deep affection on Bobby's part. One scene of bullying and abuse ends with Bobby holding a furious Marty by his neck, trying to pacify him as he pleads that Marty is his best friend and that he loves him. Such sublimated friendship is also characterized by their joint, sometimes consensual, forays into gay porn—Bobby and Marty see the recruiting of gay men to act in homemade gay porn as a potential money-making enterprise—and gay phone-sex prostitution in which Bobby pimps Marty for the money. After being raped herself, and after Ali has also been raped perversely by Bobby while being forced to watch gay porn, Lisa convinces Marty that Bobby is a hindrance and rallies a bunch of friends together: the affable but stoned Donny (Michael Pitt), the child-abused Heather (Kelli Garner), the big, clumsy, and somewhat infantile Derek (Daniel Franzese) and Ali. From the hatching of Lisa's plan, the film progresses inevitably through conspiracy and then the messy murder of Bobby and its aftermath.

Appropriately, the moments when the boys are transformed into icons of their teenage status in *Bully* happen in the scene where Fitzpatrick is first introduced. This boy, barely in his twenties but older than the rest of the characters, and running his own tract house with his other younger teeny-bopper buddies, is a resource Lisa recruits for professional advice about the murder. At one point the camera holds on a boy scarcely more than eight or nine years old looking straight on at the lens and smiling at us in all his prepubescent self-revelation.

Yet such self-revelation is also undermined. The central formal device of the desperate conspiracy scenes in *Bully* is the high-speed vertiginous 360–degree swirl of the camera that encircles the kids in close-ups of their faces as they figure out how best to murder Bobby. But since this swirl is shot from the inside of the circular space looking at the kids' faces, and since the faces get nearly blurred in this full-circle pan, the overwhelming sense is that we are witness to people who can't get far enough beyond their bodies to entertain a moral thought. Beyond the decision itself to murder Bobby, beyond the combination of bravado and blind resolve, they are better left living and satisfying their bodily urges than engaging in any real cognitive project.

In the scene where the kids first plot the murder, the camera moves languorously over the mass of twisted, confused bodies on the bed and on the floor of Lisa's room, letting the teenagers gesturally pin down with striking accuracy their own lethargy, inertia, and inability to move their weighted bodies. What is revealed to us by them is that radical embodiment does *not* sit well with real cognition, a sense of morality and ethics, and other such civilized discontents, a point reinforced narratively by the sheer naiveté and imploding failure of the cover-up in the postmurder sequences, when Lisa's cousin Derek spills the beans to a co-worker; Lisa herself unravels like a hand-wringing Lady Macbeth; and Ali boards up her room in darkness.

ANOTHER DAY IN PARADISE

Lauren Berlant discusses at length the infantilization of America: America, in the eyes of anti-porn advocates, is likened to the young girl who needs to be protected. It is in the name of this little girl that sex and morality are policed, and in opposition to her that an other "adult culture" is defined, where "adult" stands both for how pornography is marked ("adult books") *and* for the adults who protect the girl's citizenship till she passes "boringly . . . to what has been called the 'zone of privacy' or national heterosexuality 'adult' Americans generally seek to inhabit" (1995, 381). Clark occupies different sides of that debate in different films. He has spoken of *Kids* as being a warning call for parents (see Savage 1996, 9),[1] as if parents need to know what their children are thinking and, more important, what they *look like.*

Another Day in Paradise thematizes this parental-advisory mode. Set in the 1970s, the film offers a dystopic family drama in which a drug-dealing, thieving, childless couple, Mel and Sid (James Woods and Melanie Griffith), take the teenage couple Bobby and Rosie (Vincent Kartheiser and Natasha Gregson Wagner) under their wings and adopt them as enthusiastic collaborators. The foursome moves from one cheap motel to another, from one heist to another, typical of characters in a breezy road movie, celebrating every spurt of income with shopping sprees, dinners, and ominously rancorous occasional arguments till a failed heist and important differences of opinion leave one of the kids (Rosie) pregnant and eventually dead and the other kid's (Bobby's) life threatened by his own surrogate father, Sid.

Another Day seems to start with prototypical Clark imagery: the opening shot of the naked Bobby asleep with Rosie snuggled up to him recalls "Teenager Asleep, Oklahoma City," one of the photographs in *Teenage Lust.* An early scene in the film suggests a preoccupation with homosociality (that is more fully explored in *Bully*): Bobby is reclining in bed in close proximity to his friend Danny (Brandon Williams) who is naked, except for his briefs, as the two gaze vacuously at the television. In yet another early scene, as Danny wakes up and stands in his underwear, his hard-on is unmistakable if not entirely conspicuous, and marks more of the casual realism of "bodily" detail that reflects the continuing influence of Clark's photographic work and his attempt to subtly (or not so subtly) push the envelope of what can be shown on a movie screen.

That said, for the rest of its duration the film hardly relies on the distinctive visual emphases of Clark's work up to *Kids*, focusing instead on a strong narrative and character interplay and marking itself as a drama rather than as a strikingly visual document. The film—replete with scenes of domesticity—works as a parody of familial ties, and can be juxtaposed to a TV show like "Seventh Heaven" for its imitation of the modes of nuclear family well-being. What initiates the disruption of this drug-dealing family of two homeless kids and two childless parents is not an outside force, but the pregnancy of Bobby's girlfriend, the fetus within the waiflike girl-child that hits a raw nerve with Uncle Mel (who cannot have children). When the kids out-parent their surrogate parents by desiring a life of stability, reproductive sexuality, and familial bliss rather than the risks of thievery and drugs, the relationship comes fully undone. Here, Clark's didacticism is fully evident as he chronicles the drug-dealing life as a potentially redeemable utopia of collaborative and affectionate dysfunctionality within the structures of a nuclear conjugality whose tragic exemplars are Bobby and Rosie.

Both *Kids* and *Bully* suggest that iconic visions of childhood are uncomfortably close to rampantly "live sex acts." While Bobby and Rosie, in *Another Day in Paradise,* desire to make the safe move into the private zone of heterosexuality, they are singular exceptions in the light of Clark's other films. In both *Bully* and *Kids*, there is no one like Bobby and Rosie, but in both, the male teenager, far from making plans to have children and live a life of nuclear conjugal bliss with his girlfriend, is actively engaged in vandalizing an iconic young girl that needs protection. Thus, in *Kids*, a young girl, not old enough to be "deflowered," keeps watch outside the apartment where the boys smoke, watch skateboarder movies, and talk of girls. This is Clark's paternal/parental irony in its most iconic mode.

Such infantilization occurs in tandem with an implicit prelapsarian conceit that for teenagers having sex is devoid of sexuality or sexual feeling, "merely" an innocent hormonal overdrive. This aspect might well be Clark's biggest "scam," the presiding ideological trick that supports the notoriety of his filmic images and their shock value. It is more than plausible that in his earlier still photographic images, presumably devoid of a narrative, teenagers come across by default as hormonally charged sex machines. Clark deliberately transplants this possibility as a conscious choice of narrative and character delineation in his movies as if to suggest that teenagers are ontologically and intrinsically amoral, sex-crazed animals: most of the boys in his films would fit this description. In this respect, *Kids* shares remarkable, though highly qualified, similarities with a particular brand of amateur gay porn—by which I mean porn targeted at a presumably gay audience that takes as its unique attraction teenage boys jacking off together while watching straight porn. Kids shares with amateur gay porn this conceit that boys engaging in sexual acts in each other's presence are straight rather than queer, not just in its highly visible obsession with teenage boys and their bodies but also in what the boys reveal to us as *their* (straight) sexual obsessions, obsessions played out not in solitude but in shared social, geographic, and conversational spaces. The notes for one such amateur porn film say, "So . . . you love horny 'Meat' off dangerous streets! REMY & WEST are a couple of baseball athletes that were promised the opportunity to star in a video with real cheerleaders . . . WATCH, as their cocks get hard! Well . . . they did have to do a jerk off video to show the girls! Just to show the girls? Well . . . When the circus is in town the real excitement for 'KADE' the circus worker is between the legs of an 18-year-old Marine! ("Rough Street Trade!"). There's plenty of "raging" sex here. Such amateur gay porn astutely sells the prelapsarian conceit of innocent hormonal overdrives to an audience as the pleasures of the homosocial, of "social bonds between persons of the same sex" (Sedgwick 1985, 1). Clark's films, while empirically implying a wider audience than that for amateur gay porn, nevertheless reveal an acute, razor-sharp perceptiveness to homosocial space within their visceral biological agenda. Leo gets Casper to smell his fingers stinking of virgin pussy juice; Casper makes Leo suffer the smell of his sweat; in the party scene, boys go into the bathroom to urinate in toilet bowls against which other boys lie drunk, passed out, and stoned. In one seemingly interminable hypnotic slow-motion shot that introduces the Washington Square Park sequence in *Kids*, Clark's camera focuses on just the touching of fists, the crossing of elbows, the shoulder-to-shoulder "hugs" that mark the ritual of greeting one another among teenage boys.

In addition, reinforcing the generic affinities of Clark's films with amateur gay porn is the interpretive possibility that his films pander to a certain spectatorial fantasy that boys hanging out together might just "get into" each other as much as they get into the straight porn that they watch together. KADE in the notes quoted above actualizes such fantasies. It is here, of course, that a seemingly neutral figuration of homosocial space becomes a function and tool of homosexual eroticism, the sort of eroticism that validates homosexual desire, according to Michael Hatt (1993, 12).[2]

Pursuing the argument along these lines, it would seem as if Clark weren't unaware of the possibility that boys hanging out together might create a world in which girls are a problem to be reckoned with. All three films involve triangular relations that seem to suggest that girls intercede in the (perhaps erotic) friendship between two boys. *Bully* is a striking example. The first time Lisa and her friend Ali hang out with Bobby and Marty in a car, Bobby pushes Ali's head down to his crotch and in the back seat Marty plunges his head into Lisa's. But the camera interestingly blocks out Marty and frames a shot of Lisa looking at Bobby, followed by an eye-line match of Bobby looking at Lisa: Lisa has intercepted the libidinal energy Bobby and Marty are sharing. Much later in the film, as Lisa lies in bed bruised by Marty after her revelation of her pregnancy, her mind flashes to the image of Bobby looking down at her in the earlier car scene. It's at this point that, schooled in the syntactic logic of these things, *we* decide that Lisa decides that Bobby needs to die.

The most explicit moment of triangulation in *Bully* occurs in the first threesome between Lisa, Marty, and Bobby. Bobby stands naked in front of the mirror (the hand-held camera framing him head to torso, up to his pubes) readying himself for something (we do not know what) as if he cannot wait. Then he walks into the room where Lisa is riding Marty, picks up a belt, and whips Lisa. The whip serves as the cut to the next shot and to Lisa's split-second squeal and disappearance from a pictorial frame that now reveals Bobby looking down at the bed from between the legs of the naked prostrate Marty as if Bobby were about to ride him. Here, Lisa seems the point of connection through whom Bobby and Marty can unite.

As we shall see, the affinities of Larry Clark's films with amateur gay porn transform into something distinctly negative for women. Consider that the discourse of the penis by the girls in these films—the girls in *Kids* talking about the boys' penises and their sperm sticking between the teeth; in *Bully,* Ali telling Lisa about some guy with a "huge dick"; in *Paradise* a scene where Sid confesses to Rosie that her husband is "hung like a horse"—is a "heterosexual, *not* feminine discourse" (Berlant 1994, 158), a discourse for and ultimately about boys. To paraphrase Berlant, boys serve as the girls' interpretive incitement to speak, but the girls' acceptance into the space of sociality is bound to boys: it happens not through the mouth but through the vagina. Detached from boys, girls are lost. When Lisa finds out that she is pregnant she also finds out, through Marty's violent reaction and then tears, that she "finds no home in any discursive field, whether domestic, ethnic, regional or national" (1994, 147). Her sense of an entrance into any kind of space was predicated on a complete adoration of Marty that is seriously threatened by Bobby. The threat initiates her speaking on behalf of Marty to her coterie of friends in the plot to murder Bobby—"Power as pleasure comes from speaking for two" (Berlant 1994, 162). Over and over, in the homosocial world of Clark's films, as bell hooks bluntly puts it, "it is only the girls who are getting fucked and fucked over" (1996, 10) even if girls like Lisa have the right to be vicious and cruel, too.

As for Bobby, he realizes as well that the pleasure of power comes from speaking for everyone. Might it be that as he stands in front of the mirror and spits at his reflection he is spitting at the world—Marty, Lisa, Ali and all of them? And as he stands over Marty in the whipping scene he reveals himself to Marty as the person who calls the shots, for himself, for Marty, for Lisa and for everyone around, rather than wanting only to ride Marty.

My point is that even as the boys in Clark's films exist in homosocial worlds and are visually presented in homoerotic ways, their heterosexuality is only reinforced, not compromised. As support for this line of reasoning, consider Bobby's perverse mimicry of gay porn and his pimping of his buddy Marty for gay phone sex and go-go dancing. Bobby mimics the famous feminist adage that pornography is the theory, and rape is the practice; it is possible, in short, to use a mask to cover behavior. As Bobby rapes Ali, he watches (and forces her to watch) gay porn, thereby using the gay porn as a cover for his own practical study and appropriation of fascist heterosex. Leo Bersani could be referring to Bobby when he writes, "The very real potential for subversive confusion in the joining of female sexuality and the signifiers of machismo is dissipated once the heterosexual recognizes in the gay-macho style a *yearning* towards machismo . . . a *per*version rather than a *sub*version of real maleness" (1987, 207–8).

In *Bully,* early in the film, Bobby forces Marty to get on stage in a gay club and join other boys in a striptease. After they leave the club, having made quite a bit of money, Bobby is very much the happy pimp as he jokes slyly and cryptically to Marty—and much to Marty's chagrin—that Marty is a "faggot, aren't you?" For Bobby, Marty is an experiment in pedagogy. Bobby hopes that Marty will learn to be savvy enough to rid himself of scruples, that they can engage with other lifestyles and make a quick couple of hundred bucks, be good businessmen, and get out of it with their own heteronormative identities uncompromised. This might be a tall order for interpretation *on our part* given the affinities Clark's films share with gay porn and given Bobby's own cryptic comments to Marty. But this canny manipulation of homosexual lifestyles is what Clark presents as the world of his teenagers, and this is indeed how Bobby's character evolves as he eventually rapes Ali while watching, and forcing her to watch, gay porn. Clark formally notates queerness as if it were a rule of etiquette of identity-politics.

CLARK AND THE HOMOEROTIC

Asked by Mike Kelly to comment on the fact that his work often came across as "homoerotic," Clark replied by reiterating the charge: "I saw that some people might get it that way. They just can't get past the fact that it's teenage boys. Someone I know once showed Allen Ginsburg *Teenage Lust.* Allen looked at the pictures and asked, "Is he gay?" and my friend said, 'No'; Allen said, 'Wanna bet?' There is that aspect, if you have fifteen-year-old kids in your pictures with hard-ons, people are going to think that. But what can I do about that?" (Kelly 1992, 85). If this is an ingenious, and perhaps also a disingenuous, comment on Clark's part, it is also somewhat beside the point. Consistently and most unselfconsciously, he places a masculinity smelling pungently of homoeroticism side by side with a rigorously reiterated and taken-for-granted heteronormativity, as if there were no differences, antagonisms, disparities, or incompatibilities between the two; indeed, as if one doesn't affect the other at all. And yet, it is precisely this aspect that goes unnoticed in the responses to Clark's films, received either as preeminently realistic glimpses into teenage life in general, or, by the more canny viewer, as really queer texts underneath the ostensible hetero posturing. Clark's films are neither: they are not windows into authentic teenage lives, nor are they queer in any positive or at least, emancipating, sense of that word. In Clark's films, masculinity can be very homoerotic and still be desperately heteronormative, not compromised at all by the pervasive impression of male-male desire. What this says to me is that for Clark, homoerotic desire is entirely impotent, if it can even make itself visible in the domain of the heteronormative, which is for him such a very obvious domain. In light of the gay-bashing in Washington Square from *Kids;* or the scene from *Paradise* where Mel berates Bobby for being uptight about doing a deal in a gay bar, the obviousness for Clark of heteronormativity's ability to accompany homoeroticism onscreen and, presumably, in the world, comes as something of a shock. From *Kids* to *Another Day* to *Bully,* one sees the rising stakes and dramatic value of criminality in the worlds that Clark's boys inhabit: a full-blown assault on bodies by other bodies. But one also notices the fascinating costs of presenting this world homoerotically.

What consistently pops out of the films' gay closets is heterosexism, rape, and gay-bashing, not homosexuality or even homoeroticism. These are not straight films with gay subtexts: it might be closer to the truth to say that what we have here are "gay films" with straight subtexts, if their marked affiliation with gay porn can allow us to call Clark's films "gay" at all. This most peculiar transmutation of the homoerotic into the heterosexist (and even the homophobic) remains the most compelling feature of Larry Clark's filmmaking.[3]

NOTES

1. Such parental concern is echoed somewhat differently by Thomas Doherty, who sees *Kids* as coming too close to kiddie porn, in his comparison of *Kids* to Amy Heckerling's *Clueless* (1995) from the same year (1995, 16).
2. This is precisely the sense in which José Muñoz uses the word "homoerotic" in his reading of Clark's photographic work. Muñoz reads Clark from *within* a subcultural queer register, identifying Clark's boys, and indeed, Clark himself, as "trade." "Trade has been used in queer lifeworlds to describe tricks and hustlers who commit queer acts yet nonetheless produce a heterosexual identity," says Muñoz. The presiding conceit of "trade" in Clark's work and in gen-

eral, is that "the queer charge . . . requires the operative fiction of an untainted heterosexual desire." I take this to be, precisely, a reading of the kind of amateur gay porn I offer as a comparison to Clark. For Muñoz and the audience he addresses (in an essay that begins in the autobiographical mode, noting his own desire for "lean and lethargic" adolescent white boys), the homoerotic ends up being the same as homosexual eroticism, and the same homosexual eroticism that validates homosexual desire is extended into the pleasures of the homosocial. The snapping of the shutter of Clark's camera, Muñoz says, is a "queer act" even if everything before and after "is about (re)establishing heterosexuality" (1998, 168).

3. I am grateful to Elena Gorfinkel, Sam Ishii-Gonzalèz, Aparna John, and Chris Straayer for comments and suggestions on early drafts of this essay, and to José Muñoz for making available to me his essay on Larry Clark.

Works Cited

Berlant, Lauren. 1994. "America, 'Fat,' the Fetus." *boundary 2* 21, no. 3, 144–95.

———. 1995. "Live Sex Acts." *Feminist Studies* 21, no. 2, 379–404.

Bersani, Leo. 1987. "Is the Rectum a Grave?" *October* 43 (Winter), 197–222.

Cieutat, Michelle, and Phillippe Rouyer. 1995. "Entretien avec Larry Clark." *Positif* 418 (December), 18–22.

Clark. Larry. 1983. *Teenage Lust*. Meriden, CT: Meriden Gravure.

Darlington, Shasta. 2002. "Venice Awash in Scandal as 'Ken Park' Hits Screens." Online at http://ca.news.yahoo.com/020904/5/oq8h.html.

Doherty, Thomas. 1995. "Clueless Kids." *Cineaste* 21, 14–16.

Felperin, Leslie. 2002. "Bully." *Sight and Sound* 12, no. 3, 40.

Hatt, Michael. 1993. "The Male Body in Another Frame: Thomas Eakins' *The Swimming Hole* as a Homoerotic Image." In *The Body*, ed. Andrew Benjamin, 8–21. London: Academy Group.

hooks, bell. 1996. "White Light," *Sight and Sound* 6, no. 5, 10–12.

Kelly, Mike. 1992. "Larry Clark: In Youth Is Pleasure." *Flash Art* (International Edition) 164 (May/June), 82–86.

Mondzain, Marie-José. 2000. "Iconic Space and the Rule of Lands." *Hypatia* 15, no. 4, 58–76.

Mulvey, Laura. 1992. "Pandora: Topographies of the Mask and Curiosity." In *Sexuality and Space*, ed. Beatriz Colomina, 53–71. New York: Princeton Architectural Press.

Muñoz, José Esteban. 1998. "Rough Boy Trade." In *The Passionate Camera: Photography and Bodies of Desire*, ed. Deborah Bright, 167–77. London: Routledge.

Rothman, William. 1997. *Documentary Film Classics*. New York: Cambridge University Press.

"Rough Street Trade!" Film 5 (VHS). Online at http://www.thebody-shoppe.net/gay/vhs/bs041.html.

Savage, Jon. 1996. "Now: Larry Clark's *Kids.*" *Sight and Sound* 6, no. 5, 7–9.

Sedgwick, Eve Kosofsky. 1985. *Between Men: English Literature and Male Homosocial Desire.* New York. Columbia University Press.

Stephens, Chuck. 2001. "Aggressive Behavior." *Filmmaker Magazine* (Summer). Online at http://www.filmmakermagazine.com/summer2001/features/aggressive.html.

Taubin, Amy. 1995. "Chilling and Very Hot." *Sight and Sound* 5, no. 11, 16–19.

Vassé, Claire. 1995. "Kids: Saintes Vierges, Priez Pour Nous." *Positif* 418 (December), 16–17.

Williams, Linda. 1989. *Hard Core: Power, Pleasure and the "Frenzy of the Visible."* Berkeley: University of California Press.

Wrathall, John. 1999. "Another Day in Paradise." *Sight and Sound* 9, no. 8, 38.

THE BEAUTIFUL ENGLISH BOY

Mark Lester and *Oliver!*

Dianne Brooks

Oliver! (1968) was more popular in the United States than in Britain, despite its English cast, English director, English subject matter, English setting, and original author Charles Dickens. In this sense it may be linked, tenuously, to other British-boy-blockbusters like *Harry Potter and the Sorcerer's Stone* (2001) or *The Lord of the Rings* (2001–2003), which rely on the sale and consumption of an idealized English boyness. I say tenuously because although *Oliver!* and *Harry Potter* are about orphan boys in fantasy worlds, their differences trump their similarities. In some ways *Oliver!* has more in common with the staid and insightfully romantic musings on Victorianism presented by the Merchant-Ivory franchise. *Oliver!*'s setting is specific in a way in which *Harry Potter*'s is not: despite the music and dancing you can't take the Victorianism and even the Dickensian critique of such entirely out of the film. *Harry Potter* is much less specific in its time and place: it is a blend of the contemporary with the myth and magic of the pre-Christian past. Where Harry Potter is pagan, *Oliver!* can't entirely dispense with Dickens's Christian redemption even if it does turn the Jewish Fagin (whom Dickens made emphatically evil) into its hero. *Oliver!* is the last in a line of big musicals with a more or less specific nod to the nineteenth-century Old World and its values and aesthetic, not unlike its predecessors, *The Sound of Music* (1965), *My Fair Lady* (1964), *Gigi* (1958), and even *Oklahoma!* (1955). These films are adult romantic melodramas linked to an era that is now too distant for contemporary children to recognize. But the big musical has long since died and the fantasies of childhood created by baby boomers tend toward moral lessons dressed in epic Arthurian legend.

In the years since the release of *Oliver!* the film industry has profoundly changed. 1968 was a time of transition. The studio system was over, films were searching for new financing and new markets. But it was not until the mid-to-late 1970s that boys were identified and targeted as an important film market niche. *Oliver!* predates this discovery and is therefore in the tradition of the "family" film that gives something for adults to engage with (Dickens) while at the same time appealing to children (kids singing and dancing). Films like *Harry Potter* are directly marketed to children and to the child-in-all-of-us-just-can't-grow-up baby boomers (apparently tons of adults are devoted readers of the Harry Potter books). So although parents will still make the decision as to whether a child will go to the film, contemporary family films are more direct in their address to children as consumers than in the past. One example of this might be the casting credits on *Potter,* which place the three young stars' names above the title and above such well-established luminaries as Maggie Smith, Richard Harris, and John Cleese. In 1968, no one would have thought to put Mark Lester (Oliver) and Jack Wild (The Artful Dodger) ahead of the adult stars; they are instead "introduced" after Ron Moody who plays Fagin and Oliver Reed who plays Bill Sikes, because they do not drive the story, being minor characters in terms of dialogue and action.

Oliver successfully sold—and continues to successfully sell— a version of English boyhood that was more closely tied to the Dickens novel than one might think. *Potter's* fantasy English boy will become the all-powerful knight, Oliver's will become the Victorian gentleman. Despite its popularity with kids, its career boost for Mark Lester in particular, and its periodic revivals on Broadway and in dance recitals, it's not really so very kid-centered, that is, it's not as kid-centered as contemporary films that depict childhood and that are more directly aimed at the boy demographic. Harry Potter's witchy world is an idealized public school, except with girls, where the kids wander around and make and enforce rules much as in *Tom Brown's Schooldays* (1951). But in *Oliver!* neither the workhouse nor the den of thieves is portrayed as anything like a gentleman's school or club; it's almost as if Mark Lester went missing from that sort of a place. In *Potter,* the kids take power away from the adults, literally, and dictate the outcome of events. In *Oliver!* it really is up to the adults to intervene and restore order. Harry Potter is an active conjurer, an orphan who can literally transform himself. Oliver is the orphan of melodrama: dependent on inexplicable twists of fate, mostly managed by adults.

What *Oliver!* and *Harry Potter* do have in common is their being about the journey from boyhood to manhood or something short of it, all in a nostalgically English setting. But the real differences in these films speak to changing times (1968 versus 2000 and beyond) and to what it means to be a boy and a man. Oliver is a throwback to the ways of the old English gentleman, not the middle-class everyman. Harry, although he is a public school wizard-boy, seems to embody more the contemporary bourgeois pretense of classlessness than the ideals of Old World aristocracy. In *Oliver!* the adults are central to the story: they are never entirely absent, and they, rather than the children, drive the action. The narrative takes place in a world that has not yet unleashed the power of the child. Dickens liked to critique the way in which children were powerless and exploited, but he did not put Oliver Twist in the driver's seat. Thus Oliver is more object than subject in his film, whereas Harry and his cronies give the boys (and perhaps girls) fantasies of power over adults.

This essay examines how *Oliver!* constructs this earlier version of boyhood and masculinity and how that relationship is dictated by both the text on which it is based (*Oliver Twist*), the genre (musical comedy/melodrama), and the time and place the film was made (late 1960s Britain). In order to do this I will first look at how the film was adapted from Dickens and in particular how the character of Oliver was changed. I will also argue that the relationships between the boys (Oliver and the Dodger) and the casting of their roles confirms a certain Old-World nostalgia for English boyhood and manhood that was already almost anachronistic in 1968 and that is even more limited in its appeal today. Contemporary films about boys that are targeted to adults, like *About a Boy* (2002) or *Billy Elliot* (2000), have turned their backs on the old English gentlemanly ideal in favor of Tony Blair's new, less class-bound, hipper, and more masculine English boy-man à la Hugh Grant.

ADAPTING DICKENS'S MOST FAMOUS WAIF

Most of what sold Columbia Pictures, which put up 100 percent of the financing, on the idea of a filmed adaptation of a British stage musical (these were usually notorious flops in the United States) was Charles Dickens. From the beginnings of British cinema, Dickens had been seized upon as "the great source" of film material, and the adaptations began as early as 1913 with *David Copperfield*. He has been a continuous source for films and television ever since with seemingly countless adaptations of his work.

There are at least five filmed versions of *Oliver Twist:* two theatrical films (Lean and Reed) and three made-for-television adaptations. The opening credits of the Reed film say that it has been "freely adapted" from the novel (as a direct translation of the Lionel Bart musical), which is true in that much has been altered. But the bare bones of the story remain. This is why it's important to examine what choices were made in the presentation of the story, and in particular of its title character.

Although Oliver is the central character of *Oliver Twist,* he sometimes seems almost peripheral: it's as if the story swirls about him, with the usual clutter of much more interesting Dickensian characters. Oliver is the innocent straight man caught up in these circumstances, and unlike some other characters who drive the narratives of Dickens novels (Esther in *Bleak House,* David Copperfield, Pip in *Great Expectations*) he does not narrate his own story and in fact barely speaks at all. In discussing the position of the narrator in the text, Karin Lesnik-Oberstein links Oliver's silence to his construction as the "good child," by contrast with the other children in the text like the Artful Dodger or Charley Bates. Since so much speaking by characters in the text consists of duplicitous, rationalizing self-justification, hypocrisy, and outright lying, silence functions as the clearest indicator of innocence and goodness. She states: "If verbal language is therefore, to the narrator, inherently suspicious—contaminated and contaminating—we can now see that Oliver's speechlessness is an essential attribute, or constitutive of his goodness. He is the good child because both goodness and childhood are defined in the text as silent" (2001, 92).

So, as Terry Eagleton notes, Oliver's innocence, as embodied by his "blankness" in the text, "brings into dramatic focus the social forces that dominate him" (1996, 155). Oliver's silence and the other kids' garrulousness are essential ingredients in any adaptation of Dickens's story and one might argue that they are what makes this story peculiarly right for translation into musical melodrama, a form that must appeal to adults and children simultaneously but differently. One can imagine Lionel Bart thinking, "Here we have a complex story by an adult writer and here we have a reason to have lots of cute kids singing and dancing." With Oliver as the practically mute central character, one does not need to worry about the musical sequences dwarfing the hero, yet the one especially cinematic problem that remains is, with whom does the audience identify?

Following Rick Altman's genre analysis of the American musical, *Oliver!*, which he does reference (1987, 274), demonstrates the necessary evolution of the "fairy tale" musical, from European operatic/melodramatic sources and reliance on high art professionalism to the "folk" musical that expanded its universe to include families and children, had less polished operatic singers, and incorporated "folk" musical traditions in its numbers. Furthermore, although the setting is a fantastical rendering of Victorian England, and the tale of a magical familial rescue is nothing but fantasy, Dickens's social realism and the form of the film account for its popularity as a folk tale of sorts.[1]

According to the usual classical Hollywood filmmaking practices—and this film follows most of those conventions—there must be one character whose point of view we occupy: the audience needs a hero and a point of view. Oliver could not really be that character in 1968, not only because of his position in the novel but also because he is a child. Most films with children, even those distinctly about children, had them function as either objects of our desire (the site of our own lost and irretrievable innocence); or, conversely, as frightening creatures over whom adults had lost control; or both. *Lord of the Flies* (1963) might be seen as the perfect combination of these two approaches. Children's status in films is, historically, much like that of women, a parallel reflected in a society that has historically treated children since the nineteenth century as incompetent to act independently. In *Oliver!* the title character drives the narrative in almost exactly the same way that he does in the novel, by remaining at rest while the action swirls around him. Although there are key moments when the audience is placed at Oliver's point of view—when he famously asks for more gruel at the workhouse, when he first sees London, when he first sees his "surrogate mother" Nancy—he is never the controller of the gaze in the shot-reverse-shot sequences but rather remains the object to be looked at. His "beauty" further emphasizes his to-be-looked-at position: he is blond, slight, with delicate, almost feminine facial features. He in no way conveys ugliness or even the convincing griminess one would expect of the Oliver Twist of the novel.

Nor is Oliver given much dialogue. He never describes his extensive experiences of abuse or suffering, and in fact scenes of his suffering are minimized. Dickens's novel was mostly a bleak portrait of a neglected and exploited child at the hands of greedy and thieving nineteenth-century London society, but to fit this into the demands of an upbeat, sunny, happy-ending musical much had to be abandoned, for instance, the story about Oliver's half-brother who is the driving force behind much of his trouble. Unfamiliar with the true nature of Oliver's mother's exploitation and suffering, the audience is more able to comfortably enjoy the overall upbeat mood of the musical numbers. The film manages to achieve that brilliant melodramatic Dickensian balance between real-life tragedy and pain, and hopeful happy endings. Oliver in the novel is blank and silent, and Oliver in the film is a beautiful object rather than the forceful subject. And he is also blank and silent in (as he is virtually absent from) the song and dance numbers in the film, which are of course the bread and butter of musicals. Although he is objectified, he is not eroticized because his body is not on display as those of many men, women, and even in some cases children are in musicals with dance numbers. He has only one solo song, the very short "Where Is Love?" He participates in "I'll Do Anything" and "Who Will Buy?" which both really dwarf him. The latter in particular, probably the most visually and musically complex number in the film, inserts him briefly but builds up to a huge production number with a large chorus of singers and dancers. Oliver never dances at all and his singing voice is an odd whispering boy soprano that creates the effect of standing completely apart from the rest of the cast's more natural-sounding full-bodied music-hall/vaudeville/Broadway singing style. In this sense he is the retiring Victorian upper-class English gentleman whose voice and body are off limits for consumption, not the singing and dancing boy/man who instantly problematizes masculinity.

Another critical necessity in translating the novel was trimming down the count of villains. Any references to the luckless father, the half-brother, and the half-brother's mother are gone. Mr. Bumble (the director of the workhouse), his wife, and the Sowerberrys (a mortician and his family) are softened or marginalized, and most importantly, Fagin's den of thieves is more like a camp for wayward innocents than a training ground for boys devoted to a life of crime. Dickens meant *Oliver Twist* to be a deterrent to this sort of life of crime, but the musical cannot sustain his indictment of Fagin and his boys. This is interesting considering that Dickens received some comeuppance from William Thackeray for making the life of crime seem attractive at a time when public punishment was seeming to generate interest in and even sympathy for the criminal rather than achieving its deterrent effect. Fagin's

Jewishness, which Dickens made much of, is virtually eliminated in the film, and Fagin himself is made a charming rogue with a protective attitude toward the boys. The contrast mentioned above between Oliver the innocent and the more sophisticated and streetwise boys is maintained, though mainly through singing and dancing and less through any sort of indication that these children are soured or jaded already.

One way in which this is cleverly achieved is in the casting of the Artful Dodger. In the novel, the Dodger is meaner, getting Oliver into trouble at the bidding of Fagin and the half-brother Monks and winding up in jail at the end. As played in the film by Jack Wild, the Dodger seems more a composite of the novel's Artful Dodger and Charley Bates. Although there is nothing in the film to indicate that the Dodger will give up his life of petty thievery, there is also nothing the least bit dangerous or malevolent about him. The fact that Reed chose Wild to play the Dodger indicates that he wanted a more pronounced visual contrast with Oliver—so the Dodger sings and dances expertly, speaks more often than Oliver does, and looks quite different. Whereas Mark Lester is towheaded, very slight, and almost feminine in his features, Jack Wild is dark-haired and round-faced, a little plumper, and generally more robust in appearance. One might argue that Wild is truer to the orphan workhouse, Lester truer to the actual upper-class parentage that is revealed later in the story. Wild is the working-class hero, contemporary even at that time, while Lester is reminiscent of the upper-class ideals of the past.

CAROL REED AND *OLIVER!*

Most of the decisions related above were already a part of the stage version of the musical, which translated to the screen more or less directly. The book was kept intact and it was left to the producers of the film to find a director. That director turned out to be the now very well respected Sir Carol Reed, lauded as one of Britain's "auteurs" mainly for films like *Odd Man Out* (1947) and *The Third Man* (1949). Many don't realize that the director of these two films directed something as "banal" as a musical. The critic and director Lindsay Anderson (*This Sporting Life* [1963] and *If . . .* [1968]) thinks of Reed as "a very curious and sad case really. He's obviously a man of immense talent who somehow went astray. He ended up in *Oliver* somewhere. It's very strange. But you should see *The Fallen*

Idol—it's a very good film" (Dixon 1994, 169). Anderson is in many ways the complete opposite of Reed: he wanted to see the influence of the "Nouvelle Vague" swamp and transform what he saw as the staid conservatism of British cinema. Reed's work was already deeply institutionalized by the 1960s and he was exactly the kind of director Anderson was rebelling against. And Anderson was not alone in his dismissal of the film and its whole genre because, or in spite of the fact that, it turned out to be monstrously successful, with Academy Awards and huge box office. Film critics like Stanley Kaufman and Vincent Canby reviled it, while Judith Crist, Richard Schickel, and Pauline Kael praised it. It is now generally thought of as having been better received in the United States than in Britain although several British reviewers, including those reviewing for *Punch* and the *New Statesman,* liked it. Kael's review for the *New Yorker,* titled, "The Concealed Art of Carol Reed," and one of the most extensive and favorable pieces of writing about the film (apart from publicity), applauds Reed for having "just made the kind of movie they don't make anymore" (Kael 1968, 200), meaning a big-budget commercial musical that demonstrates "quiet concealed art of good craftsmanship" (205). In conclusion she states: "The period of cutups may be over among movie artists that is; the hacks are just beginning to call for scissors and strobes. In this context of a search for new ways of *integrating* material on the screen, the unostentatious work of Carol Reed may be both behind and ahead of what is now exhaustingly fashionable" (206).

The conflict between Anderson's and Kael's points of view on Reed reflects differences in taste, politics, and the true meaning and purposes of cinema. It most definitely reflects a simplistic bias against popular forms such as the musical and the melodrama, which are assumed to lack both creativity and social critique in their quest for providing pleasure. However, it does address an anachronism in terms of Reed's ideal of English boyhood that seemed still to be very much bound up in Old World class designations. Reed was working as a hired man, he was an insider in the troubled British film industry and was not, like Anderson, a young innovator agitating for change—his time in that role had passed. In fact, Reed had just come off a series of not-so-well-received films, the most recent of which had been the big-budget critical and box office flop *The Agony and the Ecstasy* (1965) for Twentieth-Century Fox. Carol Reed was doing what so many of the older well-established directors, like David Lean, had to do: take projects financed

Director Carol Reed instructing Mark Lester on how to be an "English Gentlemen" for the film *Oliver!*

by American studios, since British financing for big movies was hard to come by. By 1968, the innovative "kitchen sink" cycle of British films had run their course and although there were very good films being made there was also much "swinging London" drivel.

Reed was an excellent choice, being an actor's director who had worked very successfully with children before in, for example, *A Kid for Two Farthings* (1955). He made key choices in casting and shaped the performances of the boys and consequently the presentations of boyhood in *Oliver!* For this, reviewers consistently praise him. In *Oliver!*, as in *Farthings*, Reed's emphasis is on naturalism and restraint as opposed to the "fabricated prodigyhood that makes so many child stars in America quite insufferable" (Moss 1987, 250). Lester's Oliver is meant to suggest innocence and goodness translated onscreen as quiet, shy, nonshowmanship. Oliver is also the nonerotic object, beautiful to look at, almost ethereally detached at times, reflective with genuine emotion registering now and then. He has an upper-class accent and manner which, combined with preadolescent beauty, signals a future English gentleman in the tradition of noble failures like Ronald Coleman or Leslie Howard. Wild, too, despite his character's "worldliness," projects innocence in his round face. And where he could have been the "show off" attention grabber he is an innocently competent scene stealer, his eagerness to please appearing genuine as compared to the more obvious and cynically manipulative performances of many child actors.

LESSONS IN ENGLISH MANHOOD

Oliver! might be said to fit into a tradition of films about the journey from boyhood to manhood, like Alexander Mackendrick's *Sammy Going South* (1963), which tells of a ten-year-old boy who journeys from Port Said to Durban after his parents' death and is taught the ways of manhood by various men along the way. This is a story that is mainly targeted to an adult audience, invited to remember and examine its own transition, rather than to children, who were not yet seriously considered as an independent film demographic—not yet clearly targeted by Hollywood as independent spenders (in the way that young males are today). Dickens wrote the story of boyhood transition in many books, and although Oliver doesn't reach manhood in the course of *Oliver Twist* as Pip does in *Great Expectations* this story does seem to be pointing Oliver in a clear direction toward proper masculinity. Although the ending message is clear—a rich benefactor will save Oliver and teach him how to be a man—the vague characterization of Brownlow in the film can't really cancel the central and most appealing man in the story: Fagin. Even if we contest that Fagin primarily serves this function, Brownlow does not hold our attention in strictly filmic terms—Sikes does. In the novel, Oliver is restored to a proper home with Brownlow, who adopts him. He lives in the man's home with the doting housekeeper—his newly revealed aunt, to whom he has already become attached—in close proximity. The film briefly refers to this homecoming when Oliver steps out of Brownlow's carriage, climbs up the stairs to his house, and is greeted at the door by the housekeeper, the very last shot showing

Oliver's head in her ample bosom. But the main protagonist role shifts between Fagin and Sikes, with Brownlow receding into the background literally to open the door to proper English boyhood at the end.

Fagin and Sikes become the figures who drive the visual and narrative action rather than either the children or Brownlow. This is what makes *Oliver!* oddly anachronistic in 1968, or at least a measure of changing and confusing times. The film is still in the hands of the adults. Unlike *Harry Potter* and even *About a Boy*, *Oliver!* presents no confusion about who is in charge; the boys do not sneak about behind Fagin's back, taking matters into their own hands and saving the day. Ron Moody's universally applauded performance as Fagin is really the center of the film. He is a softened gangster, a sort of comic spiv—a type that was prominent and recognizable in British cinema, particularly in the 1940s and 1950s. The comic spiv was a sort of antihero who "fiddled" around restrictions but was not necessarily an outright criminal. The criminal version of the spiv was a roguish dandy who broke rules and tended to be malevolent, yet always invited the audience to sympathize, the archetype being Stewart Granger's Ted Purvis in *Waterloo Road* (1944). By the 1960s the spiv had almost disappeared, but Moody's Fagin is clearly a version of him.

Fagin has three song-and-dance numbers in the film: "You've Got to Pick a Pocket or Two," "Go but Be Back Soon," and "I'm Reviewing the Situation." Each of these is instructional in the art of petty thievery in a lighthearted and comical way, offering "acceptable" justifications for "fiddling." One could easily see him as fitting into the tradition of the "fixer . . . the family man who commands some admiration as a nimble dodger" (Spicer 2001, 9). Each number is performed in the presence of either the full complement of his charges or at the very least the Artful Dodger. In each number he betrays a genuinely protective, fatherly concern for them. In the scene where Bill Sikes and Nancy argue over Oliver, Sikes strikes her violently while Fagin and the boys look on. Their reaction—particularly Fagin's—is clearly disapproving.

Fagin as father figure and masculine model is the adult version of the Artful Dodger. The visual parallels between Jack Wild and Ron Moody are clear in that they are both presented as clownish caricatures in their costume. In the second to last scene of the film, Fagin and the Artful Dodger reprise "Reviewing the Situation," the song that signals Fagin's deep down good-heartedness. Fagin has managed to escape the chaos created by Sikes's murder of Nancy and the exposure of the hideout, he has lost his loot, but just afterward he finds the Dodger waiting for him. The two of them dance up a yellow brick road, arm in arm and into the sunset, with *Wizard of Oz* (1939) choreography. In the novel, both the Dodger and Fagin come to bad ends: Fagin is killed and the Dodger is jailed.

In the film, there is only the slightest suggestion of a paternal relationship between Sikes and Fagin: perhaps Sikes is the bad son, the bad seed. But although Sikes is really drawn as pure evil the casting works against such a simplistic reading, since Oliver Reed can't help but project a certain sympathetic quality beneath his burly exterior. Reed was by this time known for alienated hero roles: he is both handsome and sympathetic, reminiscent of the gothic romantic hero of earlier eras as translated into "the Angry Young Man" ushered in by Laurence Harvey in *Room at the Top* (1959) and carried forward in films like *Saturday Night and Sunday Morning* (1960). Penelope Houston's *Sight and Sound* review of *Room at the Top* characterizes the type as "A young man in a provincial lodging, precariously poised between working-class origins and professional future, openly derisive of the 'system,' the Establishment, taking out his frustrations in buccaneering talk and a raw political and social awareness" (1959, 56).

The toughness of the Angry Young Man was associated with a more macho and therefore masculine traditional northern working-class culture and in direct opposition to the poetic and more feminine associations of the urban educated elite of the south of England, notably London. An offshoot of this type is the Alienated Young Man, who is embodied by David Hemmings in *Blowup* (1966) and Oliver Reed in *The System* (1964) and *I'll Never Forget What's'isname* (1967). In these films, particularly the latter two directed by Michael Winner, the Angry Young Man is bitter, alienated, and completely dissatisfied with success, unable to achieve the alternative life he dreams of. Spicer notes that Oliver Reed here "projects a sense of barely contained physical energy and anger that can never find its occasion, becoming a powerless Byronic antihero, whose distant gaze suggests that nothing really satisfies or truly engages him and who has nowhere to go" (2001, 157).

In a musical like *Oliver!*, which does not spend time developing psychological complexity or motivation, Sikes is meant to be a standard psychopathic villain, in fact the only real villain of the film. Reed therefore bears the weight of the audience's and the other characters' hatred. But the lack of time for, and the genre restrictions on, developing Sikes's character are compensated for by Carroll Reed's casting, since Oliver Reed would have been connected to the alienated young man films referred to above. Moreover, despite attempts to make him as unappealing as possible with costuming, lighting, and dialogue delivery, it doesn't altogether work. He is not monstrous or grotesque as other Sikeses: for example, compare the Sikes of the most recent PBS "Oliver Twist" (1999) (Andy Serkis). In all of Oliver Reed's films, even his final appearance in *Gladiator* (2000), a certain beauty peeks out from behind his big, burly exterior. This makes Nancy's loyalty to Bill Sikes more understandable: when she sings her plaintive ballad "As Long as He Needs Me" or celebrates in "It's a Fine Life" we understand what draws her to him.

In Dickens's story there are many people involved in the battle over the possession of Oliver and ultimately his soul. The film has staged this battle as taking place mainly between Sikes and Brownlow as future fathers, possessors, and role models. One of Dickens's and melodrama's stock plot mechanisms involves the mystery of parentage. The film rather uncomplicatedly sets up Bill and Nancy as metaphoric and possibly literal parental figures. One never sees Oliver's parents and it is only toward the end that the identity of the mother is discovered. One can imagine that the story could go in this direction, the nightmare revelation of Bill Sikes as Oliver's "real" father tantalizingly dangled before us as in a horror film. Although it becomes clear that Nancy is not Oliver's natural mother, she functions as something more than a surrogate, acting out his own mother's history. When Oliver and Nancy first meet in the film the exchange of looks is oedipally charged, immediately followed by a number called, "I'll Do Anything." Here Oliver joins in only briefly to sing to Nancy (and she to him), clearly establishing an instinctive maternal bond. From then on, she is caught between her attempts to protect him and her loyalty to Bill. Like Oliver's mother, Nancy is misused by her lover, with Oliver figuring as a cause of both deaths. Both "mothers" sacrifice their lives to save this son.

If Nancy is the stand-in mother, the possibility that Bill Sikes is both the literal and figurative father is made even more explicit in the film. Just as Nancy feels an instinctive attraction to Oliver, so does Bill immediately seek to possess the boy. In terms of structure, Oliver and Bill are continuously paired together in scenes, Bill taking him under his wing so to speak, trying to train him in the ways of thievery. Their struggle is central and provides the climactic moment in the film. They are both relatively silent, the only two major characters who hardly sing or dance. Sikes via Oliver Reed, an angry and alienated psychopath, represents young Oliver's future: the son will become the father. In the climactic scene, Sikes uses Oliver to escape—as assistant, hostage, or companion? But Oliver botches the job (again) symbolically causing the death of the bad father and with it the potentially bad self. In this scene, the boy is balanced precariously on a pole with a rope around his small body supposedly to anchor Sikes's swing from one building to another. Oliver does not really take action here but is saved by the gunshots of police who leave Bill's body swinging beneath him for all to see. But even though Oliver is placed above Bill in this climax, he remains a somewhat passive child as compared to other more contemporary active children who are coming of age. Nonetheless, once Oliver has crossed this bridge the door literally opens to the right and good life as a good English gentleman.

Although Dickens was himself critical of the ruling classes, Carol Reed seems to have made a clear choice to summon up the ghost of the proper English gentleman. Mark Lester as his Oliver is an idealization of an English boyhood that has all but disappeared, the closest contemporary reference being Prince William with his tow-headed, shy, and restrained manner, the ultimate English anachronism. Lester, with his upper-class accent and beautiful appearance, somewhat resembles the Prince and would seem to fit perfectly—and in princely fashion—at the feet of his adoring yet stalwart nanny (Brownlow's housekeeper) on his way to Eton and Oxford. For at least the first half of the twentieth century, this male ideal of the British ruling classes was dominant and perpetuated in, for example, the public school gentlemanly "code" as well as in various cultural forms such as film. Such a boy grew up to be "the gifted amateur trained for nothing but ready for anything," a combination of "idealized medieval chivalry, the delicacy and sensitivity of the cultivated Man of Feeling, the athletic, vigorous manliness of 'muscular Christianity' and the Protestant success drive" (Spicer 2001, 9). In film, actors like Robert Donat and Leslie Howard most often played this role in the 1930s and 1940s, but by the end of World War II the English Gentleman was on the decline.

The decline of the debonair English Gentleman coincided with the rise of the Everyman as notably embodied by actors like

John Mills. In Lean's *Great Expectations* (1946), Mills as Pip acts out Dickens's critique of the Victorian cult of the gentleman by learning not to confuse the desire for a better life and goodness with class status. The Everyman gave way to all manner of more middle-class heroes into which mold *Harry Potter* might fit squarely, set as it is in a public school for warlocks from middle-class English suburbs where the snooty old-school throwbacks inevitably lose. Although Oliver's world and manner are not nearly as clubby, he himself is more Old World than New, more aristocratic than democratic. This is perhaps one of the things that Lindsay Anderson objects to in Carol Reed, whose age, class, and worldview would seem to dictate that sort of choice in the casting of Mark Lester as Oliver.

If anyone signaled the trend of future English boyhood it was the Dodger as embodied by Jack Wild. Wild had played the original Oliver in the stage version, thus connecting it to the trend of class-less singing, boy-next-door types that had become popular in the late 1950s. This may not be entirely coincidental as Lionel Bart, the writer and producer of the stage version, had his first successes writing songs for Tommy Steele and Cliff Richard, two hugely successful "rock and roll" alternatives who ushered in a wave of pop musicals demonstrating wholesome, clean-living, nonrebellious, love-your-mum-and-dad qualities. It is Jack Wild as Oliver who leads more directly to the Billy Elliots, Harry Potters, and contemporary English boy heroes who, even if upwardly mobile, can never penetrate class barriers nor even disguise themselves as aristocratic in manner. He is just too buoyant, sharp, and charismatic to have been as utterly passive as Mark Lester. Wild is probably better suited to infuse the Dodger with sharpness, charm, loyalty.

CONCLUSION

Building the filmed version of *Oliver!* with an eye toward successes like *The Sound of Music* but also with an awareness that the death knell had already been rung on the film musical genre, required shrewd choices. The film had to be true to what was the most essentially appealing about Dickens in general and about this story in particular—the family melodrama with the happy, if not completely unambiguous, ending. But the melodrama had to be tempered sufficiently to sustain the demands of musical comedy—thus turning villains into good guys or making them attractive anti-heroes. So although the genre in many ways is conservative, certain casting choices and narrative trimmings introduce complexity and ambiguity in unexpected ways. Centering the action in the criminal environment, making that the central "family" that, although ultimately rejected, stays with the audience, runs against a straight reading of Dickens's supposed intention to offer a lesson on the vagaries of the criminal way of life. As in most Dickens novels, the villains are as interesting as the heroes, if not more so, and not always simplistically evil.

The success and popularity of *Oliver!* can then be accounted for by the way in which it is both anachronistic and contemporary. Mark Lester as the "beautiful English boy" is a throwback to the innocent, powerless, silent child who through strict control and proper example will become the great man of the great Empire. On the other hand, Jack Wild with his rougher look and manner signaled the trend of the future: boys as the ultimate niche market, boys who control adults and the stories that are told about them, boys, indeed, who are "classless" or even "working-class" but who still aspire to all that is good in those core gentlemanly values (work, manners, wit) with just a touch of grit and manliness added. Additionally, by casting his nephew, Oliver Reed, to play Sikes, Carol Reed adapts to future trends. Oliver Reed already had a certain hip, serious currency, playing with stodgy English masculinity by calling attention to the alienation and dissatisfaction caused by the dictates of the upper classes and their gentlemanly "codes." So *Oliver!* shows us that English boys can still be twitty in a way that is only English and at the same time paves the way for the Harry Potters who are no longer just seen but are also actively being heard.

Children have changed, as has our romantic view of them and as has childhood itself, in the years since the pretty English boy of *Oliver!* was presented onscreen. Like Harry Potter, boys onscreen today are much more active and heroic, much less passive and innocent, as *Oliver!* idealizes them. Our culture, our parenting, so much of our experience is youth-centered or at least seems to be packaged that way with us all looking backward as we age. *Oliver!* is the end of the old-school, mighty British Empire giving way to a change that has culminated in Tony Blair's new, hip England. But *Oliver!*'s lessons in manhood were still instructive.

NOTES

1. Although Altman discusses the American Film Musical, certainly *Oliver!*'s stylistic allegiance to Hollywood filmmaking practices, its American financing, and even its reception by America make it suitable for discussion and analysis in this context.

WORKS CITED

Altman, Rick. 1987. *The American Film Musical.* Bloomington: Indiana University Press.

Booker, Christopher. 1969. *The Neophiliacs.* Boston: Gambit.

Dickens, Charles. 1999. *Oliver Twist.* Oxford: Oxford University Press.

Dixon, Wheeler Winston. 1994. *Re-Viewing British Cinema.* Albany: State University of New York Press.

Durgnat, Raymond. 1971. *A Mirror for England.* New York: Praeger.

Eagleton, Terry. 1996. "Ideology and Literary Form: Charles Dickens." In *Charles Dickens,* ed. Steven Connor, 151–58. London: Longman.

Houston, Penelope. 1959. "Room at the Top?" *Sight and Sound* (Spring), 56–59.

Kael, Pauline. 1968. *Going Steady.* Boston: Little, Brown.

Lesnik-Oberstein, Karin. 2001. "Oliver Twist: The Narrator's Tale." *Textual Practice* 15, no. 1, 87–100.

McNab, Geoffrey. 2000. *Searching for Stars.* London: Cassell.

Mallett, Richard. 1968. "Cinema." *Punch* 255 (July/December), 479.

Moss, Robert. 1987. *The Films of Carol Reed.* New York: Columbia University Press.

Murphy, Robert. 1992. *Sixties British Cinema.* London: BFI.

Perry, George. 1974. *The Great British Picture Show: From the 90s to the 70s.* New York: Farrar, Straus and Giroux.

Spicer, Andrew. 2001. *Typical Men.* New York: I. B. Tauris.

Richard Dreyfuss as Roy Neary in *Close Encounters of the Third Kind* (1977):
encounter without the weight of expectation.

7

THE MAN-BOYS OF STEVEN SPIELBERG

Murray Pomerance

Childhood, which by my own admission and everybody's impression of me, is what my life has been.
Steven Spielberg

In any modern society, especially in the context of advanced global capitalism, it is difficult to draw the clear distinctions between adulthood and childhood that seemed to characterize those preindustrial social arrangements nineteenth- and early-twentieth-century anthropology adored. Today, job restructuring and managed unemployment routinely infantilize persons who would have been considered adults (or young adults) twenty-five years ago, not to mention the intentional prolongation and stabilization of adolescence as a rabid consumer base and the proliferation of the latchkey family that lays responsibilities once reserved for adults on the knapsack-slugging shoulders of children. Useful for those who would try to understand the conditions under which adulthood is constructed now and the tacit guidelines constructers use in constructing it—given the confusions of biological age-grading—is a distinction Erving Goffman made in 1974 between natural and social primary frames. What he referred to as *social* activity is an organization of "guided doings": the *natural* world, by contrast, is taken to be "undirected, unoriented, unanimated, unguided" (1974, 22). In light of this dichotomy, the process of growth and socialization can be seen as a complex ongoing production of guidedness, an increase in the extent to which persons can be taken as skillful and capacious agents of their own activities and therefore as suitable repositories of responsibility both casual and legal. The adult owns action, if not formally and economically as property then at least morally, and to the degree that his moves can be taken as indications of his intent, alignment, and will. Children, on the other hand, exist in nature, without fully internalized—and therefore, automatic—socially constructed systems of guidance in place to assist them in navigating the world with control.

It is the natural being, not the successfully socialized one, Mark Twain brings to our attention concluding *Tom Sawyer*, surely one of the most celebrated and perceptive treatments of boyhood in modern Western literature. "So endeth this chronicle," he writes: "It being strictly a history of a *boy*, it must stop here; the story could not go much further without becoming the history of a *man*. When one writes a novel about grown people, he knows exactly where to stop—that is, with a marriage; but when he writes of juveniles, he must stop where he best can" (1946, 318). The really critical definition of the adult male rests in his capacity to get married—to exist in the state of being "married," indeed, instead of "not married," as Laura Mulvey put it in a 1989 reflection on *Duel in the Sun* (1946). When a male marries he grows up, and the boy he was disappears.

And, apparently, when a male grows up, he marries, or at least stabilizes—participates in a complex of adaptations, attitudes, projections, plans, biographical constructions, status alignments, pretenses, masks, ensnarements, modesties, surrenders, claims, hypotheses, groundings, honors, celebrations, poses, and artifacts: the wedding announcement, the wedding ring, the wedding photograph, the wedding cake, and the wedding bed. A fellow marries and announces his willingness to join what was in Twain's time, and what remains in most American states and Canadian provinces today, a heterosexual conspiracy. One plans to make children, or at least admits to no longer belonging rather exclusively in the company of them oneself. One engages in consultations before accepting dinner invitations. One is guarded in staring adoringly at persons the unknowing world could label as suitable sexual partners. One shares bank loans and tax benefits, toothpaste and favorite films and flavors of ice cream. And one apparently does not play while being seriously at work, does not have, as Stephen Schiff claims for Steven Spielberg, an "insatiable passion for video games":

> Sometimes he plays them by modem with Robin Williams, who lives in San Francisco. Sometimes he just plays by himself. He plays after the kids go to bed, and on weekends, and sometimes on movie sets.
>
> "He has little hand things," Dustin Hoffman says. "On *Hook*, while they were lighting, he shut everybody out, and he sat on the camera dolly and he played those—what are they, Game Boy? And

then for a while he was getting all the flight information from L.A. International Airport, so he's sitting on the dolly and he's listening to the pilots. And he's doing that *while* he's playing Game Boy." (2000, 184)

In such a scheme, merely to *pretend* to stabilize, even with art, is merely to play at manhood. Play, even elaborate play (such as is effected with the company of a pretend wife [Natalie Wood] and a pretend child [Sal Mineo] by James Dean in *Rebel Without a Cause* [1955]) is the serious business of boyhood, a condition (we might as well acknowledge) not always experienced voluntarily. If adulthood is forbidden or reserved, even those who are ready for it may be forced to retain childhood status and to act out their impulses through the matrix of play rather than embedding them in the socially supported structure we call "reality." This is because adulthood is not only an expectation but also a privilege, a status to which power applies; and power is not widely distributed in our society.

The truly good boy, Twain suggests, is actually bad, or at least naughty—what Leslie Fiedler called a "good bad boy" (1960, 267–72): "Tom was eating his supper, and stealing sugar as opportunity offered" (5). This is the character the history of whom must stop before he grows. There is also a good boy who is good and nothing but good, in short a bore, the sort who swallows and believes every word addressed to him reprovingly by the county judge in a chapter called "Showing Off in Sunday School":

> Knowledge is worth more than anything there is in the world; it's what makes great men and good men; you'll be a great man and a good man yourself, someday, Thomas, and then you'll look back and say, "It's all owing to the precious Sunday-school privileges of my boyhood—it's all owing to my dear teachers that taught me to learn—it's all owing to the good superintendent, who encouraged me, and watched over me, and gave me a beautiful Bible—a splendid elegant Bible—to keep and have it all for my own, always—it's all owing to right bringing up! (45)

This paragon that the judge has the bad judgment to name Thomas, let's call the *man*, since unless Tom is very careful he is going to grow up to become such a being. The man is strong, stalwart, morally responsible, a good citizen, a taxpayer, predictable—indeed insurable—and a good catch for anyone eager to find a husband who can be counted on. He is not by any stretch of the imagination Indiana Jones. Nor is he the grown-up Peter Pan configured by Robin Williams in *Hook* (1991), a person who even though welded to his cell phone is somehow still an irresponsible scatterbrain. He isn't Keys the government agent (Peter Coyote) in *E.T. the Extra-Terrestrial* (1982), desperate in middle age to reach out across the stars; or Basie the moocher (John Malkovich) in *Empire of the Sun* (1987), the goofy eccentric Dr. Ian Malcolm (Jeff Goldblum) of *Jurassic Park* (1993), Matt Hooper (Richard Dreyfuss) the innocent oceanographer of *Jaws* (1975), the Private Ryan (Matt Damon) who gets saved but always seems to have his twinkling eye, as all of these others do, on some distant pile of sugar cubes on some distant table, or even Frank Abagnale (Christopher Walken) in *Catch Me If You Can* (2002), a fellow who can dance, to be sure, but not one who can hang onto the girl he's dancing with. These, and many other characters created by Steven Spielberg, fail to become adult men—fail spectacularly, one could say, since their failure is not only note-worthy but a central feature of a well-conceived spectacle.

They are not, however, plainly and simply boys, as are other noteworthy characters centrally placed in Spielbergian narratives, such as Elliot (Henry Thomas) in *E.T.*, Jamie (Christian Bale) in *Empire*, or that adorable quintessence of insouciance and charm, Frank Jr. (Leonardo DiCaprio) for most of *Catch Me If You Can*. Often, in fact, the glowingly authentic boys of Spielberg are mature beyond their years—Elliot with a wisdom and simplicity no other human being can demonstrate; Jamie with superhuman resilience and hunger for life, a "boy who had grown up too quickly, who was becoming a flower long before the bud had ever come out of the top-soil" (Forsberg 2000, 127); Frank Abagnale Jr. with an uncanny abil-ity to measure out performance. But while the boy in Spielberg is sometimes a prescient child, he is far more often a blossoming spiritual presence inside the shell of a grown man, and as such a reflection of the filmmaker, "like an excitable prepubescent, his hormones zinging, his thoughts scooting by so fast that his mouth can't trap enough language to express them" (Schiff 2000, 176). These failed and incomplete, thus distinctively older, males retain into physical adulthood the charming immaturity and unscarred beauty of youth and in so doing reflect the transnational, conglom-erate, bureaucratic, postcapitalist world in which we live, where the ideal corporate pawn is weighed down with responsibilities (an

adult) while at the same time lacking essential power and authority (a child). If this *man-boy*, as I shall call him, is ideal for capitalism because he can be made to do heavy work while being paid and
generally treated as a child, he is also and in different ways, as I
hope to show, ideal for the Spielbergian narrative.

•◆• •◆• •◆•

"Only that which narrates can make us understand," Susan
Sontag wrote (1977, 23). To the extent that I have an argument, it
is that the characterological treatment I wish to foreground permits
certain narrative tactics. But I will also take advantage of this
opportunity to take a more detailed look at a particular moment in
Close Encounters of the Third Kind (1977), a moment that nicely
figures a stable construction I hope I can successfully point to in
Spielberg's work and that has eluded serious treatment. My
approach owes a great deal to others who have written in a different way about masculinity: for example Peter Lehman (1993) and
Steven Shaviro (1993) (as well as to Alessandra Ponte's essay on the
architectural essence in phallocentrism [1992]) without, I fear,
repaying much of that debt or dwelling as they do on the politics of
masculinity or the qualities of masculine embodiment. My fascination is for the architecture of stories. I am interested here in following Spielberg's evident interest in masculinity as an index of social
arrangements, and his writing a masked boyish version of it as a
negotiable existential moment; a way of experiencing and knowing;
a trait or set of traits that can be gained and lost. If male experience
involves method, positioning, and alignment, it is some condensation of these elements (always situated in both social space and life
history) that we find manifested within the social press as a structured role with concomitant obligations, rights, expectations,
styles of management, and embellishments.

By *man-boy* I have in mind not the insufficient and incomplete product of whatever it is that is taken as appropriate and
correct male socialization in any culture—the boy who never quite
becomes a man because for him something is missing in the
transitional mechanism—but instead the man who never quite
abandons his boyhood, although, as Albert Camus suggested in *Le
Premier homme*, he may have sufficient trouble understanding it.
Spielberg was often ridiculed as a wunderkind in Hollywood, a "boy
with a camera" boldly swimming with adult sharks and thus continually experiencing what Stephen Schiff calls "the simultaneous

urgency and impossibility of communicating what it is he sees"
(1995, 185). Nevertheless, he has never aligned his audience but
with the adult side of the man-boy's mixed perspective, so that consistently—at least until *Catch Me If You Can*, to which I will
return—the Spielbergian man-boy is cast as a type of man, not a
type of boy. To put this in terms of power and privilege, the man-
boy is not a powerless child engaging perforce in a pretense of capa-
bility and responsibility with no real resources to substantiate the
claim implicit in that engagement. He is a person subject to state
regulation, heir to the freedoms, self-determination, and culpability
that accrue thereto, yet borrowing, at a moment critical to the turning of the plot that grounds him, the wonder, helplessness, insight,
vulnerability, playfulness and guile of an "unguided" child.

If Jim Graham in *Empire of the Sun* is *not* a paradigm (it is the
fact that he is forced by circumstance to collect manly resources
and produce manly behavior, without ever losing a boy's body, that
makes his condition so deeply evocative, but he is a boy-man), his
father (Rupert Frazer) is. We see this precisely in the gala party
scene at Mr Lockwood's house, where he ponders morosely on the
future of civilized British colonial superiority in Shanghai all the
while dressed like Captain Hook transmogrified out of the classic
that Spielberg would himself play out nine years later (using the talents of that man-boy par excellence, Robin Williams). The
Lockwood party—in its structure something of an homage to the
masquerade ball scene in Hitchcock's *Rebecca* (1940)—is a pivotal,
even triggering, scene because pater Graham's realization in the
climax of it, that the enemy is at the gates and his whole sanctimo-
nious world is at an end, is the trigger that leads him to move his
family away from the seclusion of their house and into a more public, more crowded position where Jim can be separated from them
and thrown into the lonely and enchanting wartime adventure that
is the subject of this film. Watching his son, dressed as a genie,
stray beyond Mr Lockwood's property and come face to face with
the Japanese army, the shocked Graham is utterly the Old Boy in
his outlandish, exaggerated, flamboyant costume, rendered a creature of make-believe trapped in a circumstance of high seriousness.
Aware of the responsibilities all other adults would attribute to
him, Mr Graham is also, because of the sudden presence of so huge
a danger at so close a range, utterly vulnerable, frozen with incapacity: a boy trapped in a man's life.

The man-boy can be seen throughout Spielberg's body of work. In *Jaws* he is Matt Hooper, a young oceanographer called in to assist the sheriff (Roy Scheider) of Amity, Long Island, face what he fears is a killer great white shark. Matt is knowledgeable, indeed expert, and therefore has the intelligence of an adult; this we see in a gruesome scene where performing a shark autopsy he demonstrates both professionalism and intellectual superiority to the common man sheriff. But he has the personality of a good bad boy. Joining the sheriff at home for dinner, he shows off the insouciant and romantic detachment of the child-dreamer. For him, the little town of Amity is a fairyland; and the story into which he has tumbled is a fabulous myth, an adventure that can gobble him up like a shark itself. If it is true of sharks that they must move incessantly in order to live, the great white of *Jaws* is film itself, continuously unspooling, engaging, and unfolding, and the expert who is familiar with the technology of the thing but at the same time suspended in wonder and delight is Spielberg, an analogue for whom Hooper may well be.

In *Schindler's List* (1993), the bourgeois entrepreneur Schindler (Liam Neeson) is a man-boy, because the heroic business upon which he has set himself in saving Jews from extermination is, for him, not business at all but adventure. He is swept up by it, passionate and daredevil in a way that seems wholly irresponsible when considered in terms of his own career and social position, not to mention the human lives that are the markers in his game. As Schindler flew in the face of criticism from his friends and countrymen, Spielberg, making this film, flew in the face of what "people would say . . . 'It's the wrong style. What's he doing? Who does he wanna be like? Who's he trying to become?'" (Schiff 2000, 173) It is Schindler's agonized and hard-laboring assistant, Itzhak Stern (Ben Kingsley), who sees the creation of the List as a desperate, terrifying, and overwhelming act; his is a completely adult response, which is to say, one fully acknowledging the controlling political pressures to which a person in his position is subject. An anti-Nazi man-boy not entirely unrelated to Schindler is Indiana Jones (Harrison Ford) in *Raiders of the Lost Ark* (1981). His tendency is to place himself in situations that are both unthinkable for sedate, responsible, Bible-reading, mature adult males and unmanageable for powerless boys. In the sequel, *Indiana Jones and the Temple of Doom* (1984), it is just such boys that Jones must rescue, indeed; and as he does, it is clear by his strategy, style, and attitude that he has a personal affinity for a boyish style of exhibiting manly strength.

Keys, the chief government scientist in *E.T. the Extra-Terrestrial*, is a man-boy. Keys is nonmilitary, smooth-cheeked, and indiscriminably featured, like Elliot, in fact, but also a man encased in the carapace of officialdom—a high tech hermetic spacesuit. Radiating from his glowing, huge, childlike eyes is a sense of peaceful wonder, directness, perfect sensitivity, and beauty—what might be called the "natural" response. Wonder and sensitivity are certainly not residues of socialization and acculturation in Western postcapitalist suburbia, where survival depends on canniness and engaged technical capacity (the kind Elliot demonstrates with his three friends as on their bikes, boys raising themselves to the status of men, they scramble to save E.T. in the concluding chase sequence). Keys, like Elliot, is a romantic. "Elliot," he whispers, gazing at what he believes to be the corpse of the extraterrestrial, "I've been to the forest . . . that machine, what does it do?, it's doing something—what? . . ." The boy is sobbing: "I really shouldn't tell. . . . He came to me. He came to me." "Elliot, he came to me, too. I've been wishing for this since I was ten years old. I don't want him to die. I don't think that he was left here intentionally"—this last a telling observation no paranoid North American adult could possibly make, but that an aging ten-year-old boy very well might. We are looking into Keys's face as we hear this, his eyes moist with concern and wonder, his expression a mask of yearning, and the small boy reflected like an iconic moustache over his top lip.

In a passage quoted by the French art historian Philippe Ariès in his *Centuries of Childhood*, Antoine de Saint-Exupéry gives what I take to be an elegant description of this man-boy:

> He was free, infinitely free, so free that he was no longer conscious of pressing on the ground. He was free of that weight of human relationships which impedes movement, those tears, those farewells, those reproaches, those joys, all that a man caresses or tears every time he sketches out a gesture, those countless bonds which tie him to others and make him heavy. (1962, 411)

Ariès suggests that since the seventeenth century, male adulthood and family responsibility have been linked conceptually in our society. The adult male and female are *adult* by virtue of being at the center of a family, and the family is a bounded haven against the intrusions and provocations of the world. The *good bad boy* who doesn't commit himself to family life in wedded bliss with the woman of his dreams has thus been a social outcast, a failed male, through all of the history of motion pictures. It is because Keys is such a failure, a man-boy instead of a man, that his desire for E.T. can be so open and bold; and that he can recognize the same desire in Elliot. It is because he is a man-boy that Keys permits Elliot the private moment to say goodbye, a privacy, to be sure, utterly denied the boy by the territorial adult technicians who have been milling around the space and one in which, E.T. revealing himself to be not so very dead (perhaps something of a man-boy himself), the climactic apotheosis of the film comes for the first time within reach.

In *Hook,* Spielberg leads us to see that the man-boy is made— perhaps self-made—not born. Much of this film's interest lies in its being a twisted remake, with a magically overgrown hero, of an exceptionally famous children's book that had already been the basis of a noteworthy filmic adaptation (by Walt Disney Studios in 1953, "starring" a "boy") and a Broadway play and television special, with Mary Martin in the title role. That Spielberg was filming *Peter Pan* with an adult male as Peter, indeed, was a centerpiece of the publicity but, I might add, no shock to potential viewers, given that this adult was in truth only an "adult," an unbridled, even maniacal, stand-up comedian who had already established a record of being able to display himself as an overgrown child but who was yet some time away from showing fans the capacity to be reliable and mature, as he would in Penny Marshall's *Awakenings* (1990), or feelingfully (if sententiously) pedagogical, as he would in Gus Van Sant's *Good Will Hunting* (1997). If Robin Williams was going to be this new Peter, then Peter wasn't to be such an adult at all: he might be a successful yuppie, with a wife who shopped at Banana Republic and a mouth filled with trading room jargon, but nobody would doubt for a moment that in the Banning family the thirteen-year-old son Jack (Charlie Korsmo) was the one who wore the emotional pants.

The narrative conceit of *Hook* is that having abandoned Neverland for a few too many years, Pan has aged and subsequently forgotten everything of his Panic existence. He returns to the island, but accompanied by his real-life children, and there the Lost Boys are forced to re-educate him to the wonders of his lost childhood in order to reincarnate the leader who can help them defeat the malevolent, and desperately immature, Hook (Dustin Hoffman), another quasi-adult male bearing the scars of a childish psychology yet without nobility and therefore no man-boy. It is clear in this film that both Hook and Peter are masked men—Peter caught up behind the pretense of "success" and Hook hiding behind the façade of command—so clear, indeed, as to imply that the "weight of human relationships" that requires and encourages males to grow up and wear such masks, and that rewards them when they do, is a mask itself. *Hook* thus implicitly critiques a social structure in which men arrogate to themselves the power to control people's lives and communities' futures, all the while explaining their arrogation as a logical reward for sober compliance with the "needs" or "demands" of some mythical, hypothetical "society" that somehow preexists male power and requires it. Using the myth that conventional male adulthood is a proper payoff for the sacrifices young males make in order to achieve it, we have too long rationalized male dominance, perpetuated it, and made it seem like propriety.

When most males are seeking political and economic power, however, by pretending to the kinds of appetites and attitudes Mark Twain's county judge advocated and also reinforcing those appetites and attitudes as desirable, males who do not happily conform—who don't grow up, like Hook and Peter—must somehow be explained in their idiosyncrasy. With the moral reprobates, the Hooks, the explanation comes easily: these are the deviants, the losers, the would-have-beens and persisting wannabes. And here, indeed, Dustin Hoffman's captain is a whining, selfish, bitter, resentful man who believes megomaniacally (and, given that Hoffman is quite visible beneath his makeup, hilariously) that he should have been a star. How to explain the whimsicality and energy of the Pan, however, when the Pan is shown at very great narrative expense to be no youth at all but a middle-aged man with a secure family life who has made all the necessary sacrifices to social convention and yet somehow has retained the ability to be a kid? How is it that a middle-aged yuppie, successful in the stock market, center of a sedate family, and so committed to his financial responsibilities he's on a cell call in the middle of his kid's school play, can possibly be able to get involved in a food fight, or crow like a rooster, or entertain the bizarre little Tinker Bell in conversation? How can he possibly be what we recognize him for—an inflated boy?

One easy answer: he's self-indulgent. He has plenty of money and can well afford to take a few days in Neverland instead of obsessing on the job. A conventional rationale in this film, then, is that the protagonist's social class explains everything and anything we need explained if we don't want to rest on the idea that Pan is a man-boy. If we absolutely must believe that every male has to be either a boy or a man, this creature is nothing but a man who is getting away with *pretending to be a boy*, merely because it delights him to do this and because he's spoiled and privileged enough to afford this delight. But Spielberg has made this film in order to challenge such a hypothesis, a hypothesis he personally needs to challenge because Pan, it is clear enough, is him: "I certainly felt that everybody had sent me the message loud and clear," he told Stephen Schiff, "that I was, you know, bad casting. I was a kid for life. And I almost slept in the bed they made" (2000, 173). If the role of the boy and the role of the man are seen as two possible, and only, choices—if one is simply a boy until one reaches a threshold the society constructs for age-grade transitions, at which point one simply becomes a man: a view I intend here to reject—then all boys, even the warped and the damaged, like Hook, somehow make this transition; or, as Barrie put it, "All children, except one, grow up" (1987, 1). The fairly recent category of adolescence is the moratorium stage that contemporary technological mass society constructs as a holding tank between childhood and adulthood, since full male adulthood implies occupational security and mass technological capitalist society needs to be able to produce a subservient labor pool by keeping a reserve of adult males out of work. Adolescence permits us to keep a significant number of physically mature males out of significant work for an extended period. But the man-boy that is Spielberg's Pan is *not* an adolescent kept out of work: he has a full-time job, and a good one at that. Nor is he, apparently, self-indulgent in fact—he works too hard, doesn't want to stop working for an instant, takes everything far too seriously. Apparently, then, he's the perfect adult, not some guy goofing around in Neverland for entertainment. To go further—he denies that he is Pan and must be convinced by the Lost Boys, who believe he's "in denial."

What makes Peter a man-boy is that he can do something no purebred adult can do, nor any self-indulgent dabbler, nor any socialization failure with an evil heart. He has one talent for which one needs a vivid imagination—"Does a boy get a chance to whitewash a fence every day?"—and a playful mind, a feeling for movement and music, an unclear sense of the difference between dreaming and being awake—all qualities Robin Williams has shown he possesses in spades; a talent, indeed, one cannot recognize at all in oneself yet must manage to find, even though one already has it, so innocent is the man-boy of his man-boyishness; and this is: *the ability to fly.* No serious adult, overcome by the rational knowledge that flying is for the birds, can possibly achieve it; nor can any adult manage to experience Peter flying who is convinced this is only a motion picture, in which the director has employed "special effects." For Peter to "really fly," we must believe in film, just as, in the stage play, the audience must believe in fairies, childlike creatures themselves (thus, Spielberg's equally challenging casting of the much-celebrated—and rather childlike—Julia Roberts in the role of Tink). One must be convinced of the overarching and defining power of the imagination, able to say with Tom Sawyer to Joe Harper, "Well, say, Joe, you can be Friar Tuck or Much the miller's son, and lam me with a quarterstaff; or I'll be the Sheriff of Nottingham and you be Robin Hood a little while and kill me" (1946, 87). The adult with his nice new Bible, who was so very well brought up, will never be able to really imagine this—only, perhaps, to consider the implications of imagining—and will never fly.

For his part, Frank Jr. in *Catch Me If You Can* represents a new plateau altogether in Spielberg's explorations of the man-boy, since he progresses onscreen from a boy who is lost, to a boy-man who develops his talents at fraud and performance, to—finally and climactically—a man-boy. The man-boy, in other words, is the supreme achievement of the hero's life in this film, this apotheosis epitomized at a moment after Frank has been imprisoned for his many crimes, then been withdrawn from prison by agents of the FBI who would like to make use of his knowledge and talents, then spent uncomfortable days working 9 to 5 in a dingy cubicle as a government employee. Just as he appears to have fallen furthest from the noble stallion of fantasy he has been riding in the film, he suits up in an airline pilot's uniform again and prepares to steal away for a weekend of illicit masquerade. His supervisor and former pursuer (Tom Hanks) follows him through the Pan American terminal at Kennedy Airport. "Go ahead. Nobody's going to stop you." Frank strides away from him proudly, toward the domain of the man-boy where imagination and play hold sway over career, legality, insurance, security, normal life. When after the weekend he shows up back at work, he is finally free: a man who has accepted social responsibility exactly *in order that* he may have a grounding from which to caper off as the spirit takes him.

•◆• •◆• •◆•

If it is a coup of the imagination to fly over Neverland, or away from one's day job in the FBI, it is even more preposterous to believe that an immense alien spacecraft is landing on top of a mountain so that space travelers can have a touching entente with leaders of the military-industrial establishment or even, as Spielberg himself suggested, "observe growing up in the twentieth century" (Tuchman 1978, 49 quoted in Telotte 2001, 152). Peter Banning's challenge was to accept the purely cinematic reality of the Lost Boys, and thereby come to see himself as the Pan, who could fly and do other noble and wonderful things; Frank Abagnale Jr.'s challenge is to have the courage to keep walking toward that airplane, though he knows he may be arrested and sentenced again, this time for fifty years. But in *Close Encounters* Roy Neary, a working-class employee of the electric company, is challenged to see himself as a man who can yield to irresistible artistic impulses, in the process relinquishing the entirety of his everyday world. His reward in becoming a man-boy who loses—as T. S. Eliot put it in *The Four Quartets*—"everything" is encounter without the "weight" of expectation, pure being liberated from the corrupting falseness of bourgeois ideology—an escape, in short, from social class, responsibility, and human time that can be understood as either death or resurrection, depending on one's optimism.

Neary, married with three children—J. P. Telotte calls him "simply an open and playful person" (2001, 150)—is subjected one night to an electromagnetic field from a hovering flying saucer. He begins to manifest strange responses to normal social situations—like lying down and crying in the shower with his clothes on—and soon enough loses his job, finally so bewildering and alienating his wife that she takes the kids and leaves him. "I don't think I know what's happening to me," he says in some desperation, nicely giving the lie to any hypothesis that man-boyishness is invariably deliberate, conscious, and willful. Roy's problem seems to be centered on a sculptural obsession, prepared for us initially in a cute dinner table scene where he begins to make shapes in his mashed potatoes and finally played out to the full in a beautiful extended sequence I wish now to discuss at some length. This sequence is highlighted by Dreyfuss's exquisitely simple performance of a person always competent and adult in his movements, clearly directed, purposeful, resourceful, well-managed, even sober; while all the time being arbitrary, spontaneous, reckless, even poetic in his needs, his inspiration, and his fixation.

Roy slowly wakes in the family room where he has fallen asleep beside a clay mountain he has been casually building. His daughter is watching "Marvin the Martian" on TV. He tears down some newspaper clippings from a bookshelf: "UFO's: Seeing Is Believing," and "Canada: A Haven for UFO's?," crumples them and throws them away, with a line to his nervous wife, "Ronni—everything's fine. All this stuff is comin' down." The clay mountain resists his attempt to pull it apart, however, and as he struggles a hunk breaks off in his hands and he tumbles back to see a vision from which he cannot take his eyes (as offscreen Daffy Duck snaps, "That's the last straw! Now I'm going to use my secret weapon!"). Slowly moving forward he sees—and so do we, through an intercut dolly shot that simulates the perspective from an approaching helicopter—a flat-topped mountain with tiny model train–sized trees stuck in at the base. His eyes agape, he slowly, though uncomprehendingly, smiles. On the TV, a cartoon explosion marks the "insight." Outside the window we see Roy in the garden, blithely yanking up shrubs.

"What are you doing?" yells Ronni, but Roy only smiles at her and tucks more shrubs under his arm. In the kitchen she raps on the window as he continues to yank plants out of the garden, exclaiming, "You'll really love this!" As she stands at the sink, moaning, "Oh, Roy!" he throws a plant, soil ball and all, then another and still another, through the window in front of her face. We cut to the driveway outside this window, the two boys emerging to watch their father shoveling dirt from a wheelbarrow and tossing it through the window. "Dad," says the younger one (Richard Dreyfuss's nephew Justin), "After this, can we throw dirt in my window?" Ronni arrives: "Stop it!" Out of breath and still shoveling, Roy retorts, "Ronni, if I don't do this—that's when I'm gonna need a doctor." While the next-door neighbor watches in schadenfreude, blow-drying her hair, Roy collects bricks from a pile outside his house, explaining to Ronni, "You ever look at something and it's crazy and then you look at it another way and it's not crazy at all? . . . If you just close your eyes and hold your breath, everything will be really pretty."

"You're scaring us now," she says (with a chilling tranquility), and he cajoles, "Don't be scared. I feel really good. . . . I haven't felt this good in years." He is now hurling the bricks one by one through the window and into the kitchen sink. But he's still not finished. Under the neighbor's censorious gaze he stomps down the driveway and spies garbage collectors coming. Their truck stops. He wrestles with, and defeats, a garbage man, who watches incredulously as he turns the container upside-down and empties almost everything in it onto the road. What's left he marches back with in triumph, passing Ronni who is despondent in the early morning sun.

We see the garbage coming through the kitchen window, then the younger son outside helping his dad by throwing a small plant inside, too. "Chicken wire," says Roy, striding past the neighbor, who now follows him to another window as he pulls up the wire fencing around her ducks. In a sparkling imitation of Margaret Hamilton's Wicked Witch of the West, she shrieks, "Whatever you're doing's against the law!" As he dismantles the fence and throws the pieces near his house, Ronni is collecting the children. A group of neighborhood kids rise up into the frame to watch the prodigy, awestruck. The ducks are squawking. Roy's older boy (Shawn Bishop) is watching his father, disgusted and betrayed. "Stay!" Ronni commands the ducks, who are following her. Four more shrubs come through the kitchen window, into the camera. At the front door, Ronni and the children are heading for the station wagon, the younger boy whining, "Where are we going? Where are we going?" We are now inside the car, Ronni telling the kids to lock the doors. Through the windshield we see Roy advancing: "Ronni? Ronni? . . . Honey, where you goin'?" The car won't start. "I'm taking the kids to my sister's." Very sanely he rejoins, "You're crazy, you're not even dressed." Ronni gets the car in gear and backs into the street, Roy following. He climbs onto the hood. "Will you hold it one minute?" She hits the gas, dumping him into the road and driving off as the neighbors from several houses stand around silently. Seeing them seeing him, he stands up nobly, reties his bathrobe, and walks with dignity to his kitchen window where he yanks up one last shrub and tosses it in. The duck lady is trying to round up her flock as he climbs the stepladder and throws himself inside, with a cartoonlike crash. Then we see his head emerge through the window again. He grabs the ladder, retracts it, looks around, and slams the window shut.

Some time later, covered with dirt, he is picking a twig from a branch and moving around the family room. In a slow pan we discover that he has built a flat-topped mountain from floor to ceiling, a hundred times the size of the original sculpture. As he creeps around the base of the mountain to find the right spot for planting his "tree," the camera slowly withdraws and we see in the foreground a television that Roy cannot see. A soap opera is playing. We cut forward in time. Roy is looking through his window at the "normality" of suburban life outside, people washing a car or tending to a lawn. A Budweiser commercial can be heard on TV. Roy looks offscreen, disgusted, and draws the blinds. Hands on hips, he stares—still uncomprehending—at the sculpture he has made. In the extreme foreground, out of his view, Howard K. Smith of ABC News announces a rail disaster at Devil's Tower, Wyoming. Roy is on the telephone, beside his sculpture, trying to persuade Ronni to come home. "I can do other things. . . . I'm *trying* to be . . . It was a *joke!*" The news cuts to a local report where we see the Tower juxtaposed on the TV screen right next to the sculpture Roy has made: Roy's piece is an absolute replica. "Ronni! Don't hang up!" he is crying, and he slams the phone down and turns to the TV screen just as a landscape shot of the Tower fills the screen. He stares at it. He looks over at his sculpture. The music swells eerily. He kneels in front of the TV screen, then slowly stands up, his chest rising and falling as his sculpture comes into view.

If, like his judgmental neighbor and other strangers with whom people normally make society in suburbia, we know very little of Neary *except* the outrageous behavior this sequence shows, we, too, may think him insane. Part of the genius of Spielberg in this film is aligning us with Neary before this sequence, so that we are positioned to share his sense of desperate and uncomprehending alienation as he looks through his (prison) window at the normal world outside. Neary can be understood not only as a misunderstood artiste, a man-boy excluded from the rights and benefits that accrue to mature adults in a world where age-grading is a central organizing principle, but also as Everyman, fragmented and oppressed by the simplest aspects of everyday life in our society. Even his wife adopts toward him the perspective of a total stranger, beginning to withdraw from her loyalty and sensitivity the moment his capacity to support her (in a submissive domestic role straight out of the 1950s) is threatened. That Roy is in part adult is reflected in his self-aware claim, "If I don't do this, that's when I'm gonna need a doctor": this the sort of sober assessment a professional counselor might give. But his youngest kid knows that Roy has more in common with him than with other adults: "Dad—after this can we throw dirt in *my* window?"

Central to the structure of the scene is Roy's newfound ability to see through the masking pretense of social order, that elaborate police state, to establish a vision of the construction of the social universe seen directly in itself. Society, the sequence instructs, is a production from raw materials, technology, technique, knowledge, and labor. The hero deconstructs the received vision of things—a home, a neighbor, a nice lawn—substituting a vision of things as they are—bricks, mortar, furniture, living beings, more bricks, land. The garden fencing that is accepted by the neighbor as an intrinsic part of a duck pen, in short as decor, is suddenly visible to Roy as usable materiel, as are Ronni's shrubs and some of the garbage waiting to be tossed from the garbage can. Here, Marshall McLuhan's wry observation, following Freud, that one man's trash is another man's treasure (1970, 183) is almost made substantial as Roy approaches the can on the curb with a view to purloining its sloppy treasure as materiel but then, suddenly, whimsically, almost musically, changes his mind and dumps the refuse on the road while the garbage collectors, those final guardians of civilization, gaze on dumbfounded. But the inner project on which Roy is engaged is, once again, essentially filmic. The final sculpture is an alarmingly successful reproduction of a natural landscape, in which objects that have been declassified from their everyday function are reinvented, reformed, relabeled, and resocialized in the context of his creative production. Andy Warhol, another man-boy, performed precisely these actions on a Campbell's soup can label. Further, if Roy's construction is sculptural in itself, the crane and dolly shots through which we see it constitute landscape cinema. The sculpture is therefore a film set, an elaborate miniature. Seen in the right way, it becomes reality. This "right" seeing, of course, is the prerogative not only of filmmakers and other artists but also of children at play, whose use of make-do objects and materials is exactly sufficient to support the vision *they* will have of the finished play-world, a vision that often slowly swoops from above like a helicopter shot and that is imbued with the imaginative offer of emotional engagement play makes routine. "I'll be the Sheriff of Nottingham . . ."

The man-boy of *Close Encounters*, a Bakhtinian carnival unto himself (the dramaturgy of the man-boy in Spielberg seems to require scenes in which *only* he inverts the social order; for an elaborate exposition on this see *Minority Report* [2002]), is not merely an adult male who plays with his food—in this case sculpting the Tower out of his mashed potatoes, in *Hook* imagining empty plates are full of brilliantly colored goo and then hurling it in his friends' faces—but one who is susceptible to new readings of the cultural language food constitutes, to what Howard Becker once called "unconventional sentimentalities" (1964). Not only are mashed potatoes no longer edible food for him (as was the case in Europe before the sixteenth century), they are no longer even mashed potatoes. While the local adults—in this case, his wife and his precocious eldest child—think of his culinary activity as pure disengagement from the rules of table etiquette (that Claude Lévi-Strauss saw as the fundament of organized social behavior), Neary is in a state of suspended consciousness (see Winnicott, 53–56), where mundane awareness of his own activity is blocked in order that an impulse be made free, unimpeded and unguided by forces on the social level. As the plot of *Encounters* would have it, he is preparing, albeit unconsciously, to encounter (in the reedited version, join and fly away with) aliens, though this plot is only the surface rationale for a deeper moment, which is the central epiphany of Spielberg's films, in which a man heroically surrenders his manhood. We can think of oceanographer Matt Hooper seeing his theoretical knowledge become physical reality, Alan Grant (Sam Neill) in *Jurassic Park* letting go of his theories for the purity of direct experience, Pete Sandich (Dreyfuss) in *Always* (1989) surrendering to death's angel, Hap (Audrey Hepburn); Keys in *E.T.* surrendering his captured creature to the boy; Banning surrendering his Wall Street persona to the Lost Boys in *Hook;* the robotic man-boy Gigolo Joe (Jude Law) in *A.I.: Artificial Intelligence* (2001), letting go of his freedom to free the "boy," David (Haley Joel Osment); John Anderton (Tom Cruise) in *Minority Report* relinquishing his eyes in order to be able to see.

Having considered the culmination of the form Roy Neary is building (out of the same hopeless detritus of middle-class existence Antonioni exploded in his finale to *Zabriskie Point* [1970])—the form that is signaling him in some inchoate way— and the fact that though his wife has taken the children and left him he is unfazed and delirious; and that he is living in denial, detached from his socialized life and ultimately lured to Wyoming to witness what turns out to be the first visitation of aliens to earth, we need not feel satisfied that we have arrived at the deep meaning of the long scene

I have just described, although it is true that scene does further all of these narrative actions. Although ultimately Roy is indeed being an artiste, what we see and experience in the sculpture sequence is a methodical, impatient, accelerating, zealous, monomaniacal, impulsive, uncivil, intemperate, and glorious act of domestic terrorism. As Mary Douglas might have put it, purity is rendered vulnerable. The social order of the domestic institution—the rec room as a bounded zone of ritualized entertainment and sacred childhood invention—is violated in order that frenzied and unplanned (therefore, unmortgageable) play may be grossly situated. The official voice of the television (Howard K. Smith) is artfully and painlessly disattended by someone old enough to know better though not sober enough to know he is old enough. Neighborly relations are made bellicose: this is civil disobedience. Language is silenced, since Roy works in desperate wordlessness except when he pleads incoherently with his wife for sympathy. The perfect manicured microcosm of Western civilization is completely destroyed—actually *renovated*—in this inexorable sequence, all in the name of something profound, wonderful, harmonic, transcendent, and good, the view of the alien craft, which turns out to be a filmic translation of Matthew Arnold's sweetness and light. The man-boy, then, if he is a social reject also makes possible the happy undoing of social order in the name of something more important, and indeed permits the suggestion that something more important than social order can really exist. Later in the film, echoing this scene, alien scout ships—or blips—impetuously crash through a line of tollbooths without paying, all but thumbing the extraterrestrial nose at uptight State-controlled military-industrial civilization.

•◆• •◆• •◆•

However:

The story Spielberg is telling does not absolutely require the man-boy, or sociological deconstruction. We must ask what it is that can be accomplished using this tool, difficult or impossible to achieve without it, *beyond* the mere account of the plot? Three possibilities: First, chastity. The screen can contain and compose movement, visions, and vistas, but the deep subjectivity of a character can only be indexed, typically through sound. Certain moving and intensely personal human experiences—I have in mind the taste of food, abject fear, and the physical sensation of orgasm—are difficult to portray directly in motion pictures. With food, the generic quality of Spielberg's choices tends to incorporate the experience of a wide audience—Neary eats mashed potatoes, after all, not caviar. As to the second, it isn't necessary to depict a character's fear if the viewer can be brought into sufficient alignment to fear *for* the character. But sex is, at least technically, a problem. Every gaze at it is a mere approach, in the sense that gazing must be translated to become feeling. If sex can be demonstrated, and sexual pleasure hinted at, still our closest approach is through the melody of passion, which is acoustic. Basically, Spielberg's films are sex-free, at least as much because sex cannot fully be translated onscreen (and he shows an obsessive faithfulness to the screen) as because the director is himself prudish about it (in *Catch Me,* clumsy sex is alluded to). For big budget Hollywood productions in what Frank Rich has described as a pornographic climate (2001) lucrative filmmaking is difficult unless either a fetishistic replacement for sexual feeling, the icon of the sexual act, is relentlessly substituted (as in most conventional films) or some mechanism can be introduced to account for the pervasive air of chastity most directors cheerfully abandon or lack. The man-boy, understandably avoiding sex, is an ideal protagonist for a film that is purely about visual storytelling (and in which sex is therefore impossible)—the film that is not, on a philosophical level, a sell-out.

Next, social realism. The man-boy allows for a central figuration that addresses the real condition of the current film viewer, who subsists in a global economy built upon the exploitation of a fast-developing and highly technologized workplace. As work is fragmented, individuals have less control over what they do and less influence over its outcomes. Workers become replaceable. Labor is continually cheapened in order to be competitive. So adult workers are infantilized and infantilization becomes a daily condition of existence. The man who is not fully a man is an ideal form for representing the modern condition, a world full of men not empowered to be men. Thus, by virtue of the man-boys embedded in it (much more than by virtue of its fondness for technology), the cinema of Steven Spielberg is contemporary.

Finally, the man-boy is a propelling force. Conventional Hollywood narratives tend to turn on arbitrary "magical" devices—Hitchcock called these MacGuffins—that have only a tangential connection to the sinews of the tale and scant status in reality. *Citizen Kane* (1941), for instance, revolves around a man we are to believe is obsessively interested in the meaning of the last word spoken by another man he never knew. In Spielberg's films, the presence of a man-boy allows us to see a plot turn not by virtue of the imposition of a thing extrinsic to it, a kind of winding key, such as the word "Rosebud," but by virtue of a characteristic temporal meld, a past on display as a future. In each moment of the man-boy's action, we are engaged with everything he became and once hoped to be, and also with him continuing to hope and not yet actually being—since he is both a man who has grown and a boy who looks forward to growth. We move forward with constant allusion to the past but also anticipation of what we do not know. The man-boy, filmically advancing and recycling, is thus also a pure construct of the filmic surface, since film, too, is a temporal meld. Film, too, moves forward but on a track that offers an absolutely continuous reverse journey into the past; at every moment it both is, and hopes to be.

For Spielberg, then, the story in which the man-boy takes form and the form he takes in that story exist unified, in a single rhythmic and evaporating dimension.

Notes

I am indebted to Lester Friedman and Steven Woodward for discussing early versions of this essay with me.

Works Cited

Ariès, Philippe. 1962. *Centuries of Childhood: A Social History of Family Life*. Trans. Robert Baldick. New York: Vintage.

Barrie, Sir James M. 1987. *Peter Pan*. New York: Henry Holt.

Becker, Howard S., ed. 1964. *The Other Side: Perspectives on Deviance*. New York: Free Press.

Camus, Albert. 1995. *Le Premier homme*. Toronto: Alfred A. Knopf.

Fiedler, Leslie A. 1960. *Love and Death in the American Novel*. New York: Criterion.

Forsberg, Myra. 2000. "Spielberg at 40: The Man and the Child." In *Steven Spielberg: Interviews*, ed. Lester D. Friedman and Brent Notbohm, 126–32. Jackson: University Press of Mississippi.

Goffman, Erving. 1974. *Frame Analysis: An Essay on the Organization of Experience*. Cambridge: Harvard University Press.

Lehman, Peter. 2001. *Running Scared: Masculinity and the Representation of the Male Body*. Philadelphia: Temple University Press.

McLuhan, Marshall, with Wilfred Watson. 1970. *From Cliché to Archetype*. New York: Viking.

Mulvey, Laura. 1989. "Afterthoughts on 'Visual Pleasure and Narrative Cinema' Inspired by King Vidor's *Duel in the Sun* (1946)." In *Visual and Other Pleasures,* 29–38. Bloomington: Indiana University Press.

Ponte, Allesandra. 1992. "Architecture and Phallocentrism in Richard Payne Knight's Theory." In *Sexuality and Space,* ed. Beatriz Colomina, 273–305. New York: Princeton Architectural Press.

Rich, Frank. 2001. "Naked Capitalists." *New York Times Magazine,* May 20, 50–56+.

Schiff, Stephen. 2000. "Seriously Spielberg." In *Steven Spielberg: Interviews,* ed. Lester D. Friedman and Brent Notbohm, 170–92. Jackson: University Press of Mississippi.

Shaviro, Steven. 1993. *The Cinematic Body.* Minneapolis: University of Minnesota Press.

Sontag, Susan. 1977. *On Photography.* New York: Farrar, Straus and Giroux.

Telotte, J. P. 2001. *Science Fiction Film.* New York: Cambridge University Press.

Tuchman, Mitch. 1978. "Close Encounters with Steven Spielberg," *Film Comment* 14, no. 1, 49–55.

Twain, Mark. 1946. *The Adventures of Tom Sawyer.* New York: Grosset and Dunlap.

Winnicott, Donald W. 1982. *Playing and Reality.* New York: Routledge.

8

IN LOVE AND TROUBLE

Teenage Boys and Interracial Romance

Frances Gateward

Twice in the last two decades director Amy Heckerling reintro-
duced American audiences to what has become commonly known
as the teenpic. The huge critical and commercial successes of *Fast
Times at Ridgemont High* (1982) and *Clueless* (1995) reminded an
amnesiac and economically strapped industry that there were millions of young people in the United States with billions of dollars
of disposable income. The result, much to the consternation of
"mature" critics, was an inundation of comedic teen films in
multiplexes across the nation, a trend that remains unabated.
Although Heckerling's features were female-based narratives, the
comedic genre has evolved, or perhaps devolved, into stories about
the raucous male-centered sexual exploits of white,[1] middle- to
upper-class, suburban, heterosexual high school and college boys.
The conventions of recent teen movies have become so formulaic
and recognizable that Joel Gallen's 2002 release *Not Another Teen
Movie,* a parody of the teenpic, struck a chord with both popular
and critical audiences.

In the opening sequences we are introduced to the genre's
stock characters. Among the teens attending John Hughes High
School in suburban Los Angeles are: Janey, the "pretty ugly girl"
who suffers from the ugly duckling syndrome we've seen countless
times on television and in films like *Never Been Kissed* (1999),
She's All That (1999), and *The Princess Diaries* (2001); the desperate virginal nerdy boy from *Porky's* (1981) and *Weird Science* (1985);
the seductive foreign exchange student as in *Better Off Dead* (1985)
and *American Pie* (1999), who, being from Europe, is constructed
with a more mature sexuality than that of her American peers.
Almost without exception, the exchange student is female, for a
sexually experienced boy would no doubt be competition for the
American male protagonist. (The male foreign student, when present, is usually nonwhite, thus, within the context of the narrative,

undesirable and reduced to a stereotype, such as Long Duc Dong (Gedde Watanabe) in *Sixteen Candles* [1984].) All of the teenage characters in the parody are white, with the exception of one— Malik (Deon Richmond), "the token black guy," whose function in the film is, as he explains, to "Stay out of the conversation and say things like 'Damn, that is whack!'" Malik's narrative role is to remain on the periphery, to—as Robin Wood so aptly reminds us in his examination of the teen high school film—support the white male lead. His presence "at once establishes his [the white protagonist's] lack of prejudice, his openness to difference, his generosity, and asserts his *superiority:* he has the main role, he 'gets the girl,' there is never any suggestion that *he* might fall in love with a black or Asian woman, or conversely, that the (white) woman he loves, whether 'bitch' or 'nice girl,' will be sexually interested in a male from another ethnic group" (2002, 7).

Romance and sexual relationships for young people of color within the world of the racially "integrated" teen comedy films are for the most part nonexistent. Asian/Pacific American, Native American, Latino/a, and Other ethnic groups like those of Arab descent are rendered practically invisible, and because mainstream American media myopically see race as meaning black or white, if a nonwhite character appears in a romantic teenpic context, it is almost invariably a male and he is almost invariably black. In those rare instances when young black men are not neutered, their sexuality is constructed as homosexual, as in *Mannequin* (1987), where Hollywood Montrose (Meshach Taylor) functions as mammy-figure, offering emotional nurturance and advice; or in *Revenge of the Nerds* (1984) with Lamar (Larry B. Scott), who is marginalized on the college campus not because he fits the archetype of nerd, but because of his race and sexual preference. Both of these characters are extremely stereotyped by their speech, body language, mode of dress, and, in the case of Hollywood, profession (he is a window dresser in an upscale Philadelphia department store). Because mainstream teenpics are driven by heterosexual desire and remain ideologically conservative, often using gay and lesbian sexuality as the subject of jokes and treating homosexuality as the ultimate "gross-out" perversion, Lamar and characters like him can be neither desiring subjects nor objects for others. This is not to say that youth-of-color experience no romance or sexual relationships on the movie and television screens of America. They do, but in racially segregated feature films; films that despite the age of their characters or audience demographics, are not considered teen films. *House Party* (1990) and its sequels, *Poetic Justice* (1994), and *Love and Basketball* (2000) are treated as black films (while films like *Juice* [1992] and *Menace II Society* [1993] are black crime films, not coming-of-age movies); likewise *ABCD* (1999) is an Indian American feature and *Shopping for Fangs* (1997) an example of Asian American cinema. When young white people are paired with Others romantically, the films are still not positioned in the teen-pic genre, rather they are ghettoized to the realm of the social problem film.

This process of ghettoization has a significant impact on the films labeled, affecting distribution, exhibition, and reception. It is not uncommon to see the racialized descriptives in reviews by popular critics, in the plot synopses provided on the boxes of video-tapes and DVDs, and even on black film lists as a genre. The national retailer Media Play, for example, divides their films for sale into such categories as horror/sci-fi, action, drama, comedy, and black. Categorizing these features as "race films" influences weekend box office gross (black-themed films are usually released on Wednesdays and not Fridays), the number of prints released nationally, and eventually video distribution. Lewis Beale, in an article published in the *Washington Post,* reveals a disturbing trend in the video rental industry, where video store proprietors purchased fewer copies of black features than other films of comparable box office gross.

Interracial, social problem romance narratives are shaped by the intersection of ideologies of race and gender, often reflecting and reinscribing America's long history of white fears of miscegenation, with the requisite stereotypes utilized to justify the legal, and in the case of lynching, extralegal enforcement of racial segregation and oppression. Hollywood has given us, Hays Code permitting, stories of interracial sexual relations as deviant, violent, and based on coercion as in the rape fantasies of Cecil B. DeMille's *The Cheat* (1915) and D. W. Griffith's *The Birth of a Nation* (1915) and the literally bestial representation of black masculinity and sexuality in *King Kong* (1933). *Love Is a Many-Splendored Thing* (1955) and *The World of Suzie Wong* (1960) follow the long legacy of colonialism that both fetishizes non-Western cultures and privileges white men with access to women of color.[2] Fetishization has continued, in later years with films like *Mandingo* (1975), a perverse depiction of that "peculiar institution," slavery. More recent films of interracial relationships like *The Bodyguard* (1992) conclude with the impossibility of "happiness ever after." Although the film radically purports that a black woman's life is valuable enough to be protected, in the dilemma of career vs. love the job takes precedence. *Jungle Fever* (1991), as the title implies, is centered not on an emotional bond, but on objectification and fantasies of the illicit, while *Bulworth* (1998) resorts to the more common resolution of violent death to maintain cultural norms of segregation.

Films of interracial romance continue to fascinate American audiences, as evidenced by the recent controversy surrounding *Monster's Ball* (2001).[3] Now, however, one is more likely to find these romances occurring not between men and women, but between boys and girls. Older films like Robert Wise's 1961 musical adaptation of Romeo and Juliet, *West Side Story*, which transfers the family feud to rival gangs, one white and one Puerto Rican, continue to be popular with young girls and tweeners today, setting the formula for later films like Gordon Parks Jr.'s *Aaron Loves Angela* (1975) and Abel Ferrara's *China Girl* (1987). *Honky* (1971), the extremely popular *The Karate Kid, Part II* (1986), the horrendous blackface comedy feature *Soul Man* (1986), and the transformation of Shakespeare's *Othello* into the prep-school drama *O* (2001) are but a few other examples of the trend.

As with the adult romances, those involving teens are treated with deadly seriousness, and the social cost of love in these tragic tales is an often exorbitant one, for it is not unusual for these films to end with the untimely demise of their characters. If it is not the lovers themselves who are the victims of race-based hate crimes, as in *West Side Story*, *China Girl*, and *O*, then it is their immediate family and circle of friends in films like *Zebrahead* (1992). Are these concluding scenes genuine critiques of the rigid racial hegemony or do they serve as warnings for those who dare to transgress those socially drawn boundaries? The fact that teenage interracial romance is treated as melodrama rather than comedy, with heightened social consequences more dangerous than adults face, reveals the social order's excessive anxieties about race and the investment in youth as the future of the nation. Coming to terms with these anxieties is perhaps even more imperative now, as minority populations grow (whites are no longer the majority in the state of California) and teens are increasingly dating across the color line.[4]

Most films featuring teenaged characters are centered on issues of coming of age, the transition from childhood to adulthood.

Comic teen films typically mark the rite of passage as obtaining a driver's license, graduating from high school, gaining admittance into university, or the loss of virginity; while the white romantic teen narratives are driven by the goal to find that special person, the escort to the all-important pinnacle event of high school, the prom. However, recent interracial romance films define coming of age as a raising of consciousness that will call into question issues of social identity and relations of power, usually within three narrative patterns: the nostalgic story, the damsel-in-distress scenario, and the story of the cultural hybrid, each with its own particular tensions and contradictions.

YESTERDAY, WHEN I WAS YOUNG

In his essay on "Postmodernism and Consumer Society," Fredric Jameson (1983) clearly delineates the culture's excessive infatuation with nostalgia as a characteristic of the postmodern condition. As late capitalism continues to develop and expand, along with new markets to exploit, so too does dependence on the mythic past. Motion pictures and the media industries have always mined the annals of history, but the degree to which this is escalating today is alarming—from the reactionary rewriting of the past in the adaptation of *Forrest Gump* (1994) to the romanticized recollections of World War II as the "Great War" in *Saving Private Ryan* (1998) and *Pearl Harbor* (2001), the popularity of the teen-focused television sitcom "That '70s Show" (1998) and a high school boy touring with a rock band in *Almost Famous* (2000). The desire for the past is so strong that middle-aged family men attempt to relive frat boy college life in the sophomoric *Old School* (2003). It is imperative that commercial treatments of history are examined critically, for the texts are often accepted by millions as accurate reconstructions of the past; and, as Marcia Landy reminds us, representations of the past are related to conceptions of power, and may actually tell us more about the present (1996).

The nostalgic, like other forms of historical narrative, is defined by the present, dependent upon a contrast to the moods, events, and lived experience of current circumstances. A nostalgic examination of the past is not a critical one. Rather, it is invoked because the postmodern condition is one of alienation, frustration, and despair. A selective past is constructed as simplified and joyous, without the complexities and struggles of contemporary life.

Because, as Fred Davis (1979) states, nostalgic feelings may emerge during periods of abrupt social change, triggered by a fear of actual or impending change, revealing a concern over or denial of the future, I find *Liberty Heights* (1999), *A Bronx Tale* (1993), and *Foreign Student* (1994) especially compelling: films produced in a period of cultural shift and set during the coalescence of the biggest grassroots movement in America's history, the struggle for civil rights.

In *Liberty Heights*, Barry Levinson returns to Baltimore, Maryland, once again (as in *Diner* [1982], *Tin Men* [1987], and *Avalon* [1990]), to 1954, only a few months after the historic Supreme Court case of *Brown v. Board of Education*, the decision that declared the permissive and mandatory racial segregation of public schools across the United States unconstitutional. The narrative tracks the parallel trajectory of the working-class Kurtzman brothers as they engage with their respective romantic interests beyond the Jewish enclave in which they grew up. Education proves truly enlightening in this film. The elder Van (Adrian Brody), attending a local college, is introduced to the world of rich white gentiles through extracurricular parties and his pursuit of a blond, blue-eyed "Cinderella" called Dubbie (Carolyn Murphy), whom he meets at a Halloween party. His younger sibling Ben (Ben Foster), a high school senior, falls for his classmate Sylvia (Rebekah Johnson), one of the few black students permitted to attend his high school because of the recent legislation.[5]

Foreign Student, adapted from a 1956 autobiographical novel by Philippe Labro, follows a young Frenchman (Marco Hofschneider), who has just been awarded a scholarship to college in the United States. During his stay in a small South Carolina town, his education, like that of the Kurtzman brothers, extends beyond books in the classroom. When Philippe falls head-over-heels in love with a local black teacher named April (Robin Givens), he is schooled in the ways of American racism and segregation.

Robert DeNiro's directorial debut, with a script Chazz Palminteri adapted from his own play entitled *A Bronx Tale*, takes place during the 1960s. Nine-year-old Calogero (Francis Capra) is caught between his relationship with Sonny, a local gangster charmingly played by Palminteri, and his father (DeNiro), a bus driver who tries to instill in his son the values of honesty, hard work, and racial segregation. At seventeen, Calogero (Lillo

Brancato), who now goes by the moniker "C," meets the exotically named Jane (Taral Hicks), a new student who has moved to the Bronx from the East New York section of Brooklyn. As his secret affection for her develops, he must contend with the demands for race loyalty made by his bigoted circle of friends.

All three of these features approach their subjects as nostalgic reminiscences, deploying the expected conventions such as first-person narration, evocative associations made by the use of period music, and even more importantly, the emotive aspects of nostalgia that center on the yearning for the "good old days." Ben, Philippe, and C all look back on their youthful experiences with warmth and affection, despite the reactions of family and community to their flings (none of the relationships exists in the narrational present). The films are seemingly critical of American racial relations during one of contemporary history's most volatile periods, but the need to keep the films nostalgic requires the glaring omission of the Civil Rights Movement, thus contributing to the country's chronic cultural amnesia concerning the history of race relations.

The nostalgic impulse also requires that the gender roles be inverted, in spite of the fact that, as Mary Ann Doane (1987) has noted, the love story is considered a feminine discourse. Although it is refreshing to see boys smitten, sensitive, and emotional rather than tough, stoic, and hypermasculinized (an approach perhaps allowed since they are not yet men), their placement as protagonists is problematized by race. Whiteness and male identity reinscribe race and gender privilege—in narrative point of view, in the power of the gaze, and in the availability of women of color to white men. To grant subject status to the girls would require a shift in the films' tone and attitudes toward the past. We would have to consider why in *Foreign Student* April, though she is educated and employed, has to take on the additional job as a domestic worker on the white side of town; or the difficult daily experiences of Sylvia in *Liberty Heights,* as she breaks the color barrier at her predominantly white high school; or, in *Bronx Tale,* the terror of the violent race-based hate crime experienced by Jane and her family. Nostalgia necessitates a release from ideological function, so the films cannot interrogate histories of legalized racial oppression.

One compelling aspect of the boys' identities in these three films is their shared status as liminal, in all three cases because the boys are working-class, but in addition because Philippe is not

American and because Ben is Jewish. As boys coming of age, they are each trying to determine their identities as men and to seek their place in the wider social framework. These origins are significant in their linkage with the marginal status assigned black communities. Philippe's Frenchness serves a dual function—to render him an observer of American culture, untainted by the history of slavery and Jim Crow (he can be constructed as nonracist), while simultaneously giving him outsider status. He is not a suave, sophisticated French paramour (that would require a higher class status), but a naive, socially clumsy youth. C sees the labor struggle of the working man through the life of his father, and thus finds criminality seductive, perhaps the only way he can access the American Dream and the power and adulation that come with material success. Ben's encounter with mayonnaise and untoasted Wonder Bread in the second grade awakens him to the realization that he is a member of a minority community, as does the sting of anti-Semitism when he and his two friends are kept from swimming in a public pool by a fence and the sign upon it that reads "No Jews, Dogs, or Blacks." I should mention here that the ethnicities of Calogero as an Italian and Ben as Jewish also create a further association with blackness. Italians and Jews, as well as the Irish, were ranked low on the color continuum of whiteness: all were considered inferior races.[6]

No love story is without music used for heightened effect so of course it is used provocatively in these three films to stir emotion. But because they feature young lovers and are set during the rise of that new form of popular music, rock 'n' roll, it is not surprising to find the soundtracks full of girl groups, doo-wop, and rhythm and blues. But the songs are more than an indication of the time period. Music is used to signify the disparate communities, and in the case of the lovers, to facilitate the crossing of racial boundaries. In *Foreign Student* Philippe is introduced to rhythm and blues when April notices that a band touring the Chittlin' Circuit has arrived in town.[7] Intrigued, he makes his way across the tracks to hear the music. Barred from entry because the black bouncers are suspicious of his motives, he is finally admitted by the intervention of Howlin' Wolf (Charles S. Dutton). The musician ensures the doormen that Philippe is okay because he is French (an allusion not only to the treatment of black soldiers in France during World War II, but also to the history of French appreciation for black American culture and the number of prominent black American expatriates, such as

Josephine Baker and James Baldwin, who were making their homes in Paris).

In *Liberty Heights*, Ben, who listens to the "normal" radio stations, is introduced to Ray Charles while hiding on the floor of April's mother's car. A highlighted event in the film is a James Brown concert at the Fox Theatre, located on the black side of Baltimore. Ben and his friend Sheldon attend with Sylvia and one of her girl friends. The teens, though not seated together, are linked through eye-line matches, and all four of them are shown thoroughly enjoying the show. Sheldon and Ben, who had never heard of James Brown before, react to the performance with screams, shouts, and dancing. Ben's enjoyment of black popular culture is further enhanced when he listens to records in Sylvia's room after school. A fan of comedy (we've seen him earlier enjoying Sid Caesar on television), Ben laughs uproariously when Sylvia introduces him to the recorded monologues of Redd Foxx.

Of the three films *A Bronx Tale* uses popular music most creatively, from the sheer eclecticism of the music—Dean Martin, Dion and the Belmonts, the Moody Blues, Aaron Neville, The Rascals, and Della Reese—to its use as commentary on the visuals and its function in characterization. Although we have experienced the use of music to delineate boundaries before—in the Orientalism of James Bond films or in the pervasive use of rap music to warn of impending threat and criminality—style is used here to separate the white and black communities without the usual ideological baggage. The film clearly demonstrates, despite the origins of rock 'n' roll, that music is as segregated as the neighborhoods. It is not necessarily the race of the artist that separates the neighborhoods, but the type of music. The Jimi Hendrix Experience for example, is associated with whites. If music is truly going to cross boundaries, how better to demonstrate this than to use a classic Motown hit, The Four Tops' recording of "Baby I Need Your Loving," as C drives to pick up Jane on their first date.[8]

The most imaginative use of music as transportation across racial boundaries involves the song "I Only Have Eyes for You." C's father Lorenzo helps to make his bus route more tolerable by listening to a small radio that constantly broadcasts his preferred type of music, jazz, particularly bebop, much to the consternation of C, who prefers rock. One afternoon, as C complains about the music, he sees Jane for the first time. It is a great cinematic moment, for a slow series of coy eyeline matches occurs, both teens smiling shyly as we hear the strains of "I Only Have Eyes for You" interpreted by jazz artists, the Gerry Niewood Quartet. Days later, we hear the song again, this time harmonized doo-wop style diegetically by some black students in a hallway at school. Of course, we know there will be another encounter, as the song has now become the couple's motif. And we hear the song two more times, in versions by the Flamingoes and the Complexions! The song is put to good use, setting the time period while also linking the couple, as well as father and son.

The interracial romances as presented for these boys differ significantly from their adult counterparts. They are not presented as a test of liberal values, as in *Guess Who's Coming to Dinner* (1967), or as instances of "jungle fever." The kids' feelings are true. C continues to shave and get ready for his date with Jane, even though his father tells him to "stick with his own." Both Ben and Sylvia are willing to risk opposing their parents' views as well: Sylvia invites Ben to the James Brown concert even though her father forbade her to see white boys after Ben is discovered hiding in her bedroom closet. Ben, too, knows it is against his mother's wishes. Earlier in the film, she asks him how the colored kids are getting along in school. When he tells her that one of the girls is attractive, his mother's response is to moan, "Just kill me now." All of them risk more than social stigma and parental discipline. They also risk violent reprisals by bigoted communities.

Levinson tries to dispel a lot of ignorance through his characterization of Sylvia and through the ridiculous presumptions made by the Jewish boys in the film.[9] Not having had contact with anyone from the black community, and only now "discovering a world he did not know," Ben makes a number of incorrect assumptions about the material conditions of the black community, seeing Sylvia as much of America would, as an example of the homogenous uneducated and economically disadvantaged underclass. For example, when Ben decides to act on his attraction, following her onto the city bus at the end of the school day, he tells her he is going downtown to shop. He is surprised when she signals the driver before the bus has gotten to the more urbanized section of Baltimore. (Her father is a successful doctor, her mother a second-generation Spelman graduate, and they live in a large suburban house.) Sylvia confronts him, defiantly asking, "Is that where I am supposed to live?" She knows Ben has lied about his destination, and we know Ben is a boy inexperienced in the ways of courting. As they walk toward her home he makes another mistake, asking Sylvia if she knows Cab Calloway and Billie Holiday. She quickly retorts, "Do you know Albert Einstein?" His friends make even more erroneous and pernicious assumptions. As hormone-driven teens it is no surprise that they are obsessed with sex, but their concerns draw upon the hypersexualized stereotypes that have plagued black Americans since enslavement.

In phys ed class, when a newly admitted black student walks by in the background, Ben's buddy Sheldon (Evan Neumann) tells his friends that he is a good guy, talented in math and willing to help others less skilled. Sheldon continues, describing his experience in the communal shower and using it as a chance to discuss the enormity of his classmate's penis. Even after the conversation has switched to another topic, he brings the subject back to the fore by holding up the climbing rope as an illustration of his classmate's phallic power. Later, when Ben confides in his friend, telling him he spent the afternoon with Sylvia, Sheldon is disappointed because nothing sexual occurred, or more specifically, nothing sexual occurred with a colored girl. Sheldon and Ben's other buddy, Lenny (Joseph Patrick Abel), later get into a fight over an extra ticket to the James Brown concert—not because they want to see James Brown; they have no idea who he is. They are excited by the possibility of the illicit: Sylvia is bringing a friend, and colored girls "put out." Clearly this functions in the film so that we know that Ben's interest in Sylvia is innocent and of genuine affection, unlike that of his friends. It is so innocent, in fact, that intimacy never goes beyond dancing on the bed or an instance of premature ejaculation caused by an inadvertent touch on Ben's thigh as Sylvia reaches across his lap.

Foreign Student, because its central couple is older, can and does go further. Philippe and April become involved in a torrid, yet forbidden, relationship, meeting in isolated environs. She is the only person to make him feel at home, as he professes at their first meeting. Unlike the white Southerners, who call him Phil, she, having studied French, can pronounce his name with the proper inflection. There is some attempt at a cultural exchange here—through music he learns more about black culture while she learns more French. And given what we have learned of the French treatment of black people from Howlin' Wolf, the film is structured to have us believe there is a possibility of the couple continuing their lives together in Europe. The idea is further grounded by his pro-

Ben (Ben Foster) listening to records in Sylvia's (Rebekah Johnson) bedroom after school in *Liberty Heights* (1999).

posal to her after they make love. He professes his love, makes a commitment, and plans to take her back to France. This scenario and Ben's inexperience in *Liberty Heights* reveal that white boys in these films are incredibly naive about the social weight of race.

An underlying suggestion in the movie acknowledges that a life free of racial prejudice in France is nothing but fantasy, one that, even if real, would require April to sacrifice family, friends, and community. April cares for Philippe very deeply, yet she suspects that he will transfer his affections to a more "proper" partner, one of the Southern belles who attend the college. April is all too aware of the culture's devaluation of black women and the overvaluation of white women as objects of desire.[10] Although this never happens the relationship ends and Philippe returns to France.[11]

One might expect the interracial romance in *A Bronx Tale* to be radically different because it is set above the Mason-Dixon Line and because the bulk of the film takes place in 1968, the year of Martin Luther King Jr.'s assassination, four years after passage of the Civil Rights Act of 1964, and one year after *Loving v. State of Virginia*.[12] The father/son relationship is important in this film, but the romance is more crucial to C's coming-of-age process. It removes him from the company of his long-term friends, severing one of his links to childhood, and forces him to make independent decisions with serious consequences, perhaps for the first time in his life. As in *Liberty Heights* and *Foreign Student*, C's affection here is treated very much like the blossoming of first love. Like Ben and Philippe, he is unskilled in picking up girls. Maybe it is just nervousness because Jane is "so tall, beautiful, and classy," but in C's first exchange with her, he is awkward and inarticulate. She, however, can tell him she likes Italians, compliment his eyes, and even make contact as she fixes the brim of his hat. They make a date to go to the movies, but the rendezvous never transpires.

Later that day C's friends brutally attack two black young men riding their bikes through the Italian neighborhood. C tries to protect one of the fallen riders by pretending to assault him. When C meets Jane for their date in front of their school, a neutral zone between their respective housing areas, she immediately questions him about the violence. His claim of not being present is proved to be a lie when Jane's bruised and bandaged brother engages in a verbal bout. The scene and the budding romance are brought to a close when C shouts, "Fuck you, you fucking nigger," at Jane's brother. Racial tensions are further stirred as C's racist friends, armed with Molotov cocktails and a handgun, plan a drive-by in the black neighborhood. While he is wedged into the backseat of their car, C's voiceover describes his fear and apprehension though, interestingly enough, not any moral indignation about the crime they are about to commit. C is rescued from the car, and the doomed fate of his friends, by Sonny's intervention. The boys attack the film's symbol of blackness, a record shop, but are punished for their racism by burning to death. Jane, learning the truth about her brother's assault, makes up with C. Does this relationship last? The closing narration suggests not. Jane is described as one in a series of "great ones."[13]

As nostalgic films, these films use race only as a means to provide impediments for romance, failing to make complex critical examinations of America's racial hegemony. The girls and the experience of romance function here as the vehicles for the boys' coming of age. All of the relationships are treated as transitory. Although this can be excused as characteristic of young love, almost no Hollywood interracial romances, regardless of the age of the lovers, end with the suggestion of long-term relationships. After all, would long-term relationships logically lead to the symbol used as a warning against miscegenation, the tragic mulatto? What are we to make of these future men? Will they be participants in the struggle for social justice that will soon grip the nation? It is suggested that Ben will have such a future. At the close of *Liberty Heights* he and his two friends tear down the prohibitive sign from the pool, enter the area, set out three lounge chairs, and defiantly sit themselves down in the sun, each with a letter painted on his chest, collectively spelling JEW. But what of Philippe and C? Will they retreat back to their white worlds, content with their fleeting experiences of illicit love? And if we can blame the lack of long-term interracial romantic commitments in nostalgic narrative film on earlier society's entrenched prohibitions, then what about films set in the present?

KNIGHTS IN BAGGY DENIM

If we look at the historical film not as an examination of the good old days, but as a lesson on mistakes of the past, then *Liberty Heights, Foreign Student,* and *A Bronx Tale* inform us that those old-fashioned attitudes validating same-race dating should be relegated to history. America is a melting pot, having progressed beyond such antiquarian ideologies, right? Maybe not.

In 1994, the principal of Randolph County High School in Wedowee, Alabama, threatened to cancel the prom if it was attended by interracial couples. Only a few years ago, in 1999, the Alabama State Senate finally voted to repeal the state's constitutional prohibition of interracial marriages. During his presidential campaign, then candidate George W. Bush started a national furor, giving a speech in February 2000 at Bob Jones University. His presence on the campus, which bans interracial dating, was interpreted as a confirmation of the institution's values. Even more recently, Senator (and House Majority Leader) Trent Lott, a government representative with an anti–civil rights voting record, publicly valorized segregation, suggesting racial integration is the cause of the United States' current ills.

It was in this context that two more teen films of interracial romance were released, *Crazy/Beautiful* and the immensely popular *Save the Last Dance* (both 2001). These films were more accepting of the relationships they depicted, suggesting that the contemporary Generation Y has a more progressive outlook than its baby-boomer parents do. Yet closer examination reveals that the acceptance may be more restricted than it seems, for the discourses both films support are contradictory, and ultimately supportive of conservative ideology.

These two films, marketed specifically to audiences of teenaged girls, are about the redemptive power of love, following the pattern that John Cawelti in *Adventure, Mystery, and Romance* terms the "fantasy of all-sufficiency love, centering on the overcoming of some combination of social and psychological barriers" (1976, 42). The social barrier is, of course, race, and the psychological barrier is the absent mother.

Crazy/Beautiful and *Save the Last Dance* revert back to the formula of the feminine discourse, with the girls as protagonists. In this way both films return to an agenda not of feminist ideology but of racist *and* sexist reinscription. The films function as star vehicles for Kirsten Dunst and Julia Stiles, highlighting their white characters, Nicole and Sara respectively, who are paired with boys (played by relative newcomers). The girls manage to dictate their perspectives of the narratives even as they passively wallow in the depths of psychological nihilism awaiting the boys who will save them. Although the girls are rescued by nonwhite boys, their cultures, black and Latino, are constructed as so pathological that they require escape.

In his analysis of interracial romance films, Ed Guerrero identifies a compelling characteristic of films that pair white women with nonwhite men. The films may be read as radical in their pairings, yet "interracial unions are often flawed by rendering them between subjects who are distinctly unequal in ways that inversely underscore the superiority of the all-powerful white norm. Consequently, the white woman depicted with nonwhite men is devalued in some subtle way. She is plain; she is blank; she is handicapped, etc. suggesting that the sign of her whiteness should be enough reward for the person of color" (1993, 173). Surely this scenario applies to *Crazy/Beautiful.* While watching the film it is hard to fathom a reason for Carlos's (Jay Hernandez) attraction to the seventeen-year-old Nicole.[14] She is an alcohol and drug abuser, has no interest in school, and in these days of deadly sexually transmitted diseases she is promiscuous without practicing safe sex. Later we learn that Nicole has attempted suicide numerous times, suffering from psychological traumas caused by her mother's suicide and her father's neglect. Carlos, by contrast, is a studious scholar/athlete, leaving his house before dawn to travel two hours for the privilege of attending high school in an exclusive suburb of Los Angeles. His dream is to attend the Naval Academy in order to become a pilot. Sara in *Save the Last Dance* also suffers from the loss of her mother, who died in a car accident en route to her daughter's audition for admission to Juilliard. Sara blames herself for her mother's death, giving up ballet when she moves in with her estranged father. The intervention of Derek (Sean Patrick Thomas), an aspiring doctor, inspires her to realize her dream.

Nicole's degradation is so severe that when we are introduced to her, she is picking up litter on the beach as punishment for getting caught driving under the influence. This is where Carlos and his friends meet her, and his buddies continue to refer to her as "trash girl" later in the film. Her initial interest in Carlos is a fetishized one—she insists that he speak Spanish to a food vendor, despite his protestations that the woman speaks English; when she brings him to her room for sex she declares that her liberal congressman father would be proud that she has a person of color in her bed, and is excited about the sight of their comparative skin tones. In fact, he has very little power in the narrative. Nicole not only has the power of point of view, she also literally has the power of the gaze. As an amateur photographer, she is constantly snapping photos of her boytoy, even putting words in his mouth as she draws dialogue balloons on the photos she adds to her scrapbook. Her power is also realized as sexual aggression. She jumps in his lap early in the film, ignoring his pleas to slow down. She even initiates sex, always in her space. As their relationship progresses, her lifestyle impedes on his. Carlos abandons his friends, loses sight of his goals, ignores obligations to his family, and fails to meet his responsibilities. Even her father sees the effect she has on the boy, and the congressman instructs Carlos to dump her. Carlos refuses to abandon Nicole, and through the power of his love, he restores both Nicole's self-esteem and her relationship with her father.

The film depicts female independence and rebelliousness as self-destructive, blaming it on the lax parenting of liberal baby-boomers who were probably members of 1960s counter-culture. By placing Nicole back in the care of her enlightened father (kids need boundaries, especially girls on the cusp of womanhood) the film restores patriarchal power, using a minority boy as the tool. But not just any boy, one who as a real-life "top gun" pilot will commit violence on behalf of the greater social order led by middle-aged white men like the congressman.

Save the Last Dance, the first feature-length production from MTV films, smartly capitalizes on its production company's musical associations. The film simultaneously acknowledges the economic and social impact of hip-hop musical styles, while exploiting white youth's fascination with black youth culture. Hip-hop, and its most recognized incarnation, rap music, has surpassed rock 'n' roll as the dominant youth musical form. In addition to the black artists who make up the majority of Billboard's rankings, its co-optation has resulted in the careers of soul-inflected white boy bands like N'Sync, pastiche artists like Beck, the phenomenon of Eminem, and the nymphets Britney Spears and Christina Aguilera. Sara's move from the suburbs to the heart of black Chicago allows us entry into the strange and hidden world of hip-hop—not the political or ideological form, but the MTV incarnation, all surface and style, defined by clothes, hairstyle, and dance.

Dance is central to the film. (The producers and director Thomas Carter acknowledge that no studio would touch the film without this component.) Although Sara is not the only white student in her high school, she remains the odd-girl-out because she knows nothing of hip-hop music or dance. The film goes so far in racializing dance forms that the world of ballet is depicted as one of exclusion.[15] Derek introduces Sara to hip-hop, helping her to work out the right dance moves and requisite attitude after school. They grow closer during these dance sessions and dates at the local club, eventually falling in love. She uses her newly learned dance skills, incorporating hip-hop movements into her ballet routine, and draws from his support and encouragement at a second, and finally triumphant, Juilliard audition.

Both girls are in need of a strong masculine presence in their lives. The gap is filled by boys with vision who will provide them with the love and stability the girls' preoccupied fathers lack. How odd, then, that these boys should come from cultures depicted as severely in need of both love and stability. Neither Carlos nor Derek has a father. Derek cannot even benefit from the support of a mother, for she is a crack addict in prison. The academically talented boys, with long-term goals, have no comparable peers either. Stereotypes of poverty, single-motherhood, and communities of violence populated by ex-cons surround them. Although in *Crazy/Beautiful* it is actually the excesses of white bourgeois culture that threaten Carlos, whiteness still defines the norm, and communities of color are worlds of entrapment from which escape

Sara (Julia Stiles) gets her groove on with Derek (Sean Patrick Thomas) in *Save the Last Dance* (2001).

is necessary: for Carlos to Annapolis and for Derek to Georgetown University.

If these romantic pairings are to be equitable relationships, then neither participant would be required to abandon his or her culture, the expected sacrifice of females we have seen time and again, even in films like *The Little Mermaid* (1992). Carlos's feminized position within the narrative and the ease with which he acclimates to Pacific High suggest that he would suffer the loss, not Nicole. Conservative films like *Crazy/Beautiful* typically present minority communities as less tolerant than the white ones, a view typified here by the scene at the *quiceañera*.[16] The celebration is treated like a strange ritual, one in which Nicole is not made to feel comfortable. Shortly after her arrival at the party, feeling alienated and unwelcome, Nicole rushed out. As she flees, Carlos's willingness to abandon his home, family, and ambitions in order to run after her reveal that his assimilation into her world is complete. In *Save the Last Dance*, Sara lives in the black community for only a short period of time—the duration of her senior year. Many viewers attributed her appropriation of language, fashion, and dance to an endeavor to fit in, not as an attempt to act black. But she is soon to enter the environment of Juilliard's prestigious ballet program, which the film has defined as white. Will she then revert to white-ness, in order to assimilate once again?

Maybe what is needed is a more complete cultural crossing, a subversion of the social order that is rendered as more than the tourism and cosmopolitanism presented in the five films discussed thus far.

Beyond the Binary

Mikhail Bakhtin differentiates two types of linguistic hybridiza-tion: the conscious, where integration is deliberate, and the uncon-scious, where aspects of language are joined unintentionally, "preg-nant with potential for new world views" (1981, 360). When it is applied to the racialized youth culture of hip-hop and its global popularity, this concept clearly delineates the difference between the radical potential of hybrid identity and cultural exchange as compared to the racial masquerade of wiggas and wannabes.

The terms *wiggas* (white niggers) and *wannabes* (a conflation of "want to be") refer to the phenomenon of white and other non-black youth who adopt what *they understand* as essential signifiers of blackness; employing aspects of dress and body language and the phonology, grammar, and lexis of African American Vernacular Eng-lish, often incorrectly. This racial impersonation is nothing new, exemplified by Norman Mailer's 1957 essay on the White Negro (1992), which suggested an affiliation with black culture to culti-vate hipness in the midst of post–World War II conformity. The affinity of nonblack youth for hip-hop culture and its expressive forms has had long-lasting effects on contemporary popular culture, too many to discuss here, but one aspect important to note is the treatment of hip-hop culture as a site of contestation: issues of pro-priety and authenticity arise as the process of co-optation by the mainstream occurs.[17]

These tensions surface in Timothy Chey's *Fakin' da Funk* (1997), and in *Zebrahead* (1992), directed by Anthony Drazan, fea-ture films in which teenaged boys who are not black adopt "black identities." *Fakin' da Funk* is distinctive, challenging the racial order by refusing whiteness as the norm. It is not white and Other that are paired, but black and Asian American. Filipino American[18] actor Dante Basco plays a Chinese teenager who was adopted as an infant by a black couple, a clergyman (Ernie Hudson) and his wife (Pam Grier). Years later, when the family moves from Atlanta to South Central Los Angeles, Julian, who identifies as black, experiences a crisis of identity because the community sees him as Asian. His befuddled state of mind is further complicated by his attraction to Karyn (Tatyana Ali), a black girl who, able to speak Japanese, knows more about Asian cultures than he does.[19]

In *Zebrahead*, a Jewish teenager falls for the new girl in school. Like Julian, a Chinese teenager, Zack's (Michael Rapaport) identity is heavily invested in black culture through his fondness for hip-hop and his intimate associations. (For Julian it is his immediate family, for Zack his deep friendship with Dee [DeShonn Castle].) When Zack begins to get seriously involved with Nikki (N'Bushe Wright), Dee's newly arrived cousin, trouble is caused by a black student also attracted to Nikki.

In both films the boys are accosted for what is taken as racial impersonation, perhaps understandable given the long history of appropriation. They are not involved in conscious code-switching, yet the boys are ignorant of the privilege they possess within the U.S. racial hierarchy. (Both are clearly ranked lower than WASPS on the race and ethnicity scale, yet they are still higher than blacks.) Still, they differ from deliberate hybrids who adopt black identities as a form of rebellion or an attempt to be cool. As organic, unconscious hybrids, they come by their identities "naturally," Julian by his adopted family and community, and Zack through his family's long associations: his grandfather was a talent agent; his father manages a record store that specializes in jazz and R & B; and, as Zack himself mentions, he grew up in the predominantly black city of Detroit. If we consider the use of music as a means of transgression, Zack's identity is even more solidified. He doesn't just listen to hip-hop music, he creates it, selling his homemade mix tapes from his school locker.

In one of *Zebrahead*'s most striking scenes, Zack flirts with Nikki as he works his turntables during practice for a school fashion show. Students dance on the runway and on the floor of the converted gym as Zack demonstrates his skill. When he blends Puccini, Captain Beefheart, and a bluegrass fiddle into his break beats, it is a wonderful postmodern moment. What better way to demonstrate boundary slippage than with a type of music that originated from an eclectic African diasporic cultural mix of music and poetry forms, one that uses pastiche! As Zack coyly says to Nikki in a double-entendre, "You can sample anything."

And he does, as his relationship with Nikki progresses quickly from physical attraction to a full-fledged sexual and emotional bonding. Although their feelings for each other are expressed as genuine, their peers view the relationship as suspect, as another case of "jungle fever." Community distrust is also presented in *Fakin' da Funk*, when the black community questions Julian's investment in black culture. But unlike the films noted earlier, peer pressure, parental disparagement, and even violence fail to end either relationship. *Fakin' da Funk* goes even further, by offering the budding of a second romance—between a Chinese exchange student (Margaret Cho) who is mistakenly placed in the neighborhood and a young black man. Unfortunately, much of this is undermined by the film's strained humor that homogenizes Asian cultures and relies on cliché stereotypes of both Asian and black Americans. Similarly, *Zebrahead* attempts to challenge expectations, yet draws on the image of the dysfunctional, fatherless inner city black family and the gangsta archetype.

Media critics have noted that popular culture often deploys racialized narratives in periods of extreme economic distress or during moments of challenge to mainstream values, for example the recurrence of the mammy figure and scapegoating, and the re-emergence of the "magical black man."[20] The interracial teen romance can be seen to function as a site to reveal and work through contemporary racial anxieties, attempting to shift the paradigms of race and gender rather than reinscribe the conservative ideology of the trends noted above, even if the modifications are not as far-reaching as we would hope.

Of the films discussed here, only one, *Save the Last Dance*, was a bona fide hit, with a box office gross of more than ninety million dollars in the United States. Much of this MTV-produced feature's appeal is its focus on teens as protagonists, for a specifically youthful audience. By capitalizing on contemporary hip-hop music and dance, in a period when the styles of the subculture have now become dominant, Thomas's film reached into the pockets of the most desired demographic—teens. *Save the Last Dance* does not *feel* as retrograde as the other films because it not only sounds like a music video, it looks like one as well. Although ideologically problematic, the film may have resonated with its audiences specifically because of its link with other forms of popular culture. In almost every entertainment realm except mainstream cinema, one can find examples of interracial relations between youth that reveal feature films to be more conservative, such as in the Marvel Comics series *Runaways* or on television in the UPN series "One on One." The conventions of the classical Hollywood narrative—reducing complex social issues to simplistic individualized melodrama that relies on stereotypes, the use of a star system that almost exclusively posits white characters as the protagonists, the need for spectacle that fetishizes (hetero)sexual relations, and the treatment of interracial romances as transitory—impose a discourse that ultimately fails to address these race and gender power relations adequately.

NOTES

1. Despite it being well established that race has no biological basis (scientists have proven that there is more similarity between races than within them), the classification of human beings based on phenotype, in this case the particular physical characteristics of skin tone, hair texture, body type, and facial features, has a very real effect on every aspect of everyone's lives. The ability to "pass," to transgress the socially defined racial boundaries; the one drop rule that applies solely to the definition of blackness; the treatment of Latino as a race rather than as an ethnicity (also problematic because it assumes homogeneity); the lumping together of specific distinct and disparate East Asian cultures as one (counting only China, Japan, and Korea while excluding Laos, Thailand, and other nations located farther south); the confusion as to where to place Arabs, Indonesians, people from the Indian subcontinent; the belief that all Africans are necessarily black; the inability to place mixed race people, and even the hierarchy of whiteness, with WASPs at the pinnacle and Jews, Italians, and Irish at the bottom, reveal the irrational and indefensible processes of racial ideologies. However, because race is perceived as real and is manifested in social policy and social interaction, within this essay it will be treated as such, with references to groups as commonly defined.

2. See Marchetti (1993) for an in-depth study on interracial sexuality between whites and Asians in Hollywood film.

3. The granting of actress Halle Berry an Academy Award for Best Actress for her performance in *Monster's Ball* (2001) was the subject of consternation and criticism for many Americans. The content of the film was incendiary: a white death row prison guard from a racist background falls in love with the black wife of a recently executed

prisoner. Fuel was added to the fire when Berry received her award, the first black woman ever to win an Oscar in that category. Many found her character demeaning and felt she was rewarded for what they judged an unrealistic portrayal, another example of women of color's availability to white men.

4. In a study conducted by David Knox, more than 50 percent of college students polled were open to involvement with someone from another race, while almost 25 percent had already been so involved. A 1997 *USA Today* Gallup poll conducted nationally revealed that 57 percent of teens that date (aged 13–19) have dated interracially.

5. Although the relationship between Van and Dubbie is of interest, particularly because of the way the film constructs upper-class WASP identity, I focus here on the friendship/romance between Sylvia and Ben. One reason is because Ben's experiences frame the film through his narration. Another is because Jewishness is commonly defined not as race, but as religious practice or ethnicity. Jews are normally considered white.

6. Racial and ethnic links between these communities have been explored by Sander Gilman, for example, who, in *Difference and Pathology*, details the stereotypes of sexuality and pathology commonly attributed to blacks and Jews in "scientific" texts and those of popular culture. Eric Lott's *Love and Theft* and Michael Rogin's *Blackface, White Noise*, both studies on minstrelsy, offer compelling treatises on how the form of entertainment contributed to cultural definitions of blackness and other ethnicities as well. Rogin's work illustrates how Jews and blacks became linked in liberal politics, and also the process by which Jews became "white." See as well Brodkin 1998.

7. The Chittlin' Circuit was a string of nightclubs, theaters, and honky tonks that featured black performers for black audiences. The term is usually used to describe such venues during legalized segregation, when many performers and audiences were barred from other locales, though it is still used today.

8. Motown, the Detroit-based record label with artists like Stevie Wonder, The Supremes, The Temptations, The Miracles, Marvin Gaye, and The Jackson Five, released quite a large number of cross-over hits in the 1960s, records that were equally popular with black and white audiences. This was an important feat at the time, for many songs written and recorded by black artists were unknown to white fans of contemporary rock and pop. Many of their songs were covered by white artists who enjoyed national attention and great profits. Some examples include "Hound Dog," originally recorded by Big Mama Thornton, Joe Turner's "Shake Rattle and Roll," and "Tutti Frutti" by Little Richard.

9. This is not to say the film's representations of blackness are not with-

out issue. Little Melvin, played by Orlando Jones, is one of the most retrograde black characters to appear in contemporary American film.

10. For more on this subject see bell hooks (1981).

11. *Foreign Student's* characterization of white womanhood in the character of Sue Ann (one of the Southern Belles at Philippe's college) is strikingly similar to that of Dubbie in *Liberty Heights*, rendering both girls undesirable because of psychosis.

12. This is the Supreme Court case in which prohibition of interracial marriage was judged unconstitutional.

13. "A great one" refers to Sonny's description of the rare woman who comes along in a man's lifetime, a woman who is giving and provides comfort and support. The gangster tells C that race doesn't matter, suggesting to C that he give Jane a test to see what kind of girl she is. His instructions are to lock both car doors as he exits to go and pick up his date. After greeting Jane, he should unlock the passenger door first. The test is to see whether or not she will reach over to unlock the driver's side. She passes. But strangely enough, Jane is willing to date a boy who uses racial epithets easily and toward her brother. She is even willing to walk around at night looking for C in the neighborhood where her brother was beaten!

14. The explanation given in the film is that because his life is so structured and focused, he is attracted to her impetuousness and spontaneity.

15. All the dancers in the ballet recital Derek takes Sara to enjoy are white. The admissions committee, for whom Sara performs at the film's climax, consists of three white people and one black person. The white male chair speaks all of the lines and is featured most often in close-ups. When this chair shares the frame, it is almost exclusively with the white woman who sits to his left. The black faculty member is seated at the opposite end of the row. Throughout the scene, as the camera tracks to display the committee's reactions, it stops before he comes into frame! How equivocal for a film in which the ballet choreographer is Randy Duncan, a black man.

16. This elaborate gathering of family and friends to celebrate a girl's fifteenth birthday is common in many Latin American countries and diasporic communities. More than just a birthday party, it is a rite of passage, usually involving religious ceremony as well as the bestowing of symbolic gifts.

17. For more about the appropriation of black American culture, see Tate (2003).

18. The interchangeability of Asian ethnicities in casting is problematic here, as is the way Asian cultures are homogenized. The film does provide some constructions of the black community as different from the usual stereotypes, but falls back on criminality and the

potential for violence in an attempt to create narrative drama.

19. Interestingly, Tatyana Ali is of both Asian and African American descent.

20. For treatments of the mammy consider Oprah Winfrey and the film roles of Whoopi Goldberg; regarding scapegoating see the construction of stereotypes of the fraudulent welfare mother, the hyperviolent black male youth, and the unending tide of illegal immigrants; and for examples of the supernatural black man who comes to the aid of white protagonists note films like *The Green Mile* (1999), *The Legend of Bagger Vance* (2000), and *The Family Man* (2000) with Don Cheadle and Nicolas Cage.

WORKS CITED

Bakhtin, Mikhail. 1981. *The Dialogic Imagination.* Trans. Caryl Emerson and Michael Holquist. Austin: University of Texas Press.

Beale, Lewis. 1992. "Boyz in Your Hood?" *Washington Post,* March 8, p. c1.

Brodkin, Karen. 1998. *How Jews Became White Folks and What That Says about Race in America.* New Brunswick, NJ: Rutgers University Press.

Cawelti, John G. 1976. *Adventure, Mystery, Romance.* Chicago: University of Chicago Press.

Davis, Fred. 1979. *Yearning for Yesterday: A Sociology of Nostalgia.* New York: Free Press.

Doane, Mary Ann. 1987. *The Desire to Desire: The Woman's Film of the 1940s.* Bloomington: Indiana University Press.

Gilman, Sander. 1985. *Difference and Pathology: Stereotypes of Sexuality, Race, and Madness.* Ithaca: Cornell University Press.

Guerrero, Ed. 1993. "Spike Lee and the Fever in the Racial Jungle." In *Film Theory Goes to the Movies,* ed. Jim Collins, Hilary Radner, and Ava Preacher Collins, 155–69. New York: Routledge.

hooks, bell. 1981. *Ain't I a Woman.* Boston: South End Press.

Jameson, Fredric. 1983. "Postmodernism and Consumer Society." In *The Anti-Aesthetic: Essays on Postmodern Culture,* ed. Hal Foster, 111–25. Port Townsend, WA: Bay Press.

Knox, David. 2000. "Interracial Dating Attitudes among College Students." *College Student Journal* 34, no. 1, 69–71.

Landy, Marcia. 1996. *Cinematic Uses of the Past.* Minneapolis: University of Minnesota Press.

Lott, Eric. 1993. *Love and Theft: Blackface Minstrelsy and the American Working Class.* New York: Oxford University Press.

Mailer, Norman. 1992. "The White Negro." In T*he Portable Beat Reader,* ed. Ann Charters, 586–609. New York: Viking,

Marchetti, Gina. 1993. *Romance and the Yellow Peril: Race, Sex, and*

Discursive Strategies in Hollywood Fiction. Berkeley: University of California Press.

Rogin, Michael. 1996. *Blackface, White Noise: Jewish Immigrants in the Hollywood Melting Pot.* Berkeley: University of California Press.

Tate, Greg. 2003. *Everything but the Burden: What White People Are Taking from Black Culture.* New York: Broadway.

Wood, Robin. 2002. "Party Time or *Can't Hardly Wait* for that *American Pie:* Hollywood High School Movies of the 90s." *Cineaction* 58, 2–10.

⑨

THE "WEE MEN" OF GLASGOW GROW UP

Boyhood and Urban Space in *Small Faces*

Peter Clandfield and Christian Lloyd

In Gillies and Billy MacKinnon's *Small Faces* (1996), thirteen-year-old Glaswegian Lex MacLean (Iain Robertson) undergoes a catalogue of masculine coming-of-age experiences: boozing, fighting, choosing role models, claiming territory. However, the extent to which the film incorporates familiar situations and motifs has led some critics to miss the complexity of its treatment of these motifs, and to assess the film under a generalized innocence-to-experience rubric (see Shulgasser 1996). In this essay we will attend to the layers of generic elements that drive the narrative, but will also foreground the cultural and historical specificities that are crucial to the film's distinctive take on boyhood. *Small Faces* is set in 1968, when Glasgow itself was "growing up" in a particular sense, as large numbers of inner city tenement dwellers were relocated to monumental modernist developments dominated by tower blocks. Although oblique, the film's critique of this process is one of its key features: Lex's development is significantly influenced by architectural developments in the city. The film dramatizes the particular pressures—for both sexes—of growing up in a place where space is both contested in stressful ways and changing in dramatic ways. We will draw on Mikhail Bakhtin's theory of chronotope, "the intrinsic connectedness of temporal and spatial relationships" (1981, 84) that "provides the ground essential for the . . . representability of events" (250) in narrative, in order to explore the film's depiction of a site-specific boyhood.

"OOR HOOSE": LEX, BOBBY, ALAN

Lex lives with his mother Lorna (Clare Higgins) and two older brothers in a nineteenth-century sandstone tenement in the south-central Glasgow district of Govanhill. Their flat, like those of many working-class Glaswegians of the era (see Pacione 1995, 161–62), is crowded: the three boys' beds are crammed into one smallish room, where the film opens with Lex drawing a large map of the city from his own perspective. Thus, while the film begins in domestic space, it immediately points outward. The map includes representative features of the city, but focuses less on physical geography than on gang territories and the personalities (or "faces") that inhabit them. As Glaswegian writer Andrew O'Hagan notes in a 1995 *Sight and Sound* article on the making of the film, these details are based broadly on actuality: "Whatever was happening elsewhere in the world [in 1968], in Glasgow, and on the front of the *Daily Record*, there was news of razor-slashing young gangs scouring the city in search of some terrifying character known only as 'The Face'" (8). The map thus points toward the film's concern with the details of particular spaces at particular times. At the same time, though, it establishes that this is an "art" film: one organized at least in part by subjective individual perception and by self-reflexive awareness of the implications of particular representational techniques.

This opening sequence also maps Lex's family. Not only does Lex draw himself and his two brothers inside "oor hoose," but also the act of drawing the gang-focused map brings together his brothers' contrasting influences. Eighteen-year-old Bobby (J. S. Duffy), drawn as a hammer-wielding figure bawling with rage, is sullen, semiliterate, and heavily involved in the local gang, The Glen. Alan (Joseph McFadden), perhaps a year younger, drawn as an innocent, haloed figure, is handsome, gentle, and an aspiring painter. Lex's brothers represent two alternative traditional images of Glaswegian working-class masculinity: the volatile, territorial "Hard Man" (see e.g., McArthur 1997, 20) and the detached, outward-looking thinker. These models are *not* mutually exclusive, as the Mac-Kinnons point out (1996); however, the film suggests that they do not coexist easily, and their interaction in the film is the basis for its distinctive generic mixture. Lex draws himself as a pitchfork-brandishing little devil, and in so doing points to the way in which he will exhibit throughout the film, in unpredictably varying ratios, both Bobby's rebelliousness and Alan's creativity.

Clearly enough, *Small Faces* is a coming-of-age narrative: Lex evolves as the film progresses, gaining an increased awareness of the roles and perils of adulthood. Like many works in the genre, such as Truffaut's *Les Quatre cents coups* (1959) with its implicit commentary on the condition of postwar France, the film suggests parallels between the progress of its protagonist and that of a surrounding community. Just as strikingly, though, *Small Faces* combines two of the most recognizable—and most apparently dissimilar—coming-of-age subgenres: the youth gang story and the *Künstlerroman*, or tale of the development of the artist. Coming of age frequently involves moving permanently, yet also gradually, from one space to another; more specifically, for males, at least in a patriarchal society, it entails leaving home to claim space in a wider and often indifferent or hostile world.[1] Gangs claim an environment physically; artists do so imaginatively. *Small Faces,* however, does not simply depict Lex as choosing between these alternative modes of self-assertion. Rather, the film gains much of its vigor and specificity from the juxtaposition of the two modes (and the corresponding genres) in Lex's life and in his Glasgow. Repeatedly, and in some of its most striking sequences, the film shows convergences or collisions between efforts at creativity and acts of violence. This generic hybridity—a recontextualizing rather than a rejection of genre conventions—helps the film to move beyond formulaic ideas about boyhood in general and 1960s Glaswegian boyhood in particular.

The combination in Lex of his brothers' traits also helps to emphasize that they, too, are still in many ways boys themselves. In different ways, in fact, he seems more advanced than either of them: he is more self-aware than Bobby, and more streetwise than Alan. Positioned literally (in that they share a room) and figuratively between these contrasting role models, Lex also has his own distinctive combination of qualities. His preadolescent body is bulky, ungainly, and ill coordinated, but his personality is inquiring, spirited, and articulate. The conflicting forces at work upon and within Lex make him a kind of walking drama in himself, and the allusive, episodic, and sometimes elliptical plot of the film is driven by his efforts to cope with these forces as they impel him to move around the city in increasingly ambitious ways.

Both Lex's position between his brothers and the film's resourceful ways of indicating its complication of his development are further illustrated in another early sequence. Bobby, first seen gleefully feeding Lex's goldfish to death, awakens screaming from a nightmare and has to be comforted by Lorna ("I was dead! I was dead, Ma!") as Lex looks on. Then, overlapping sound links Bobby's trauma obliquely to troubles of Lex's own: the repeated crack of strap hitting flesh ushers in a pan through Lex's classroom, where he is undergoing corporal punishment for some unspecified offence. Lex asserts himself against the brutality of the punishment by pulling his hands away from the strap and saying, with memorable decisiveness, "No, that's enough!" Sent to report to the principal, he meets Alan, who pulls him into a room where another aspiring artist, Fabio (David Walker), is completing a painting. This sequence may seem to sketch an optimistic trajectory for Lex, from fear and violence through self-assertion to liberation through the opportunities afforded by art. Yet the film pauses on Fabio's painting, which depicts Christ suffering on the cross, suggesting that neither Lex's path nor the film's generic path will be simple or linear.

Contributing further to the film's juxtaposition of contrasting elements is a sequence soon after, which features a party in the MacLean home in honor of the visit from America of Uncle Andrew (Ian McElhinney), expatriate brother of the boys' long-dead father. As his visibly inebriated uncle embarks on a song about a "Hard Man" (in itself a fusion of art and violence), Lex liberally samples the bottles in the kitchen. Once Andrew has finished his performance, which includes falling over and pretending to have electrocuted himself on a lamp, the adults go off to carry on the party elsewhere. Left with Alan, Lex goes into a drunken fit. Dashing to the floor the insultingly small glass of beer that his brother offers him, he leaps, yelling, at the living-room curtains, bringing them down onto himself in a pile, from which Alan extracts him just in time for the arrival of Bobby, whom Lex proceeds to charge, topple, and pummel in retaliation for the goldfish episode. Lex then collapses in a crash of breaking glass as the screen goes dark. The parallels between Lex's behavior here and his uncle's earlier performance imply that Andrew, easily the most substantial adult male character in the film, is less than ideal as a father figure. Moreover, occurring as it does in the confines of the flat, and in less than thirty seconds of screen time, the sequence conveys the strong sense that Lex can no longer be contained in his home by the adults in his life and is on the verge of an inevitable move into the city and into its violent subcultures.

THE WEE MAN

The aftermath of the party sets up the key event of the first half of the film, which does indeed push Lex toward new surroundings. The day after the party, Bobby gives a hung-over Lex an air gun as "an offering, to keep the peace, OK?" Ironically, in light of these words, but predictably given the film's generic associations and context, Lex soon uses the gun unwisely, firing it semiaccidentally at a group of footballers in a park and hitting one in the head. To Bobby's amusement, the victim proves to be Malky Johnson (Kevin McKidd), feared leader of the Garaside Tongs, powerful archrivals to The Glen. Lex's feat attracts the attention of The Glen's own leader, Charlie Sloan (Garry Sweeney), as do Alan's artistic talents. The sharply dressed Sloan embodies the convergence of the Hard Man and the intellectual, and of the film's subgenres: he has a passion for art books, his collection of which ("all nicked") fills the room into which he summons Lex and Alan when they walk past his tenement one day. Gillies MacKinnon implies in his comments on the film that Sloan is not entirely invented: "We wanted to tell a story about working-class Glasgow teenagers in 1968 showing some of the contradiction familiar to us—boys with a consuming passion for art growing up among the gangs; a gang leader whose hobby is stealing books and building up a massive personal library" (1996).

It is on this occasion that Sloan christens Lex "the wee man." This is a common working-class Scottish epithet for "boy," but Sloan attaches it in a particular way to Lex, as does the film as a whole. Sloan's interest in Lex implies a canny recognition that Lex's precocious audacity has talents that may make him an effective agent for the quasi-adult ends of The Glen; yet the adjective "wee" suggests Sloan's confidence that he can control the younger boy. As the film progresses, the implications of the nickname are developed, and Lex comes increasingly to define "wee" manhood on his own terms.

For his part, Alan—though older than Lex, and though he is flirting with a girl, Joanne McGowan (Laura Fraser), whom Sloan also admires—is willing enough to accept the gang leader's patronage; Lex remains wary, and with reason. Lex's and Alan's first escapade with The Glen is relatively harmless, and perhaps even subversive of cultural and class boundaries; it certainly displays the combination of criminal and imaginative daring. Using Lex's wee size, the gang breaks into a museum so that Alan can draw Sloan into one of the exhibits, a collage of faces. While this exploit highlights Sloan's naively dandyish desire to see his face immortalized, his next appearance exposes his sinister side. He and a lieutenant pick up Lex in a car and tell him that they are "going for a cup of tea wi' Malky Johnson." They drive to "Tongland," introducing both Lex and the viewer to the vast estate of concrete blocks which is the home territory of Malky and his gang, and which will figure

Lex (Iain Robertson)
dominated by the urban
jungle of Tongland.

prominently later in the film. They threaten to abandon Lex in this
hostile environment: "Maybe they'll render him unconscious wi' a
hammer and drop him doon the nearest manhole," remarks Sloan
before they retreat.

The violence promised in this episode is realized soon after.
Fabio, who has been helping Lex with his art, crosses paths with
The Glen as the gang is gearing up for a confrontation with the
Tongs, and is severely beaten at Sloan's behest, apparently for no
other reason than that he is an outsider. When Lex happens on the
scene, he too falls victim to the gang's arbitrary brutality. Sloan,
who has been drinking in preparation for the brawl, greets him
expansively: "Hey, wee man! Come and say hello to your Uncle
Charlie!" Sloan's "hello" proves to be a head-butt to Lex's face. One
of Sloan's own henchmen expresses disgust, but Bobby—worried
about his place in the gang's hierarchy—merely laughs as his
brother staggers away. In the subsequent battle between Glen and
Tongs, Bobby smashes Malky's nose with a brick. Cut into the
brawl is a shot of Alan ministering to Lex's own damaged nose and
asking if Bobby is responsible. The parallel nature of Lex's and
Malky's injuries not only underscores the fact that Bobby *is*, indi-
rectly, responsible for what has happened to Lex, but also links Lex
visually to Malky in an important hint of events to come.

It is at this point that the film offers at least a partial explanation of the MacLean family's dynamics. After the brawl, Lex and
Bobby have a tense encounter in their kitchen. Bobby accuses Lex

of treachery to The Glen ("There's an informer. A clay pigeon") and Lex mocks Bobby's deficient literacy by telling Alan, "it's time B-o-b-b-y went for a w-a-l-k . . . he's a m-o-r-o-n!" But upon hearing what has happened to Fabio, Lex storms out. Alan then offers Bobby what amounts to an oblique apology, and a way of understanding his anger: "Jesus, Bobby. D'you remember when we were kids? . . . D'you remember Dad? . . . I couldn't do anything wrong, but he was always on at you." Bobby first disavows any such memories, then insists that their father apologized to him before he died. Aside from a brief reference by Uncle Andrew, this is the film's only mention of the father. It is not clear whether his abuse was the cause of Bobby's troubles or a response to them (or both), but Bobby's denial serves to confirm that some sort of abuse has affected him. The denial may also be seen as Bobby's vestigial effort at using his imagination to cope with his situation (as his brothers do theirs) and to escape the cycle of violence.

"YOU ARE NOW ENTERING TONGLAND"

However, Lex's own actions at this juncture also contribute to this cycle. Ironically, Bobby's suspicion of him proves retroactively justified, as Lex sets out to join the Tongs and thereby gain revenge on The Glen for his and Fabio's injuries. In a pivotal sequence, he ventures alone into "Tongland." Wide-angle shots of him gazing up at the high-rise slab blocks that dominate the bleak estate emphasize its vastness and his own wee-ness. The blocks are reflected in pools of water, which further accentuate their scale and Lex's isolation among them. The sequence dramatizes the way in which for boys growing up, the world looms as a monumental challenge. The high-rises were created, after all, by men who once were boys looking up at the world and dreaming of what they could build. The only other person visible is a boy about his own size, who flees when Lex hails him. Lex finds him again, however, on the access deck of one of the lower blocks, and they converse with a mixture of suspicion and empathy:

> LEX: You in the Tongs?
> GORBALS: Nah. I'm a pacifist. Between you and me, the
>   Tongs is a load of crap.
> LEX: What's your name?
> GORBALS: Gorbals. My family moved from the Gorbals two

> years ago. My real name's George.
> LEX: I was thinking of joining the Tongs.
> GORBALS: How old are you, son?
> LEX: Thirteen. You?
> GORBALS: Sixteen.
> LEX: You're awful wee for sixteen, Gorbals.
> GORBALS: I smoke a lot.

As Lex's comment on Gorbals's size suggests, he recognizes the other boy as a peer: a fellow "wee man" (someone wiser than his size) and a potential ally. The fact that Gorbals (Mark McConnochie) has adopted the name of his former home—the legendary working-class district that was among the areas of Glasgow most drastically redeveloped in the 1960s—emphasizes his own displacement in Tongland. Combined with the visual emphasis on the bleakness of the estate, Gorbals's name signposts the film's implicit commentary on the importance of space to the growth of young men and on the specifics of Glasgow's redevelopment.

Bakhtin's theorization of the chronotope (literally, "time space") offers a way of describing how particular narrative genres are characterized by particular kinds of setting in, and particular relations between, time and space. Picaresque novels, for example, employ the chronotope of "a road that winds through [the hero's] native territory," and along which the hero (and the narrative) moves through time and space (Bakhtin 1981, 165). Bakhtin does not offer a specific assessment of coming-of-age chronotopes, but of obvious relevance are his remarks on the threshold, whose "most fundamental instance is as the chronotope of *crisis* and *break* in a life," and which always has metaphorical as well as literal importance (248; original emphasis). As critic Phil Powrie notes (without explicit reference to Bakhtin), the threshold "acts as a complex metaphor" in *Small Faces:* "It is both developmental and spatial ... It is also clearly a temporal metaphor, the location between the past of childhood and the future of adulthood, a kind of precarious present" (2000, 322). Concerning the crisis that Lex faces, Gillies MacKinnon remarks, "At that age—and I think this is universally true and true of boys today—boys live in a world where they have certain threats that nobody else has. If you know teenage boys, there are some roads that they won't go down because of the things that might happen to them" (1996). As the film progresses, it places increasing emphasis on both literal and metaphorical thresholds and on Lex's movements between his relatively safe domestic space and the danger and adventure of the city beyond. Particularly note-worthy in emphasizing this "precarious present" is the rhythm of the editing in the sequences that depict Lex's explorations: rather than beginning with conventional establishing shots that treat the city simply as a backdrop, these sequences often begin with medium shots of characters and then introduce longer shots of their environments. The effect is to emphasize characters' subjec-tive perceptions of the city, and to dramatize the ways in which their sense of time-space relations are in flux along with their hor-mones.

A further, and crucial, point about chronotopes is that they are not just formal generic devices that organize what is represented within a given work. As Martin Lefebvre notes, Bakhtin stresses that it is "out of the actual chronotopes of our world" that there "emerge the . . . chronotopes of the world represented in the work" (in Bakhtin 1981, 253). "Bakhtin sees the chronotopes of narrative as being related to those of the real world, to the chronotopic com-plex in which the work is created and consumed. . . . [T]herefore, chronotopes in literature or cinema are in constant dialogue with chronotopes in life and are to be understood as historical and cul-tural products" (Lefebvre 1998, 89, 90). While time-space relations in novels, films, or other narratives do not simply correspond to time-space relations in actuality, the concept of chronotope draws attention to material connections between texts and contexts. Thus this sequence is the film's most imposing fusion of art and gang worlds.

Critic Duncan Petrie points out that in *Small Faces*, "The city is . . . powerfully rendered in terms of a contrast between the traditional sandstone tenements of Lex's neighborhood and the imposing high-rises, empty waste grounds and foreshortened brick walls that constitute 'Tongland,' the latter filmed in such a way as to suggest a highly stylised dystopia owing more to the imaginative universe of Lex (and MacKinnon) than modes of documentary real-ism" (2000, 204). As Petrie implies, the film suggests that being a man (wee or otherwise) is not just about claiming predefined space but also about imagining and representing space for oneself; in this respect the sequence we have described above takes up the opening images of Lex's drawing. So too does the phrase "You are now entering TONGLAND," which is painted on a wall at the threshold of the estate. This piece of graffiti can be seen as signing the estate not only in the sense of announcing its unofficial identity, but also in the sense of claiming it as, in part, an imaginative construction.

Petrie's phrase "highly stylised dystopia," while it captures the film's emphasis on Lex's (and its own) subjective perceptions, could also be a near-literal description of some of the dysfunctional housing estates created, both in Britain and elsewhere, by grandiosely abstract thinking on the part of ambitious architects, politicians, and planners. Glasgow has been an especially important site of large-scale housing schemes. Following the Second World War, according to social geographer Michael Pacione, "one-seventh of Scotland's population was crowded into three square miles of central Glasgow, and houses often lacked basic sanitary amenities" (1995, 161–62). In the 1960s the Gorbals became the center of "the largest redevelopment scheme in the United Kingdom" (Pacione 1995, 168), and other areas of the city also underwent radical architectural change. Connoting purposeful efficiency, modernist high-rises—"machines for living," in the famous phrase of Le Corbusier, the Swiss architect who was one of their principal exponents (see Hall 1988, 205)—were particularly appealing to those in charge of the city's development. "Between 1961 and 1968 high flats accounted for almost three quarters of all housing completions. . . . In 1969, 163 tower blocks were occupied" (Pacione 1995, 171).

Thus it was that Glasgow itself not only grew but grew *up*. The new projects included Red Road, whose 31– story blocks were the tallest residential blocks in Europe when completed. Tongland itself is "played" by another of the city's most imposing developments, Sighthill, built between 1963 and 1969 on the former site of the St. Rollox chemical works (see Glendinning and Muthesius 1994, 231). Pacione notes that it was the high density of low-income tenants in these super-sized projects that began to reveal serious drawbacks to high-rise housing in Glasgow. These drawbacks were exacerbated by design flaws, poor maintenance, and social problems associated with the economic stagnation of the 1970s and 1980s (Pacione 1995, 170–71). Jeff Torrington's 1992 novel about the redevelopment of the Gorbals, *Swing Hammer Swing!*, christens the new high-rise estates "Legoland" (307), neatly suggesting, in this allusion to the well-known building toy, the naiveté and the residual boyishness of men who have spent their lives dreaming of ways to change the way the world looks, and whose dreams have been concretized. Nevertheless, Glasgow's modernist developments have had defenders: even planning historian Peter Hall, a sharp critic of Corbusian excesses, suggests that schemes for the Gorbals and comparable areas were relatively successful. However, Hall's comments on these schemes actually serve to point to some of their key flaws. Writing in 1988, he suggests that Glasgow high-rises presented "few consistent problems . . . except for those with children, unsurprising since four in five children lived above the fourth floor" (225). He appears not to regard this as a major exception, as though children were a slightly esoteric minority interest rather than an ordinary, indeed necessary, part of human life.

The comparisons Hall draws between Glasgow and other environments also suggest more than they are intended to. Hall asserts that the "Corbusian city of towers" worked well enough "for the solid, tough traditional tenement-dwellers of Glasgow, for whom the transition from a Gorbals rear-end slum to the twentieth floor seemed like the ascent to paradise. But for a welfare mother born in a Georgia shack and dumped in St Louis or Detroit with a brood of uncontrollable children, it proved an urban disaster of the first magnitude" (1988, 240). However, several of the new Glasgow buildings—including some of the most prominent: Basil Spence's award-winning blocks at Queen Elizabeth Square—functioned so badly and became so dangerous that, exactly like several of the American projects to which Hall compares them favorably (235–38), they were demolished with explosives in a public extravaganza only a few decades after their erection (see Glendinning and Muthesius 1994, 327). Pacione, writing in 1995, observes that "the Gorbals would be an automatic inclusion in any catalogue of planning disasters" (170; see also Campbell 1993, 24). Some tower blocks in the city have been more successful, but development since the late 1970s has concentrated on less monumental and more flexible projects (see Pacione 1995, 171, 180–82; Reed 1999, 223–28). *Small Faces* is certainly based on its makers' subjective vision of their city's recent past rather than on any identifiably orthodox documentary approach: high-rise blocks, despite their plentifulness in Glasgow, are almost never visible, and certainly never foregrounded, except in connection with the Tongs. However, the vision of such blocks as forbidding and dysfunctional is rooted at least partly in the specifics of local history.

Hall's remarks can serve, too, to link *Small Faces* to other representations of people dominated by monumental kinds of architectural and social engineering. Hall's suggestion that Glaswegians are made of inherently sterner stuff than African Americans may be implicitly racist, but it does highlight the fact that it is the presence of housing-estate dystopias, as well as of gang culture, that gives *Small Faces* noteworthy possibilities of comparison with American representations of disadvantaged young men.[2] Nobody in *Small Faces* comments directly on the bleakness of Tongland, but the film's critique of housing schemes is all the more telling for being implicit: it suggests that the inhumanity of such places—both in Glasgow and in the world viewers inhabit—is now almost axiomatic. In fact, the modernist housing-block dystopia—architectural artwork turned gang battleground—can be regarded as a recognizable chronotope in itself. Part of the distinctiveness of *Small Faces*, then, is the range of ways in which it uses chronotopic motifs that link it both to its genre and to its specific setting. This dual linkage allows the film to make its insider's take on Glaswegian boyhood intelligible for viewers who have never been to the city.[3]

A KIND OF EXPERIMENT

In the second half of *Small Faces*, the "wee men," Lex and Gorbals, join forces to negotiate the "grown-up" world around them. Gorbals reveals that his stepbrother belongs to the Tongs and offers to introduce Lex. As they walk along the concrete passage toward his home, he describes his family, where adults are even less prominent than they are elsewhere in the film:

> GORBALS: It's just me, my stepbrother, and two stepsisters.
>   And wee Harry till he got put away.
> LEX: No adults?
> GORBALS: Nah. They live their own lives next door.
> LEX: But isn't that against the law or something?
> GORBALS: We don't really see much of the law down here.
>   Anyhow, it's a kind of experiment. Like a Kibbutz.

There is no explanation of who wee Harry is or why he was "put away," but the allusion raises the possibility that even "wee men" can be dangerous. The phrase "put away," moreover, resonates ironically here, for the whole family has in a sense been "put away" in Tongland by the authorities who have abandoned them

there without "much of the law." More explicitly, of course, Gorbals's reference to an experiment implies an ironic parallel between
his family's living arrangements and the large-scale experimenta-
tion with humans that modernist housing schemes in effect
entailed. The repeated use of low-angle shots in this sequence posits
an analogy between the relatively small stature of the wee men in
an environment they had no say in making and the insignificance of
high-rise dwellers to the planners of machines for living.

Gorbals's stepbrother, leader of this "experiment," proves to
be Malky Johnson himself. He is both amused by Lex's small
stature and (though unaware at this point of Lex's surname and
thus of his family connections to The Glen) suspicious of his geographic provenance: "What's the Tongs going to do wi' a stunted
midget from Glenland?" He demands information on Bobby and
Sloan, and on Joanne McGowan, with whom he, too, is involved.
Scared, Lex mentions that Sloan takes weekly skating outings
unaccompanied by his "team" of gang members. Intrigued by the
possibilities of ambush that this information offers, but still suspicious, Malky later subjects Gorbals to an even more menacing
interrogation: he has his lieutenants hold his stepbrother by the
ankles, head down, over the edge of his block's access deck. This
sequence is introduced by a shot from Gorbals's inverted and highly
unstable point of view, in which nearby tower blocks lurch upside-
down around the screen. Superfluous to the main narrative, the
shot serves to highlight the vertiginousness and disorientation of
being a wee man in a "grown-up" world. While one traditional conception of boyhood—alluded to in *Small Faces* by shots of the
MacLean brothers' baby pictures, for example—treats it as an idyllic natural state, in which individuals are free to experiment in the
development of their own autonomous identities, this sequence
vividly reminds the viewer that the boyhood of Lex and Gorbals has
always been vulnerable to the dangers and constraints of the imperfect, built world around them.

More generally, Malky's treatment of Gorbals here could also
be seen as dramatizing the oppression-by-architecture that the less
powerful members of the family, and people like them, are experiencing on a more quotidian basis, and even as suggesting that redevelopment itself has been inherently destabilizing and dangerous.
At any rate, Malky learns from Gorbals the full extent of the
MacLeans' activities against him. Gazing grimly over the surround-

ing expanse of housing blocks, he expresses grudging admiration: "I mean, you've got to hand it to them. That's a remarkable family." This does not, however, prevent Malky from pursuing his vendetta against the MacLeans, which appears to eclipse even his hatred of The Glen.

"You're Dead!"

At the skating rink, as Lex looks on, Malky's henchmen target not Sloan but Bobby, who is struggling on his skates in a way that provides a visual synecdoche for his difficulties throughout the film. Stabbed in the ribs, Bobby collapses and bleeds to death on the ice. In a shot from directly overhead, his body is shown being dragged away and leaving a wide stripe of blood in its wake. This is one moment in the film that conspicuously lacks subtlety, yet the graphic image serves to link Bobby to his brothers, however gruesomely and ironically, since his trail of blood on the vast rink strongly resembles a stroke of paint across an empty canvas. The image also serves as a gruesome reminder that in a sense it is artlessness that has doomed Bobby. After Bobby's death, Lex rushes home, where his mother is chatting with friends, but he cannot tell her what has happened and sits in helpless silence (which, naturally, is interpreted as adolescent moodiness). This sequence neatly expresses both the close bond and the communicative difficulties between Lex and his family.

After Bobby's funeral, and tormented by guilt, Lex leaves home. He is found wandering by Gorbals, who warns him against the further danger Malky presents to him and Alan and gives him a knife ("It's against my principles, but you'd better take this"). Lex then confronts Sloan on the front steps of his tenement and appeals to him to protect Alan against Malky (who is jealous over Joanne). The Glen's leader, however, has become shy of violence: "Sorry, wee man. Can't help ye. Strictly organized crime from now on." Gazing down the stairs, Lex responds contemptuously: "Organized crime? So is that why you're doing the shopping for your Mammy? You're a washout, Sloan." As Lex storms away, Sloan can only gaze after him before hoisting his shopping bags and trudging up the stairs. Seen from the top of the stairs, Sloan is both physically and spiritually diminished here, made to appear as a dutiful boy on the threshold of a mundane adulthood.

This sequence is the first of several that register a change in the status of the wee men: they grow up in part by bringing bigger boys metaphorically down to size. Left to rely on himself, Lex contemplates returning home, but as he gazes in through his bedroom window (another threshold) at a sleeping Alan, the film cuts directly to a shot of Tongland, expressing his movement out into the dangerous adult world. After threatening Malky by phone— "You're dead!"—Lex goes to Malky's flat and attempts a break-in with the knife Gorbals has given him, but Malky comes to investigate. Catching sight of Lex cowering on his threshold, Malky reacts first by screaming in fear; Lex too screams before dropping the knife and escaping. Here, as in his exchange with Sloan, Lex exposes the vulnerability of an apparently much bigger boy. Malky takes out his anger on Gorbals, head-butting and kicking him savagely. Gorbals then takes his own revenge on Malky. As the Tong leader lies passed-out in his room, Gorbals turns on the gas. Awakened by the odor, but groggy, Malky unthinkingly lights a cigarette and blows himself up. This moment may be seen as representing not only the victory of the wee men over their larger oppressors, but also the symbolic revenge of the Gorbals itself on housing-estate dystopia: Malky meets his end in an explosion, like Queen Elizabeth Square a few years before *Small Faces* was made (see Glendinning and Muthesius 1994, 327).

"When I woke up I was still a boy"

Malky's self-demolition cuts to Lex waking with a start in a cinema full of children attending a variety program. A film is just finishing, and "The End" appears on the screen. As this visual pun suggests, both Lex's immediate troubles and *Small Faces* itself are nearly over. As the smaller children around him sing along to a familiar song, Lex gradually joins in. This moment appears to corroborate Gillies MacKinnon's suggestion that Lex "finds his childhood again, he renews himself" (1996). However, the film's closing sequences are much more complex and ambiguous than this remark would imply. Visiting Gorbals in his damaged flat, Lex tries to assuage his friend's guilt (as Gorbals has done for him after Bobby's death). But Gorbals responds grimly: "I did it. So now I'm the killer, OK? I saved you, that whore Joanne, that idiot brother of yours. . . . I murdered the fucker." In his final line, face in shadow, he asserts, "I'm the leader of the Tongs, now." This statement not only implies the end of his pacifism but also hints that, like Malky and Bobby, he may be doomed to fall into a spiral of violence; in generic terms, his life, it seems, may be locked into the rules of gang power structures.

The final sequence of *Small Faces* explains—apparently in conventional closure-confirming fashion—what has become of Lex's family. Lex reports in voiceover that Uncle Andrew married his mother and came to live in Govanhill, and that Alan went to art school and moved into his own flat. ("I don't worry about him any more.") Even Bobby has a happy ending of sorts: Lex relays a dream of his mother's in which, not dead, his brother goes north, becomes a fisherman, and attains acceptance. But Lex then describes a dream of his own: "My dream was different—more like a nightmare. I grew hair all over me. I had body odor. I suffered from uncontrollable senseless impulses. Yeh–I felt responsible for everything. I dreamt I was a *man!*"

If being a man entails suffering from "uncontrollable senseless impulses" yet feeling "responsible for everything," it amounts simply to a never-ending and particularly stressful boyhood. It may be the nightmare of a thirteen-year-old, but this startling definition of adult masculinity is the most explicit one the film offers. Coming where it does, it invites renewed attention to the film's oblique critique of conventional gender roles and relations.

If *Small Faces* focuses on traditionally masculine chronotopes such as the indoor-outdoor threshold and the gang battleground, it does so in order to challenge the sexist elements of Glaswegian working-class culture. Admittedly, Lorna, for all her fortitude, is rarely seen outside the MacLean home, while Joanne, as Gorbals suggests, apparently helps to exacerbate gang rivalries. However, on closer inspection, Joanne's conduct looks less like irresponsible sexual promiscuity than like a strategy for maintaining her autonomy. Critic Colin McArthur observes that in conventional representations of the Hard Man, "Mothers or lovers" of this figure "are allowed no space for their own sense of what it means to be a woman in Glasgow" (1997, 20). Joanne moves around the city more easily than any other character in the film, creating space for herself by negotiating relations with males on her own terms. She sees through the Hard Man personae of the gang leaders: she mentions that Malky "still cries himself to sleep at night" and that Sloan looks "like a wee boy" (not even a wee man) while skating. She initiates her relationship with Alan, intercepting him on his (archetypically boyish) paper route and upbraiding him flirtatiously on his delivery technique ("Hey! Can't you just push it in properly?"). Fittingly, it is she who eventually escorts Lex home after his adventures. In fact, despite her youth, Joanne is the most successfully grown-up figure in the film, and her presence, combined with the film's debunking of masculinity, suggests that with a new generation may come lasting changes to relations between gender and space in Glasgow.

Yet if *Small Faces* can be seen as cautiously optimistic about prospects for wee men, and for young women like Joanne, the fact that the film looks retrospectively at Glasgow complicates everything about its ending. The final sentence of Lex's voiceover reports the end of his nightmare of masculinity: "Luckily, when I woke up I was still a boy." The accompanying final shot finds him by a sunny window, painting in the bedroom that is now his alone. He has apparently attained an ideal spatial balance: he is safe, yet he has room of his own. But this idyllic scene—and its suggestion that Lex may follow Alan into a successful life of the imagination—is immediately undercut by the song that plays throughout the end credits, Zager and Evans's 1969 hit "In the Year 2525," and its solemn vision of a series of dystopian future possibilities ("In the year 2525, / If man is still alive, / If woman can survive, / They may find . . ."). Moreover, while the film's focus on the 1960s, "an optimistic period," as Billy MacKinnon notes (1996), could in itself be seen as nostalgic, since the decades since have seen worse social problems in Scotland than gangs, still the treatment of Tongland has hinted strongly at the drawbacks of the city's upward growth. Lex's future is particularly uncertain, since he will be an adult in the 1970s and 1980s, when class and regional inequities in Britain will be exacerbated.

Here again the film illustrates how chronotopes relate not just to genre but also to contexts of production and consumption. Powrie discusses *Small Faces* as an example of a specific type of heritage film, "The rite of passage film set in the past," which engages "through the eyes of a single child protagonist" with "difficult moments in the national past which indicate contemporary fears" (2000, 316). Powrie argues that such films "act as an allegorical mapping of the imagined re-membering of the national body politic traumatised over time into geographical fragmentation" (324), and ultimately undermine the idea that either an individual or a nation can attain a stable identity (326). We would stress, however, the ways in which the film's uncertain ending invites viewers to consider the possibilities for the future that Scotland faces in the 1990s. Although it was made with Scotland on the threshold of a new era of increasing autonomy (most tangibly in politics, with the devolution of powers from London that followed the election of 1997), the film notably avoids making the progress of its wee protagonist stand too obviously for that of his small country. In the end, it is the combination of vivid genre details and nuanced ambiguities in Small Faces that makes it a particularly notable example of the cinema of boyhood.

NOTES

1. *Les Quatre cents coups* offers a benchmark for the cinematic treatment of coming of age in terms of a search for both literal and metaphorical space. Even more dramatically than Lex, Antoine Doinel moves from crowded conditions at home to daunting freedom outside. (See as well chapter 11 in this volume. —eds.)
2. Roughly contemporaneous with *Small Faces* are two particularly vivid African American takes on the exacerbation of interracial and intergenerational tensions by dysfunctional architecture. Spike Lee's *Clockers* (1996) sets its story of amoral drug gangs and contemptuously complacent police (and eventual challenge to these attitudes) in a decaying Brooklyn high-rise project. "Scene of the Crime," a 1996 episode of the television police drama "Homicide: Life on the Street," is set and shot in the slab blocks of Baltimore's Highland Terrace housing project, which it depicts as—like the project in *Clockers* and Tongland in *Small Faces*—a place in which whole communities of people have effectively been abandoned to fend for themselves, and in which gang activity is to some extent a logical response to surroundings. Parallel problems with housing projects are all the more noteworthy given the fairly obvious historical differences between Scotland and the United States.
3. The vigorous but nuanced activity of chronotopic and generic motifs in *Small Faces* contrasts notably with their almost ostentatious absence in another notable Scottish film about boyhood, Lynne Ramsay's *Ratcatcher* (1999). Like *Small Faces*, *Ratcatcher* revolves around a working-class Glaswegian boy entering adolescence in the era of large-scale urban redevelopment (in this case the early 1970s). Like Lex, Ramsay's protagonist James Gillespie is menaced by older, gang-affiliated boys; the gang in *Ratcatcher*, however, lacks any sense of organization, purpose, or charisma: its members, though even more brutal than The Glen or the Tongs, are aimless and impulsive,

and in appearance and speech they are virtually interchangeable. Like Lex, James is driven to wander the city. However, James has little of Lex's wit or artfulness; like almost all the film's characters he is notably inarticulate, and his lack of inner as well as outer resources seems, by the end, to have doomed him. In the absence of genre motifs, the film's emphasis is on its own visual artfulness, particularly in the ambiguous final sequence in which James appears to drown himself in the canal behind his family's tenement home, yet also to envision his family's longed-for move to a spacious new house on the edge of the city.

WORKS CITED

Bakhtin, Mikhail M. 1981. "Forms of Time and of the Chronotope in the Novel." In *The Dialogic Imagination: Four Essays*, ed. Michael Holquist, 84–258. Trans. Caryl Emerson and Michael Holquist. Austin: University of Texas Press.

Campbell, Beatrix. 1993. "The "Queenies That Betrayed the Gorbals." *The Independent*, September 15, 24.

Crawford, Robert. 1993. "Scotland." In *The New Poetry*, ed. Michael Hulse et al., 278. Newcastle: Bloodaxe.

Glendinning, Miles, and Stefan Muthesius. 1994. *Tower Block: Modern Public Housing in England, Scotland, Wales and Northern Ireland*. New Haven: Yale University Press.

Hall, Peter. 1988. *Cities of Tomorrow: An Intellectual History of Urban Planning and Design in the Twentieth Century*. Oxford: Blackwell.

Lefebvre, Martin. 1998. "A Sense of Time and Place: The Chronotope in *I Confess* and *Le Confessionnal*." *Québec Studies* 26 (Fall/Winter), 88–98.

MacKinnon, Gillies, and Billy MacKinnon. 1996. Interview. Kamera.co.uk. Online at http://www.kamera.co.uk/interviews/mackinno.html. Accessed October 4, 2001.

McArthur, Colin. 1997. "Chinese Boxes and Russian Dolls: Tracking the Elusive Cinematic City." In *The Cinematic City*, ed. David B. Clarke, 19–45. London: Routledge.

O'Hagan, Andrew. 1995. "Gangs in the Hood." *Sight and Sound* (July), 8–11.

Pacione, Michael. 1995. *Glasgow: The Socio-Spatial Development of the City*. Chichester: John Wiley.

Petrie, Duncan. 2000. *Screening Scotland*. London: BFI.

Powrie, Phil. 2000. "On the Threshold between Past and Present: 'Alternative Heritage.'" In *British Cinema, Past and Present*, ed. Justine Ashby and Andrew Higson, 316–26. London: Routledge.

Reed, Peter. 1999. *Glasgow: The Forming of the City*. Edinburgh: Edinburgh

University Press.

Shulgasser, Barbara. 1996. Review of *Small Faces*. *San Francisco Examiner,*
September 20. Online at http://www.sfgate.com/cgibin/article.cgi?f=-
/e/a/1996/09/20/WEEKEND11506.dtl. Accessed June 10, 2002.

Torrington, Jeff. 1992. *Swing Hammer Swing!* London: Secker and
Warburg.

10

THE BOYS' PRICE IN MARTINIQUE
Visions of the Bildungsroman in *Sugar Cane Alley*

Tarshia L. Stanley

It has been the literary definition of the *bildungsroman* to articulate the coming of age of the male child, a process necessarily fraught with exodus and death as the child is divested of the things and people that connected him to his youth. This essay examines Euzhan Palcy's translation of the literary into the visionary bildungsroman in her film *Rue cases nègres (Sugar Cane Alley)* (1983).[1] The film is effectual and compelling because she taps into universal allegories about boyhood by way of a uniquely postcolonial prism.[2] Through the eyes and in the voice of Jose, the narrative speaks to the ways in which boys surreptitiously become men in a society that would deny them the opportunity. Coming of age is difficult for any boy, but it is particularly so for one who must fashion his definition of manhood from the social, cultural, and economic wreckage of colonialism.

Since its initial screening *Sugar Cane Alley* continues to be the emissary of Caribbean cinema (Cham 1992, 6), with studies of authentic Caribbean cinema still centering on it nearly two decades after its premiere. This is due in part to the limited number of films emanating from the Caribbean, but is also attributable to the reception of the film itself (Warner 1995, 266). It is a film with which a wide variety of audiences identify because it invokes specific psychic archetypes about growing up. In it we find the kind of story Jung says every society tells itself to understand and survive its psychosocial structuring (Shelburne 1988, 50). We watch Jose as he excels in school despite abject poverty. We are charmed by the quintessential struggle of good vs. evil, right vs. wrong, and the individual against the establishment. Palcy manages to tap into a primordial theme common across time and cultures. Jose becomes David and the postcolonial society against which he struggles is Goliath; he is Beowulf and the cane field is Grindel. He is the black American child in the era of the Civil Rights Movement who has been nursed on King's dreams and suckled by the blood of the countless men and women who struggled in their own cane, tobacco, and cotton fields so that their collective "child" could have a better life.

Indeed even the history of Martinique itself is laden with the desire of her people to overcome. In 1848 several factors contributed to the slaves rebelling against the masters and demanding their freedom. Slavery had been abolished in the English-held islands in 1833, and the same abolitionist fervor that was sweeping America was prevalent in Martinique. In addition, there were almost ten times as many slaves on the islands as there were white owners. When the slaves in Martinique revolted, France had little choice but to abolish slavery. Yet, as is evidenced in the stories the young protagonist hears of his peoples' history, while the slaves were officially set free their living conditions and their political and economic status remained largely the same (Watts 1998–2000).

Sugar Cane Alley continues to be popular among Western audiences precisely because it recounts the parable of picking oneself up by one's bootstraps. In the film the assurance is reiterated that intellect, self-determination, education, and a sacrificial parent are what one needs to "beat the system." Yet, there is much more to *Sugar Cane Alley* than the assurance that postcolonialism can work if you work at it. At the crux of the film is the story of what it means to come of age in the wake of colonialism. While the Horatio Alger myth is alive and well at the film's surface, when we look carefully we can see another story about coming of age and this one may be more nightmare than fairy tale.

In *Ten Is the Age of Darkness: The Black Bildungsroman* Geta LeSeur scripts the formula for the European bildungsroman and illuminates the way in which writers of the African diaspora have adapted the form to fit their literary needs. According to LeSeur the black bildungsroman uses the same foundation as the original: "The European bildungsroman in the 19th and 20th centuries concerned itself with the development of a single male protagonist whose growth to maturity was the result of both formal and informal education, the latter acquired largely through his relationship with various women" (1995, 30).

She goes on to emphasize the leave-taking, the journey upon which the young man must embark in order to meet his destiny and acquire his identity (LeSeur 1995, 199). In addition to these foundational elements of the European delineation of the bildungsroman, LeSeur sees the black writer, and in particular the Caribbean male writer, as immersed in the notion of community and engaged in writing the way in which this literal and figurative journeying into destiny, identity, and individuality will necessitate a break with one's community which is often synonymous with exile (38).

Since Palcy's film is not only an adaptation but also an homage to fellow Martinican Joseph Zobel's novel *La Rue cases-nègres,* it is feasible to appropriate LeSeur's literary theory of the black bildungsroman in an analysis of the film.[3] Palcy herself elucidates the synergy between her vision of the film and Zobel's book: "It is because there is a meeting between the book and the filmmaker. When the novel is saying exactly what I would say and conveys the same feelings as I would, there is no point in one trying to write something different, because I found someone who can be my voice" (in Cham 1992, 298). Whether Zobel is Palcy's voice or Palcy is Zobel's, *Sugar Cane Alley* remains an assemblage between the two. Palcy elucidates Zobel's vision, bringing *Rue cases nègres* to life. Although Zobel's novel was first published in 1950 it was not widely available in Martinique and was not translated into English until 1980 (Warner 1997, xiii). Thus, much of the indigenous and indeed international reception of *Sugar Cane Alley* is a first reaction. Many people's initial encounter with the Zobel story is as Euzhan Palcy's film. Specifically the people of Martinique saw it as their own cinéma vérité. It was said to be the first time they saw themselves, and not narratives about themselves, on-screen (Menil 1992, 156).

Even the opening shots in the film are symbolic of Palcy's desire to show the people of Martinique their story. We see old sepia-tinted postcards and pictures as scenes of life in Martinique circa 1930 flash across the screen. There are intermittent images of blacks standing in front of dilapidated lean-tos with stalks of sugar cane framing them. Amidst the vignettes are scenes of streets and schools in Fort-de-France predicting the journey the protagonist will have to make. As the pictures fade from sight we hear a voiceover, Jose Hassam (Garry Cadenat), in his roles of interpreter and griot, participant and witness to life in the cane fields. Jose's importance and presence as the center of the narrative are quickly established as his grandmother, M'man Tine (Darling Légitimus), warns him to stay clean and out of trouble as the adults of Black Shack Alley head off to their daily labor in the cane.

As the cornerstone of the bildungsroman, education is of crucial importance in *Sugar Cane Alley*. In the formal sense, Jose is educated at the local school and does so well he is allowed to sit for examinations that will enable his admission to the upper school in Fort-de-France. Yet, Jose is being taught much more than grammar. Written on the board of the schoolroom is the mantra of postcolonial education, "Learning is the key that opens the second door to our freedom." The import is not lost on Jose who embraces scholarship and sees it as the way to get himself and M'man Tine out of Black Shack Alley. Herein lies one of the ways in which the black bildungsroman differs from the classical white tradition. In the archetypal bildungsroman the protagonist must obtain a key and unlock a door, usually the one marked "membership in affluent, white, patriarchy" to gain access to manhood. Black boys not only have a different set of keys to a different kind of door, but they also have another door a priori. Although it may seem that the first door, marked resistance or "post" (as in postcolonial) has been opened already, Jose's informal education will dictate otherwise. While Monsieur Roc (Henri Melon) makes Jose and his friends write every day that learning will open the second door to their freedom, the purveyor of Jose's informal education, Monsieur Medouze (Douta Seck), tells him that the first door has never really been opened.

Madeleine Cottenet-Hage and Kevin Meehan assert that the formal education of the ex-colonized is a snare that yields ambivalent results, for in "acquiring certain forms of knowledge . . . [one] risks appropriating the myths of a society in which discourses of equality and brotherhood are contradicted by the reality of social institutions and prejudices" (1992, 76). While Jose is defining the difference between singing and cackling, the nature of his education does not encourage him to question the system under which he lives. He is not encouraged to inquire as to the equity in having any doors to one's freedom at all. Even when Jose does decide to testify in the form of a school essay about the injustice he has seen in the cane fields his work is dismissed as plagiarism, not because the story is so awful it must be fiction, but because the teacher in Fort-de-France does not believe Jose could master metaphor in that way. In the end, when the schoolmaster corroborates that Jose's experience was real, there is no more discussion of the matter. Jose is given a scholarship immediately afterward as a kind of hush money designed to stop him from contemplating the matter further. We see no more reflection on the cruel death of Medouze or the life awaiting the "petites bandes," children who go to work in the fields. Instead in the next scene we see Jose counting the money from his new and improved scholarship assuring M'man Tine that she will no longer have to work so hard to provide for him.

The lack of further discourse on the plagiarism charges leveled at Jose or on the content of his essay bespeaks the insidiousness of postcolonial formal education. It suggests that traveling the educational route marked by the ex-colonial is the way out of the fields, therefore out of poverty. Yet this same course often requires the journeyman to appropriate a way of thinking that renders his own culture and domestic education inferior. In effect he must disassociate himself from what he has seen. In the solution set forth by the "lycée," the protagonist is required to separate himself or forget himself in order to live a life beyond the cane fields. He is encouraged to see the suffering of his people through the eyes of a reporter or a recorder, an observer who is not at all, or no longer, directly affected. He is persuaded to see the failure of the masses to flourish under the colonizers' structure as their own failure and not as the intention of a system inequitable at its core.

"Le Deuxième Porte" to Manhood

Jose's formal education is paramount to his understanding of what it means to come of age, to be a man, in that society. If the definition of manhood in patriarchal societies is inextricably linked to power and privilege and therefore whiteness, then the "manhood" possible for Jose will be something altogether different.[4] In Jose's society those in control are the white male landholders and government officials. They are directly descended from the French colonialist and are known as the "béké" in the Creole language. If he can never hope to occupy the same spaces and be accorded the same definition of manhood as these béké, then he is left with what they tell him through education and show him as "manhood" through their treatment of blacks. The black teacher in Petit Bourg, Monsieur Roc, preaches the gospel of life beyond the cane fields via an education at the lycée in Fort-de-France. All roads out of the cane field for Jose and those like him lead to respectable professions like teacher and government worker. However decent these occupations may be, they are ones in which occupants still have no real access to power. They still have no ability to change the prevailing system from the inside. The official education proclaims that manhood for the blacks is not having to work in the cane field, while manhood for whites is owning the field, the store, and the societal structure itself.

We witness this limited definition of manhood as the workers of Black Shack Alley are "paid" for their labor. Ti Coco St. Louis is docked because the bosses saw him relieving himself in the field. He grudgingly accepts his fate but it is his wife, so far into her pregnancy that she must tie a scarf around her waist to support her bulging stomach, who protests. She begins to scream and shout about the injustice of the wage system but the bosses dismiss her with sarcasm and derision. The béké spews at her, "Anastasie bigbelly!" while her husband drags her away and admonishes her to save her breath. Julien "Twelve-Toes," too, curses and swears against the low wages, but he does not direct his anger at the ones responsible. Rather, he violently beats part of a porch with his machete and decries why he has not died already. Old man Medouze accepts his money silently, throwing only an acerbic look at the bosses as he hobbles away. Thus Jose learns important lessons about being a man in Black Shack Alley. A black man is unable to adequately provide for his family, he is unable to adequately protest, he has no outlet for his anger, and he is effectively silenced. In essence, Jose learns that the men who work in the field are impotent when compared with the béké—and in some cases even when compared with the women. These lessons are indeed a part of Jose's formal education though they occur outside of the schoolroom.

In juxtaposition to the men of Black Shack Alley stands Jose's schoolteacher in Petit Bourg. How could Jose not admire Stephen Roc? He is dressed nicely when the men of the fields are in little more than rags, he speaks French while the men of Jose's home speak Creole. Jose never sees him disrespected or humiliated by the béké because he is in effect a purveyor of postcoloniality. It is Monsieur Roc who shows Jose a concrete way of ascending in the fields. Of the many examples available to him, it seems only natural that Jose would gravitate to the model set forth by Roc.

However, Jose's relationship with Medouze complicates his transition into the postcolonial form of black manhood modeled by Monsieur Roc. Medouze is Jose's link with the past and a major proponent of his cultural education. In a ritualization of the "titim" (riddle), Medouze quizzes, cross-examines, and lectures Jose in the

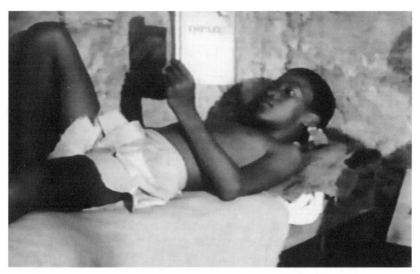

Jose (Garry Cadenat) studying his way out of postcolonialism.

manner of a schoolmaster. It is Medouze who tells Jose of the history of black people in Martinique; we do not see him learn this at school. The old man functions as the man must in the bildungsroman, providing Jose with his culture and history. Medouze names him by telling him who he was meant to be. His tales of Africa and her children in Martinique, their rebellion and ultimate defeat, are told so that Jose can remember. Medouze and Jose sit before the cooking pot, the flames bouncing off their faces. Medouze is old and gray, sweat leaking from his skin, and Jose is the younger version. Jose still has promise and a future. The old man tells him the story of the slave rebellions in Martinique. According to Medouze's father, "I ran so much. I ran all around Martinique. When my feet refused to go on, I looked ahead and behind. I saw I was in Black Shack Alley again. It was back to the cane fields. We were free but our bellies were empty. The Master had become the boss". Medouze knows that there are not really any open doors because the "post" in postcolonial society has not manifested itself: colonialism isn't over. Medouze continues, "The law forbids their beating us, but it does not pay us a decent wage." Slavery has not ended in Martinique but merely changed forms. Much like the sharecropping system in the post–Civil War south, blacks in Martinique quit one slave master only to find themselves at the mercy of another.

Yet Medouze's lesson is not that Jose should reject his formal education, but that he should not reject his informal one. All of their lessons take place outside against the backdrop of the landscape. Whether it is at a cooking fire in the village or a clearing in the forest, Medouze is teaching Jose that he is connected to the land and its people. When Medouze declares that fire and water do not negate each other but are the "elements of creation," he is indicating the kind of amalgamation that will have to go on between Jose's two forms of education because he is inextricably a hybrid. Medouze has charged Jose with recollecting the real story of Martinique and creating his own definition of manhood outside of the one dictated to him by the postcolonial system. Understanding this will make him a more complete man than he would be with only the béké's definition. Medouze can see that Jose is fashioned by, and evidence of, a society in which he will experience W. E. B. Du Bois's infamous two-ness. For Cottenet-Hage and Meehan the character of Jose embodies the hope of integration, "the figure for a new generation of Caribbeans, rooted in an indigenous history and freed by their capacity to control and synthesize diverse forms of knowledge" (1992, 88). However Jose's so-called freedom is questionable if at every moment that he utilizes it (for example, in his writing of the essay) he is effectively silenced.

Jose's struggle to become a young man against the backdrop of the cane fields is heavily structured by his formal education and his grandmother is integral to that structuring. M'man Tine has made it clear to any one who will listen that her Jose will not work in the fields. He will use his intellectual abilities to lift himself beyond the life of abject poverty in which they live. Of course she can make sure that Jose achieves this only at great expense to herself, and in this film, as in much of Caribbean literature and film, it is an acceptable and indeed an expected sacrifice.

M'man Tine is the quintessential black mother character. She is the epithet of self-sacrifice and tough love. Indeed, in his foreword to Zobel's novel Christian Filostrat, a Martinican, writes, "We all had a M'man Tine" (1997, vii). Images of the mother in Caribbean literature and film are often of this self-effacing superwoman who lives for and through her children (Liddell 1994, 321). While she is in many ways what Cherene Sherrard calls the "colonizing mother," M'man Tine is more than the specter of colonialism birthing new mental slaves into a postcolonial society. Sherrard writes that mothers often perpetuate the precepts of colonialism in their childrearing practices as a way of protecting their children. I would add that mothers often advance colonial premises as a way of elevating their children as well (1999, 126). M'man Tine's major concern is making sure Jose does not work himself to death for the béké's benefit in the cane fields. Although she does suckle Jose on the importance of education, M'man Tine in and of herself is the force that sculpts Jose. She is his disciplinarian, motivator, and only family. While the influence of the community and particularly of Medouze as surrogate father are apparent in Jose's upbringing, his grandmother is by far the most influential force. The old woman saves scraps of newspapers and has Jose read them to her while she makes his dinner. M'man Tine moves to Petit Bourg so that she can make Jose's lunch during the school year. She is so confident that he will pass his exams she has a suit made for him in advance. When he earns only a partial scholarship to secondary school, she travels to Fort-de-France and takes up residence in an abandoned boxcar so that Jose will have every opportunity. Her devotion to her grandson never ceases. Jose watches his grandmother's wisdom and charity cut short by the grueling work she endures in the fields, and he learns his lesson.

No mention is made of Jose's father and we learn that his mother is dead. Although the mother (Delia) exists in Zobel's novel, Palcy effectively melds the mother and grandmother into one character. After all, their functions are virtually the same, they are both of specific narrative importance because they aid in the development of the protagonist. It is precisely this sacrifice that enables and motivates Jose's success. We see M'man Tine refuse to let Jose work in the fields even when, after the fire the children set, the békés require the children to go to work with their parents. While the others mock M'man Tine and Jose, she does not veer from the course. M'man Tine says, "I won't let you end up in the cane fields. Like all blacks without pride who throw their kids into the same misery!" She is even resigned when Anastasie's baby is stillborn and sees it as one less child born to suffer in the fields.

Although M'man Tine and Medouze are the overwhelming sources of Jose's education, he does have other influences. Palcy chooses to introduce the mulatto character Leopold (Laurent Saint Cyr). If the definition of "manhood" seems to be synonymous with "white manhood" then the mulatto men occupy as precarious a space as the black men. Leopold is further evidence that Jose must fashion his own definition of what it means to be a man beyond the limitations set for him by the fields or by the system. As the child of a mulatto woman and a béké father, Leopold is instructed not to associate with the black boys with whom he attends school. It is clear that Leopold is trapped between the two worlds and sees the inconsistencies of his place in the colonial scheme of things, and that this conundrum is representative of many of the people in his position. There is a scene in which Leopold's mother scolds him for playing with "those black boys" despite his father's wishes. By referring to "those black boys," the mother is refusing to acknowledge her own heritage and the father is denying that his own son is in some part black. This is until Leopold's father is fatally wounded. Leopold's mother pleads with him to give Leopold not just his property but also his name. The father refuses and tells her that de Thorail is a white man's name and as such too good for Leopold, even if he is his son. In the end, de Thorail is unwilling to really ignore or incorporate Leopold's black heritage. He sees Leopold as impure. Postcolonialism continues to construct definitions of manhood even for the mulatto. If the black man's only chance at manhood, even in its scripted and limited form, is life away from the fields, then the mulatto can only hope to reside one tier above the black man. The black man may be able to obtain a good job. The mulatto may have a good job and land. Neither of them will ever be allowed legitimacy. De Thorail's refusal to name his son, his refusal to acknowledge Leopold as the heir to his name, articulates the hierarchical constitution/constriction of the post-colonial structure.

What separates Jose's hybridity from Leopold's is that Jose has been taught his history. As the mulatto child whose father will not name him white and whose mother will not name him black, Leopold lacks Jose's connection to ancestry, collective memory, and purpose. There is a lesson for Jose in Leopold's life. While in Fort-de-France, Jose meets a young black woman who after being robbed by a black man shrieks, "I hate my race." Jose reprimands her for the remark, and she explains how she is not really black. She says, "Except for my color, I'm not black. My character is white," and proceeds to explain to Jose that she needs to marry white so that her children will be light skinned. Jose is confronted with a mindset of self-hatred and self-effacement. Rather than probe a system that would encourage her to hate her own skin color the young woman seems wholeheartedly colonized. The look on Jose's face is one of incredulity and disappointment. Even at his young age Jose's informal education has taught him better than self-loathing. As he looks at the young woman behind the bars of a ticket counter he understands that she is trapped both physically and mentally. He comprehends that the answer to the system in which they live is not to become white. He recognizes that blacks are not white people who failed at being white, but are a viable people who've been disadvantaged. He understands that he must define himself and that his self-definition must go beyond a reaction to postcolonialism.

Carmen (Joël Palcy) is the boy/man whose life ambition is to become an actor and who is bereft of the wisdom of survival and success in postcolonial society that M'man Tine imparts to Jose. Of all the characters Palcy recreated for the screen, Carmen is the one who is most her creation. Carmen has gotten Jose to teach him to read and write because he thinks it will help him get to Hollywood. The irony of Palcy's statement is not lost on the audience. It is a long way from Martinique to Hollywood, and an even longer way from black boatman and houseboy to film star. Carmen is obviously influenced by the movies that have been imported to Martinique. He has begun to identify with the leading men who are all white. Not Medouze and Monsieur Roc but the movies have been Carmen's schoolmaster. In between the frames he sees a vision of manhood beyond that of fieldworker or domestic servant, even beyond that of son of the béké. He wants to become the béké himself.

Even if such a life were probable Carmen himself makes it impossible for the viewer to imagine it for him. In one scene, as he reenacts his seduction by his white employer, Jose loses all respect for Carmen. Having come to Carmen for consolation (after his teacher accuses him of cheating) Jose finds little encouragement but instead Carmen pretending to be master of the manor while the real owners are away. He describes his relationship with the mistress as if he is in control. Rather than recognizing that he is being prostituted in yet another way, Carmen thinks that he is irresistible. After all, as Jose mentions, even his very name means "charm." It is precisely this charm of Carmen's that will be his undoing. The viewing audience sits with a mixture of apprehension and antipathy as Carmen dons the white woman's robe and lies across her bed. Carmen looks and sounds foolish as he mimics the woman calling his name. The camera cuts to a black-and-white picture of the woman, a headshot reminiscent of Hollywood starlets. She is in effect the leading lady to Carmen's pretense of leading man. Because this woman has deemed him worthy to be used, Carmen feels as if he has the béké stamp of approval. Like the young woman who hates her race Carmen hates himself and no longer sees himself but instead sees a caricature onscreen. He is so caught up in the fantasy in his mistress's bedroom that it is impossible not to wonder if Carmen sees himself as white when he imagines himself as a screen actor.

As one watches the scene it is impossible not to recall Toni Morrison's Pauline from *The Bluest Eye*. Pauline is the black maid who sits in a movie theater and imagines that she is the white woman with the handsome husband and the perfect life she can see onscreen. What devastates the character is her ability to distinguish fact from fiction and prefer the latter. Morrison writes, "Then the screen would light up, and I'd move right on in them pictures. White men taking such good care of they women, and they all dressed up in big clean houses with the bathtubs right in the same room with the toilet. Them pictures gave me a lot of pleasure, but it made coming home hard, and looking at Cholly hard" (1970, 97). When she goes home to her problematic household and her black husband, and even her own black reflection in the mirror, she begins to reject what is real in favor of what is fantasy. Pauline abandons her family emotionally and spiritually and opts to spend more and more time with the white family for which she works because she had rather participate in whiteness vicariously than live out blackness in its often-painful authenticity. The same seems to be true of Carmen as he opts for the fantastic in lieu of the reality of domestic service.

Although it is Jose's story, Leopold and Carmen are part of the narrative about boyhood in *Sugar Cane Alley*. In seeking to show the people of Martinique their story, Palcy excavates some important theories of manhood in postcolonial society. *Sugar Cane Alley* is a bildungsroman, a coming-of-age story that critiques the way in which black males are encouraged and allowed to develop into men. In *Sugar Cane Alley*, to be a man means to be a white man, which is synonymous with legitimacy and power. Manhood for black males is limited. Black men either work themselves into early graves on the békés' land and in their houses or a very few acquire an education as a way out. However, while it is a way out of the fields or from behind the wheels of béké limousines it is not necessarily a way into the places where one would own the land or command the limousine. Yet, in Jose lies the potential for another definition of what it means to be a black man. It is one infused with pride in one's culture and the affectations of the postcolonial education. It is one where to emerge as a man from the cane fields is not dependent on definitions by the system but is the result of a collective effort and sacrifice on the part of some kind of family, and on behalf of some segment of the community. Black boys can make the transition into men whether they work in the fields or in a government office, but they will have to move beyond emulation of, or dictation by, the béké for their new and vital definitions of manhood.

NOTES

1. The bildungsroman is a novel that chronicles the coming of age of an adolescent, in particular a male child. The form is based on Goethe's *Wilhelm Meisters Lehrjahre,* an apprenticeship novel published in 1795. "Apprenticeship novel" is the translation of bildungsroman.
2. Postcolonialism is a contentious term and many scholars have addressed the fallacies inherent in its use. However I find it the most appropriate expression, particularly for a critique of a film portraying 1930s Martinique.
3. I also make use of Gloria J. Gibson-Hudson (1991) as way of translating literary criticism to film studies.
4. I do not intend to project a definition of "manhood as white male patriarchy" as correct or even desirable. It is, however, the most "powerful" manhood, in terms of privilege and access, available to Jose.

WORKS CITED

Cham, Mbye, ed. 1992. *Ex-Iles: Essays on Caribbean Cinema.* Trenton, NJ: Africa World Press.

Cottenet-Hage, Madeleine, and Kevin Meehan. 1992. "Our Ancestors the Gauls: Schools and Schooling in Two Caribbean Novels." *Callaloo* 15, no. 1, 75–89.

Filostrat, Christian. 1997. "We All Had a M'man Tine." Foreword to *Black Shack Alley,* by Joseph Zobel, vii–xii. Boulder, CO: Lynne Rienner.

Gibson-Hudson, Gloria J. 1991. "African American Literary Criticism as a Model for the Analysis of Films by African American Women." *Wide Angle* 13, no. 3–4, 44–54.

Givanni, June. 1992. "Interview with Euzhan Palcy." In *Ex-Iles: Essays on Caribbean Cinema*, ed. Mbye Cham, 1–43. Trenton, NJ: Africa World Press.

LeSeur, Geta. 1995. *Ten Is the Age of Darkness: The Black Bildungsroman.* Columbia: University of Missouri Press.

Liddell, Janice Lee. 1994. "The Narrow Enclosure of Motherdom/ Martydom: A Study of Gatha Randall Barton in Sylvia Wynter's *The Hills of Hebron.*" In *Out of the Kumbla*, ed. Carole Boyce Davies and Elaine Savory Fido, 321–30. Trenton, NJ: Africa World Press.

Menil, Alain. 1992. "*Rue cases-nègres* or the Antilles from the Inside." In *Ex-Iles: Essays on Caribbean Cinema*, ed. Mbye Cham, 155–75. Trenton, NJ: Africa World Press.

Morrison, Toni. 1970. *The Bluest Eye.* New York: Washington Square Press.

Shelburne, Walter A. 1988. *Mythos and Logos in the Thought of Carl Jung: The Theory of the Collective Unconscious in Scientific Perspective.* Albany: State University of New York Press.

Sherrard, Cherene. 1999. "The 'Colonizing' Mother Figure in Paule Marshall's Brown Girl, Brownstones and Jamaica Kincaid's *The Autobiography of My Mother.*" *MaComère* 2, 125–33.

Warner. Keith. 1997. Introduction. In *Black Shack Alley*, by Joseph Zobel, xiii–xxiii. Boulder, CO: Lynne Rienner.

———. 1995. "On Adapting a West Indian Classic to the Cinema: The Implications of Success." In *Cinemas of the Black Diaspora*, ed. Michael T. Martin, 266–73. Detroit: Wayne State University Press.

Watts, Richard. 1998–2000. "Martinique." In *Microsoft Encarta Africana.* Microsoft Corporation. 3rd ed. CD-ROM.

11

PORTRAIT OF THE ARTIST AS A YOUNG BOY

François Truffaut, Antoine Doinel, and the Wild Child

Patrick E. White

To speak about the autobiographical nature of much of François Truffaut's work has long been a critical commonplace. Certainly the series of films focusing on the character of Antoine Doinel, played by Jean-Pierre Léaud beginning with *Les Quatre cents coups (The 400 Blows)* (1959) and continuing as Léaud aged with *Antoine et Colette*, an episode in *L'Amour à vingt ans (Love at Twenty)* (1962), *Baisers volés (Stolen Kisses)* (1968), *Domicile conjugal (Bed and Board)* (1970), and concluding with *L'Amour en fuite (Love on the Run)* (1979), constitutes one of the most sustained autobiographical sequences in film. Truffaut acknowledges that much in *The 400 Blows* reflects his own childhood in details of setting, character, and action. He notes for example that he lived with his parents in a cramped apartment where he slept in the entryway, that his mother was often furious with him, his father was a kinder more jocular pal, and that if he happened to break a plate he would drop the pieces in the sewer rather than admit to his parents what had happened—all elements of character and action that are replicated in detail in *The 400 Blows*.[1] In Truffaut's various recollections of his childhood he remembers himself as a lonely, inquisitive, rebellious boy, one not afraid to lie, who finds solace in reading and film, but not in school-work, who comes to at least a momentary bad end, consigned by his parents to a juvenile detention center (1987, 11–12, 16–17).

The physical similarity between Léaud and Truffaut is much commented on by critics and enjoyed by Truffaut himself. Even before he grew into the thin, sharp-featured echo of the director in *Bed and Board* and other films, Jean-Pierre Léaud was seen as a young Truffaut and even mistaken for his son (Truffaut 1971, 7). At the same time, Truffaut has said that the central impulse of *The 400 Blows* is not fidelity to his own life (1987, 59). Truffaut's interest in boyhood and youth goes beyond the autobiographical. Although the number of his films where children dominate is relatively few—his first short film, *Les Mistons* (1957 [almost always noted in French, translated variously as *The Mischief Makers* or *The Brats*]), *The 400 Blows, L'Enfant sauvage (The Wild Child)* (1969), and *L'Argent de poche (Small Change)* (1976)—the world of boyhood seems Truffaut's natural milieu, the place of his heart.

Looking at Truffaut in the context of other writing about boyhood in film encourages me to shift the discussion from an analysis of his work as autobiography to an exploration of how Truffaut's films enrich our understanding of boyhood more generally. By placing the evidently autobiographical *The 400 Blows* next to *The Wild Child,* clearly historical and not autobiographical in any obvious way, we will be able to illuminate his vision of boyhood and the nature of his art and explore how the two are profoundly interrelated.

Truffaut's films are central to a study of boyhood in film because he probes the conventional view of boys as rowdy, undisciplined, and rebellious troublemakers. This convention is an old one in literature and film, finding expression in broad comedy such as Hal Roach's *Little Rascals* shorts in the 1930s, in fantasy rebellion in Jean Vigo's 1933 *Zéro de conduite (Zero for Conduct)*—a film Truffaut greatly admired—and in teen melodrama in Nicholas Ray's *Rebel Without a Cause* (1955), much praised by Eric Rohmer, Truffaut's fellow *Cahiers du cinéma* critic ([1956] 1985). Truffaut does not deny the partial truth of the convention. As his first short film *Les Mistons* shows, boys *are* brats, mischievous rule breakers, but the convention does not tell the whole story, for it is in that rebellious streak, that creative undiscipline, that the artist is born. From his own childhood, Truffaut sees something more, not only in exceptional boys, but also in all boys: in the rebel boy, in the apparent incompetent slacker, in the silly goof-off he sees something admirable and necessary, the boy as artist. His boys are admirable not because they are rebels and mischief-makers, but because out of the chaos and disorder of their boyhood comes invention, creativity, and artistry. In Truffaut's films he reimagines the conventions of boyhood. He sees the chaos, the trouble, the pain, and the rebellion, but reclaims the boy as artist.

THE 400 BLOWS

At school Antoine Doinel is an indifferent student and often in trouble. He plays hooky to hang out with his pal René (Patrick

Auffray) and go to the movies and the amusement park; he tricks his parents, forges excuse notes saying he is ill, and lies about where he has been. To get out of one scrape with a teacher when he has no excuse, he even says that his mother has died. When his parents appear at the school, his formerly kindhearted father slaps him. That evening Antoine runs away and, after trying to sleep in an old printing factory, wanders the city streets all night. After this incident his mother is momentarily kinder and even confiding, but when he steals a typewriter from his father's office, he is arrested and his parents have him sent to a reformatory, where only his mother visits. Antoine eventually escapes and runs away to the sea where the film ends.

The title of *The 400 Blows* comes from the French idiom "faire les quatre cents coups," "to raise hell" (Insdorf 1994, 173), a behavior that Truffaut particularly associates with the chaos and confusion of adolescence. Unsympathetic parents, tyrannical and insensitive school teachers, loyal chums, days spent playing hooky or running away, and a brush with the law are all familiar aspects of adolescent rebellion narratives in autobiography, fiction, and film. Antoine lies and steals, and he does not seem to worry about the effect his behavior has on anyone around him. The audience learns little of his motivation or of what he wants to become. This is not a tale of frustrated great expectations. Truffaut conveys, nonetheless, sympathy for the pain and loneliness Antoine feels, and that feeling is sharpened because it is hidden by toughness. Jean-Pierre Léaud's Antoine Doinel is not crying out for anyone's love, perhaps because he only vaguely discerns its possibility. His father's slap across the face is not resented as much as absorbed. His night in jail spent crowded out by prostitutes into an even smaller cell is not resisted. And the tear as he is taken away in the paddy wagon is significant because this is the first time we see any sorrow, any suggestion that the world should be different for Antoine. Low expectations may be at least one subtitle here. Antoine does not explain himself to mother, father, teachers, or police. In an important scene near the end of the film, he does partially reveal himself to the psychiatrist at the juvenile detention center, but even here he is sly and amused by the questions, a boy/man with a secret to keep.

Antoine Doinel's secret is both particular and general and says much about Truffaut's vision of boyhood. Antoine suffers a particular kind of youthful malaise; his is a portrait of an artist as a young boy. In the first scene in the film, the camera peers over

Antoine (Jean-Pierre Léaud) has his freedom curtailed in *The 400 Blows* (1959).

the shoulder of a schoolboy looking at a pinup nude. The picture is passed from boy to boy in the classroom until it comes to Antoine, who draws a mustache and beard on the pinup and is caught by the teacher. He is then told to stand behind the map as punishment. Other boys looked, other boys passed the picture, but Antoine is caught because he takes time to alter the picture, in short because he is an artist. The sketch is not sophisticated, but it does transform the pinup into a comic image, and is the first glance at the artist's desire to transform his world. When he is behind the map, Antoine accentuates the cause of his punishment by writing on the wall that he has been "unjustly punished by Little Quiz for a pinup that fell from heaven." This sense of injustice is nothing new in adolescent stories. But the sense of outrage becomes a kind of manifesto of artistic freedom and pride, flung against arbitrary repression of the artist's impulse. The first moments of the film thus offer a cue to see Antoine's story as a portrait of an artist.

Antoine, however, shows little awareness of himself as an artist. After school in the first scene in the apartment, Antoine makes the fire and wipes his hands on the curtains, a nice touch of habitual rebellion. He then goes to his parents' room and sits down at his mother's dressing table. He smells the perfume, tries her eyelash curler, and then leaves. This scene is shot from behind, and we see Antoine reflected in three different mirrors, the main in front, a small one to his left, and one on the door. All three give different incomplete visions of the boy, and Antoine reveals no special interest in probing his own image. When compared to the frontal self-analytic gaze of Ingmar Bergman's characters or Woody Allen's self-reflective narrators, Truffaut's gaze here resists the temptation to self-contemplation associated with the mirror and the artist's self-portrait.

The aspect of Antoine that most infuriates his parents and teachers is this lack of reflection, a seeming lack of self-understanding and maturity. But much that seems mere happenstance in the action of the film or unreflective impulse in Antoine's character can be understood as a portrait of the artist as a young boy, or more precisely a portrait of the boy as potential artist. Why, for example, does Truffaut show Antoine taking out the garbage in two sequences? These show the boy doing household chores, one of the few times he is a good kid; but, as Truffaut follows Antoine down the steps past each landing of the other apartments and allows us to hear with Antoine the conversations and echoed radio or television programs going on in the apartments of his neighbors, these reveal Antoine as pleased eavesdropper, a voyeur into the lives of others. This motif is reinforced when Antoine is sent to get the bread that he forgot and is left waiting in a queue with women who discuss their problems with their families. Antoine listens, takes no evident notice, and the scene ends without an obvious point. Similarly, from his cramped bed set up in the entryway of the apartment he hears his parents arguing when his mother comes home late. His mother has to climb over the supposedly sleeping boy. Even the ignored child is a nuisance, but he also becomes a listener, who becomes a memoirist, and a storyteller. When Antoine lies about his mother's death, he creates a story that serves his purpose for a while. His other lies and stories are made up for the delight of others and to get the youth off the hook. Antoine models the story-telling of all children, expeditious in its response to the moment ("Why don't you have your homework?") and carrying with it the more profoundly fictive impulse of the artist in making a story about the self that in effect creates the self.

Throughout *The 400 Blows*, Antoine's lies begin to form a pattern. In forging a signature, he takes on another personality; in telling lies to avoid punishment, he becomes a storyteller; and in becoming a plagiarist, he becomes a pseudo artist, but an artist nonetheless. Antoine, like Truffaut, a great reader, is enamored of Balzac. He places a picture of Balzac in a makeshift shrine in his apartment and lights a candle to him. That he forgets the candle and it starts a fire comically undercuts Antoine's dedication to literature but does not deny his attachment to the made world of the artist. The Balzac fire immediately precedes the one unmitigated happy scene with his parents. They go out to a movie to get out of the smoky apartment, and we see them laughing and enjoying the film and one another in the car on the way home. It is also telling that Antoine gets in trouble in school when he turns in an essay with text copied from Balzac. Another artist might turn this into a wronged youth story—it really is the kid's work! à la *Finding Forrester* (2000)—but Truffaut's understanding of the artist is richer. What Antoine does is a forgery, but in grounding the borrowing in real admiration of Balzac, Truffaut recognizes an authentic artistic impulse.

When Antoine and his pal René leave a movie theater and steal a picture of Monica Vitti, they are echoing the many times Truffaut and his friends stole film stills for their own pleasure and for resale, but it is one more example of the boy's inchoate desire to possess and create art. Truffaut repeats a similar scene in *La Nuit américaine (Day for Night)* (1973) and thus emphasizes that the theft of the film still is an attempt to appropriate the work of art and engage the milieu in which the young director wishes to work. The ultimate theft in the film, Antoine's taking a typewriter from his father's office, is grounded in Truffaut's past, but accentuates the emblematic nature of the theft: the snatching of the word machine is almost a Promethean act for the young writer/filmmaker. In fact, young Truffaut stole the machine from his father's office and sold it for 4,000 francs to support his film club (Baecque and Toubiana 1999, 37). In the film, the motivation behind the theft is not so noble, and Antoine is caught only when the deal with the fence goes sour and he is in the process of returning the machine. Committing a crime may not pay but trying to undo a crime is even worse.

In imitating and plagiarizing Balzac, stealing film images or the typewriter, Antoine is not a self-conscious artist. He makes no declaration that he wants to be an artist, and at times he is a very poor one. His lies are often transparent; his forgeries are never deft. When he does not know what to write in a faked excuse letter, he copies an old note from his friend René, but he is too faithful, and simply writes, "Please excuse René," then says *merde* and starts over. Similarly his plagiarism of Balzac is word for word. As an artist, Antoine is immature, still a boy. Truffaut does not bestow Antoine's acts with the retrospective purpose they came to take on in his own life nor do we see the passionate precocity with which young François as budding *cinemane*, film critic, and director pursued reading and filmgoing.

In this resistance to romanticizing his own development as an artist, Truffaut is not plying a false modesty here. Rather he reveals the vitality of a more generic creativity, the artistic, creative, and rebellious spirit in all boys at the cusp of adulthood, which for him is the absolute essence of what it is to be an artist. Truffaut therefore ultimately pays tribute to the artist in all boys. One of the most curious shots in the film occurs shortly after Antoine is sentenced to stand behind the map. The boys are told to copy a poem as the teacher dictates it. One fellow starts, blots his paper and tries again and again. In the business of the film, this shot has no particular purpose. The boy is not a character we engage again, though he has a hip finger-snapping swagger when he breaks away from the gym teacher's march in that notable scene, a bit of bravado that might mark this minor character as an artist. This is a potentially painful adolescent moment, but Truffaut has other purposes here. The teacher takes no notice, and the perpetual starting over becomes less a schoolboy's embarrassment than a painful artist's moment, the confrontation of continuous mistakes no matter how hard you try.

Truffaut has noted the fear and anxiety that comes with being an artist, and the joy. "I demand that a film express either the *joy of making cinema* or the *agony of making cinema*" (Truffaut 1994, 6). Inez Hedges notes that the word translated as *agony* in the original French is *angoisse*, anxiety, an edgier and more everyday emotion (1991, 69). In this Truffaut signals his link to one of his masters, Alfred Hitchcock, especially to the primal scene of Hitchcock's life, in which his parents take him to jail as an object lesson for misbehavior (Truffaut 1984, 25). Within Truffaut's confidence and Antoine's seeming nonchalance, we still see the self-doubt of the artist. This mixture of anxiety and joy, tension and exhilaration, confinement and escape composes the rhythm of Antoine Doinel's life, the life of the adolescent boy knowing that he is no longer a child and not yet a man, knowing that whatever joys of childhood—and Antoine acknowledges few—are soon to be replaced by the great freedom and anxiety of adulthood.

One of the reasons Truffaut chose Jean-Pierre Léaud for the role of Antoine is his evocation of longing and nervousness. Truffaut notes that in casting Antoine he was looking for a "moral resemblance to the child I thought I had been" (1971, 8). Léaud was a little older than he wanted, but Truffaut was attracted to him by how "tense and anxiety ridden" he seemed and by the conviction that he desperately wanted the role (8).

The 400 Blows presents little of the joy of the artist or of the boy, but one scene that shows the exhilaration, the fearlessness, and the daring of the boy artist occurs when Antoine and René play hooky at the amusement park. In one ride a room-sized drum rotates while the floor drops out leaving the riders pressed against the side of the wall. Antoine enters the ride and René watches from above. Antoine plays with the ride, making it his own as he crawls up the wall to become parallel to the floor. None of the other riders, all adults, make this move. In cuts back and forth from Antoine's point of view to a straight-on shot whirling with Antoine, we see the altered perspective Antoine has gained, and we share one of the few times in which he is smiling and enjoying himself. This is not an easy move, it is a struggle for him, but it is a struggle that gives joy. That this might be a metaphor for the artist is suggested further by the fact that one of the other riders is Truffaut himself, in a Hitchcockian cameo that marks a telling partnership with Antoine, his joy, and his altered vision.

Antoine's great escape at the end of the film is a muted release. When Antoine slips away from the soccer match at the detention center, the audience, and perhaps Antoine, has no idea where he is going. The camera follows him in flight for many minutes, including long tracking shots in which we are running along with Antoine. When seemingly by accident Antoine arrives at the sea, he experiences no simple triumph, no realization that he has beaten the adult world. He jogs up and down the beach, almost measuring his boundaries, wondering where to go next. Then Truffaut focuses in on Antoine's face and ends the film with a freeze-frame in which the anxiety of the adolescent and the artist is as discernible as the joy of freedom. This portrait of the artist as a boy is by no means a paean to the unalloyed joy and power of either boy or artist, but rather a portrayal of the boy artist in escape, in motion, and a portrait of the anxiety that comes with that power and freedom.

Although grounded in the particularity of François Truffaut's own life, *The 400 Blows* shows the condition of the artist in the young boy. Less a portrait of the particular artist Truffaut as a young boy, *The 400 Blows* is more the portrait of the representative young boy as artist, in that moment of transition from childhood to adulthood when the child lives in the joy and the agony of creative life, marshaled in opposition to which lies every aspect of his social world. The teachers are tyrants or easily tricked buffoons. His parents are unfaithful to their roles (his mother is having an affair) and unclear about what they should do to raise a son. His father, who like Truffaut's is not Antoine's biological father, is a sometimes pal, but is more interested in his weekend adventures with his auto club than he is in Antoine. His mother rarely says his name and speaks of him as "the kid," but Antoine is more mature than either of his parents. Antoine the artist can at least imagine adulthood, where his parents and teachers seem not to know what to do with the apparent adulthood they have. His friend René's father's apartment is like a nursery with a large stuffed horse. One reason it is so hard for Antoine to become an adult is that there are no models of creative, free, and joyous adults in his life.

What qualities of the young boy as artist does Truffaut hold forth? An eavesdropper and a voyeur, he is a spy on other people's lives. Always in motion and taking delight in that motion, he is ready to escape both literally and figuratively the bonds that his world will place upon him. He is a liar—think of the colloquial parental accusation of falsehood, "Are you telling stories?"—a creative person willing to steal from the best. He is willing to look at the old world with a new vision, and in the race to the sea, willing, perhaps driven, to go where he has not gone before, in a kind of escape to he knows not what—adulthood and his potential as an artist. All of the adults of *The 400 Blows* are fixed; in his own incompleteness, Antoine, like all boys, like all artists, is an unfinished character.

THE WILD CHILD

Even as he continued the Antoine Doinel cycle, Truffaut's exploration of the artist as young boy moved with *The Wild Child*, which is based on a historical incident, to a less personal, more abstract level (see Shattuck 1980, the most accessible account in English, containing a short commentary on the film). In the forest near Aveyron in France in 1800, a child was discovered, a child who apparently since infancy had survived alone. The child could not speak and was thought for a time to be deaf as well. Child development had long been an interest of Truffaut's. As early as 1958, Truffaut was aware of the famous "experiments" of Emperor Frederick II, who tried to discover the original language of humans by placing several newborns in the hands of wet nurses who were instructed never to give them comfort and most definitely never to speak to them. The children all died. At the time he made *The 400 Blows*, Truffaut saw this story as a cautionary tale for the importance of language and interaction in the normal development of children, including Antoine Doinel (1987, 57–58). In the story of the feral boy of Aveyron, Truffaut chose to cast himself as Dr. Jacques Itard, the scientist who gained custody of the wild child and took on his education. It is also significant that the film was dedicated to Jean-Pierre Léaud, who since *The 400 Blows* had increased his identification with Truffaut through the completion of three more films in the Antoine Doinel cycle. It might be that the dedication to Léaud is recognition that just as Itard plays a complicated role as the teacher to the wild boy, Truffaut's role in the early life of Léaud, giving him language, and indeed self-consciousness, is fraught with joy and anxiety.

As *The 400 Blows* ends in motion with an escape, *The Wild Child* begins in flight as the wild boy (Jean-Pierre Cargol) is discovered, pursued, and captured. The rest of the film marks the boy's rise in education and humanity, an ambiguous ascent. In an early scene, the child inspects his image in a mirror, not understanding the nature of the reflection. Itard grabs an apple and holds it above and slightly behind the child. The boy repeatedly reaches into the glass for the offered apple, yet soon realizes the image is an image and the real apple is behind the person in the mirror who must be himself. He then reaches behind to grab the apple. More than the dressing table mirror scene in *The 400 Blows*, this scene invites the questions of who is looking at whom, who is gazing, and what the gaze of self-understanding means, though neither mirror brings the self-reflective understanding that might be connected to an artist's self-portrait. The innocence of the wild child and the naiveté of Antoine will not admit this awareness. Meanwhile the child is put on display to visitors. The functionary who handles these visits is portrayed as a carnival huckster, moving the guests through quickly to make room for the next visit. In one moment as he goes to welcome the next group, he carries out a large doll-like puppet, a neat nod to the classic illusionist question, "Is this real?" and the Pinocchio puzzle, "Is this a real boy?"

In the film, Itard slowly teaches the child language. In this process, *The Wild Child* becomes a meditation on boyhood, an exploration of human creativity, and again an exploration of the ways in which the young boy carries within himself all the strengths and not a few of the anxieties of the artist. The wild child's life is one of constant creativity. Itard notes that all that the wild child is doing, "He is doing for the first time." He learns to eat at a table after a number of tries, to gesture for what he wants, and eventually to say the word lait to ask for milk. In preparing for this film, Truffaut and cinematographer Nestor Almendros studied among other films Arthur Penn's *The Miracle Worker* (1962), the story of Anne Sullivan's bringing Helen Keller to language (Baecque and Toubiana 1999, 263). There are a number of clear echoes: the stark bare rooms, the thrown food, the tantrums and kicking the floor. But for Truffaut the coming to language is not the threshold and culminating experience it is for Penn's Helen.

For Truffaut, and for the child whom Itard names Victor, the coming into language, into the role of artist, is a more ambiguous triumph. Itard finds in Victor a passion for order, a desire to keep things in their place, but very little emotion. He notes early in the film that he has never seen the boy cry, not even when tormented by other children, yet Victor possesses a longing for motion and change. He looks forward to his walks with Itard, delights in wheelbarrow rides, and one night, near the end of the film, he climbs out into the yard to sway in the moonlight.

When his experiments with Victor learning to understand language have progressed to a certain point, Itard experiments with the sense of justice. Even though the boy brings him the correct objects when asked, Itard scolds him and locks him in a closet. This experiment, which sees in rebellion against injustice an emblematic humanity, is also reflective of Truffaut's understanding of the artist. Itard gets the reaction he wants. The child rebels and cries. As Antoine Doinel's tears in the paddy wagon evoke sympathy, they also tell us that he knows what is happening to him is unjust, that he does not deserve this. This self-awareness that he is distinct from the judgments of others is a sign of Antoine's moral growth as it is for Victor. The boys gain their own perspective on the world necessary for their coming of age and shadowing forth the independent moral angle of vision essential to the artist.

The Wild Child, like *The 400 Blows*, culminates in flight. Victor runs away and is pursued by strangers, escapes, and finally returns home. His return comes less with triumph than resignation. When Itard takes him back, he speaks a judgment that could apply to both Antoine Doinel and the Wild Child, "He is no longer a wild child but not yet a young man of great expectations." This ending has been read as too sentimental and optimistic, as though the education is somehow complete (Allen 1985, 9). However, as the child goes upstairs an iris lens narrows on his face, and this portrait carries not quite resignation, and certainly not triumph. Like the freeze frame on Antoine Doinel at the end of *The 400 Blows*, this iris portrait captures the unsure awakening of the boy artist. Antoine has told stories, stolen the Promethean pictures and the word machine, and stood in an original relation to the world at the rotor and in his discovery of the sea. Victor has, to Itard's joy, invented a chalk holder, learned a new language, discovered injustice and the rightness of his own vision, and chosen to return to a life where he will grow up. Both have suffered the repression of their societies, but managed, however painfully, to create their own way of being in the world.

The endings of these two films hide very different conclusions. In the strictly autobiographical reading of *The 400 Blows*, the confused Antoine Doinel grew up to become one of the great directors of world cinema. The Wild Boy of Aveyron never learned to talk with any facility and, neither fully adult nor human, he lived out his life caught between the wild and the civilized. But at the center of both these films is a straightforward look at how a boy, in both cases very much against all odds, shadows forth the possibility of becoming that creative, anxious, moral, and joyful creature—an artist. In Truffaut's vision, the autobiographical bildungsroman becomes not just a story of growing up, but also a *Künstlerroman*, a story of the development of an artist. And as he looks at these boys who are not only potential artists but already artists in their understanding of the world, in their rebellion against injustice, in their creative manufacture of their own worlds, and in their indomitable spirits, his work becomes a profound exploration of the nature of boyhood.

The primal act of many modern boyhood narratives is a sexual coming of age. In *The 400 Blows* and *The Wild Child* this moment is preempted in the viewer's and the main characters' attention by the realization of the young boy's fate as artist. When handed the pinup at the start of *The 400 Blows,* Antoine proceeds to claim that image as a canvas to be redesigned by the artist—not as aid for what could otherwise come to be a conventionally dominating sexual imagination. That Truffaut's boys lay claim to the perspective of the artist before they become men presents a priority in value as well as chronology. They stand outside the controlling malehood of Western culture. This does not mean that the youths of Truffaut films are any less distinctively male, but they are boys before they are men and their identities as artists adhere to the freedom, courage, rebellion, and anguish of their lives as boys, not to their promise as protomen. Antoine and the Wild Child are both caught frozen at the end of their films, awake in a moment to both the complexity of the world and their power over it as artists even as the inevitable cataclysm of growing up lies in wait for them.

Antoine Doinel and Victor the Wild Child are inarticulate speakers for the agony they feel, but at the end of their respective films, they know only that they are stepping into a new world, a world they must make by their rules, that they must invent. This gives each of them great freedom and joy, but also fear and anxiety. Truffaut has said that those who have happy memories of childhood are people with defective memories (Truffaut 1987, 47). In *The 400 Blows* he does not sentimentalize his own childhood or in *The Wild Child* the childhood of the human race, but he seeks to reveal the power of boyhood as well. In that turmoil of misperception, lies, motion, escape, and return, can be found not only the particular past of one artist, but also the agony, joy, and moral power within all art, within all artists, and the potential artist within all boys.

In his films about boyhood, is François Truffaut irredeemably lost to those of us who must see male gender identity more than anything else as a perduring locus of cultural and political power? Is he, in short, prefeminist? I would not characterize his gender perspective in these films as prefeminist as much as boy-centered. In this Truffaut may be considered locked in autobiography, even puerile and narcissistic in his self-involvement, if one wants to put it in negative terms. However, as I have tried to show, one aspect of the genius of *The 400 Blows* lies in the discovery by the boy/artist of an alternative to the trials and tribulations of conventional boyhood—one does not have to become a conventional man to triumph or even survive. Indeed, the men in these films offer no clear models for the boys to grow up to. Antoine Doinel's father is a cuckold and at best adolescent. The teachers are figures of tyranny and petty cruelty. Even Itard in *The Wild Child* is largely cool and controlling in his scientific temperament. This artist role is certainly not the particular prerogative of a male child for Truffaut: in *Small Change* there are girls who partake of artistic temperament and, among the early films, Jeanne Moreau's Catherine in *Jules and Jim* may be worth exploring as a Truffauldian artist figure as well. But while a substantial exploration and critique of Truffaut's perspective as generally "prefeminist " may be worth doing, and may reveal an evolving feminist reaching to enlarge the boundaries of action and expression for both boys and girls, it is not the subject here. My focus has been on the way in which Truffaut's self-portrait of the artist as a young boy in *The 400 Blows* reaches beyond the autobiographical to lay claim to the special character of boys in particular moments as artists discovering, naming, and creating a world, with all the anguish and joy of that creation. His exploration of boy artist in *The 400 Blows* and *The Wild Child* develops into a portrait of the adult male artist figure in such films as *Day for Night, La Chambre verte (The Green Room)* (1978), and *Le Dernier métro (The Last Metro)* (1980). *Small Change,* in the sympathetic adult male teacher, the girl artists, and the exploration of positive sexuality, may be read as Truffaut's attempt to give the world of the boy artist more access, to make the artist's identity more inclusive. Yet because his project *is* autobiographical in central ways, it is the boy artist who captures Truffaut's attention more than any other character in the films I have discussed; the boy artist who became, and who remained, Truffaut.

SMALL CHANGE

In many aspects, *Small Change*—where Truffaut revisits with affection the energy, creativity, and vulnerability of young adolescent boys on the verge of becoming artists of their own experience—is a lighter and happier film than *The 400 Blows* or *The Wild Child.* The schoolrooms are places of real learning managed by sympathetic teachers who are seen in the community, part of the children's world. The boys are still hell-raisers and occasional voyeurs, often shown in motion, like Antoine Doinel, running through town and sneaking into movies. Although there are important individual stories, such as the coming of age of Patrick (Geory Desmouceaux) as he transfers his love for an absent mother to the mother of a friend and then at the end to a nascent romance with a girl his own age and the story of the resilience of baby Gregory who falls out a several-story-high window only to land unhurt and laughing, *Small Change* is in many ways a communal portrait. However, one boy does stand out as a boy with a secret. Julien (Philippe Goldman), we discover, is not just a petty thief, a scruffy poor kid, and a loner. Living in a shack, he is severely beaten and abused by his mother and grandmother. Julien is a more desperate and downtrodden Antoine Doinel. Truffaut makes this connection explicit when he shows Julien dropping pieces of a plate he has broken down a sewer to hide them from his mother, a precise emblematic echo of Antoine's action and Truffaut's own. Julien's family condition is much worse than Antoine's. In addition Julien lacks Antoine's resources as a creative actor in his own life. Julien is finally saved not by his own flight to the sea or his own lies and imagination but by the intervention of the teachers and police, the very people who oppress Antoine.

In the long penultimate sequence of the film, the sensitive teacher Richet (Jean-François Stévenin) explains to his boys what has happened to Julien, now a ward of the state, and assures them he will be taken care of. But he does not diminish the damage that has been done to Julien, noting that it will be many years before Julien is free and calling the abuse of children, of the innocent, the greatest crime. In this speech the teacher admits that he had had a terrible childhood himself, and he became a teacher to help other children avoid what he has endured. He also shows an important understanding of the special moment of late boyhood, of the power, vulnerability, and creativity of that moment, as he urges his charges to not only make the most of their youth but also band together and seize the power to stop the oppression of children. The teacher here is the spokesperson for Truffaut whose understanding of the special state of boyhood becomes a plea to see the qualities of sensitivity, perception, courage, adventure, and vulnerability in all boys as ripe with the rebellion, sense of justice, and creativity of the true artist.

If all boys are artists, then the social conditions that Truffaut, the teacher, Julien, Victor, and Antoine Doinel had to suffer are more reprehensible. Adults and the larger worlds of school, society, and state created by adults are not just restraining brats, but oppressing the innocent, the helpless, and creative humans at a time, their late boyhood, when they at once are the most vulnerable and the most full of potential for discovery and creativity. The fact that the artist boy triumphs in Antoine Doinel and endures beyond all expectation in Victor the wild child may be a tribute to the strength of the boy, but does not make the social world and blind repressiveness of adulthood any more forgivable, nor the damage done to Julien even in the sunny world of *Small Change* any less horrible.

NOTES

1. Antoine de Baecque and Serge Toubiana's *Truffaut: A Biography*, 11. This work is the standard biography. Also important for understanding the young Truffaut are his "Introduction: Who is Antoine Doinel" in Truffaut 1971, a collection of the treatment of *The 400 Blows* and the screenplays of the four other Antoine Doinel films, all save *Love on the Run*. Also useful are the interviews compiled in Truffaut 1987, especially the first chapter, "Autobiography," and of course the section on *The 400 Blows*. (For further discussion of *The 400 Blows* see chapter 9 in this volume. —eds.)

WORKS CITED

Allen, Don. 1985. *Finally Truffaut*. New York: Beaufort Books.

Baecque, Antoine de, and Serge Toubiana. 1999. *Truffaut: A Biography*. Berkeley: University of California Press.

Hedges, Inez. 1991. "Truffaut and Cocteau: Representations of Orpheus." In *Breaking the Frame: Film Language and the Experience of Limits*, 52–65. Bloomington: Indiana University Press.

Insdorf, Annette. 1994. *François Truffaut*. New York: Cambridge University Press.

Rohmer, Eric. [1956] 1985. "Ajax or the Cid." *Cahiers du cinéma* 59 (May). Reprinted in *Cahiers du cinéma, The 1950s: Neo-Realism, Hollywood, New Wave*, ed. Jim Hillier, 111–15. Cambridge: Harvard University Press.

Shattuck, Roger. 1980. *The Forbidden Experiment: The Story of the Wild Boy of Aveyron*. New York: Farrar, Straus and Giroux.

Truffaut, François. 1971. "Introduction: Who is Antoine Doinel," in *The Adventures of Antoine Doinel: Four Screenplays*, 7–13. Trans. Helen G. Scott. New York: Simon and Schuster.

———. 1984. *Hitchcock*. With the Collaboration of Helen G. Scott. New York: Simon and Schuster.

———. 1987. *Truffaut by Truffaut*. Texts and Documents compiled by Dominique Rabourdin. Trans. Robert Erich Wolf. New York: Harry N. Abrams.

———. 1994. *The Films in My Life*. Trans. Leonard Mayhew. New York: Da Capo Press.

12

OUT WEST
Gus Van Sant's *My Own Private Idaho* and the Lost Mother

Matthew Tinkcom

> Western fiction has traditionally been clean. Where the coyotes howl and the wind blows free was never a place for promiscuous sex, kinky sex or perversion. Since the early sixties, however, all this has changed.
>
> C. L. Sonnichsen

In "How to Bring Your Kids Up Gay," in her book *Tendencies,* Eve Kosofsky Sedgwick offers a thoroughgoing critique of the complicity of contemporary therapeutic and psychoanalytic practice in the pathologization and stigma attached to queer sexualities. In particular, in that essay Sedgwick argues that perhaps the greatest danger to queers comes not so much from the variety of religious and social commentators who earn their livelihoods from the demonization of queers, but more perniciously from those professionals (psychiatrists and therapists included) who claim as their mandate the improvement of the lot of queers as sex/gender has become more central to the public discussion of sexuality in the U.S. setting. She (rather devastatingly, to my mind) asserts that "revisionist analysts seem prepared to like some gay men, but the healthy homosexual is one who (a) is already grown up, and (b) acts masculine" (1993, 156), implying that the psychoanalytic explanation of the existence of queer adult men is preserved largely by the fiction that for the most part queer children do not exist—that the child or adolescent who announces queer desire or affiliation is an anomaly and can be treated, medically and psychologically, in order to avoid becoming a queer adult.

Therefore, the "problem" of the queer child or adolescent is that he or she fails to inhabit one of the more powerful cultural teleologies of sex/gender, namely that queers simply appear fully formed as adults on the social landscape. In point of fact such children and teens grow and develop as queers throughout the early parts of their lives. Yet the psychological professions, according to Sedgwick, have afforded little possibility of such development. She writes: "[There] are huge blank spaces to be left in what purports to be a developmental account of proto-gay children," and the absence of such accounts indicates a less than benign activity at work in the treatment of gay and lesbian youth, leading to what she describes as the net effect of such discourses and practices that although "the associated strategies and institutions are not about invasive violence," nevertheless, "what they are about is a train of squalid lies. The overarching lie is the lie that they are predicated on anything but the therapists' disavowed desire for a nongay outcome" (Sedgwick 1993, 161). Sedgwick bases her interrogation of the "treatment" of queer youth on the rather startling fact that gay and lesbian teenagers are, by the admission of the United States Department of Health and Human Services, two to three times more likely to attempt suicide than their straight counterparts. Her accusations are not without their statistical merit.

Elsewhere, though, Sedgwick suggests in passing that the techniques of psychoanalysis might be helpful in understanding the experiences of queer children and teenagers as they grow up in a homophobic culture, a culture that continually enjoys the harassment, insult, and sometimes murder of queers, young queers not excepted. What she calls "the possibly spacious affordances of the mother texts" of psychoanalysis might make room for us to see how the condemnation of queer desire and pleasure fuels a culture in need of outlets for its rage. Sedgwick's playful turn to psychoanalysis as a discourse that mothers children, rather than fathering them by inserting them into the patriarchal arrangement of the socius, fosters this essay's impulse to consider the function of the mother for the queer teenager.

For the queer adolescent the movement from childhood to adulthood is a process fraught with various prohibitions against discussing the erotic dimensions of boys and male teenagers in relation to adult sexualities and genders. We should understand Sedgwick's comments as an attempt to underscore how little commentary we have about the fact that children (male and female) are expected to arrive in the world of adult "choices" regarding pleasure and reproduction with astonishingly sparse acknowledgment of their own erotic capacities. I address Gus Van Sant's *My Own Private Idaho* (1991) because that film almost singularly offers a vision of male adolescent same-sex sexuality in a manner that is neither utopian nor condemning. Van Sant's film, whatever its perceived shortcomings, has the virtue of arguing that teenage boys nurture queer thoughts and fantasies, and indeed that such mental activities may do two things: (1) link them to other kinds of familial bonds (in particular to the figure of the mother) and (2) shape a way of seeing the surrounding world with a gaze very different from that customarily associated with heterosexual desire.

Further, the remarkable achievement of this film is that it sets aside the question of origins that haunts the medical and therapeutic practices that seek to understand where homosexuality "comes from"—how it develops in individual subjects and how its origin shapes the eventual identities and practices we think of as "queer." By ignoring the very force of this language, *My Own Private Idaho* offers another story of queer boys; the film invents a particular language of dreams and memories and depicts a fiercely heteronormative world in which queer pleasure might be a haven, and one that links the queer teenager back to boyhood recollections of the mother, the most central emblem of shelter and protection within the vagaries of "civilized" life. In this regard, we can read the film through its depictions of a lost, vaguely remembered childhood, a childhood that holds meaning for the late adolescent boy who is the central figure of the film.

In order to make sense of *My Own Private Idaho*'s narrative and formal devices as they depict the coming of age of a queer working-class male, the character of Mike as portrayed by River Phoenix, I turn first to the "mothering discourses" within the writings of Sigmund Freud as he addresses himself and the psychoanalytic project to the figure of the queer male, and the queer boy in particular. Worth retrieving in Freud's account of the homosexual man's remembrance of his youth, I would argue, is the figure of the mother who nurtures the queer boy within the Oedipal family. I then return to a closer examination of Van Sant's film in order to trace through its narrative a subtle confirmation that the love of the mother for the queer boy is the sole confirming figure in an often violent world.

Freud and the Maternal Penis

In one of the central theoretical psychoanalytic texts that address the experience of the queer male teenager (and perhaps one of the most provocative of all of the psychoanalytic case studies) Freud offers an often speculative psychobiography of Leonardo da Vinci. Here Freud makes his case regarding the etiology of queer male desire as it emerges in the family. His argument, in brief, analyzes a few fragmented texts from da Vinci's own diaries and decides that they offer clues as to how da Vinci's homosexuality emerged from the strong bond with his *mothers*—and the plural is deliberate. Da Vinci, Freud reminds us, was born out of wedlock to a prosperous middle-class functionary and a peasant woman. Raised by his birth mother for the first five years of his life, da Vinci was then (under circumstances that remain unclear) removed to his father's household, where he was subsequently raised until early adolescence by his father's wife, who seems to have been unable to have children. Freud reads this complicated domestic scene through the fragment of a dream that da Vinci recollected in adulthood, a dream that consisted of his being visited as an infant in the cradle by the figure of a vulture that presses its tail to his lips repeatedly. Without dwelling at length on the techniques of psychoanalysis by which Freud arrives at his conclusions,[1] we can see in Freud's account that he seems to traffic with some of the more predictable stereotypes of queer male life but, I would argue, in perhaps inadvertent fashion Freud offers a provocative and not entirely pathologizing account of male same-sex desire and its nurturance in family life. The pathological dimensions of Freud's account seem more likely to be an element of his successors' readings of his work than of his work itself. In terms of the former, portions of Freud's discussion of da Vinci's biography at moments read like the originary text for every panicked depiction of the male homosexual as the boy who once grew up too close to his mother, and Freud would appear to be only too willing at points to subscribe to the theory that, in sum, mothers make their sons gay. The reasoning behind such a theory runs thusly: because of too intimate and too longstanding a bond between mother and son, the boy child can never fully make his sexual drive and his sexual aim toward a woman coincide. He fails to understand woman as bearer of the sign of sexual difference and thus, in some mysterious fashion, makes his sexual aim the same as that of his mother: that is, men. The basis of this account of the development of male homosexuality takes its form in the Oedipal myth, which for Freud functions as the defining experience for the gendering of all modern subjects. The details of this structure and its accompanying narrative are probably so well known as not to need too great an elaboration here, but worth remembering about the Oedipus narrative is that it centers around the child's fantasy that the mother, at some point previous to the child's entry into the world, had a penis; in some act of violence that the child cannot know, she was deprived of it so as to become the bearer of the sign of sexual difference because of her lack and the forms of power and domination associated with it. The queer male child, it would seem, develops strong attachments to men because he too strongly identifies with the mother and never fully breaks affections with her in order to side, in normative fashion, with the father.

Yet in his reading of da Vinci's dream materials, Freud's reasoning on the matter of the function of the Oedipus narrative for the queer boy is considerably more complicated, and here he reaches beyond the stereotypical to a more nuanced understanding of the appeal of the mother for the queer child. (Worth emphasizing here is the fact that Freud's theories seem to imply that the boy child's queer sense of himself comes into being at an early moment in his life, an idea upon which Sedgwick's essay amplifies significantly.) The appeal of the mother as an intimate companion for the queer boy is occasioned by her potential to be a masculine figure, and Freud's assertions about the matter are worth quoting at length, because he takes as an assumption the strange fact that the mother can bear for the queer child a phallic presence. In sum she can have a counterintuitive hold over the boy. He writes:

> There really was a time in which the male genital was found to be compatible with the representation of the mother. When the male child first directs his curiosity to the riddle of the sexual life, he is dominated by the interest for his own genitals. He finds this part of the body too valuable and too important to believe that it would be missing in other persons to whom he feels such a resemblance. As he cannot divine that there is still another equally valuable type of genital formation he must grasp the assumption that all persons, also women, possess such a member as he. (1947, 68)

Knowledge that woman does not own the phallus thus becomes *the* fact that informs the male child's development toward possessing the sexual aim toward women—the "straight" child stops identifying with the mother and sees her as castrated object. But the queer boy's discovery of his mother's lack of a penis occasions the transformation of his identification with her "into its opposite and gives place to disgust, which in the years of puberty may become the cause of psychic impotence, of misogyny and of lasting homosexuality" (Freud 1947, 68). This, however, is only a feeble explanation. Freud in that same account offers the mother as a figure of strong affiliation with whom the queer boy never breaks, and the stereotypical explanation of the queer male's domination by the mother can be imputed to be the powerful threat of the seemingly uncastrated woman—a figure that Freud suggests is widely acknowledged in the various historical and mythological legends he summons in that essay.

Indeed, he comments that the woman who always bears the phallus is a longstanding image in the straight patriarchal imagination, but that she seems to offer little threat because she is limited to the production of queer boys! Freud writes about this that, "none of these observations explain the psychological riddle, namely, that the fantasy of men takes no offense at the fact that a figure which was to embody the essence of the mother should be provided with the mark of the masculine power which is the opposite of motherhood" (1947, 67). This riddle, as Freud calls it, might more summarily be named "the infantile assumption of the maternal penis" (71), whereby the queer boy is nourished in a world of same-sex desire (i.e., desire for a figure who bears a penis) by his failure ever to renege on the pre-Oedipal fantasy that the mother has a penis. In short, this fantasy allows the mother to bear the phallus that the boy comes to enjoy in others. The interpretive advantage that Freud gains by the assertion of the mother as continued bearer of phallus for the queer adult male is that Freud can then detect in Leonardo's art an ongoing fascination with women as paradoxically homoerotic masculine emblems, where the famously enigmatic figurations of women (such as Mona Lisa del Giaconda and the images of Mary and Saint Anne in *The Holy Family*) repeat for the artist an early love for the maternal figure who bore the phallus and continues to do so in adult fantasy.

It is worth emphasizing this important rethinking of the Oedipus narrative within Freud, since what his account of da Vinci indicates is another Oedipal formulation based on a childhood fantasy other than that of the castrated mother. The queer boy gives the phallus to the mother early in his psychic life and does not then fantasize the mother's deprivation of it. More properly put from the viewpoint of patriarchal privilege, the mother retains the phallus in the queer boy's fantasy and is never dispossessed of it. While Freud continues, then, to argue that Leonardo's homosexuality was not so much expressed through erotic affiliations with men as sublimated in his art (what Freud labels pruriently the artist's "ideal homosexuality"), the implication I want to take from Freud's conception of the queer male Oedipus is that in same-sex attraction the queer man reenacts the queer boy's desire for the phallic mother. Freud's comments are unclear as to whether the boy in post-Oedipal life *re*-attributes the phallus to the mother, having gone through the more typical Oedipal scenario of perceiving her as castrated, or if he never perceives her as castrated at all, maintaining throughout his maturation the sense of the mother as an ongoing phallic presence. Regardless of what we might decide upon this matter, the threat of queer male desire, for both the more normative dimensions of Freud's figuration of the Oedipus narrative and masculine patriarchy, is that such desire gives the mother a phallic presence in the world, one that at all costs must be denied her by others. The menace that Sedgwick detects at work in the "treatment" of gay youth derives perhaps from the possibility of the mother as (apparently too) empowered an actor in the Oedipal drama, an actor whose legacy happens to be the queer boy. It is no wonder that the queer boy and queer adolescent must so strongly be disavowed, even by those institutions that claim to help him, because at stake in the enterprise of counseling, along with the avoidance of a view of queer adulthood as the result of a queer childhood, is the intense bond between boy-child and mother as anything but a sign of pathology.

COUNTRY BOY: THE MOTHER AND THE LANDSCAPE

The narrative of *My Own Private Idaho* oscillates for the most part between two spaces: that of the country (Idaho) and that of the city (Seattle and Portland). These spaces become associated in hardly atypical fashion with a recognizable set of ordinances that are by now so well known as to nearly become cliché: the country (here, the expansive American prairie) associates itself with a sense of limitless expansion, new possibilities, regrowth, and sexual innocence, while the city (paradoxically in this film, a city west of the wilderness, and not east as is more usual) becomes the space of moral degradation, institutional corruption, and the compulsion toward brutal normativity. At key moments in the film—the beginning, conclusion, and when he travels to Idaho with Scott (Keanu

Reeves)—we see Mike standing in the midst of the prairie and framing the distant horizon into a face. I would read this moment as being about the playful engagement between the human and the natural world that allows Mike to see the flat open land and wide blue sky as something friendly, inviting, and, in Freud's terms, maternal. Alternately, the film's depiction of metropolitan life puts its characters in the starkest of economic circumstances, working the streets as hustlers and dwelling as squatters in abandoned buildings, living at the behest of the law of the father—in Scott's case, literally. However, this split between country and city life brings to bear an important set of reversals beyond these more customary associations to the degree that *Idaho* explicitly associates the country with the maternal and the metropolitan with the patriarchal and depicts this oscillation between the mother/rural and the father/urban as about a need to escape from the latter into the former. This movement, I would argue, bears remarking upon because it emphasizes the father's role in the production of corruption and heteronormativity while holding out, in perhaps utopian fashion, a wish to return to the mother and her sponsorship of the unrestricted desire and pleasure of the queer adolescent boy. Even a passing familiarity with the structure of the classical cinematic western will alert the reader to the fact that the western in its Hollywood incarnation bases its narrative movement on the expansion of the law and patriarchy into the domain of the "savage" and uncivilized, but paradoxically installs the figure of the woman into the newly civilized space as the keeper and guarantor of domestic order and familial reproduction. *My Own Private Idaho*'s innovations in the genre of the western appear in its inversion of expectations for the queer male. The desire to escape the city to the rural landscape of the prairie signals the queer man's fantasy of return to the maternal.

My Own Private Idaho situates this movement through two narrative vectors, one set in the film's present-day American West (in the early 1990s) and the other in the memories of the film's central figure, Mike, as he recalls his own childhood through dreams, hallucinations, and memories. The nexus that draws these two narratives together is Mike's narcolepsy, itself foregrounded at the beginning of the film through a shot of a highlighted dictionary entry of the term. At moments of stress and challenge, Mike falls into a sleep that seems to offer him some protection from the world

he inhabits, a world largely structured for him through his employment as a male prostitute in the cities of Seattle and Portland.
Crucial for understanding—within the context of the film's conventional diegesis—the editing of Mike's recollected fantasies of his
youthful memories of his mother is this apparent symptom, not
least because the theory of psychoanalysis takes such physical and
psychic manifestations as indicators of the Unconscious emerging
into psychic life at key moments where something can no longer be
repressed. In a quite explicit sense, one thing that Mike shares with
his mother is illness, since it unfolds that the mother herself has
been hospitalized for unspecified hysterical symptoms. Thus, the
occasions in which Mike faints into a narcoleptic spell are
immensely important for the film's correlation of his queer desire
with his affection for his mother: he faints when he looks at the
landscape of the prairie (richly associated with his mother) and
when he finds himself in a sexualized interaction with an (older)
female client, one who evokes maternal love in the context of the
sexual economy that for the most part excludes women—male
prostitution.

The importance of prostitution for the film, I would argue, is
that it becomes the defining metaphor for virtually all sexuality in
the film; when Mike and Scott travel to Rome in order to find
Mike's mother, they land among that city's own male hustlers,
hanging out looking to trick in much the same way we've seen
them in their own American cities. The film then offers us a challenge to find a sexuality not locked into the exchange of money for
gratification. In its continual recuperation of the memory of Mike's
mother, the film suggests that the one lone emblem of a nonex-
ploitative sexuality would be that of the mother's affection, which
might be dispersed—if only in fantasy (and regret)—to other
moments, most centrally the moment where Mike expresses an
erotic tenderness toward his closest ally, Scott.

In order to make sense of this key scene, though, we should
remark upon the explicit equivalence of sex-for-money as it is
played out in a scene in which the film's two central figures are
discovered together in bed by policemen who have been dispatched
by Scott's father (the mayor of the city—a most powerful emblem
of patriarchal power and corruption) to summon Scott. When the
cops raid the squatters hotel, we see them barging in on two figures beneath the bedcovers; expecting as we might looks of shock

or disgust on the faces of the cops, we instead see them leering and smirking at the two young men in bed—revealed to be Scott and Mike—and obediently backing away from the erotic scene taking place before them. The importance of this scene resides in its implication that two men could only, even for the cops, be in bed if they were engaged in a financial arrangement that needs to be respected if not ignored. That the cops walk in on the two central figures in bed and are satisfied with the explanation of male homosexuality as a financial transaction indicates that the police (like everyone else) seem less concerned with the taint of homosexuality than with the problem of profit, here apparently neatly resolved in a scene of erotic play as playing out an alibi of financial gain. In short, homosexuality paradoxically confirms the law (and by implication, the father) when it can be construed as a monetary transaction and nothing else. Even the struggle over Scott by two older men in the film (his own father and the figure of Bob Pigeon) signals a desire to own his body for some kind of profit—either as son of the mayor or as heir to the beggar-king.

While the struggle over Scott forms an ostentatious Oedipal scene worth dwelling upon, for the purpose of this essay I want to consider it in regard to how it informs the movements of Mike through the film. It does so by way of putting into relief the mother who cannot be found except in fantasy. While Scott declares that he loves Bob more than he loves his own father or mother, and Scott's life is determined by his apparent choice to live as a street hustler against the wishes of his mayor/father, nevertheless late in the film, after he has fallen in love with a woman he meets in Italy, Carmella, Scott disavows Bob and sides with the world of power, affluence, and heterosexuality. Yet the importance of this narrative thread in the film indicates a choice that Mike can never have because, on the one hand, he has no recourse to a father who might guide him into the world of straight masculinity, and, on the other, he cannot situate his erotic attractions to men solely in the activities of hustling, where ostensibly sexual contact with other men is only a function of the economic. For Mike, desire for either of the figures of the father—the mayor or Bob—means having to situate his attraction to men as an excuse for patriarchal recognition and prestige, which at the end of the film entice Scott away from the debased economic sphere of squatters and hustlers and toward the world of municipal politics and marriage. Mike's attraction to men, and to Scott specifically, figures as part of his larger impulse to find his mother, the figure who might serve to explain his confusion (and his narcoleptic tendencies).

The film marks Mike's compulsion to seek his mother through a particularly noticeable formal technique, where Mike's flashbacks to his childhood experiences of joy in his mother's company are indicated through the use of grainy 8mm home-movie stock, swerving in close-up and long-shot to depict the figures of his childhood. Implied by the inclusion of this footage is the question of who might have taken such movies, and the most obvious candidate would be Mike's own father, fathers forming the more customary users of home-recording technology in the making of cinematic household memory. Such an attribution, though, implicates a father who seems to mean little to Mike, because Mike seems to have little interest in finding or knowing his father, a fact made uncomfortably clear in the sequence where Mike and Scott visit Mike's brother in Idaho and the brother suggests that Mike's father was probably a distantly remembered drifter with whom their mother had fallen in love. Mike disavows this explanation by countering that he knows that his brother is his father, an idea the brother drunkenly scorns by suggesting that Mike "knows too much." Surprisingly, this bit of titillating incestuous information isn't pursued in the film. Instead, the film makes a point of demonstrating that, however perverse or sordid Mike's paternity may be, it matters little to him in the face of his need to find his mother—she can serve ultimately as explanation for who he has become.

The dynamics of parentage and desire in the film, then, fall into a dyadic structure that associates Scott with conventional masculinity, money, power, and the need to ally with the father, even if only after the father has died, and situates Mike in terms of all that the lost mother might help to recuperate: sex and love without monetary impulse, and the utopian possibilities of the prairie. This fantasy of the mother—as an emblem of a nonalienated sexual love that might be possible between men—is driven home in what I take to be the central scene of the film, where, on the road from Portland to Idaho, Mike confesses his attraction and love for Scott. Mike tells Scott that he wants to kiss him, and in turn Scott replies that he only has sex with other men for money. One might expect a more usual dynamic to play itself out, where Scott might violently reject Mike, but Van Sant, through the movement of the actors' bodies in

River Phoenix (l.), with Keanu Reeves in *My Own Private Idaho* (1991).

this scene, implies a kind of maternal love that remains between these men, as Scott holds Mike in a Pietà-like embrace of comfort and consolation.

Finally a perhaps naive question: whose Idaho is implied by the film's title? The probable answer is Mike's, because he is the film's central figure and because more than anyone else in the film he travels to Idaho. I would argue, however, that the "my" of the title invokes the figure of Mike's mother, who indeed becomes so associated with the idea of privacy as not to be represented outside Mike's fantastic recollections of her; the states of privacy and of Idaho (literally) belong to the mother. This leads to a perhaps not-so-naive question: why can't the mother be represented in the world of the queer youth?

The answer to this question returns us to Sedgwick's claims that even the most seemingly "open-minded" accounts of queer gendering and sexuality cannot abide the thought that something—more specifically, someone—has brought a queer boy or girl into the world and helped them to be and to become queer. In this regard, the mother of the queer boy can serve only as a reminder of another kind of Oedipal scene, one that Freud's accounts only hint at and that *My Own Private Idaho* summons in the nostalgic and hallucinatory footage of Mike's remembrance of his childhood and his mother.

NOTES

1. Readers interested in a more expansive treatment of Freud's interpretive techniques might consult his own introduction to the matter, *The Interpretation of Dreams,* trans. James Strachey (New York: Avon, 1983), as well as any of the case studies, where Freud practices upon his patients. For a fascinating rendering of lesbian desire, see for example *Dora: An Analysis of a Case of Hysteria* (New York: Touchstone, 1997).

WORKS CITED

Freud, Sigmund. 1947. *Leonardo da Vinci: A Study in Psychosexuality.* Trans. A. A. Brill. New York: Random House.

Sedgwick, Eve Kosofsky. 1993. *Tendencies.* Durham: Duke University Press.

Sonnichsen, C. L. 1978. *From Hopalong to Hud: Thoughts on Western Fiction.* College Station: Texas A&M University Press.

13

MAMMA'S BOY

Counting on Ghosts, Sending Smoke Signals, and Finding Surrogate Fathers in Contemporary Film

Nicole Marie Keating

Mothers and daughters/fathers and sons—these dyads seem fixed in our cultural patterns of binary formation. Yet the complementary pairs (mothers/sons and fathers/daughters) also offer profound opportunities for discovery, for in these relationships we are able to learn about what we are *not*. Still, for many years the mother-son relationship seemed all but ignored by the academic community. Although there has been a recent surge of interest in the mother-son connection (see Forcey 1987; Silverstein and Rashbaum 1994; Smith 1995; Rowland and Thomas 1996; Pollack 1998; Kivel 1999; Backes 2000; and O'Reilly 2001), the fact remains that the intricacies of this relationship have been relatively unexplored onscreen. Some might account for this avoidance by citing sexual undertones in the mother-son relationship (as alluded to in *Spanking the Monkey* [1994] and *The Grifters* [1990]). Because cinematic representation is a cultural touchstone with immense symbolic value, it is worthwhile to examine how the mother-son relationship has been portrayed in contemporary American film.

If the mother-son relationship has sometimes been ignored in cinematic representation, it has certainly been pathologized. Images of boyhood typically involve rituals such as playing ball (with Dad), but what happens when Dad is out of the picture? After viewing recent American films, one might think that when Dad is absent, all normalcy disappears as well. Sons raised primarily by women are often portrayed as typical "mamma's boys": passive, odd, and ill equipped to deal with life's challenges. In the following pages, I examine mother-son relationships in such films as *Men Don't Leave* (1990), *What's Eating Gilbert Grape* (1993), *Heavy* (1995), *Smoke Signals* (1998), *The Sixth Sense* (1999), *Finding Forrester* (2000), and *You Can Count on Me* (2000) (referring to various other films along the way). Overall, films dealing with mothers and sons tend to involve one or more of the following: (1) a son who is debilitated in some way, (2) a fixation on a missing father or a search for a father replacement, and/or (3) a son who must become the father replacement himself. Although many films incorporate the above themes, my choice of films for this essay was narrowed by a desire to concentrate on American films released in the 1990s or later and to include a range of films representing cultural diversity as much as possible. Using textual analysis within a cultural studies framework, I demonstrate that films seemingly focused on mother-son relationships are usually more oriented toward missing father-son relationships. Ultimately, I argue that there is a lack of films portraying textured, meaningful (perhaps even "healthy") mother-son relationships considered valuable in their own right.

Since media forms reflect and construct cultural ideologies, this tendency to denigrate and/or ignore mother-son relationships in media presentations sets an alarming example. As scholars have noted, a close, loving relationship with both parents fosters healthy development in sons and daughters alike. After all, if sons can't communicate with their mothers, how will they ever learn how to communicate with the female half of the population? If we want to support well-rounded masculinity—and if we're serious about resolving the gender wars—then strong mother-son relationships must be encouraged and seen onscreen.

In recent years, members of the academic community have started to advocate mother-son closeness, though they are battling years of strongly ingrained opposition. In *Mothers and Sons: Feminism, Masculinity and the Struggle to Raise Our Sons*, Andrea O'Reilly writes that "the hegemonic narrative of mother and son attachment—as scripted in parenting books, psychoanalytic theory, and popular wisdom—assumes that sons must separate from their mothers in order to acquire a 'normal' masculine identity" (2001, 14). Olga Silverstein and Beth Rashbaum (in *The Courage to Raise Good Men*) also make the case that mother-son closeness is thought to "feminize a boy, to make him soft, weak, dependent, and homebound" (1994, 11). They argue that "most women, like most men, fear that a mother's influence will ultimately be harmful to a male child, that it will weaken him, and that only the example of a man can lead a son into manhood. Single mothers in particular are haunted by the dread of producing a sissy" (9). This assumption reverberates throughout much popular, literary, and academic literature dealing with masculinity. Even the poet Audre Lorde assumes that "[our sons'] way is more difficult than that of our daughters, for they must move away from us, without us." Still, Lorde feels that maternal influence is a positive thing: "Hopefully, our sons have what they have learned from us, and a howness to forge it into their own image" (1984, 73). Robert Bly, author of *Iron John*, feels differently. He asserts that men suffer from emascula-tion and "father-hunger" due to closeness with mothers, and that in order to develop a strong masculine identity they must separate: "When women, even women with the best intentions, bring up a boy alone, he may in some way have no male face, or he may have no face at all. . . . A clean break from the mother is crucial" (1990, 17–19). In contrast to Bly's view, recent work (by O'Reilly 2001, Silverstein and Rashbaum 1994, and others mentioned previously) emphasizes that forced separation from the mother, often perceived as rejection, ultimately interferes with well-rounded masculine development.

The film version of the theoretical dance described above has yet to be produced. Most contemporary American films subscribe to the old-school approach to mother-son relationships (i.e., mother-son closeness stifles boys and must be curtailed). This ideology is set into sharp relief in films dealing with single mothers since these films isolate the mother-son relationship (though surrogate fathers are usually inserted at some point).[1] In Hollywood films generally, a father's influence on his daughter is presented in positive terms, while mother-son closeness is presented negatively and linked with the "mamma's boy" syndrome. As Silverstein and Rashbaum com-ment: "To be a 'Daddy's girl' is a charming and desirable goal, but a 'Mamma's boy' is a terrible thing" (1994, 3–4; see also De Vaney 2002). In essence, male influence (associated with strength) is considered empowering, but female influence (associated with weakness) is considered disempowering. This essay examines how contemporary American films reflect and reinforce these deeply embedded cultural ideologies.

One of the first films to catch my attention in this regard was *You Can Count on Me* (2000), an independent film dealing with sin-gle mother Sammy (Laura Linney), her brother Terry (Mark Ruffalo), and her eight-year-old son Rudy (Rory Culkin). The film opens with the arrival of Terry, a rambling man who's been in trouble with the law and with his girlfriend. He and his sister have a close relation-ship, but it is also dysfunctional in a typically "codependent" way.

Terry is a roguish troublemaker, adventurous yet tormented and unreliable. His sister is a responsible rescuer: she covers for him, bails him out, loans him money, and invites him to stay with her while he tries to get his life together. These dependencies create resentments on both sides, yet brother and sister are forever bound by traumatic childhood experiences. Their parents were killed in a car accident when Sammy and Terry were quite young, so they inevitably turn to each other for love and support. This theme of parental loss becomes a recurring one when Terry shows signs of concern that his nephew is growing up without a father (or other male role model). At first Terry seems ready to take on the job. He takes Rudy fishing, teaches him how to use a hammer, how to play pool, etc., thus generating a series of images that evoke father-son bonding. These moments are often intercut with scenes of Sammy on dates with various men, suggesting a parallel between the search for a husband and a father. Ultimately, Terry isn't ready for the role of surrogate dad, and he overstays his welcome by forcing a confrontation between Rudy and his estranged biological father. Needless to say, Terry's stay with his sister quickly comes to an end.

Embedded within *You Can Count on Me* is the assumption that mother-son closeness can be harmful to sons. Some might argue that the lack of male role model per se rather than the presence of mother-son closeness causes harm; these two factors are easily confounded. Rudy is clearly wounded by his lack of a father. He spends much time wondering about his lost father and fantasizing that his father is an action/adventure hero. It is thus hard to differentiate between the potentially deleterious effects of the loss of a father, the experience of not having a father, and closeness with a mother. In such cases, it is difficult to weed out the various issues at stake; in most of the films examined in this essay, multiple factors are involved. Many of the boys in these films are dealing with the death or abandonment of a father, and so their subsequent lives are inevitably fraught with grief and instability. Still, it is clear that there is much societal unease about single mothers raising sons. In her essay entitled "On Throwing Like a Girl," columnist and lawyer Patricia Williams refers to this anxiety:

> I am not exaggerating when I say that scarcely a day goes by without the worried chiding of one male friend or another . . . the pressure seems to deploy sport as a cipher for anxiety about [my son's] fatherlessness. I have had men actually ask me why I adopted a boy rather

than a girl. . . . There is an undercurrent to it that seems to assume that I will be the ruination of my son, that I will crush the fledgling male instinct with the unchecked voodoo of single-mother sissification. (1999, 214–15)

This fear of "single-mother sissification" is a major concern in *You Can Count on Me*. Consider the scene in which Terry confronts Sammy after a night of playing pool at a local bar: "I think his problem is that he's totally sheltered. You treat the kid like he's three instead of eight, so that's how he behaves. . . . I don't think he should have to run and tell Mommy every time he does something that you might not approve of." The subtext of Terry's comments is unmistakable: Rudy is sheltered and overprotected by his "Mommy" and therefore at risk of "sissification."

But what does the end result of such "sissification" look like? Part of the anxiety surrounding the mother-son relationship is no doubt related to homophobic aspects of the mamma's boy syndrome. Consider, for example, the Arthur Gayle character in *This Boy's Life* (1993): Arthur, son of a single mother, is teased by his classmates because he "walks like a girl, runs like one, talks like one, throws like one." There is also the fear that "mamma's boys" will grow up to be weak or ineffectual (i.e., effeminate) regardless of sexual orientation. One film that provides a particularly compelling sketch of this feared outcome is *Heavy* (1995). This film deals with Victor (Pruitt Taylor Vince), a thirty-ish man who lives with his mother Dolly (Shelley Winters); Victor also works for Dolly in her greasy spoon called "Pete and Dolly's." Pete is Victor's father and Dolly's ex-husband, but he is out of the picture, leaving Victor alone with his passive-aggressive mother. Victor is a great cook, but he is extremely timid, overweight, and socially awkward. He develops a crush on Callie (Liv Tyler), the beautiful new waitress in the restaurant, but he is painfully shy around her through most of the film. It soon becomes obvious that Victor's masculinity has been stunted, presumably due to his unhealthy relationship with his mother. Throughout the film, we see evidence of Dolly's controlling yet dependent behavior. At one point, Callie observes Victor making pizza and comments that Victor is a great chef and that he should consider going to the well-known cooking school across the river. Dolly counters that "they would just charge us a lot of money to teach him what he already knows. I don't think so." When Victor says that he hates making pizza, Dolly tells Callie: "But he loves making breakfast. This young man takes very good care of his mother. He makes me a whole buffet every single morning."

As the film progresses it becomes increasingly evident that although she is well-intentioned, Dolly holds Victor back because of her own dependency issues. Victor plainly feels oppressed, but he is too passive to set himself free. He drags his heavy body around his mother's restaurant, and the whole film seems to lumber along with him in the small-town, slow-paced barren landscape. He has perpetually shifty eyes, not so much from furtiveness as from timidity, so he is incapable of "bearing the look." He peers at Callie through doors held ajar and other narrow openings, but he can't look her in the eye. As he works away in the kitchen, a song playing in the background is quite fitting: "Sometimes it seems I can barely breathe" (from "Carry Me," performed by The Vidalias). Victor is slowly suffocating, but he never asserts himself and is ostracized and ridiculed as a result. In one scene, Victor looks through a local barfly's stack of pinup cards. As Victor glances through, Leo (the barfly [Joe Grifasi]) comments that "if you don't use it occasionally, it falls off." Symbolically at least, Victor has been castrated by his oppressive mother. Later in the film Victor's mother dies and gradually Victor becomes stronger. Although he is so paralyzed by grief that he is unable to tell anyone that his mother has died, there are subtle signs that he also feels liberated. In a gesture that reveals a growing confidence, he visits the local culinary institute mentioned by Callie. And finally (if only for a minute) he does get the girl.

Heavy provides a good example of why people fear mother-son closeness, which is often assumed to be stifling. Another interesting example is *Smoke Signals,* though in this film boys without fathers become either "sissies" or "bullies."[2] The story begins with a flashback to 1976, when the Coeur d'Alene Native American tribe is celebrating the bicentennial Fourth of July. After the party, Arnold Joseph (Gary Farmer), drunk from holiday celebrations, accidentally starts a fire that kills members of the tribe. Once the fire is blazing, a baby boy named Thomas Builds-the-Fire is thrown out the window and caught by Arnold, who also has a baby son, Victor. When the film cuts to the present, we see that Thomas (Evan Adams) and Victor (Adam Beach) have grown up very differently. Thomas represents the "mamma's boy" (or in this case, the grandmamma's boy since he was raised by his grandmother after his parents were killed in the fire); he is a likeable but highly eccentric "sissyish" male described by Dennis West and Joan West as "an engaging cross between a mamma's boy and a traditional seer" (1998, 28). Victor represents the bully—he is a detached, uncommunicative "angry young man." In one scene, Victor tries to teach Thomas how to "look mean" so he doesn't seem foolish, but Thomas teaches Victor how to smile. In some ways, the film challenges our thinking about these binaries by revealing Thomas's strengths and Victor's weaknesses, but by focusing solely on father-son relationships it marginalizes mother-son connections. In the film, Victor hears of his father's death and then travels with Thomas to get his father's ashes. During the journey we learn that Thomas and Victor both lost their fathers the day of the fire: Thomas's father died, and Victor's father was never the same again. It makes sense, then, that the film begins with the lines, "How do we forgive our fathers?" and ends with the following piece of narration: "How do we forgive our fathers? . . . Do we forgive our fathers for leaving us too often—or forever—when we were little? . . . Do we forgive our fathers in our age or in theirs? Or in their deaths, saying it to them or not saying it? . . . If we forgive our fathers, what is left?" Father-son relationships are thus presented as highly charged, primal, and all encompassing. As a result, mother-son connections may well be "what is left," or rather "what is left out." Although father-son narratives are extremely important, so are mother-son narratives. If this film is a characteristic case study, then sons raised by single mothers are given two rather limited options: they can become either ostracized "mamma's boys" like Thomas, or wounded "bullies" like Victor. There is one scene in which Thomas returns home to his grandmother, and as he walks in the door we see that he and his grandmother are exactly alike. At that moment, the audience bursts into laughter, for we see why Thomas is so odd. Of course—it was the grandmother who did it! Thomas was raised by a woman, and an elderly one at that. This scene is so hilarious because it taps into our cultural anxiety surrounding such arrangements. Victor, by contrast, is determined to defy this stereotype and overcompensates by becoming hostile and proud (i.e., "macho"). He may have taught Thomas how to "look mean," but in the end it is Thomas who teaches Victor how to forgive his father. As the film concludes, Thomas is presented as something of a hero, which brings new status to the "mamma's boy" figure. Mamma's boys are perhaps able to forgive their fathers in a way that is difficult for macho men.

If *Heavy* and *Smoke Signals* provide examples of the difficulties experienced by boys raised or controlled by single women, other films resolve these problems through the insertion of a father figure. Interestingly, *You Can Count On Me* stops just short of taking that step. Terry almost becomes a father substitute for his nephew Rudy, but isn't able to follow through on his intentions (perhaps reflecting unresolved grief concerning his own lost father). Other films such as *Men Don't Leave* and *Finding Forrester* do use surrogate fathers to fix the "problems" caused by single mother–son arrangements. In *Men Don't Leave,* for example, full-time mother Beth McCauley (Jessica Lange) is leading an idyllic small town existence when suddenly her husband John (Tom Mason) is killed in a car accident, leaving her alone with two young sons. They have no life insurance so Beth is forced to sell their cozy home and move into a cramped apartment in downtown Baltimore to pay the bills. Things quickly deteriorate: Beth falls into a severe psychological depression and both sons get into trouble (particularly the younger one Matt [Charlie Korsmo], who begins stealing and skipping school). Once Beth meets a new man, Charles (Arliss Howard), things start to improve dramatically. Charles has a son of his own from a previous marriage and at one point Beth comments to Charles's ex-wife: "They sure do love their daddies, don't they?" Beth feels these words viscerally; the first scenes of the film were devoted to revealing the closeness between her own sons and their father. In these early scenes, Beth contentedly bakes in the kitchen while her two sons playfully frolic with their daddy, who takes them in his beloved pick-up to his construction site, teaches them how to use power tools, and bonds with them at a "guy flick." Beth, meanwhile, looks wistfully on, feeling left out yet loving all of her "boys" just the same. With the death of her husband, this wistfulness turns to depression, and the rest of the film provides a sharp contrast to the blissful opening scenes—until Charles enters the picture. Charles functions as a father replacement, thereby ensuring the proverbial happy ending.

At one point in the film, Beth and her eldest son Chris (Chris O'Donnell) are in the middle of a spat when Beth comments that since his father isn't there anymore she must make the rules. Chris blurts out, "I wish it were the other way around." These words reflect the overall tone of the film, which reinforces societal angst concerning the prospect of single mothers raising sons. This message is conveyed cinematically through abrupt stylistic shifting between various film segments. In the opening scenes, for example, the film contains all of the telltale signs of a Hollywood "feel good" movie: soft lighting, comforting background music, heartfelt voiceovers by the youngest son, and a mise en scène tastefully accented by symbols of domestic tranquility (a roaring fire, plush furniture, and good housekeeping). The McCauley home looks like something out of a catalog, but when the father dies, a strain of cinematic realism emerges. Perhaps because Jessica Lange is so adept at playing "crazy women" (see especially *Frances* [1982] and *Blue Sky* [1994]), the film convincingly loses its gloss and becomes messy, cluttered, and out of control; it seems almost like a different movie. There is also a noticeable absence of sentimental voiceovers—until the final scene, when a surrogate father has been secured. In this way, the film is "bookended" by picture-perfect scenes populated by fathers or surrogate fathers, with a miserable phase of "realism" (i.e., single motherhood) sandwiched between them.

Another film in which a surrogate father plays a pivotal role is *Finding Forrester*. In this film, Jamal (Rob Brown) is an African American high school student living with his single mother (Stephanie Berry) in the projects when he discovers that a reclusive white writer, William Forrester (Sean Connery), is living in the same neighborhood. Jamal is a budding writer himself—he started writing prodigiously when his father left his family (apparently using the process of writing to deal with his grief), and he yearns for a mentor. Jamal's need for guidance and his pursuit of a friendship with an older man suggest that he is searching for a father replacement. He finds this substitute in Forrester, a literary legend who wrote one classic novel years earlier and was never heard from again. Initially, Forrester becomes something of a writing tutor to Jamal, but as time progresses their friendship becomes more textured. Forrester gives Jamal advice about women: "I learned a few things along the way that might be of help with this young woman you're always talking about." He also advises him about teachers: "Just keep in mind that bitterly disappointed teachers can be either very effective or very dangerous." Most importantly, he helps him with self-confidence and identity formation. Jamal is a gifted writer, but he is also a talented basketball player, and he wins a scholarship to a private school due to a combination of his test scores and basketball prowess. He faces a number of obstacles at this new school, and he is particularly frustrated by the fact that he is stereotyped as the "basketball star" because of his race. Ultimately he comes into his own with the help of Forrester, who also benefits from the friendship; as the film moves forward, Jamal feels increasingly confident and Forrester gradually comes out of seclusion. Although this film is interesting in terms of its portrayal of interracial, intergenerational friendship, it once again reinforces the notion that all boys need to thrive is a male role model. At the end of the film, Forrester reads aloud from one of Jamal's stories called "Losing Family": "Losing family obliges us to find our family. Not always the family that is our blood, but the family that can become our blood. And should we have the wisdom to open our door to this new family, we will find the wishes we once had for the father, who once guided us, for the brother, who once inspired us." Those wishes come true for Jamal in the form of Forrester as surrogate father. Note that in the above excerpt, there is no mention of mothers.

The film thus gives voice to the general consensus that women simply cannot serve as role models for boys. Jamal's mother is rarely seen; she has a marginalized presence, and when she does appear in this film she seems frustrated, confused, and out of touch with her son (though she does cheer for him during the big game). In fact, the film opens with the sound of her voice awakening Jamal in the morning, but she is off-camera, so even by way of introduction her visual presence is erased. Only when Forrester opens his door does Jamal's life start to fall into place. Of course, male role models are no doubt necessary for boys, but female role models are also important, just as male role models are helpful for girls.

Finding Forrester also deals with race-specific issues at stake in parent-child relations. In "Masculinity, Matriarchy, and Myth: A Black Feminist Perspective," Claudette Lee and Ethel Hill Williams argue that "the major challenge to a black mother raising sons today remains the same as that of yesterday—survival" (2001, 56). Since "one out of every twenty-one African American males will be murdered,"[3] many African American mothers are especially fearful of raising "mamma's boys" because they want their sons to have the "toughness" necessary to function in an environment characterized by fear and violence. One approach to this urgent situation is dramatized in *Boyz N the Hood* (1991), in which a single mother Reva (Angela Bassett) gives up custody of her ten-year-old son Tre once he starts getting into trouble at school. Apparently Tre's father, Furious (Laurence Fishburne), had been pushing for this arrangement for quite some time, so when Reva finally agrees he asks her what changed her mind. "Just like you said," she replies. "I can't teach him how to be a man." With this line, Tre's mother expresses succinctly the dominant ideology concerning mother-son relations emerging in contemporary American cinema.[4]

In his review of *Finding Forrester*, Stephen Holden refers to a "surrogate father-boy genius subgenre" or "rising tide of shameless male weepies" (2000, E3). Other films that might be considered part of a "surrogate father subgenre" include *Good Will Hunting* (1997), *This Boy's Life* (1993), *The Karate Kid* (1984), even the *Star Wars* series (1977–2002). *About a Boy* (2002) fits the pattern quite closely. In short, it deals with a single mother Fiona (Toni Collette) whose son Marcus (Nicholas Hutchison) is ostracized by his peers. One scene in which fellow schoolboys mercilessly tease Marcus when they overhear him saying "I love you" to his mother is particularly telling: Marcus is clearly a mamma's boy. And, as usual, this single mother is dysfunctional: it is Fiona's attempted suicide that brings Marcus closer to Will (Hugh Grant), the adult male with a Peter Pan complex who becomes Marcus's surrogate father. Once Will surrenders to the responsibility of surrogate fatherhood (i.e., by teaching Marcus how to wear cool clothes and listen to hip music, etc.) everything turns out okay.

Men Don't Leave, Finding Forrester, and *About a Boy* have clean resolutions and happy endings, but what happens if a father substitute isn't found? *Boyz N the Hood* (1991) gives us some indication: things end happily for Tre (raised by his father), but they end very unhappily for his two best friends raised by a single mother (they both get killed). A similar pattern can be found in other films where fathers (or surrogate fathers) are in short supply. In *What's Eating Gilbert Grape*, for example, Gilbert (Johnny Depp) is forced to take care of his family after his father kills himself, so rather than finding a father replacement he becomes the father replacement (his mother's "prince in shimmering armor"). His mother (Darlene Cates) was devastated by her husband's death, and has become so obese that she can barely fit through the front door (as in *Heavy*, weight is used to convey a sense of suffocation). In shot after shot, her obese body dominates the frame—her fat billowing down and filling not only her sofa but even the screen. The mise en scène of the film is also filled with signs of this corpulence, most notably the house (built by the father) sagging under the weight of her body/grief. All spaces, in fact—the car, the doorway, the bed—seem cramped and overcrowded when inhabited by her enormity. The result is a sort of visual infantilization of her children, since they appear quite small in her presence, and are consistently diminished by the magnitude of her size.

The youngest child Arnie (Leonardo DiCaprio) is mentally retarded, and Gilbert has assumed almost full responsibility for him while still a teenager himself. Although the film deals with a family's difficulties in coping with the loss of a father through suicide, the more salient aspects of the story concern the problems associated with this single mother's presence. The story thus functions as yet another example of a highly dysfunctional family led by a single mother. The obese mother's children, including two daughters, are all burdened by the problems in the family. Although Arnie has been retarded since birth, in symbolic fashion this retardation points once again to the disempowering influence of single mothers. "Mamma Grape" is presented as literally all-consuming: she eats and eats and eats until the floor starts to collapse beneath her. Her eating disorder also consumes Gilbert, who must become both mother and father to his younger brother. Gilbert, however, is also in need of a surrogate father, as he is having his own difficulties coping with his father's suicide while dealing with the normal trials and tribulations of teenage life, including his feelings for Becky (Juliette Lewis), an interesting young woman who is passing through town. Needless to say, no real father substitute is forthcoming, and the ending of the film is quite tragic. By providing yet another negative portrayal of single mothering, this film affirms the stereotype that sons raised by single mothers cannot develop healthfully. Although the final scene in the film suggests some hope for Gilbert and Arnie, they are plainly scarred by their upbringing.

If *What's Eating Gilbert Grape* presents a disturbing picture of single mothering,[5] then M. Night Shyamalan's *The Sixth Sense* (1999) is a nightmare scenario. Here, a young boy named Cole Sear (Haley Joel Osment) is able to "see dead people." Single mother Lynn Sear (Toni Collette) is frantic with worry about her nine-year-old son's odd behaviors (he is anxious, depressed, ostracized by his peers, and in trouble at school for violent writing/drawing). (Collette also plays the single mother in *About a Boy*; there, in a moment of wry intertextual humor, her son Marcus refers to Haley

Joel Osment, commenting that if he were Osment he could be quite happy because he'd be a movie star.) Cole's problems are apparently related to the recent divorce of his parents; most of his symptoms started after his father left. He is clearly grief-stricken by the loss of his father, and has developed a habit of wearing his father's old clothes (glasses, watch, winter gloves, winter hat, socks, etc.). One scene in particular conveys Cole's anguish regarding his parents' divorce. After a brief montage of fairly happy mother-son scenes, the camera cuts to an ad for cough suppressant medication in which a young boy is pampered by both of his adoring parents. The ad captures the nuclear family ideal, and Cole responds by throwing a shoe (perhaps his father's) at the TV set, causing the screen to go black. Juxtaposed with this televised ideal is a shot of Cole sitting alone at a card table waiting for dinner while his mother fiddles with the thermostat. Both Cole and his mother are bundled up; Cole wears his father's winter gloves (which his mother tells him to remove). Once they are both sitting at the table eating dinner, the camera starts with a straight-on medium shot and then pans back and forth ever so slowly from mother to son, conveying a certain bare loneliness. Reinforcing the point, Lynn comments that "our little family isn't doing so good." Indeed this "little family" seems gutted by the father's absence, and the ghost of a young boy in the next scene embodies the perfect visual metaphor for this devastation. The back of his head has been ravaged by an accident involving his father's gun.

Because Cole is clearly in need of professional help, a therapeutic relationship develops between him and child psychologist Dr. Malcolm Crowe (Bruce Willis). Dr. Crowe helps Cole deal with his fears and accept his ability to see ghosts. Only as the film winds down do we realize that Dr. Crowe is in fact a ghost himself (interestingly, he was killed by a former patient who also experienced post-divorce trauma as a young boy). In some ways, Dr. Crowe becomes the kind of surrogate father discussed above, but with a slight variation —this surrogate father isn't even alive. Despite this rather formidable "handicap," he is still able to function as a father figure. This film thus provides yet another example of a damaged son of a single mother, only this time the child is so affected by the ghost of his lost father that he is literally haunted by it. He sees ghosts everywhere, and ultimately finds the perfect father substitute in the form of Dr. Crowe.

The above interpretation is particularly compelling when considered in the context of *Unbreakable* (2000) and *Signs* (2002), the next installments in M. Night Shyamalan's body of work. Both of these films also focus on lost fathers and distraught sons. In *Unbreakable,* the child is Joseph Dunn (Spencer Treat Clark), a schoolboy facing the possible breakup of his parents' marriage. As Joseph struggles with fears of losing his father David (also played by Bruce Willis) through divorce, he almost loses him in a terrible train accident in which David is the sole survivor. Gradually we learn that David is no ordinary father—he is in fact a human super-hero. The theory that David has superpowers is first proposed by comic book art dealer Elijah Price (Samuel Jackson) who suffers from osteogenesis imperfecta—a rare ailment causing extremely brittle bones. Elijah (called "Mr. Glass" as a child by his ridiculing peers and—unsurprisingly—the son of a single mother) is con-vinced that there is someone who exists on the opposite end of the strength continuum; just as he is so breakable, he believes that there must be someone who is extremely unbreakable. Joseph has no trouble believing Elijah's theory since he has absolute faith in his father's strength and power. He is so attached to his father that he sleeps with him at night and wraps his arms around him like a lasso. The thought of losing his father is unbearable to Joseph.

If *The Sixth Sense* and *Unbreakable* suggest Shyamalan's ori-entation toward a "lost father" theme, then *Signs* confirms it. *Signs* deals with a lost father on two levels. Graham Hess (Mel Gibson) is a former priest who left the priesthood due to a loss of faith occur-ring after his wife was killed in a car accident. He thus becomes both a lost Father and a lost father since his grief also causes him to become emotionally unavailable to his children (son Morgan, played by Rory Culkin and daughter Bo, played by Abigail Breslin). Throughout the film, townspeople continue to call Graham "Father" despite the fact the he consistently corrects them. "Please stop calling me Father," he utters to a local police officer (Cherry Jones), and then turns and walks away. "What's wrong?" Officer Paski asks. "I can't hear my children," Graham replies, forging a connection between the two aspects of his identity. Morgan knows that he can't be heard; he tells his father "I hate you," and mutters "I wish you were my father" to his Uncle Merrill (Joaquin Phoenix). In the end, this lost father/Father is found, due to his heroism in a battle against aliens; Graham Hess finds his faith once again, saves his son, and returns to the priesthood.

These Shyamalan films (*The Sixth Sense, Unbreakable,* and *Signs*) could thus be read as young boys' fantasies concerning lost fathers. *The Sixth Sense* is a dark fantasy in which the ultimate father substitute appears as a ghost, and *Unbreakable* is an action film fantasy in which the father himself becomes the ultimate father figure—a superhero. *Signs* is a sci-fi fantasy in which a boy's father also serves as a Father to the larger community, making his loss all the more devastating and his recuperation all the more poignant. All of these films are obsessed with male role models (fathers, Fathers, action figures, superheroes, etc.), and the perfect actors are chosen to dramatize these fantasy fathers—Bruce Willis and Mel Gibson, action heroes par excellence.[6]

In all three Shyamalan films, mother-son relationships are marginalized. In *Signs,* Morgan's mother is dead. In *The Sixth Sense,* Cole's relationship with his mother cannot save him from the ghosts (it perhaps calls up the ghosts to begin with), and it pales beside the deeper connection between Cole and Dr. Crowe. In *Unbreakable,* Joseph's mother Audrey (Robin Wright) is presented as not much more than a contingency prize when considered alongside the excitement of life with a superhero. In both *The Sixth Sense* and *Unbreakable,* life without a father but with a single mother is presented as the real horror story.

If, as Shyamalan's films suggest, the action/adventure film is the masculine fantasy narrative, then where does this leave mothers? Are mothers destined to be either marginalized or demonized in the lives of their sons? Based on the films examined in this essay, sons of single mothers are either debilitated in some way, in search of a surrogate father, or forced to become a surrogate father themselves.

Numerous examples of dysfunctional mamma's boys, overbearing mothers, missing fathers, and father substitutes are surely to be found, but are there any American films that simply focus on meaningful relationships between mothers and sons without fixating on father figures? Although there are some intermittent cases of textured representation—consider *Alice Doesn't Live Here Anymore* (1974), *Little Man Tate* (1991), and *Mother* (1996)[7]—the pattern is clear. Hollywood has yet to match the progress made in the academic community, where the value of strong mother-son relationships is now increasingly championed. Hopefully, Hollywood will not be far behind.[8]

NOTES

1. Films about the reverse scenario—single fathers and daughters—do appear occasionally, but the daughters are typically portrayed as

charming, empowered tomboys (consider such films as *Armageddon* [1998], *Paper Moon* [1973], and *To Kill a Mockingbird* [1962], among others).

2. West and West (1998, 28) relate how Sherman Alexie (the screenwriter of *Smoke Signals*) has noted that "American culture recognizes only two major Native American profiles: the warrior and the shaman." These profiles could be considered the equivalent of "sissies and bullies." Although Alexie is interested in subverting these stereotypes, he begins by affirming them.

3. This statistic appears at the beginning of *Boyz N the Hood*. Consider also that "nearly one-third of African-American males between 20–29 are under some form of criminal supervision" (Mauer 1999).

4. Much has been written about the "failure of motherhood and the championing of the black father" (Wiegman 1993, 183) in *Boyz N the Hood*, a topic that Jacquie Jones in particular has explored extensively. In her article "The New Ghetto Aesthetic," Jones comments that "Singleton comes dangerously close to blaming Black women for the tragedies currently ransacking Black communities" (1991, 41). Michael Eric Dyson concurs: "Singleton gives rather uncritical 'precedence' to the impact of black men, even in their absence, over the efforts of present and loyal black women. . . . He is [also] less successful challenging the logic that at least implicitly blames single black women for the plight of black children" (1992, 126, 133). See also Doherty and Jones (1991), Mimura (1996), and Seelow (1996).

5. An even more extreme example of unhealthy mothering can be found in Alfred Hitchcock's 1960 film *Psycho*. This film echoes in highly twisted fashion the stigma associated with mother-son closeness. In *The Women Who Knew Too Much: Hitchcock and Feminist Theory*, Tania Modleski comments on this theme: "fear of the devouring, voracious mother is central in much of Hitchcock's work, even where it is not immediately apparent. By 'voracious,' I refer to the continual threat of annihilation, of swallowing up, the mother poses to the personality and identity of the protagonists . . . the mother's psychic obliteration of her child in *Psycho* is paradigmatic of the fear haunting many Hitchcock films" (1988, 107). Just as Gilbert is metaphorically consumed by his mother in *What's Eating Gilbert Grape*, so is Norman "psychically obliterated" in *Psycho*.

6. Rudy in *You Can Count On Me* also fantasizes that his missing father is an action hero, and an animated missing-father-as-action-hero fantasy sequence occurs in *The World According to Garp* (1982).

7. Interestingly, Jodie Foster appeared in *Alice Doesn't Live Here Anymore* as a child, and as an adult she directed *Little Man Tate*. The mother-son relationships in these films are not perfect, but they are significant relationships (rather than narrative stimuli for missing father fantasies) involving sons who are not totally disempowered. Also, in films such as *White Heat* (1949) mother figures do empower

their sons—but only to lead the life of crime (in other ways encouraging dependency). This is a recurrent device based on an ironic subversion of stereotypes—the tough guy actually turns out to be a real mamma's boy!

8. Special thanks to Tosh (my baby son), Maya (my baby daughter), Phuc, my whole family, Christine Cox, Erin Smith, Jessica Fishman, and Greg Bisson.

WORKS CITED

Backes, Nancy. 2000. "Beyond the 'World of Guild and Sorrow': Separation, Attachment, and Creativity in Literary Mothers and Sons." *Journal of the Association for Research on Mothering* 2, no. 1, 28–45.

Bly, Robert. 1990. *Iron John.* New York: Random House.

De Vaney, Ann. 2002. "Pretty in Pink? John Hughes Reinscribes Daddy's Girl in Homes and Schools." In S*ugar, Spice, and Everything Nice: Cinemas of Girlhood,* ed. Frances Gateward and Murray Pomerance, 201–15. Detroit: Wayne State University Press.

Doherty, Thomas, and Jacquie Jones. 1991. "Two Takes on *Boyz N the Hood.*" *Cineaste* 18, no. 4, 16–19.

Dyson, Michael Eric. 1992. "Between Apocalypse and Redemption: John Singleton's *Boyz N the Hood.*" *Cultural Critique* 21, 121–41.

Forcey, Linda. 1987. *Mothers of Sons: Toward an Understanding of Responsibility.* New York: Praeger.

Holden, Stephen. 2000. "Got Game. And Pen. And Mentor." *New York Times,* December 19, E3.

Jones, Jacquie. 1991. "The New Ghetto Aesthetic." *Wide Angle* 13, 3–4, 41.

Kivel, Paul. 1999. *Boys Will Be Men: Raising Our Sons for Courage, Caring and Community.* Gabriola Island, BC: New Society.

Lee, Claudette, and Williams, Ethel Hill. 2001. "Masculinity, Matriarchy, and Myth: A Black Feminist Perspective." In *Mothers and Sons: Feminism, Masculinity, and the Struggle to Raise Our Sons,* ed. Andrea O'Reilly, 56–70. New York: Routledge.

Lorde, Audre. 1984. *Sister Outsider.* Freedom, CA: Crossing Press.

Mauer, Mark. 1999. "The Crisis of African American Males and the Criminal Justice System." U.S. Commission on Civil Rights (The Sentencing Project).

Mimura, Glen Masato. 1996. "On Fathers and Sons, Sex and Death: John Singleton's *Boyz N the Hood.*" *Velvet Light Trap* 38, 14–27.

Modleski, Tania. 1988. *The Women Who Knew Too Much: Hitchcock and Feminist Theory.* New York: Methuen.

O'Reilly, Andrea, ed. 2001. *Mothers and Sons: Feminism, Masculinity, and the Struggle to Raise Our Sons.* New York: Routledge.

Pollack, William. 1998. *Real Boys: Rescuing Our Sons from the Myths of Boyhood.* New York: Random House.

Rowland, Robyn, and Alison M. Thomas. 1996. "Mothering Sons: A Crucial Feminist Challenge." *Feminism and Psychology* 6, 93–154.

Seelow, David. 1996. "Look Forward in Anger: Young, Black Males and the New Cinema." *Journal of Men's Studies* 5, no. 2, 153–78.

Silverstein, Olga, and Beth Rashbaum. 1994. *The Courage to Raise Good Men.* New York: Penguin.

Smith, Babette. 1995. *Mothers and Sons: The Truth about Mother-Son Relationships.* Sydney: Allen and Unwin.

West, Dennis, and Joan M. West. 1998. "Sending Cinematic Smoke Signals: An Interview with Sherman Alexie." *Cineaste* 23, no. 4, 28–32.

Wiegman, Robyn. 1993. "Feminism, 'The Boyz,' and Other Matters Regarding the Male." In *Screening the Male: Exploring Masculinities in Hollywood Cinema,* ed. Steven Cohan and Ina Rae Hark, 173–93. New York: Routledge.

Williams, Patricia J. 1999. "On Throwing Like a Girl." In *Between Mothers and Sons,* ed. Patricia Stevens, 211–17. New York: Simon and Schuster.

14

SLACK, SLACKER, SLACKEST
Homosocial Bonding Practices
in Contemporary Dude Cinema

John Troyer and Chani Marchiselli

Etymologically, the *dude* has no origin, but is a transitive figure peculiar to American Modernity. Webster's has him as "fastidious in dress," especially as in the case of an adventurous urban dandy out of place in the filthy American West. The dude is also a "city man" whose inappropriate manners and geographic mobility, despite the term's unknown origin, reveal his class status and an originary moment of sorts. The dude surfaces in the Wild West as the curiously dandified mascot of manifest destiny. This ahistorical notion of a performative fate, a residue of Calvinist logic, is also that which means to justify a specifically American sense of entitlement. It has been argued that the United States often conceives of its expansion as the fated end of Western Europe's teleological progress. Having severed itself from the paternal origins of the Old World, the United States imagines the space of the new nation as the Promised Land. The Wild West is a future utopia made possible by the mobilized heroics of dandies and pioneers.[1] Unhindered mobility, of course, is reserved for men of means whose entitlement is always predicated on privilege. Thus the "dude" as Webster describes him is the embodiment of American progressivism, antipaternalism, and masculine entitlement.

In allegiance with Michel De Certeau's suggestion from *The Writing of History* (1988) that "the past is the fiction of the present," we are in the process of constructing an imaginary history, one whose invention may illuminate the narratives of contemporary dude cinema within the context of American modernity. If the dude is a liminal subject, simultaneously at ease and out of place in the New World, then his adventures may be understood as allegorical imaginings of America's awkward adolescence, replete with age-appropriate anxieties. Themes of parental rejection, the forma-

264

tion of sexual identities, and the recuperation of lost memory are entrenched in the haphazard heroics of dude cinema narratives.

The dudes of today are not the dandies of yesterday, but socioeconomic products of progressivism. By birthright, they are white middle-class Californians, the brothers of surfers and other Western go-luckys. They have forgotten their Eastern fineries and the manners that once distinguished them. New dudes are slobs, slackers, idiot savants whose achievements are fated and manifest. The obliteration of history that is always implicit in dude films works to obscure the gender and class privileges that new dudes share with their predecessors. Paradoxically, in fact, the films call for the recuperation of history in order for dude heroes to achieve the utopic end of progressivist teleology, the saving or remaking of the universe. Exemplary "dude" narratives frequently involve anxious and sometimes literal recollections of lost memories and historical pasts. Yet simultaneously the dude is always in the process of rejecting his origins. He defies expectations produced by his socioeconomic status and shuns the advice of his progenitors, fathers, or other configurations of the patriarch. Like the dandy, the dude is a man on the make, a larva in the process of coming into being through a break with tradition and paternal authority.

Exemplary dude films such as *Bill and Ted's Excellent Adventure* (1989) and *Dude, Where's My Car?* (2000)—not to mention *Animal House* (1978), *Up in Smoke* (1978), *The Jerk* (1979), *Meatballs* (1979), *The Blues Brothers* (1980), *Caddyshack* (1980), *Porky's* (1981), *Fast Times at Ridgemont High* (1982), *The Adventures of Bob and Doug McKenzie: Strange Brew* (1983), *Bachelor Party* (1984), *Weird Science* (1985), *Young Einstein* (1988), *Bill and Ted's Bogus Journey* (1991), *Slacker* (1991), *Encino Man* (1992), *Wayne's World I* and *II* (1992; 1993), *Dazed and Confused* (1993), *Tommy Boy* (1995), *Beavis and Butt-Head Do America* (1996), *Black Sheep* (1996), *Kingpin* (1996), *The Big Lebowski* (1998), *Half Baked* (1998), *Deuce Bigelow, Male Gigolo* (1999), *American Pie I* and *II* (1999; 2001), *Road Trip* (2000), *Saving Silverman* (2001), and *Not Another Teen Movie* (2001)—or proto-dude films like *Easy Rider* (1969) are akin to the boy's adventure tale. As with other juvenile heroes, the new dude's subjective awakening always takes the form of an epic quest, the pursuit of some Holy Grail: missing objects such as cars, guitars, and historical figures may stand in for the otherwise elusive powers of the phallic father. The retrieval of these objects heralds the dude's adulthood, his entrance into the phallic order with all its corresponding rights and privileges. Invariably, however, his ability to stumble through his adventures is made possible by his position within a fraternal group of two. In dude pairings, the young men mirror each other's dress, speech, manner, and philosophy. Theirs is a masculine intimacy characterized by narcissistic mimicry. Because dudes always appear in such mimetic pairs, their relationships are loaded with erotic implication.

In *Bill and Ted's Excellent Adventure*, a product of conservative Reagan-era Hollywood, the homoerotic potential of Bill and Ted's unerring friendship is constantly occluded by homophobic humor and gratuitous heterosexual love interests. Bill and Ted's coming of age, in fact, pivots on their desires to save two "medieval babes" from execution, a wish that also magically leads to the recuperation of Western history. The protagonists of *Dude, Where's My Car?* on the other hand, give full play to the homoerotics of masculine intimacy and thereby reveal the mechanics of the subgenre's humor and narrative conventions. As we will see, these two boys never entirely ascend into phallic adulthood but exist in a kind of adolescent stasis. In both films, the twosomes are charged to save the universe from total destruction, a heroic project that hinges on the recuperation of lost memory. The later film, however, makes such homosocial adventures ironic, flippantly snubbing bourgeois American notions of heroic masculine adulthood.

MASCULINE CITIZENSHIP, THE PRIMAL HORDE, AND THE ORIGINS OF HEROISM

Freud posits that the origins of heroism lie in a fraternal conspiracy that sets Western history in motion. The primal horde is described (Freud 1967) as a band of brothers who, enraged by the patriarch's unlimited access to women, murder him and then devour his body. It is not "brotherly love" that bonds young men to one another but shared hatred of paternal authority and the rapes by which it legitimates itself. Women are excluded from the murder and incorporation of the primal patriarch and subsequently betrothed to the brotherhood of man. Thus, implicit in the logic of fraternal orders and social institutions is a pervasive sense of entitlement. The church, the army, and the modern nation state are haunted, Freud suggests, by repressed memories of the original patricidal conspiracy.

The brotherhood of man is meant to guarantee its access to the remote bodies of women, saved from the father's brutality through the execution of the original conspiracy: when boys band successfully, they get girls. In contemporary society, we obscure the original patricide and subsequent rapes by which the modern nation state is founded (see Pateman 1988). Men's ability to enter into contracts with other individuals or state institutions is always contingent on masculine privilege; adult citizenship is reserved for members of the fraternal order. The homosocial order is befuddled by women, who bear the mark of the father. If, for Freud, heterosexual object choice heralds adulthood, fraternity only works through brotherly love based on shared hatred of the father. The dudes who bond can have girls, and ultimately The Girl, only if they relate correctly to Dad.

Thus, boys in groups are fettered with impossible tensions. Repressed memories of the primal horde carry guilty rage as well as antipaternalist sentiments. Conversely, groups cannot remain coherent without the paternalism of a charismatic leader. Further, the identification of individual group members with one another is ensured by mutual love/hatred of the father.

The boy on the make desires to exceed the fraternal order and replace the primal father. These desires are much like those of the modern rock star on the rise and recall the logic of Freud's mythic hero. Hence Bill and Ted's aspirations revolve around the rock band Wyld Stallions. For Jesse and Chester from *Dude, Where's My Car?*, aspirations are relegated to adolescent sexual conquest. In this way the dude movie is fraught with homosocial anxieties: its heroes are confused adolescent homophobes, frightened of, yet also bent on escaping, paternal controls and fixated on the talismanic bodies of women. The films we have chosen, *Dude, Where's My Car?* and the now-classic *Bill and Ted's Excellent Adventure*, play out with special clarity the perilous antics of male bonding, girl getting, and awkward homophilic father bashing. By remaining juvenile, the dude evades guilty memories of the original patricide on which his privileges pivot.

Dudes are free from the responsibilities of a self-conscious adulthood. In this sense, the haphazard hero is anti-intellectual, apolitical, and ahistorical. Bill and Ted's reconstructed masculinist history attests to the fantasy of a persistent boyhood through which the onus of self-awareness and historical consciousness is transcended. Slackness (being stoned, being out to lunch, being off-balance, being stupid) becomes the exercise of privilege on which the accidental heroism of the dude film pivots.

BILL AND TED'S EXCELLENT ADVENTURE

Sigmund Freud, with corn dog in hand, peruses the mall food court in San Dimas, California. Although he roams the shopping center with other historically displaced figures (Billy the Kid, Socrates, Joan of Arc, Genghis Khan, etc.), it is Freud, arguably one of modernity's defining intellects, who feels most ill at ease in the "modern" world of San Dimas. Billy the Kid and Socrates, meanwhile, swagger toward a table of flirtatious teenage girls with whom they exchange delirious banter. In this scene, Billy the Kid retrieves a "Wanted: Dead or Alive" poster from the inner pocket of his western overcoat and brags: "We're from History." The flirtation ends abruptly when Sigmund Freud appears and inappropriately suggests that the big-haired mall babes "seem to be suffering from some type of hysteria." His diagnosis solicits snickers and a counterprognosis: "What a geek!" Freud's corn dog immediately goes flaccid.

In *Bill and Ted's Excellent Adventure,* two wayward but good-natured high school buddies travel through time to retrieve this host of historical figures. The recuperation of said notables is the project by which Bill S. Preston, Esquire (Alex Winter) and Ted "Theodore" Logan (Keanu Reeves) haphazardly pass their history exam, graduate from high school, and form a band, Wyld Stallions, whose poignant lyrics inspire a new harmonious world order. In this film's narrative, the utopia of the future is contingent on re-collecting significant figures of the past. The young heroes' task, to resuscitate primarily Western masculinist history, also redirects its teleological progress. Apocalypse is evaded and utopia achieved by the perpetual reiteration of such phrases as "Be excellent to each other" and "Party on, dude."

Bill and Ted's adventure is ultimately one in which the homosocially prone, midriff-baring duo must assemble a host of "significant" historical figures in order to pass their pedestrian high school history class in order to eventually inspire a utopic future resembling San Dimas shopping malls. An envoy from this utopic future, the protodude George Carlin, locates Bill and Ted in 1989 using a Tardis-like time machine clearly reminiscent of Dr. Who's

Bill (Alex Winter, l.)
and Ted (Keanu
Reeves) collecting
together.

phone booth device as seen on the BBC television series, only
absent the infinite space. Once it is full of historical figures, Bill
and Ted's finite Tardis recalls an old school fraternity phone booth
stuffing episode, a spectacle that clearly manifests a specifically
American kind of homosocial order. Along these same lines, the
only female figure retrieved from history is the androgynous Joan of
Arc who discovers, at the San Dimas shopping mall, her true calling as an aerobics instructor. In the end, of course, the world is
saved by the re-presentation of these figures: including, significantly, a Billy the Kid displaying all the characteristics of *the*
"American Spirit," a heterosexual Socrates, and a socially awkward
Sigmund Freud unable to keep his corn dog up.

It is the childish simplicity of Bill and Ted's language that
inspires western civilization's return to a kind of prelapsarian

consciousness. *Bill and Ted's* narrative, like many others, suggests that utopia lies on the brink of manhood. In this case the masculine, adolescent coming-into-being, that is, the "Excellent Adventure," operates as the metaphor for modernity's progressivist promise. Utopia can also be understood as a return to the place before the fall, or that guilt-free preconspiratorial moment when daddy was king. In the dude film narrative, this paradoxically regressive progressivism is haunted by memories of the primal horde and consequently by the project of psychoanalysis. Dude films like *Bill and Ted's Excellent Adventure* simultaneously mock the Freudian specter and rely on a pervasive if rudimentary cultural knowledge of psychoanalytic language. The audience knows that the corn dog is a phallus, and a limp one at that.

It is significant, then, that the dude film is foremost a comedy that banks on juvenile discomfort with the body and the physical high jinx of classic slapstick. *Bill and Ted's Excellent Adventure*, a film that established many of the dude-movie conventions, uses a series of often-repeated situations found in films driven by juvenile dude characters chasing after missing objects. For example, penis jokes involve exaggerated reference to size and/or shape as well as blows to the groin (i.e., the ubiquitous kick to the balls). Breasts are tantalizing monstrosities, distractions made visible by wet T-shirts, push-up bras, and tight framing. The hypervisibility of female anatomy, however, may function to stave off the possibility of homosexual encounters. The most common form of adolescent humor in the dude film involves uncomfortable touches between men and male bodies in dangerously close proximity to one another. Frequently, double entendres allude to the homoerotic potential of masculine intimacy.

For example, after a near death experience with a medieval guard in armor, Bill and Ted, overjoyed at having evaded danger, embrace. Suddenly wary of the homoerotic implications of their affection, Bill and Ted recoil from each other, shouting in unison: "Fag!" The filmmaker pointedly restates the duo's chaste fraternity in the following sequence in which Bill and Ted attempt to meet a couple of royal "babes." The awkward heterosexual encounter seems superfluous to the plot itself but it is the moment in which Bill and Ted's heterosexuality is re-established, significantly, by the presence of the king's daughters. The presence of the feminine body in these films thus reconfirms the privileges of the homosocial order while staving off the possibility of homoerotic desires.

Feminist theorists have noted that in narratives such as these, women act as talismanic figures against the possibility of sexual love between men. Female bodies may also function as conduits for forbidden desires that are latent within the fraternal order. Gang-bang fantasies can be symptomatic of misplaced homoerotic urges. The "babes" appear again at the end of the film, after the twosome has redirected history and saved the universe. Bill and Ted rush to complete their tasks so that they might spare the princesses torture in an iron maiden and subsequent execution. The possibility of sex with these young women inspires the twosome to continue their quest, and hence provides the motivation for a more deliberate kind of heroism.

If the fraternal order hinges on oedipal logic, that is, on men's entitlement to the bodies of women through the act of patricide, then the homoerotic implications of fraternity must be perpetually evaded. Exclusionary social relationships are maintained only by the constant affirmation of overt heterosexuality. We might say that the maintenance of heterosexual identificatory practices escalates in the modern era. This is the era in which, Michel Foucault argues, homosexuality is "diagnosed" and thus recognized as a distinct and significant aberration (1978). The label "homosexual" provides a handy discursive foil for heterosexual identification. By calling each other "fags" Bill and Ted reconfirm a homosocial bond that is also heteronormative. Even at the level of semantics their declaration is tenuous.

Bill and Ted's Excellent Adventure is also particularly significant in terms of articulating a contemporary middle-class masculine "crisis." The film can in some way be understood as a narrative that attempts to reconcile, deliberately or as a manifestation of pop culture's unconscious, a perceived loss of social and historical agency—an agency that has for straight white men always been contingent on the homosociality of Western philosophy and a corresponding idea about historical progress. The post–1970s era dude is notably symptomatic of a particular kind of masculine privilege, an especially middle-class American combination of apathy and entitlement. Contemporary dudes co-opt the socially perceived slackness of characters like Cheech (Marin) and (Tommy) Chong in their film *Up in Smoke*. In its displaced references to Socrates, Freud, Billy the Kid, and Joan of Arc, *Bill and Ted's Excellent Adventure* illuminates a crisis in the concept of history and in the production of what qualifies as historical knowledge. Further confounding Western history the filmmaker implies that Socrates was on a babe hunt, a suggestion that obscures the relationship between Greek philosophy and the institution of pederasty. In other words, if Socrates is a dude, then Western philosophy was not founded on the homosocial and sometimes homosexual relationships between Greek men.

DUDE, WHERE'S MY CAR?

The title of the ironic and arguably postmodern dude movie, *Dude, Where's My Car?* reads like a query directed to the audience. "Dude" refers not only to the haphazard team of diegetic heroes, but also to members of the pop cinema crowd. A question mark indicates the viewer dude's interpolation in the filmic event. This viewer is asked to participate in the construction of the film's narrative, to help the protagonists find the missing vehicle. If the audience member is imagined as a dude like the film's protagonists, then *Where's My Car?* can be understood as a self-reflective commentary on audience participation and generic convention. Viewer expectations are both coddled and denied at various points throughout the movie's relentlessly ludicrous narrative.

In this film, two young men of deliberately ambiguous age, Jesse Montgomery III (Ashton Kutcher) and Chester Greenburg (Seann William Scott), must recollect the events of the previous night in order to *dude, find their car* and incidentally save humanity with an object called "the continuum transfunctioner." As in *Bill and Ted*, the recuperation of lost memory propels the plot. As previously noted the excellent adventure is laden with sentimentality and Hollywood romanticism. Its heroes moved by the possibility of love eventually ascend to the tasks. For Jesse and Chester, however, the well-being of the universe is an afterthought, and heterosexual love becomes fodder for crude satire. One sequence in particular playfully exposes the banality of Hollywood romance in which all plot and narrative foibles are transcended through love. On the couch in their apartment, where an anonymous roommate periodically emerges to take a leak on their plant, Jesse and Chester ponder how to reunite with their incensed girlfriends Wilma and Wanda (Marla Sokoloff, Jennifer Garner). The dudes suspect they have left anniversary gifts for their girlfriends in the car, but since they cannot remember any events from the previous evening, all of their assumptions are entirely dubious. Unlike the Western history from which Bill and Ted recollect significant figures, the most important memories for Jesse and Chester are those that may lead to sexual pleasure. In return for these missing anniversary gifts the two perpetual adolescents hope to be rewarded with "special treats," which they imagine will include sexual favors. In terms of narrative structure, their quest is made especially urgent by the oblique warnings of aliens and space nerds, who crop up periodically in order to terrorize and warn the hapless duo. For example, a cult of science fiction geeks, intent on saving the universe from hostile aliens, insists that Jesse and Chester hold the key to salvation, that they are indeed in possession of "the continuum transfunctioner." These two dudes, however, are completely uninterested in the aversion of apocalyptic disaster, let alone the utopic end of Western history.

Chester is especially reluctant to participate in such arduous tasks as finding the car or appeasing their girlfriends. Jesse, on the other hand, driven by the most regressive, libidinal urges, hopes to convince his chum that the missing car is extremely important because its retrieval will lead to sexual encounters. In boxer shorts, Jesse declares from the couch: "Screw the universe! You know that feeling in the pit of your stomach? That's love, dude." Chester, however, retorts that "feeling in the pit" of his stomach is simply the urgency of Jesse's bowels. At the end of his motivational speech about the virtues of romance, Jesse discovers that he indeed does need to use the bathroom. He has confused romantic love with the need to defecate. Chester responds coyly, "Do I know your body!"

In this way the precarious intimacy of homosocial relations topples into the homoerotic. Chester's knowledge about his friend's gastronomic functions and the overt anality of the scene makes clear the screenwriter's intentions. Audiences come to expect squishy romanticism present in much of American cinema. Earlier dude films, because they evolve around the adventures and intimacies of young men, often supplement their narratives with gratuitous heterosexual subplots. Bill and Ted's brief and superfluous encounter with medieval babes, for example, attests to the persistence of plot devices meant to deny homoerotic potential. In *Where's My Car?* this expectation is satirized and later replaced by Jesse and Chester's clear encounters. The viewer who is well versed in the romantic convention of previous dude movies will appreciate this scene for its heavy-handed homoeroticism and perhaps for its potent nihilism.

In this 2000 update of the American dude movie, our hapless dude heroes make explicit the homoerotic potential always present, but typically masked, in fraternal orders. In a scene that clearly references a history of dude movie allusions, Jesse and Chester have a curious run-in with the romance novel icon Fabio. Driving a convertible rented the previous night, the twosome stop at a traffic light next to a similar car driven by the longhaired Harlequin novel model. A nondescript woman, the very image of the interchangeable dude movie babe, sits next to Fabio. She looks bemusedly at Jesse and Chester, who nod and smile in return, to Fabio's macho chagrin. A game of explicitly masculine one-upmanship begins. After some necessary revving of automobile engines Fabio makes a brilliant endgame move by suddenly making out with the babe sitting next to him. With little recourse other than losing face to some abstract game of masculine posturing, Jesse and Chester shock their rival by kissing each other with even greater enthusiasm. Fabio and the babe look somewhat appalled and drive off, leaving Jesse and Chester to their self-congratulatory high-fiving. Despite the couple's horrified reaction, Jesse and Chester are delighted with themselves, indeed carried away, having utterly lost track of the game's explicitly heterosexual regulations.

Differently than in other dude films before and after *Bill and Ted's Excellent Adventure*, the heteronormative regrouping that usually takes place immediately after a potential or, in this case, blatant homoerotic encounter is delayed. At no point do Jesse and Chester, per Bill and Ted, pull away from each other to yell "Fag!" or a similar pejorative. In the film's next scene, however, Jesse sucks suggestively on a large red popsicle with Chester at his side. It is only after the two labor over the film's central question—where's Jesse's car?—that they are approached by a group of self-described "hot chicks" in black jumpsuits from outer space. The leader and spokeswoman for the group of extraterrestrial babes takes Jesse's popsicle and swallows it in one quick move, causing Chester countless fantasies throughout the remainder of the film. If Jesse and Chester agree to assist the women in their mission to destroy the universe, they will both be rewarded with "oral pleasures." As totally clueless protagonists, however, the dudes do not immediately realize the mission of the space babes. Instead, blowjobs become more important to them than saving the universe.

Even though *Dude, Where's My Car?* is an explicit example of the dude movie, it uses the conventions of previous films in the genre to cleverly produce a commentary on the homosocial. As the twenty-first-century Bill and Ted, Cheech and Chong (from *Up in Smoke*), or Garth and Wayne (from *Wayne's World* [1992]), Jesse and Chester find themselves in a fraternal bond that lacks any kind of responsibility. Without a clear origin or purpose, these two dudes are completely ahistorical. Their juvenile bumbling is of course the foundation of most dude movies, dramatizing the accidental hero-ism of men stuck in the false utopia of boyhood. Jesse and Chester do not suffer or display a Peter Pan syndrome. Rather they are the personification of male slacking in the early part of the twenty-first century. As the film shows, dude characters can, by their liminal-ity, negotiate homosocial relations by simply avoiding all responsi-bility. Jesse and Chester are able to placate their girlfriends and save the universe by simply partying too much the night before.

Concluding the Dude Movie

Much of Western philosophy understands its own history as a forked trajectory—moving in only two possible directions. On one path civilization heads for utopia, really a return to some prelapsar-ian consciousness, to Eden or the primal father, to the privileged fraternal stupidity exemplified by dudes. On the other trajectory, humanity races toward an apocalyptic catastrophe, the loss of social and political agency, the loss of the phallus constantly pur-sued by Western history. It is fitting, then, that the missing objects of dude film narratives include air guitars, cars, large red popsicles, and, significantly, the historical narrative itself. Bill and Ted must together reconstruct history in order to avert personal catastrophe, that is, their separation. Jesse and Chester must reconstruct history to find the car and along the way save all of civilization.

The utopia, however, is an impossible stasis somewhere between boyhood and the inevitable decline that characterizes adulthood. The liminal space of the dude, between the freedom of boyhood and the breakdown of adulthood mediated by the ever-present talismanic female body, is often represented by the neces-sary pursuit of a missing object to replace the absent phallus, that is, a car and/or a high school diploma. Pursuit of the lost or miss-ing phallus in the dude movie usually begins in the locus of contemporary American progressivism: the suburban shopping mall so uncomfortable for Sigmund Freud. In the cultural stasis represented by the suburban shopping mall, the contemporary

American Dude movie articulates a specific kind of imaginary "boyhood." In terms of filmic narrative, this boyhood is contingent not on "real" age but on intimate characters who are trapped in a perpetual state of adolescence.

The modern masculine coming-of-age story can be understood as a situation in which everything must be a rejection of what is old or past (i.e., no longer fashionable) and an embrace of the new and the now, a rejection of abstract paternal authority. To bond with one another, and to reject father and everything he has, the boys in dude films attempt to incorporate and justify homosocial relationships with homoerotic desires; to reclaim for themselves the trajectory of masculinist, Western history and its projected futures.

The dude movie becomes a genre about the hapless male subjects who are both incompetent in paternalist terms, and heroic. The dude will be victorious without trying and free from any remorse in failure. In the uncanny mindscape of Jesse and Chester in *Dude, Where's My Car?* a new kind of mantra emerges for a rejuvenated twenty-first-century Western history: love is crap, screw the universe.

NOTES

1. Expansion into the "uncharted" territories of the western United States, particularly during the nineteenth century, has been romanticized as a time of unbridled freedom and escape from the last vestiges of Old World civility in the East. Pioneers in covered wagons, fur traders, missionaries, ranchers, and other venture capitalists pushed westward, often butchering Native American populations, in the name of progress. This expansion was imagined as America's "manifest destiny." The country's westward travelers legitimated encroaching on Native American lands by imagining that their movements were fated, an outward sign of God's will and providence.

WORKS CITED

Certeau, Michel de. 1988. *The Writing of History.* Trans. Tom Conley. New York: Columbia University Press.

Foucault, Michel. 1978. *The History of Sexuality, Vol. 1.* Trans. Robert Hurley. New York: Vintage.

Freud, Sigmund. 1967. *Group Psychology and the Analysis of the Ego.* Trans. James Strachey. New York: Liveright.

Pateman, Carole. 1988. *The Sexual Contract.* Stanford: Stanford University Press.

15

PURSUITS OF HAPA-NESS
Kip Fulbeck's Boyhood among Ghosts

Gina Marchetti

> Chinese-Americans, when you try to understand what things in
> you are Chinese, how do you separate what is peculiar to child-
> hood, to poverty, insanities, one family, your mother who
> marked your growing with stories, from what is Chinese? What
> is Chinese tradition and what is the movies?
>
> Maxine Hong Kingston, *The Woman Warrior*

Looking at memoirs focusing on boyhood entails teasing out the
intertwined stories of the boy and the man looking back on the boy.
No boyhood essence can be distilled from memory; rather, boyhood
becomes a photo album of moments, reminiscences, impressions,
and emotions that can become the wellspring of the man's account
of his own past for a specific purpose in the present.

When looking at videomaker Kip Fulbeck's oeuvre (Fulbeck
2002), it is imperative to note that Fulbeck, the young man, working on his bachelor's and M.F.A. degrees, gradually metamorphoses
into the more mature artist, the new faculty member, and, eventually, the tenured associate professor. Fulbeck, the boy, born in
California in 1965, the obsessive object of the artist's gaze, changes
as well. Distance makes some aspects of boyhood seem less significant and others move more sharply into focus. The preoccupations
with sexual prowess and vulnerability of an early piece like *Vicki in
3:30* (1990) give way to a more subtle rendering of similar issues just
a year later in *Banana Split* (1991) or a move beyond the personal
into the greater body politic in videos like *Some Questions for 28
Kisses* (1994), *Asian Studs Nightmare* (1994), *Sweet or Spicy?* (2000),
and *Sex, Love, and Kung Fu* (2000), where the boy's perspective on
Bruce Lee, Shang-Chi, interracial romance, and other aspects of popular culture becomes the man's analysis of the depiction of race in
Hollywood film and television. Although Fulbeck's ruminations on
himself and his family seem to be quite separate from his videos on

popular culture, the personal always intrudes. At the conclusion of *Some Questions for 28 Kisses,* for example, he says his critique of the depiction of interracial romance in Hollywood was precipitated by his desire to just get a video at a Blockbuster in Los Angeles. However, the broader question of cultural representation swings back to Fulbeck's own identity as a biracial man trying to situate his own desire within the context of a culture in which the politics of ethnicity and race cannot be separated from dating patterns and marriage preferences.

Primarily focusing on *Banana Split,* Fulbeck's most developed autobiographical video to date, this examination of the depiction of boyhood from the perspective of a young man coming to grips with his own identity with respect to race, ethnicity, language, religion, class, and social status will highlight the ways in which Fulbeck explores this "split" perspective as a narrative of maturation and metamorphosis. Within this autobiographical narrative, key issues come to the fore, including a developing sense of a racialized self within a racist America, the relationship between ethnic identity and the loss of Chinese culture within the American "melting pot," the interconnections among race, ethnicity, and an evolving heterosexual masculinity, the generational differences that mark his Anglo-American and Chinese American family relationships, and the institutions that frame this emerging sense of self from the nuclear to the extended family, from public schools to popular culture and American politics. As Fulbeck presents his maturation process, the key fact of his biracial identity underscores the contradictory nature of self in the last three decades of twentieth-century American society, and Fulbeck does not shy away from the implications of these contradictions as he struggles against his own participation in the racial hierarchy.

Fulbeck generally uses the term "hapa" as the preferred way to refer to his biracial identity. Coming from the Hawaiian phrase "hapa haole," which usually translates as "half outsider" or "half non-Hawaiian," the term has been used to refer to people who are of mixed European and Polynesian descent or Eurasians, although, in recent years, the phrase has been used to refer to Amerasians more generally. The term has crept into the vernacular within Asian American communities across the country, but particularly on the West Coast, where Fulbeck grew up. The implications of the term "hapa" as "half," and not wholly of any specific race, become a prominent feature of Fulbeck's sense of himself as not entirely

Kip Fulbeck and his
father, Jack Fulbeck.

Anglo-American or Chinese American, but as wholly Asian American (Fulbeck 2001b).

However, the community of "hapa" individuals that the term also implies does not figure prominently in Fulbeck's work. Even within his own family, Fulbeck seems isolated. His father, Jack, is the son of a working-class English immigrant, who was an alcoholic. A successful author, professor, and former soldier, Jack Fulbeck appears to have had Kip late in life, and this side of the family does not figure prominently in *Banana Split*. Kip Fulbeck's mother has been widowed twice and has children from two previous marriages in China, so Kip's siblings come from China. Her second marriage, in fact, was to Chi Tong Chan, a high-ranking Kuomintang (KMT) official, a onetime governor of Hainan Island; and the demands of Seckyue (Mary) Fung Chan Fulbeck's extended family and connections to a larger Taiwanese/KMT/Chinese American community became a vital part of Fulbeck's formative years. *Just Stand Still* (1990) and *Nine Fish* (1996), for example, deal with Fulbeck's relationship to his elderly grandmother, Fung Waitsing, who came from China in 1967 to be with her family, and the strained relationship she had with Fulbeck's mother as well as other members of the family as she became increasingly infirm.

Rather than connoting a community of people with similar Amerasian backgrounds, being hapa isolated the young Kip from his Chinese as well as his Anglo-American family, from the predominantly white suburban community of Covina, California, where he grew up, and from the Chinese American/Asian American world he encountered when he entered college. Just when Fulbeck seemed reconciled to one aspect of his identity, another emerged, accompanied by violent culture shock that seemed even more dramatic because the new culture, at least in part, was his own. While many of Fulbeck's experiences as filmed resonate with other Chinese American stories of the pains of racist exclusion and desires for assimilation into a white, middle-class mainstream—stories that are particularly common among those who grew up in predominantly white suburbs after World War II (when the Civil Rights Movement, changes in the immigration laws, and other factors enabled an Asian American middle class to move out of Chinatown and into an upwardly mobile, integrated population)—his tales also bear the mark of the further duality of a doubled racial difference. Fulbeck points out that he can never be one race or the other. Thus, although being hapa in Hawaii had been common for generations and many biracial children were being raised in blended households by war brides, exiles from mainland China, and others who had benefited from relaxed immigration policies that had excluded Asians since the nineteenth century, Fulbeck found himself isolated as Chinese in white America and as a "half-ghost" in Chinese America, where all non-Chinese have a marginal, spectral status in the vernacular as white ghosts or black ghosts (*bak gwai* or *hak gwai* in the Cantonese used in the Fulbeck household).

Actually, Fulbeck's sense of isolation is itself generational. Fulbeck grew up with a specific biracial identity, in a specific place—predominantly white Covina—at a very specific time, the post–Baby Boom or Generation X era when the hapa component of Generasian X was just beginning to emerge. In fact, Fulbeck notices many changes in the composition of his boyhood neighborhood as he looks back, noting African Americans playing in the schoolyard and the proliferation of Asian businesses over time. Thus, while Kip is paired up with the only other "Chinese" in his suburban elementary school class, he is immediately recognized as "hapa," not "Chinese," when he asks a Chinese American coed for a date while in college. Throughout his oeuvre, Fulbeck unveils the often painful process of constructing one's own identity without the benefit of a clear community, but with the considerable hope that social as well as personal transformation will lead to an acceptance of an identity that refuses to be homogenized, essentialized, or marginalized within the larger body politic.

SPLIT SCREENS

Kip Fulbeck works within a particular genre of experimental film/video that has its origins in the diary, the confessional, and the autobiographical film tradition. He also can be grouped with those film- and videomakers who look at childhood or take a childlike perspective on themselves and the world around them, including Peggy Ahwesh, Sadie Benning, Dan Reeves, Jay Rosenblatt, Lisa Hsia, and Valerie Soe. Within Asian American filmmaking there is a particularly strong tradition that features portraits of parents by their children, including work by Janice Tanaka, Rea Tajiri, Richard Fung, Mina Shum, Lise Yasui, Arthur Dong, and Sharon Jue (Leong 1991, Xing 1998, Hamamoto and Liu 2000, Garcia 2001, Feng 2002). Fictionalized accounts of childhood and adolescent experiences have also been a staple within Asian American cinema, including Stephen Ning's *Freckled Rice* (1983), Jon Moritsugu's *Terminal U.S.A.* (1983), and Pam Tom's *Two Lies* (1989). Moreover, several Asian American filmmakers have taken up the subject of biracial identity, including Lise Yasui, Valerie Soe,[1] and Ruth Lounsbury, among many others.

There is a deeply rooted connection between Asian American filmmaking and literature, particularly within the genre of autobiographical fiction that blends the memoir with fables, dreams, and pure fiction. Several Chinese American writers figure prominently in this genre, including Maxine Hong Kingston, Amy Tan, Gus Lee, Frank Chin, and Shawn Wong (Kim 1982). In fact, Fulbeck has entered their ranks with his book, *Paper Bullets: A Fictional Autobiography* (Fulbeck 2001a).[2] Many of the stories Fulbeck recounts resonate with other Chinese American artists' portraits of Chinese culture in America, from the "ghosts" that inhabit Kingston's fiction to the racist "Chinese, Japanese, dirty knees" chants that find their way into Shawn Wong's and Valerie Soe's accounts of their own childhoods. In fact, Fulbeck's oeuvre deals with many of the themes that Jachinson Chan highlights as key parts of Chinese American literature, written by men, about masculinity, youth, and maturation, including questions of physical prowess (being picked on, having trouble getting a date and/or getting laid, only dreaming of fighting back), oedipal tensions (feelings of inadequacy and/or rage against father figures, both Chinese and non-Chinese, generational tensions within the family with elders symbolizing the old order that must be overturned), the paucity of male role models, and issues of ethnic self-loathing and the pressures of assimilation (Chan 2001).

Although not the only biracial filmmaker in this assembly, Fulbeck has crafted his own aesthetic and found his own voice in this tradition. Particularly aware of the tensions within his own psyche, Fulbeck enacts those contradictions in the formal choices he makes within his videos. Still photographs, for example, act as counterpoint for his hyperkinetic voiceover monologues. The tension between the stillness of the image and the vivacity of the stream-of-consciousness soundtrack acts to split the attention of the viewer and allows for an experience of duality on a formal level that Fulbeck also takes up thematically.

Fulbeck is very self-conscious about his aesthetic choices. He begins *Just Stand Still*, for example, by commenting on the "slide show" quality of the tape and his commentary as well as the way he uses his grandmother as an object for the camera. However, the images do not illustrate, but, rather, contradict or veer away from the voiceovers. Movement occurs between shots, rather than within them, and sound washes over images rather than linking them together logically. Titles, quotations, and other textual elements punctuate the videos. Split identification, the inability to absorb and totally process everything that is on the screen and on the soundtrack, the constant possibility of miscommunication, misunderstanding, and misinterpretation all allow viewers to experience aesthetically the racial, cultural, and ethnic "split" Fulbeck recounts in the stories of his biracial childhood, adolescence, and young adulthood. *Banana Split* begins with a title that reads: "I always thought if I was dying I'd think about whatever woman I was infatuated with at the time. I'd whisper my last 'tell her I love her' to a bystander or die scrawling her name on the sidewalk in blood. But all I could think about was my parents."

Referring to a racist assault that Fulbeck believed would be fatal, this title succinctly sets up all of the major issues opened up for closer scrutiny in the video. First, it establishes the perspective of the young man becoming cognizant of his own immaturity and histrionic notions of heterosexual romance. When thinking of his own mortality, Fulbeck's mind moves to his parents; that is, to his place within the family and the cultures his parents represent, his own potential to carry on their legacy possibly eliminated. His parents' interracial, cross-cultural union forms the bedrock of his identity as Fulbeck "splits" himself between Anglo-America and Asian America by losing and finding himself as Chinese. Thus, Fulbeck moves from a desire to pursue his own romantic relationships to his bond to the past; that is, to the parents who created and nurtured the boy.

After the opening title, the following appears onscreen:

What do you check on the ethnicity box?
Chinese
Not white
No
Why not?

These words also serve to introduce a theme that plays throughout the video and returns again near the conclusion when Fulbeck's analyst poses this question to him as part of his therapy. When the psychologist questions Fulbeck about his decision to check "Chinese" on the ethnicity box, Fulbeck answers that he is "not white." The analyst recognizes the contradiction between Fulbeck's tendency to date white women (with a single exception) and his insistence that he is "not white" and that he absolutely does not identify as white in any way, but solely as Chinese (Fanon 1967). Fulbeck's dating preferences become linked to his racial identity, and another series of words appear onscreen—banana, apple, coconut, Oreo—that refer to various slang terms for being "white on the inside" and Asian, Native American, Hispanic, or African American on the outside. Kip immediately sees both the appropriateness and inappropriateness of the use of these terms in his case, and he shares with his analyst the title of the piece he is working on, *Banana Split*. For Fulbeck, not all the white is "on the inside" and the fact that it spills out to complicate his identity in a racially polarized society becomes the foundation for his examination of his coming of age in racist America.

Even before junior high school, Fulbeck recognized that his gender and emerging sexuality were inflected by race. The first story Fulbeck recounts in voiceover involves his classmate Laura and a field trip to Watts Towers, the massive structure of concrete and junk, once considered Simon Rodia's obsessive folly and now on the National Register of Historic Places, within the heart of a district that saw some of the worst racial violence of the 1960s. Thus, Fulbeck subtly links madness, beauty, racial tensions, and violence in his narrative. Kip goes on to list all the field trips Laura and he went on paired together ostensibly because of their predisposition to carsickness, including Chinatown and Mann's Chinese Theater. Because they were paired together, the general consensus favored the view that they were in love and would eventually marry. Kip, however, has never been attracted to Laura nor she to him. Rather, the childhood pairing arose from the fact that they were the only two Chinese children in their class, and a coupling based solely on race formed the norm even in early childhood. Because neither could find dates for the high school prom, they went with each other. Grouped within the "model minority," they shared the honor of class valedictorian.

However, from an apparently early age, they also shared a romantic attraction to whites. Although a title that reads, "My mom's still mad that I'm not dating Chinese," appears to refer to Laura's situation in relation to her parents, it may also refer to expectations Kip's mother has for his future bride. Images of a wedding with a Chinese bride that may be the wedding Laura plans to attend and photos of Kip and his date at the prom show the idealized veneer in relation to the actual feelings Laura and Kip have about the prospect of marriage based on common race or ethnicity rather than mutual attraction. In fact, images of weddings, brides, reception halls with the traditional Chinese character for marital "double happiness" flanked by the female phoenix and the male dragon for good luck, red envelopes filled with money for wedding gifts, wedding announcements, discussions of marital fidelity, and other reminders of other people's expectation that he would marry punctuate the video. A patina of harmony hides what may be a nagging element of ethnic self-loathing arising from a racist environment in which whiteness connotes bourgeois entitlement, the attainment of the American Dream, and sexual allure.

However, "success" also strikes a blow at self-esteem, a theme Fulbeck treats in his account of his only date with a Chinese woman. As images of a Chinese restaurant and gift shop appear onscreen, Fulbeck recounts the story of his date destroyed because of "Buddha's Feast," a Chinese vegetable dish that Laura loves and Kip cannot stomach. Whenever he tries to kiss her, the smell of the dish interferes, and Kip hiccups convulsively. "Buddha's Feast" represents Laura's "Chineseness" and everything that Fulbeck finds undesirable within himself because of the way racism has linked ethnicity to the old (the sauce used in the dish smells like the Tiger Balm his grandmother uses) and the foreign (e.g., the "otherness" of Buddhism in predominantly Christian America). Fulbeck's inability to kiss Laura indicates his incapacity to come to grips with himself as Chinese.

"Lawrence Is Two"

A poem entitled "Lawrence Is Two" composed by Fulbeck's father, Jack, to celebrate his son Lawrence/Larry/Kip's second birthday—

> That each of us is double—I, and you—
> And unsuspecting Lawrence, who is two.

—also acts as a structuring device throughout *Banana Split*. The "two," of course, functions on multiple levels in the poem as well as within the video, referring to the dual aspect of the toddler as hope for future immortality through the progeny of future generations, a reminder of past youth, and the "two-ness" of Kip's biracial identity and transcultural upbringing. The "two-ness" also evokes W. E. B. Du Bois's discussion of race in *The Souls of Black Folk:* "One ever feels his two-ness,—an American, a Negro; two souls, two thoughts, two unreconciled strivings; two warring ideals in one dark body, whose dogged strength alone keeps it from being torn asunder" ([1903] 1994, 2). Although Du Bois wrote these words in 1903 to describe the condition of African Americans, many of the sentiments expressed in this quotation also hold true in Fulbeck's video. His "two-ness," in fact, seems to be exacerbated by the experience of being biracial in a racist society. Fulbeck feels the tensions and contradictions of this split identity and struggles throughout his childhood and early adulthood with the violence of these forces that threaten to tear him apart, rob him of self-consciousness by imposing an identity on him, and, ultimately, throw his sexuality into doubt (Lowe 1996).

Throughout *Banana Split*, Fulbeck searches for "cultural alternatives" dialectically. He organizes his anecdotes about race in antithetical pairs, so that the tension of his own split identity dramatically surfaces. *Banana Split*, in fact, includes a series of incidents involving varying degrees of prejudice that Fulbeck handles in radically different ways. For example, he describes his father's difficulties being accepted in his wife's family. With minimal Chinese, Jack Fulbeck needs notes to help him play *tien gao,* a game similar to *mahjong,* with his in-laws. Although he only drinks white wine, Jack Fulbeck's in-laws give him Johnny Walker Red every Christmas, while complaining behind his back that he drinks too much. They also complain that he smells bad and talks too loudly.

However, later in the video, Kip picks up on many of these complaints when he shares a bed with his dad, who has not washed his feet. But Kip notes that, "It's not that bad this time." When discussing his white male roommate from Rhode Island, Kip also reiterates many of these prejudices. Over the strains of Johnny Winter's "Rock and Roll Hoochie Koo," he complains about his roommate's habits, which he sees as peculiarly "non-Asian." Appalled by his roommate's going to the gym to gawk at the "California girls" and his desire to put up a macramé hanging of a tiger because the wall looks empty, Fulbeck rationalizes his feelings as follows:

> It's not like it's prejudice; it's just easier. We could do the same things we've been doing since we were born. Take off your shoes, don't look funny eating with chopsticks . . . respect each other's privacy, don't drink, don't smoke, don't grow a mustache, keep your body clean. . . . We don't want your beard hair in the sink. Simplicity. Why do you have to have clutter?

Fulbeck longs for an ABC (American Born Chinese), an FOB (Fresh Off the Boat Asian), but will not tolerate an FCO (Fashion-Conscious Oriental), again linking racial prejudice with a certain degree of ethnic self-loathing. However, these prejudices pale in comparison to the racist violence that Kip endured during his youth. Bullied by older boys at the bus stop when he was five years old, he suffered a string of racist insults as his head was pressed over a broken mailbox post:

> Eat wood, Chinaman. Ching Chong Chinaman. Nigger skin, brownie, burnt potato chip, live in a hut. Ah so, ah so. Ass hole, ass hole. Right side bowl cut. Kung fu, Buddha Head, Fu Manchu, Chinese, Japanese, dirty knees, look at these. Woo, Wee, Wang, Long Dong Wong. Use dental floss for a blindfold. Kwai Chang Chinky chink, eat wood and have the splinter go all the way to your butt.

Although Kip got help from his older brother, who was in high school at the time, and his father brought the incident to the attention of the principal, the family suffered a final blow with a cherry bomb planted in their mailbox. Ultimately, institutions of public education do little to alleviate the problem of racism beginning in childhood. The public schools in *Banana Split* become institutions for the systematic perpetuation of racism, rather than arenas for understanding and tolerance. The brutality of this childhood assault resonates with a milder version of the story later in the tape, in which Kip uses racist invective to revenge another instance of bullying. In this case, he realizes one of the bullies, younger than himself, is black. As a title announces, "Jaime's a nigger," Fulbeck describes the younger boy's reaction in voiceover: "I just say, 'Shut up, nigger,' and his eyes flare up and he doesn't say anything. He just flips me off hard. I just smile, and he stops bothering me." Victimized by race in one instance, Kip uses racial privilege in another to mark his place in a social hierarchy based on color that seems to dominate schoolyard disputes.

For Fulbeck, public education means an education in race and racism. When Kip claims not to know what he learned in college, a friend counters, "You learned to be Chinese." In fact, the counter statement could be made about his elementary and high school years, during which time he learned not to "be" Chinese but to deny, at every opportunity, his racial and ethnic difference from his predominantly white classmates. An adult remarks, "All the Chinese has gone out of that boy," and Kip describes his reaction as follows: "And it makes me smile. Say it again. Speak English. It's my language. Don't talk Chinese in front of my friends."

Ethnic self-loathing, linked to white racism, becomes complicated by the demands of Chinese tradition and the expectations of Chinese American society. Again, Fulbeck is split between the two worlds.

However, three other childhood stories Fulbeck recounts in *Nine Fish* work toward healing that split by coming to grips with the inevitable difference and the sometimes shocking similarity between his two "halves." In one episode, he recounts going to the market in Hawaii with his grandmother. As the older Chinese women haggle over the prices in the malodorous market that Kip describes as "fish gut, pig head dirty," the seven-year-old boy loses his balance and upsets a pile of fish. His grandmother turns on him, yells at him, and, later, explains to the family that there is no fish for dinner because Kip embarrassed her at the market. While this story may, at first, seem to illustrate both the cultural difference of a Chinatown market and a more traditional attitude toward child-rearing that counts the misdeeds of the child as a reflection of the public "face" of the family in the Chinatown community, a parallel incident related later in the tape belies this reading, at least to a degree. In the second incident, the young Kip is at an American supermarket with his mother. Left alone with a shopping cart, he upsets a display of glass Scope mouthwash bottles. Although his mother offers to pay for the damage, the store manager just asks her to take her son and leave. Actually, the incident and outcome, inside and outside of Chinatown and involving different generations of Kip's female relatives, show that the cultural divide may not be so very broad. Rather, boyhood tomfoolery can be equally embarrassing, distressing, and memorable across cultural borders.

In another account in *Nine Fish*, Fulbeck tells of his German shepherd, Pepper, whom his father punished for killing a pet goose by tying the dead bird around the dog's neck. After describing the grotesque scene of the dog trying to rid itself of the bird, Fulbeck concludes that the dog absorbs the carcass's stench and "becomes one with the bird." Given the weight of Chinese filial tradition, metaphorically embodied for Kip by his grandmother, and the pain of his grandmother's impending death and his often-difficult relationship with her, the fact that Kip sees himself in the fate of his childhood pet cannot be denied. It is with the assent of his Anglo-American father that he learns to make peace with this burden. Eventually, like Pepper, he absorbs and "becomes one" with the troubling aspects of Chinese tradition. As he goes dramatically against Chinese custom by building a shrine for his grandmother's memory while she remains alive, he adjusts the traditions of his boyhood to suit the new circumstances of his adulthood within a hybridized American society.

CHILDHOOD HEROES: MEMORIES OF BRUCE LEE AND SHANG-CHI

Throughout his oeuvre Kip Fulbeck frames his own sense of racial and ethnic identity through the lens of popular culture. In addition to using it as a recurring theme in *Banana Split*, Fulbeck has devoted several videos entirely to the examination of the representation of Asians in American screen culture, including *Game of*

Death, Some Questions for 28 Kisses, American Studs Nightmare, and *Sex, Love, and Kung Fu.* However, Fulbeck's exploration of the Bruce Lee star image and the Marvel comic book character of Shang-Chi, both popular in the early 1970s when he was in elementary school, merits special attention within the context of any examination of Fulbeck's boyhood in his videos.

Bruce Lee and Shang-Chi function as yardsticks against which Fulbeck measures white America's perceptions of Chinese men. Although Fulbeck does not point it out, Lee and Shang-Chi are both Eurasians. One of Lee's grandparents was English, and the fictional Shang-Chi's mother was white (Chan 2001). Thus, the similarity Fulbeck sees between himself and these heroes may be compounded by their biracial identities.

During a cross-country road trip with his Asian American friend Hiroshige that Fulbeck calls the "Asian invasion," the pair startles a white man dressed as a cowboy, who seems to think the two Asian American young men are violent. A still of Bruce Lee links the reaction to popular cultural representations. This anecdote blends into a verbal enactment of a comic book panel from *Shang-Chi—Master of Kung Fu,* whose confused titular hero seeks to rid the world of his father, the diabolical Fu Manchu. In the strip, Shang-Chi encounters a white policeman (Fulbeck gives him an Irish accent) on the way to Chinatown. The policeman confronts Shang-Chi with crossing against the walk signal. Shang-Chi counters that the signal light cannot see traffic, while he can and that he would certainly stop, even if the signal told him to go, if he saw any cars. Since the signal does not know or care about pedestrians or traffic, Shang-Chi argues that he should simply be allowed to use his own judgment. Exasperated, the policeman finally says, "Go back to Chinatown where you belong." The episode is closed with another still of Bruce Lee whipping the staff out of the hands of his white opponent with his *nunchaku* and a voiceover revealing that the "cowboy" turns out to be "really nice" when it dawns on him that Kip and his friend are not robbers after all.

However, the association of Asian masculinity with violence lingers, as does the exotic mystique associated with Asian martial arts. For the young Kip growing up, Bruce Lee and Shang-Chi represent impossible ideals as well as markers of empowerment.

In Fulbeck's video rumination on Robert Clouse's *Game of Death,* the connections between race, masculinity, and youth appeal become salient. Fulbeck uses titles during the credit sequence of the film to underscore the racial identity of each character and the implications of Anglo-American Clouse's casting choices. Thus, the scene from an earlier film, *Return of the Dragon* (a.k.a. *Way of the Dragon* [1972]), in which Bruce Lee's character, Tang Lung, rips off the chest hair of Colt (Chuck Norris) in a duel that takes place in the Roman Coliseum becomes emblematic of the ascendancy of the oppressed (nonwhite, physically smaller, working class) against the power of the West (white, larger and heavier, bourgeois) within the literal ruins of Western civilization (Chiao 1981). Holding Colt's chest hair in his hand, Tang Lung blows it away in disgust. (Fulbeck, in fact, includes a title, "(disgust)," that includes the parentheses, in order to highlight Lee's ability to minimize white, male physical attractiveness as well as potency.)

For young men (Chinese as well as non-Chinese), Lee functions as an easy object of identification.[3] As Sheng-Mei Ma points out in *The Deathly Embrace: Orientalism and Asian American Identity*: "Bruce Lee has . . . been elevated into somewhat of a cult figure in the teen world. Undergoing drastic physical and psychological changes, adolescents yearn to be in control as in an idealized adulthood and to transcend limitations of the body. Teenagers, therefore, are especially susceptible to the kung fu mystique: sudden empowerment via a facile union of the body and the spirit, of the Western self and the Orient" (2000, 69–70).

Apparently small, vulnerable, naive, and impotent, Lee vanquishes the old order to make way for the emergence of a new generation. However, although Lee clearly had (and still has) a significant fan following among white youth (particularly preadolescent and adolescent boys), the fact that race figures so prominently as a factor in Lee's starring vehicles makes him a particularly potent object of identification for African American, Hispanic, and Asian American boys. In 1977, for example, at the age of twelve, Kip sees *Game of Death* on its opening day, anticipating a fantasy that will resonate with his own experiences, identity, and concerns. However, the replacement (after his death) of Bruce Lee by Bruce Li, the substitution of the fake for the authentic, disturbs Kip's enjoyment. Rather than finding a firm hero with an unquestionable identity, Kip encounters a split hero, played by two different people, one dead.

Fulbeck's relationship to Bruce Lee and Shang-Chi is not unproblematic, and he also looks elsewhere for models of heroism. In *Banana Split*, Lee's and Shang-Chi's theatrical aggression finds a complement in Kip's stories about his father's World War II military career in which martial prowess takes a back seat to the heroism of waiting for all members of the squadron to be accounted for, forgiving a comrade for a friendly fire incident, and maintaining friendships with fellow soldiers for years after the end of the war. Direct action gives way to the nuances of emotion, and Lee/Shang-Chi and Jack Fulbeck represent poles of identification for the young Kip. The "bad" white power of the American establishment, whether the capitalist underworld of *Game of Death* or the irritating pettiness of the police officer in *Shang-Chi—Master of Kung Fu*, must be negotiated as part of Kip's upbringing. Given that Kip comes of age at the end of the Vietnam War, the ways in which characters like Tang Lung and Shang-Chi resonate with a slightly older audience's questioning of white, male, American, military hegemonic violence lie buried in Fulbeck's analysis. Still, Kip's identification splits. He must construct a hybrid position that can accommodate the contradictions of his life in order to work through the aesthetics of the video and establish a social position.

Video Reflections on Ethnic Constructions

Fulbeck is quite cognizant of the implications of his technical and aesthetic choices throughout his oeuvre. In *L.A. Christmas*, for example, he uses a Fisher-Price toy Pixelvision camera to record the family's holiday gathering. Although Fulbeck is an adult when the film is made, the use of the child's toy indicates visually and viscerally that the images shown onscreen must be appreciated from a child's perspective as wall as an adult's. This split identification emerges here through the choice of technology as Fulbeck looks at himself and his family simultaneously from an adult's and a child's perspective. For example, he picks up on many of the themes he had previously explored in *Banana Split*, including the appeal of Asian martial arts to young Chinese Americans and the expectation of math genius within the Asian American community. Departing from the stillness of the images that characterize *Banana Split*, *Just Stand Still*, and *Nine Fish*, Fulbeck holds the toy while practicing kicks with a "black belt" nine-year-old and prompting his other nephew to recite pi to two hundred digits. Throughout the video, Fulbeck also comments on his use of the toy technology as he trains his mother to shoot video and asks for her opinion on the appropriateness of this choice for a work he plans to show in festivals. Seckyue Fulbeck questions the choice not to use the "best equipment" and treats her son like a child throughout the Christmas festivities by asking him not to chew with his mouth open, be kind to all the relatives, and not to use insecure, outdoor ATMs. Fulbeck, of course, eggs her on by asking questions from a child's perspective. For example, he asks why a household of Muslims, Buddhists, and atheists should sing Christmas carols, and her only reply is, "I think we are quite normal." Seckyue's eye looms large as she looks through the wrong end of the lens and visually turns around any idea of "normalcy" in the multicultural Fulbeck household.

Similarly, throughout *Banana Split*, Fulbeck reminds the viewer of the constructed nature of the video and the self-consciousness of its address to its audience. In a title, Fulbeck reveals that the games of *tien gao* shown were staged for the video: "Ma, Dad, and me go to Uncle C.K.'s and Auntie Barbara's to play 'tien gao.' We haven't played in years, but I want the sound and I need the shots so we go. It's a nice place. There's a shrine upstairs and the house is full of those little Chinese things I shoot that you like to look at." Throughout the video, Fulbeck includes "those little Chinese things I shoot that you like to look at" from game tiles to koi fish to household decorations in order to use objects to indicate the constructed quality of his own ethnicity and give visual clues to expectations about the "essence" of Chineseness.

Fulbeck concludes *Banana Split* with a voiceover that returns to one of the key visual themes of the work, fish, by relating a story about the purchase of a predatory fish that devours the "born-to-die" feeder fish bought at the same time. As we hear this story, the images onscreen move backward chronologically from Kip as a child to his parents' wedding with black-and-white photographs of the couple being pelted with rice as they leave the altar. A black border frames the final image as the voiceover intones, "Frame it right, and everything is okay." In order to come to grips with his own identity, Kip Fulbeck must "frame" his parents' interracial, multiethnic, cross-cultural union "right" to make "everything okay." He needs to step back from the pain of killing feeder fish to enjoy his predatory pet, just as he must step back from the agony of living in a racist society to accept himself and his place in his family. By making the traumas of his childhood, adolescence, and young adulthood into an object of aesthetic contemplation, Fulbeck "frames it right" and works to purge the pain of racism and his own sometimes willing, sometimes unwitting, complicity with it.

NOTES

1. Much of Soe's work resonates particularly strongly with Fulbeck's, including *Picturing Oriental Girls* (1992) and *Mixed Blood* (1992–94). See Soe 2000.
2. Although not as well known or widely discussed, Ben Fong-Torres, *The Rice Room: Growing Up Chinese-American: From Number Two Son to Rock 'N' Roll* (New York: Penguin, 1995) may be worth noting. Although he represents an older generation, Fong-Torres's relationship to the youth counterculture and his involvement in popular culture make his autobiography resonate in some interesting ways with Fulbeck's work.
3. Although she does not make a direct connection to youth culture, Meaghan Morris does note the fact that many martial arts films are structured around master-pupil relations, and, certainly, narratives involving pedagogy have direct appeal to boys trying to navigate issues of what to learn and from whom, as they mature. See Morris 2001.

WORKS CITED

Chan, Jachinson. 2001. *Chinese American Masculinities: From Fu Manchu to Bruce Lee.* New York: Routledge.

Chiao, Hsiung-Ping. 1981. "Bruce Lee: His Influence on the Evolution of the Kung Fu Genre," *Journal of Popular Film and Television* 9, no. 1, 30–42.

Du Bois, W. E. B. [1903] 1994. *The Souls of Black Folk.* New York: Dover.

Fanon, Frantz. 1967. *Black Skin, White Masks.* Trans. Charles Lam Markmann. New York: Grove.

Feng, Peter X., ed. 2002. *Screening Asian Americans.* New Brunswick, NJ: Rutgers University Press.

Fong-Torres, Ben. 1995. *The Rice Room: Growing Up Chinese-American: From Number Two Son to Rock 'N' Roll.* New York: Penguin.

Fulbeck, Kip. 2001a. *Paper Bullets: A Fictional Autobiography.* Seattle: University of Washington Press.

———. 2001b. "Stealing Vision." In *Out of the Shadows: Asians in American Cinema*, ed. Roger Garcia, 211–12. Milan: Edizioni Olivares, produced in conjunction with the 54th Locarno International Film Festival.

———. 2002. Seaweed Productions Web site, http://www.seaweedproductions.com/.

Garcia, Roger, ed. 2001. *Out of the Shadows: Asians in American Cinema.* Milan: Edizioni Olivares, produced in conjunction with the 54th Locarno International Film Festival.

Hamamoto, Darrell Y., and Sandra Liu, eds. 2000. *Countervisions: Asian American Film Criticism.* Philadelphia: Temple University Press.

Kim, Elaine. 1982. *Asian American Literature: An Introduction to the Writings and Their Social Context.* Philadelphia: Temple University Press.

Kingston, Maxine Hong. 1977. *The Woman Warrior: Memoirs of a Girlhood among Ghosts.* New York: Vintage.

Leong, Russell, ed. 1991. *Moving the Image: Independent Asian Pacific American Media Arts.* Los Angeles: UCLA Asian American Studies Center and Visual Communications.

Lowe, Lisa. 1996. *Immigrant Acts: On Asian American Cultural Politics.* Durham, NC: Duke University Press.

Ma, Sheng-Mei. 2000. *The Deathly Embrace: Orientalism and Asian American Identity.* Minneapolis: University of Minnesota Press.

Morris, Meaghan. 2001. "Learning from Bruce Lee: Pedagogy and Political Correctness in Martial Arts Cinema." In *Keyframes: Popular Cinema and Cultural Studies,* ed. Matthew Tinkcom and Amy Villarego, 171–86. London: Routledge.

Soe, Valerie. 2000. "Fighting Fire with Fire: Detournement, Activism, and Video Art." In *Countervisions: Asian American Film Criticism,* ed. Darrell Y. Hamamoto and Sandra Liu, 177–85. Philadelphia: Temple University Press.

Xing, Jun. 1998. *Asian America through the Lens: History, Representations, and Identity.* Walnut Creek, CA: Alta Mira Press.

16

CINEMATIC SOLUTIONS TO THE TRUANCY TREND AMONG JAPANESE BOYS

Christopher Ames

> The educational problems children are raising pose to us a difficult question: what should adults be like?
> Kawai

Boyhood truancy is not a new theme in Japanese films. When two brothers in elementary school cut class in Ozu Yasujiro's silent film *Umaretewa mita keredo (I Was Born But . . .)* (1932), their parents scolded them. Nearly seven decades later, Fukasaku Kinji's *Batoru Rowaiaru (Battle Royale)* (2000) depicts a far more severe punishment for truancy and disobedience: in accordance with a new national law, each year one entire classroom of junior high school students are selected, given weapons, sent to an island, and forced to kill one another as their teacher provides guidance from a command post. Fukasaku, the master of Japanese *yakuza* mafia films, uses extreme violence to parody the frustration parents and teachers feel about perceptions of adult loss of authority over young people in contemporary Japan. Indeed, truancy is a central focus of the filmic treatment of boyhood in Japan. If troubled and troublesome boys are a perennial theme in Japanese film history, narrative films directly addressing the specific issue of chronic truancy *(futoko)* have become something of a subgenre only recently.

Historically, some of Japan's best-known directors have produced boy's films *(shonen eiga)*. These include films by Ozu Yasujiro and a series of films by Shimizu Hiroshi. The most noteworthy of Shimizu's creations about boys is *Kaze no naka no kodomo (Children in the Wind)* (1937), a film in which two young brothers work to free their wrongly imprisoned father who has become embroiled in a property dispute. A boy "revitalizing" his selfish adult benefactors is the theme of the Ozu film *Nagaya shinshiroku (Record of a Tenement Gentleman)* (1947), a classic example of Japanese film demonstrating how seemingly naughty little boys can serve as catalysts for the spiritual betterment of adults. Amid the chaos and limited material resources of the early occupation, a middle-aged man brings a young boy—who is either lost or abandoned—back to his neighborhood. An aging widow reluctantly takes the boy in only to find that he warms her heart just in time for his father to return to claim him. Often, as in *Battle Royale,* children are basically good until made to do evil by parents. This assumption underlies much of Yamada Yoji's work—he is director of the *A Class to Remember* series discussed in this essay as well as the more famous *Otoko wa tsurai yo (It's Tough Being a Man)* series. In Oshima Nagisa's *Shonen (The Boy)* (1969), morally bankrupt parents force their son to run into automobiles as they speed through the city in a scheme of extorting money from the motorists. Kitano Takeshi's *Kikujiro no natsu (Kikujiro)* (1999) offers a contemporary example of this moral's application in Japanese film. A lonely nine-year-old boy named Masao lights out to search for a mother he has never seen. He ends up being accompanied on the road by a gambling loudmouth named Kikujiro (played by the director appearing under his stage name Beat Takeshi). The adult Kikujiro ends up "learning the heartwarming lesson that sometimes it takes a child's games to help us see exactly what went wrong with our own lives" (1999 Cannes International Film Festival program).

The present essay explores contemporary cinematic representations of boys who struggle with truancy in Japanese schools. Among the films examined, *Battle Royale* offers the most exaggerated cinematic delineation of social breakdown in contemporary schools. Many parents, teachers, and politicians nationwide objected to this film vociferously, resulting in it receiving an R-15 rating (Machiyama 2001). On the other hand, adults concerned with education frequently find merit in futoko films such as Yamada Yoji's *Gakko IV: Jugo-sai (A Class to Remember IV)* (2000) and Nakayama Setsuo's *Akane-iro no sora o mita yo (Hope beyond the Crimson Skies)* (2000). Often, adults are attracted to these conventional narratives because they promise to elucidate and perhaps even to remedy truancy problems. The happy endings offered by Yamada and Nakayama fulfill adult desires that futoko is not a permanent condition. Outside of the theater, however, many parents and teachers fear that students who refuse to go to school will be irreversibly marginalized in a public educational system dominated by pressure on students to pass entrance examinations at the high school and college level. Children who refuse to attend school raise the specter of adult failure. Somewhat ironically, it is at least partially due to the rigors of the educational system that the majority of Japanese value education and work highly (White 1984). In general, society expects parents and teachers alike to be able to socialize and control children.

Addressing futoko through punishment and rewards (ame to muchi—literally "candy" and "whips") has been shown to be unsuccessful (Inamura 1997). Parents and teachers become desperate for solutions as well as anxious to avoid blame. Futoko has received so much attention in the media and at PTA meetings that it would be unusual for parents concerned about education to be entirely free from fear that their children will one day abruptly refuse to attend school. One of the challenges of this problem is that it is often the "most serious" students who refuse to go to school (Inamura 1997). Still, children passively resisting education are less common than the level of attention the issue has received would appear to indicate; less than 2 percent of middle school students and less than 1 percent of elementary school students miss more than fifty days of school per year (Inamura). At the individual level, perhaps interest in the subject is high because the stakes for the children are so extreme; once a child leaves the system it is very hard for him or her to be reintegrated. A rising trend in chronic truancy augurs loss of adult authority, future economic problems, and a general loss of control; in short, all of the things that *Battle Royale*'s opening titles identify as leading the government to force children to kill one another.

The melodramatic depictions of boyhood offered in *A Class to Remember IV, Hope beyond the Crimson Skies* and *Battle Royale* may be painted with heavy hands, but these films provide palpable clues to the challenges that boys face in contemporary Japanese society. In a manner similar to the economic instability that has troubled their parents' generation for over a decade, Japanese boys today face an uncertain future in which the predictable "life-cycle" trajectory financed by nearly constant postwar economic growth can no longer be relied upon. For many boys, the pressure to enter prestigious high schools and colleges is greater than ever as fewer and fewer new graduates find stable careers. Boys whose goals are less ambitious face even bleaker futures. The rewards of boyhood academic toil are uncertain. Gone are relatively pristine role models of dedicated bureaucrat and businessman; today, the media bathes these figures in unprecedented levels of blame for economic malaise and the concurrent social ills that accompany it. In this situation, many boys are overwhelmed and simply withdraw. Futoko is a temporary stage for most who experience it; however, greater and greater numbers of boys withdraw completely from social interaction becoming *hiki komori* (social withdrawal), a condition that overwhelmingly affects boys more often than girls. Paradoxically, the realization of Japanese prosperity through decades of extreme toil by generations of Japanese has created conditions wherein young boys, who are accustomed to relatively affluent lives during their childhood, can neither imagine working like their parents nor being as well off as them when they reach adulthood.

Boys must also come to terms with changes in power distribution in gender relations. Japan's slow progress toward becoming a more gender equitable culture has led many boys to see girls' gains as boys' losses. High school age boys today can recall their early elementary school days when sexism was institutionalized via "boys first" rules from role call in homeroom to the tacit practice of electing boys to the executive positions in student government and girls to the secondary or "vice" position. Although in the long run, more equitable gender relations are in the interest of Japanese society and boys themselves, boys feel this loss of concentrated power acutely, perhaps more so than girls feel the diffuse and subtle gains that may accompany the redistribution of power. Traditional valorization of different stages in the putative Japanese lifecycles of males and females assures that Japanese boys sometimes feel placed in a double bind, stretched in different directions between progressive reform and regressive "traditional" social practices. In general, males in Japan do not achieve power until relatively late in life, based upon the objectification of their socioeconomic position (men as paychecks). Females, particularly those who are deemed "cute" (*kawaii*), are subject to objectification in their teen years, receiving "power" under patriarchy through the valorization of their physical beauty and youth (women as aesthetic commodities). This disjuncture in the timeline of the distribution of power between genders under Japanese patriarchy has been associated with contemporary manifestations of prostitution (a.k.a. "compensated dating") in which older men compensate schoolgirls for their attention (including companionship and sex).

D. P. Martinez (1997) analyzes how British documentary filmmakers "otherize" the Japanese school system, conditioned as their method is by prevalent foreign stereotypes of the Japanese educational system, for instance, that it is "quasi-militaristic" or that in it "all learning is rote learning." The resultant films say more about British fears of economic and educational decline, Martinez suggests, than they do about the "realities" of the Japanese school system. The necessity of making choices about what to include and exclude in the script and cinematography ensures that all films are mediated products situated within specific cultural and political milieux and arising from the intersection of subjectivities of artists and audiences. Most recent Japanese "social problem" films taking on the subject of chronic truancy were principally mediated through the consciousness of elderly adults; the directors of *Battle Royale, A Class to Remember* and *Hope beyond the Crimson Skies* are all over seventy years old.

This is not to say that elderly filmmakers cannot effectively evoke children's perspectives. Yamada, who is known for his sentimental style, has indicated in interviews that he identifies with today's youth and their difficulties. In an interview with Japanese actor Muta Teizo on the *A Class to Remember* series, he states, "Since I was born just before the war, like the current generation I spent my adolescence, which is the most important period for children, thinking that 'this is no place for a kid'" (Yamada 1999, 220). Yamada experienced a period of social withdrawal during his college days at the prestigious Tokyo University's Faculty of Law. Finding his courses difficult and the competition steep, he kept to himself and spent much of his freshman year in bed reading and sleeping. Eventually, one of his friends talked him into returning (*Nichiyobi no hiro* column, *Nikkan Supotsu*, October 10, 2000). Fukasaku, in contrast, has readily acknowledged the challenge of making social problem films about children from a different generation. In an interview with Tom Mees and Jasper Sharp, Fukasaku remarks, "I am fully aware that there is a generation gap between where I stand and where those kids stand. How we fill this gap was one of the issues we had to deal with during the actual shooting of the film" (n.d.). As veteran filmmakers in their seventies, both directors have achieved success in creating realistic portrayals of radically different perspectives. Japanese director Harada Masato, director of *Bounce Ko-Gals* (1997) and *Kamikaze Taxi* (1995), notes that the structure of the mainstream Japanese film industry, which operates on the apprenticeship system, makes it difficult for younger directors to get a chance to make "fresh" films (Interview with Harada, Ann Arbor, Michigan, February 1, 2001).

In some respects, these films say more about adults and the chronic truancy phenomenon than they do about the myriad realities of futoko or children's perspectives on the issue. For many contemporary adults, whether directly affected or not, the truancy problem is emblematic of the difference between themselves and the present generation of students (for further discussion see Clarke, Hall, Jefferson, and Roberts 1972). Truancy is a sign that since the late 1980s the school system might be failing just as the economy has been weakening, two indicators of social problems that *Battle Royale* uses to illustrate why "the nation collapsed."

A CHALLENGED JAPANESE EDUCATIONAL SYSTEM

In the 1980s the popular and the academic presses in Japan and abroad frequently depicted Japan's public education system as highly successful at producing disciplined students who fuelled Japanese economic growth and scored high on international achievement tests (see in particular the work of Merry White [1984; 1993; 2002]). When the "bubble economy" burst at the end of the decade, however, domestic confidence in the putatively traditional values of Japanese society, including the educational system, began to wane, contributing to the increase in prevalence and popularity of what Susan Napier (2000) calls an "apocalyptic mode" in Japanese film. In tandem with foreign interest in Japanese management that lingered beyond the bubble's bursting, many non-Japanese scholars and pundits continued to view the Japanese education system monolithically. In Japan, however, the emergent economic ebb tide had long since revealed not only industrial inefficiencies but also social problems that were often partially obscured by decades of unbridled optimism. The central government embarked on educational system reform in the 1980s to "internationalize" schools at the local level and "individualize" the general educational environment, but more pressing problems were emerging by the end of the decade (Burnett 2002). Truancy and school violence began receiving greater and greater attention in the media as the number of students refusing to attend school expanded rapidly. The national education ministry began to address the problem as futoko (chronic truancy) rather than simply kids who "hate school" (*gakko girai*). Eventually, futoko became a household word as children, parents, teachers, commentators, and government officials struggled to find ways to address the problem. Despite extensive government research and policy adjustment, solutions did not emerge. From 1977 to 1993 the number of children refusing to go to school for more than fifty days per school year in Japan increased five-fold from roughly 12,000 elementary and junior high school students to approximately 57,000 students.[1] By 1999, according to the Japan Teachers Union, nearly 130,000 primary and middle school children were chronically truant.[2]

Although children's refusal to attend school has been the subject of social research in Japan since the 1950s, the amount of scholarship in this field has increased dramatically since the early 1990s. Ultimately, the contemporary social milieu, as well as researchers' biases, strongly conditions the causes that have been identified, notable among which is bullying (see Morita 1991; Inamura 1997). However, bullying is merely one factor among many. Unlike futoko, bullying is not regarded as a new social problem. Certainly, earlier films, including Ozu Yasujiro's *Umaretewa mita keredo (I Was Born But . . .)* do not shy away from depicting boys bullying one another. Research has confirmed, however, that there is tremendous variation in the situations and motivations of children who refuse to attend school. From 1991 the Japanese education ministry has employed a seven-category typology to classify cases of school refusal, ranging from causes arising from lifestyle, a desire to play, lassitude, anxiety, willful refusal, compound cases and "other" (Inamura 1997, 61). Yet, these causes do not identify what makes *Class, Hope,* and *Battle* so interesting and what appears to concern adults the most: responsibility and blame. Teachers blame parents. Parents blame teachers. Nearly everyone—including truant children—fault kids. Extreme conservatives such as former Prime Minister Yoshiro Mori contend that contemporary school-related behavioral problems should be addressed by a reinstatement of the Imperial Rescript on Education (*kyoiku chokugo*), a prewar document that stressed maintenance of traditional hierarchical relations in the family state under the paternalistic emperor system.[3]

THE ROAD AND REALISM

Well-known film critic Sato Tadao has suggested that audiences of films addressing futoko may be primarily hoping to find solutions to it. Indeed, based on my conversations with viewers and industry representatives, many adult spectators of futoko films such as *Gakko IV* and *Hope beyond the Crimson Skies* seem to come to the film with such a desire, hoping that the film will suspend their tension by offering a fictitious solution to nagging and seemingly unsolvable, potentially *personal* problems. Preexisting tension is momentarily resolved only to return after the fantasy ends with the film. Thus, paradoxically, the film brings merely an ersatz resolution that heightens preexisting tension by creating contrast between the all-too-easy fantasy solution and the myriad, complex problems that viewers bring to the theater. Futoko represents to many Japanese parents and teachers not only the threat that children will not reach their career and personal potential, but also the suggestion that loss of control over children is symbolic of an increasing challenge of inability to control the self due to denial of traditional authority by an insubordinate other.

Yamada's *A Class to Remember IV* limits issues of causation to the microlevel, emphasizing the boy's immaturity as well as the roles his parents, a worrisome mother and an authoritarian father, play in fomenting truancy. As Yamada indicates in a monologue accompanying the Shochiku studio's trailer for the film, he wants *A Class to Remember IV* to render visible the invisible causes of futoko for the audience. In the opening scene, the protagonist Daisuke, a fifteen-year-old boy, states his reasons for not wanting to go to school as the camera pans the classroom where his absence is marked by a goldfish bowl on his desk: "I hate school. Why do I have to go to school?" He thinks school is boring and he hates his teachers' inflexible, scripted teaching methods. Daisuke's question has the resonance of what has been on every child's mind at some point during his or her school years. This was also the question, directed at Yamada by a male student at a school lecture the director gave in the mid-1990s, that provided Yamada with the idea for the film (Yamada comments in Shochiku's promotional trailer). Nevertheless, the ostensible reasons given by Daisuke do not exhaust the audience's desire to know the *true* cause of his truancy. Daisuke, and the audience as well, must go on an odyssey before his behavior becomes comprehensible.[4]

One day Daisuke sneaks away from home while his parents are at work, leaving only a note for his mother saying, "Don't worry, I'm on an adventure." He has been thinking for some time that if he could visit a 7,000-year-old cedar at Yakushima, an island off of the coast of Japan's southernmost large island of Kyushu, his vigor would return. His trip does not start off well because the elderly man who gives him a lift becomes suspicious, asking Daisuke why he is not in school, berating him for his truancy. Daisuke jumps out of the car and tries to hitchhike again. The adults that he meets during the rest of the film are far more understanding. A male truck driver from the Kansai district expresses empathy when he learns that Daisuke is chronically truant. His next ride is with a middle-aged female trucker. She is quiet at first but when she asks why he is not in school it is unclear whether or not she is sympathetic. Ultimately, however, they warm to each other. Upon arrival in her hometown, she takes Daisuke home to stay for the evening. There, he discovers that she has a high school age son, Noboru, who is not only not going to school but has almost completely withdrawn from all social relations. Noboru simultaneously represents Daisuke's possible fate as well as his possible redemption.[5] Daisuke befriends the silent Noboru, helping someone even more alienated than himself. In return, Noboru gives Daisuke one of the jigsaw puzzles he completed with a poem on the back. The poem is about a medieval masterless samurai who proceeds through life at his own pace. Noboru has provided Daisuke with the key to his recovery. Later, when Daisuke arrives on Yakushima, he has already realized that he simply wants to live life at his own pace, a contemporary theme among young people (*mai pesu*); now the hike to the ancient tree is no longer so important. His next encounter is with a young adult female hiker who travels with him to see the giant tree. She accepts Daisuke's decision to avoid school but on the condition that he become a self-sufficient human being. He is not sure what this means until he gets lost in the mountain forest during a severe storm upon returning from the awe-inspiring tree. He fears he will die, but musters the strength to survive. Later, his growth is complete when he befriends an old Yakushima man who gives him a ride. He intends to stay with the old man—who hates his son—for a short period at first, but then decides to take care of the old man after he gets ill and wets himself. Going against the old man's wishes he calls the man's son, who works on the distant mainland. When the son arrives with an ambulance in tow, he embarrasses his father by commenting aloud at how much his incontinence has made his bedding stink. The film climaxes as Daisuke angrily scolds the son for being so insensitive, saying, "You wore diapers when you were an infant!" Essentially, Daisuke has become an adult by recognizing the childish behavior of another adult. At the end of the film, Daisuke returns home to reconcile his relationship with his parents. Ultimately, he returns to school.

The cinematic solution that Yamada's film offers to remedy Daisuke's case of "chronic truancy" is that the boy needed space to grow on his own at his own pace. As the trailer for the film suggests, "He traveled by himself to Yakushima where he found a school for him alone." This theme and others in the film—depicting a boy taking off on a long journey by himself, for instance, and representing teachers as aloof or unsympathetic to kids who are experiencing futoko—irritated some teachers. An editorial on the Japan Teachers Union's Web site excoriated the film for its representation of Daisuke's teacher as unsympathetic as well as for the "irresponsible" portrayal of a junior high school boy embarking on a trip across Japan on his own. Missing the film's point that solutions to futoko are individualized, this teacher thought that the film would incite boys to run away from home. This solution is highly appealing to those who feel threatened by chronic truancy because it operates through an evolutionary logic propelling Daisuke toward resolution of his problems. For children experiencing futoko, resolution—if it comes at all—might not follow such a linear trajectory. I watched and discussed these films with a fifteen-year-old named Tanaka Makoto who went through futoko during his second year of middle school. Makoto felt that *A Class to Remember IV*, despite its syrupy-sweet sentimentality, provided parallels with his own experiences. In particular, he identified with the protagonist Daisuke's boredom with school and his feelings of nausea on school day mornings that retreated in the afternoon. Yet, for this real fifteen-year-old, the filmmaker's decision to drive the narrative with Daisuke's conscious odyssey of personal growth appears as a conspicuously adult imposition of causation—and resolution—for a situation characterized in many accounts as a vague emotional state rather than a conscious motivation (Inamura 1997).

Ironically, the only educational film (*kyoiku eiga*) among the films discussed in this essay turns out to be the least overtly didactic. Nakayama Setsuo's independently produced *Hope beyond the*

Promotional leaflet for *Hope beyond the Crimson Skies* featuring the title and asking "Do you hate me for not going to school?" in large characters (upper right).

Crimson Skies does not attempt to root out clear causation or blame. One reading, of course, is that it too easily lets culpable adults "off the hook," reassuring them that it is not their fault that children have problems. This film has been shown throughout Japan to a generally receptive audience through self-sponsored screenings at community centers. Tanaka Tomoko, my correspondent Makoto's mother, contends that compared to *A Class to Remember IV*, parents receive less blame in the dramatic educational film *Hope beyond the Crimson Skies*. Sato Tadao likewise recognizes this as the principal strength of the film. In his view, the film's appeal is located precisely in its avoidance of clearly ascribing cause or blame for the boy protagonist's bout with futoko (1995). Resolution in this film takes place without blame, sparing specters of extreme personal conflict for members of the audience who face futoko daily. When resolution arrives in Nakayama's film, it is through a comparatively circuitous route in a story that emphasizes the protagonist Hiroshi's subjectivity.

Hiroshi yells "Get lost, bitch!" at his mother Kazuko, who cries all day. He has been futoko for five years, since the second semester of his third year in middle school. He has attempted suicide more than once out of frustration. Every time he tries to kill himself, his mother tries tearfully to stop him. Mitsuo, the boy's father, is at a loss. By Hiroshi's fifth year in this situation, his parents are only concerned with his physical protection. The boy's older brother, Akira, also struggled trying to find his future direction. Akira encourages Hiroshi to become independent. Despite not attending school, Hiroshi automatically graduates from middle school under the Japanese public education system. He decides to go to a special high school where classes are held at night. Hiroshi begins to live by himself in an apartment in Okayama Prefecture, working at a noodle shop during the day and attending high school at night. Hiroshi has started to establish his own life at work and school. For the first time in his life he makes friends, warming to his classmates and his homeroom teacher. He begins to cheer up and even starts participating playing volleyball at school. However, before long he somehow stops going to school and work again. This leads him to recall the pain he experienced during his earlier futoko phase. The difference now, however, is that he is aware of his parents' and friends' concern for him. He finds sympathy in a female friend named Masami as they communicate through poetry. Hiroshi also learns from his friends as they manage to overcome life's small troubles one at a time. Developing strong bonds, Hiroshi and his pals begin to find their own way in life as they prepare to graduate. In the end, Hiroshi gives a graduation address before the parents and students assembled.

Unlike *A Class to Remember IV*, which is the product of one of Japan's oldest and biggest commercial studios, Nakayama's film was primarily produced to be shown at PTA meetings, support group meetings for parents of truant children, and schools. It is one of a limited number of educational films to become a Japanese Ministry of Education, Culture, Sports, Science and Technology's

(MEXT) special selection in addition to being a special selection of the national-level PTA. A group of concerned parents in Okayama Prefecture raised money for its production. The film is based on a book written by a man who grew up in Okayama and refused to go to school from fifth through ninth grade. Nakayama, the film's director, is a veteran maker of educational films. Although Nakayama has been making films about the problems children face for decades, he did not consider making a film about futoko until he read this book. Lacking the resources of a major studio, he employed amateur actors for this film. All of the children in the film, including the protagonist Hiroshi, are children from Okayama. The film is available for screenings by local parents' groups for nominal fees.

Hope beyond the Crimson Skies was completed before Yamada's *A Class to Remember IV* went into production; according to Nakayama, the first thing he did when he finished the film was to take it to Yamada to screen it together. Nakayama sees the two films as belonging to discrete genres. Although the films address the same problem, their points of intersection are limited because Yamada's film is a purely fictitious, entertainment film (*goraku eiga*) whereas *Hope beyond the Crimson Skies* is an educational film based on the experiences of someone who struggled with futoko. Still, the films share a fundamental premise, and one that makes sense to me, essentially that boys need to proceed through life at their own paces. The Japanese educational system does not offer many avenues for people who screw up early. The idea of adult education or second chances for people who were not stellar students in adolescence is gaining currency in Japan as evidenced by more flexible entrance exam policies and increasingly individualized curricula. Unlike *A Class to Remember IV*'s protagonist, the lead character in this film is troubled deeply enough to attempt suicide many times. Likewise, his absence from school has extended well beyond the "typical" several months depicted in Yamada's film. Nakayama's film explores the internal world of its protagonist with a touch of realism. Hiroshi's recovery is never a sure thing. According to Nakayama, the greatest challenge of making a film about futoko was having sufficient action to hold the audience's attention. The director's earlier films on the struggles of children in the Japanese educational system, especially *Yagate . . . haru (Spring Is Coming)* (1986), which addresses school bullying

Chronically truant lead character Hiroshi encounters his peers outside school in *Hope beyond the Crimson Skies.*

(*ijime*), were comparatively easier to make because they featured more action and did not concentrate as much on the subjective world of their protagonists.[6] The challenge of creating a dramatic film with subtlety when action is limited in some sense mirrors the nature of contemporary Japanese educational problems: as incidents of bullying are decreasing, the number of children passively refusing to attend school is growing. It is hard to make a dramatic film on futoko without imposing linearity, cause and blame. The nebulousness and personal nature of futoko's causes is one of the things that motivated Nakayama. He notes that the age at which children experience futoko is getting younger and younger while the causes—formerly ascribed to bullying—have apparently diversified. He contends that something is radically amiss in contemporary Japanese schools, something individual as well as social. Thus, government educational policies alone will not be able to address the problem effectively.

A MODEST PROPOSAL

The challenge of futoko for parents and teachers extends beyond the phenomenon itself; it is perhaps symbolic of the threat implicit in perceived radical changes in notions of Japanese childhood, and, by extension, of the power position of Japanese adults vis-à-vis children. For some conservatives, such as Tokyo governor Ishihara Shintaro, the current generation is seen as weird and weak (Ishihara 1999). Ultranationalist Ishihara resembles former Prime Minister Mori in his support for seeking solutions to current problems in the authoritarian prewar past. Today's "weak" youth are viewed as the products of postwar individualism and materialism. It is precisely the revival of such government control over individual lives that director Fukasaku argues against in *Battle Royale.* Early in its production, the Japanese motion picture ethics committee, Eirin, gave the film an R-15 rating based on the violence in its script. Opposition to the film mushroomed as politicians, officials in the education ministry, and PTA groups spoke out opposing it. As elsewhere in the world, literature on youth crime in Japan is replete with speculation about the influence of films and videogames on children's behavior. As Machiyama Tomo (2001) points out, Fukasaku's film is directed against this questionable position; Machiyama states, "He thought today's teenagers needed to know the difference between real killing and DOOM . . . to do that, *Battle Royale* should look as disgusting as possible" (Macias and Ujihashi 2001, 150–51).

Although the children in *Battle Royale* murder one another, the film blames adults for making them violent. Criticism of *Battle* often includes parallels with *Lord of the Flies,* although in the latter adults are fundamentally absent and in *Battle* they actually lead the kids into violence. A series of titles during the film's opening moments states: "At the dawn of the millennium the nation collapsed. At 15% unemployment, 10 million were out of work, 800,000 students boycotted school. The adults lost confidence and fearing the youth, eventually passed the Millennium Educational Reform Act, a.k.a. the BR Act." The titles are followed by a voiceover in which a boy character explains how adults have betrayed him. He says that his mother left when he was in elementary school; as the camera follows him into his home he finds his father has hung himself. The boy retches in the toilet. The camera wanders from the scene of the suicide as the boy states that he has no one to guide him, moving to a standard Japanese group class photo that shifts from monochrome to color as it zooms in, first on the teacher (Beat Takeshi) and then on the lead characters. The morphing of the photograph suggests that although the story is set in the future, it could just as easily be about the past. Parallels with the past are not an accident. In response to criticisms by conservative politicians of *Battle Royale*'s adolescent bloodshed, Fukasaku has drawn explicit connections between the imaginary violence by and against children in his satirical film and the very real violence perpetrated against children by Japan during the Pacific War (Machiyama 2001, 152). The voiceover of the boy's story continues as the camera moves to a classroom where the teacher is seated on a desk looking at a message left by the class, reading "Takin' the day off 'cuz we want to." The plot of the film essentially turns on the ironic tension between collective punishment via the draconian law and the individual loyalties and betrayals that arise from the policy of allowing only one survivor. This may be read as something of an exploration of the friction between any collective and its individual members. Friends must kill one another in a zero-sum game resembling the competitive environment in which Japanese youth are immersed: from their third year in middle school, the student must prepare for high school entrance exams; if he does not want to "fall through the cracks" into eternal part-time employment and day labor, he must rise to the occasion and compete with his schoolmates for limited slots in the "good" high schools. The pressure mounts as masses of students rush to improve their position all at once, making it very difficult to get ahead. If preparation for the entrance exam system received less attention and children were permitted to learn about things that interested them, school might become a more attractive place. But in this and other contemporary Japanese films, public schools are almost without exception represented as rigid institutions. Unlike real futoko students, however, kids in the film who are forced to kill one another cannot withdraw from a situation that terrorizes them. *Battle Royale*'s exaggerated cinematic solution to truancy eliminates the possibility of passive resistance via withdrawal. Participants must either fight or die, as the previous game's winner, who was inserted into the game as a "ringer" to fix the results, reminds the protagonists Shuya and Noriko. Despite this existential dilemma, Shuya and Noriko refuse to kill their classmates and end up surviving.

Futoko is a special problem in Japan today, particularly as it relates to boys. Caught between traditional gender roles and more progressive alternatives, raised in relative affluence yet faced with uncertain economic and social futures, trapped in the transition between erstwhile rigid school policies and experimental reforms, today's boys increasingly turn inward. This complex problem has received enormous media attention, yet no clear-cut solutions have emerged. More boys than ever refuse to go to school and ever-greater numbers of boys cut themselves off completely from all social interaction, including that within the family. Passive resistance can be a very powerful strategy when its goals are clear. Boys who experience futoko, however, almost always do not harbor any explicit ideas about what they are resisting. Thus futoko is a slippery social phenomenon perhaps best explored through art. Filmic representation, unlike the rational strictures of social analysis, does not require contradictions to be disentangled to offer potential solutions.

Audience desires for cinematic solutions to boyhood truancy in contemporary Japan may be seen as a specific manifestation of theoretical notions of film as dream and thus wish fulfillment in psychoanalytic terms. Wish fulfillment regarding futoko unifies characters onscreen, the social reality of truant boys, and those who perceive these boys and their filmic representation. Films tackling such social problems raise tension as much as they promise to raise consciousness. Cinema offers a temporary fix for those concerned—either personally or at a distance—but wishes are fulfilled only on celluloid. *A Class to Remember IV, Hope beyond the Crimson Skies* and *Battle Royale* tease and titillate worried adult audiences and offer reflections of possible selves to contemporary boys. In a manner similar to the futoko problem itself, these depictions illustrate the complexity of individual psychologies and their problematic relationships with social phenomena. As searches for fantasy solutions to this complex nexus of individual and social problems are revealed to have been in vain, filmgoers may encounter their own fractured subjectivities as negated dreams when the credits roll. Audiences may want to see the forest, but these filmmakers have it in mind to provide only shots of trees. Rather than offering once-and-for-all solutions contemporary futoko films end up affirming that there is no single solution as there is no singular cause—only solutions as varied as the boys themselves.

NOTES

1. See Japanese government education ministry white paper available online at http://www.monbu.go.jp/hakusyo/eng/f1-1-12.gif.
2. See the Japan Teacher's Union Web site, http://www.jtunet.or.jp/kiji/00/07/26n6.htm. In contrast, *Battle Royale* opens with a litany of statistics, one of which is "800,000 kids now refuse to attend school." Considering the rate of increase in futoko cases and the figure of 130,000, the number in *Battle Royale* does not seem as exaggerated as the draconian government policy that addresses it.
3. See the Japanese daily *Mainichi Shimbun*, May 10, 2000; Mori made this suggestion roughly one year after the Columbine shootings led conservative American politicians to call for posting the Ten Commandments on the walls of American classrooms.
4. Yamada is at home in the road movie genre. He is best known for the long series *Otoko wa tsurai yo (It's Tough Being a Man)* that lasted decades.
5. This film is part four in the *A Class to Remember* series by Yamada. Each film is a dramatization of Japanese educational experiences. The first (released in 1994, followed by the second and third in 1996 and 1998) is about a nighttime middle school. Students, such as the character Daisuke in part IV, end up at night schools if they could not or did not want to finish compulsory education (middle school) in the traditional manner and at the traditional age. Thus, for viewers who have seen the entire series, of which parts I and IV have been the most well received, part I in some ways represents another potential future for Daisuke.
6. Yamada claims to have been wanting to create his *Class to Remember* series decades before the 1990s. Nakayama, on the other hand, has been addressing school issues one after another throughout his thirty-year career (Nakayama Setsuo, personal communication, July 12, 2002).

WORKS CITED

Burnett, Bruce. 2002. "Unpacking the Japanese Educational Reform Debate." *Electronic Journal of Contemporary Japanese Studies*. Online at http://www.japanesestudies.org.uk.

Clarke, John, Stuart Hall, Tony Jefferson, and Brian Roberts. 1997. "Subcultures, Cultures, and Class." In *The Subcultures Reader*, ed. Ken Gelder and Sarah Thornton, 100–111. New York: Routledge.

Gateward, Frances. 2002. "Bubblegum and Heavy Metal." In *Sugar, Spice, and Everything Nice: Cinemas of Girlhood*, ed. Frances Gateward and Murray Pomerance, 269–84. Detroit: Wayne State University Press.

Hosaka, Toru. 2000. *Gakko e ikanai kodomo tachi.* Tokyo: Tokyo Daigaku Shuppan.

Inamura, Hiroshi. 1997. *Futoko no Kenkyu.* Tokyo: Shinyo-sha.

Ishihara, Shintaro. 1999. *Bokoku no to ni to.* Tokyo: Bunshun bunko.

Kawai, Hayao. 1992. *Kodomo to Gakkou.* Tokyo: Iwanami Shoten.

Macias, Patrick, and Happy Ujihashi. 2001. *Tokyoscape: The Japanese Cult Film Companion.* San Francisco: Cadence Books.

Machiyama, Tomo. 2001. "The Most Dangerous Movie Ever Made: Behind the *Battle Royale* Controversy in Japan." Online at http://www.pulp-mag.com/archives/5.04/feature_br.shtml.

Martinez, D. P. 1997. "Burlesquing Knowledge: Japanese Quiz Shows and Models of Knowledge." In *Rethinking Visual Anthropology*, ed. Marcus Banks and Howard Morphey, 105–19. New Haven: Yale University Press.

Mees, Tom, and Jasper Sharp. n.d. Interview with Fukasaku Kinji. Online at http://www.midnighteye.com/interviews/kinji_fukasaku.shtml.

Morita, Kiyoshi. 1991. *"Futoko" gensho no shakaigaku.* Tokyo: Gakubun-sha.

Napier, Susan. 2000. *Anime: From Akira to Princess Mononoke.* New York: Palgrave.

Rohlen, Thomas. 1980. "The Juku Phenomenon: An Exploratory Essay." *Journal of Japanese Studies* 6, no. 2, 207–42.

Sato, Shusaku. 1968. *Tokokyohiji.* Tokyo: Kokudo-sha.

Sato, Tadao. 1995. *Nihon eiga 300.* Tokyo: Asahi Bunko.

White, Merry. 1984. *The Japanese Educational Challenge: A Commitment to Children.* New York: Free Press.

———. 1993. *The Material Child: Coming of Age in Japan and America.* New York: Free Press.

———. 2002. *Perfectly Japanese: Making Families in an Era of Upheaval.* Berkeley: University of California Press.

Yamada, Yoji. 1999. *Taiwa Yamada Yoji: 2 Eiga wa omoshiroi ka.* Tokyo: Kuho-sha.

17

L.I.E., *THE BELIEVER,* AND THE SEXUALITY OF THE JEWISH BOY

Steven Alan Carr

When one looks at a Jewish boy, one traditionally looks away. Abraham looks away from Isaac before he is about to slit his own son's throat, an averted glance that saves the boy's life:

> God's angel called to him from heaven and said, "Abraham! Abraham!"
> "Yes."
> "Do not harm the boy. Do not do anything to him. For now I know that you fear God. You have not withheld your only son from Him." Abraham then looked up and saw a ram caught by its horns in a thicket. He went and got the ram, sacrificing it as an all-burned offering in his son's place. Abraham named the place "God will See" (*Adonoy Yir'eh*). (Genesis 22: 10–14)

God will see Isaac, but Abraham and other humans will not. Potiphar's wife desirously looks at Joseph, well-built and handsome, and he runs from her gaze:

> "Sleep with me," she said.
> He adamantly refused. He reasoned with his master's wife. "My master does not even know what I do in the house. He has entrusted me with everything he owns. No one in this house has more power than I have. He has not kept back anything at all from me, except for you—his wife. How could I do such a great wrong? It would be a sin before God!"
> She spoke to Joseph every day, but he would not pay attention to her. He would not even lie next to her or spend time with her.
> One such day, [Joseph] came to the house to do his work. None of the household staff was inside.
> [The woman] grabbed him by his cloak. "Sleep with me!" she

pleaded. He ran away from her, leaving his cloak in her hand, and fled outside. (Genesis 39: 6–14)

Looking away from Joseph preserves his integrity, for a longer look might evoke the boy's sexual desire. Potiphar's wife sees Joseph, and the reader sees her looking at Joseph, but one never sees Joseph looking at Potiphar's wife. In "The Story of Isaac," Leonard Cohen brilliantly reverses the perspective of the story of Abraham and Isaac. Astonishingly, the song dares to suggest that Isaac might have some degree of consciousness as his father is about to sacrifice him.

> You who build these altars now
> to sacrifice these children,
> you must not do it anymore.
> A scheme is not a vision
> (Leonard Cohen, "The Story of Isaac")

The moment is a rare instance in which one does not look away from the Jewish boy. Rather, the Jewish boy stares back, and sees plenty of modern-day Abrahams eager to sacrifice their children, with or without temptation from "a demon or a god."

Two recent American independent films, Michael Cuesta's *L.I.E.* and Henry Bean's *The Believer* (both 2001), prominently feature the sexuality of their Jewish boy protagonists. For a number of reasons both films have prompted a great deal of controversy. *The Believer* has yet to get a full-fledged theatrical or video release in the United States, purportedly after its narrative of a Jewish neo-Nazi received a chilly reception from Rabbi Abraham Cooper and a special screening at Cooper's institution, the Simon Wiesenthal Center in Los Angeles. Cooper, an expert on extremist hate groups, has become a powerful voice within the film industry. Media executives, fearful of alienating audiences, extensively rely on Cooper's imprimatur, as well as the imprimatur of the Wiesenthal Center, which remains active in areas related to anti-Semitism, the Holocaust, and Israel. On *L.I.E.*, meanwhile, although its video release now sports a so-called R rating, the Motion Picture Association of America (MPAA) initially bestowed an NC-17 rating, usually reserved for highly explicit representations of violence, sex, or "aberrational behavior." While *L.I.E.* depicts a relationship between a pedophile and a fifteen-year-old boy, it hardly depicts this relationship or, for that matter, any of the film's dysfunctional relationships, in hardcore fashion. For all of the controversy that both films have prompted, their distribution woes and subsequent status as causes célèbres in the press obscure a closer examination of the kind of representations of Jewish boyhood that both films convey. In some respects a radical departure from depictions that deny the Jewish boy as a sexual being, these representations ultimately activate concerns and assumptions regarding boyhood sexuality and masculinity arcing back to antiquity. That both *L.I.E.* and *The Believer* make the sexuality of the Jewish boy inscrutable marks both films as unique. Yet neither film invents the ambiguity of their respective representations; rather, both films follow the practice of looking at, and then looking away from, the Jewish boy. The averted gaze—and the ultimate inscrutability of Jewish boys' sexuality—is as present in these films as it is in the stories of Abraham and Isaac or Joseph and Potiphar's wife.

The representations of Jewish boyhood sexuality in these films—which have much in common with each other—operate within a broad historical, cultural, and political context. In discussing these representations, one cannot and should not lay claim to a number of related though not mutually exclusive concerns. For example, I do not seek to find some essential or biological truth about the nature of Jewish boyhood sexuality. To the contrary, the emphasis on representation seeks a more nuanced view of Jewish sexuality that accounts for the cultural perceptions of ethnic sexuality that work in tandem with whatever other signs of conscious or unconscious motivation surge forth from the ethnic boy's body. These cultural perceptions may or may not elucidate some essential aspect of the sexual identity of Jewish boys; but as perceptions, they certainly have their own reality and thus bring to bear a particular set of consequences that impinge not only upon the bodies of Jewish boys but also upon a wider cultural consciousness that perceives and defines these bodies, perceives and defines Jewish sexuality, and perceives and defines a number of other aspects of ethnic identity and sexual norms.

In addition, I cannot and should not lay claim to the strengths or failings of a censorship apparatus and how this apparatus denies or enables Jewish stereotypes present in Hollywood films—or more precisely, Jewish stereotypes present in the New American Cinema and American independent film. While the de facto prior restraint exerted on both *L.I.E.* and *The Believer*—a proscriptive rating in one case; an ad hoc ban on theatrical exhibition in the other—does have some relevance to the larger issue of the representation of Jewish boyhood sexuality, the fact that this implicit censorship has turned these films into causes célèbres has clouded rather than clarified their importance as representations. Finally, while both films are indeed important as representations of Jewish boyhood sexuality, a rare enough subject in mainstream film, closer examination suggests that these representations are not exactly liberatory. So while there is definite value to viewing, analyzing, and discussing these particular representations, one must bear in mind that the most remarkable aspect of both *L.I.E.* and *The Believer* is not so much to what extremes they go, as how radical the ambiguity they display—an ambiguity present from the time of Genesis—now seems at the beginning of the twenty-first century.

The crucial linkage between *L.I.E.* and *The Believer* is one that connects the subjectivities of the two young male leads. Existing only to be seen, these twin subjectivities function as little more than ciphers. Yet the films are linked in how they similarly position their ciphers to be both looked at and seen through. As a cipher neither boy acts; rather, each is acted upon. Even in the case of *The Believer,* which represents the protagonist as possessing seeming autonomy, the film obscures the passivity involved in Danny's motivation for becoming a neo-Nazi, as opposed to becoming a garden-variety so-called self-hating Jew.

The act of looking, and perceiving subjectivities are two facets of any filmgoing experience. Both point to the complexity of filmgoing, since both involve not just the looks exchanged between characters within the world of a film but also the master look constructed through staging the action, positioning the camera, establishing the lighting, designing the set, and accomplishing the editing and other components of film craft. The viewer is always engaged with both the convergence and divergence between this master look of the camera and the permutations of looks that are motivated by the subjectivities that help form the narrative.

The pedophilia functions as the taboo counterpart to *The Believer*'s Jewish self-hatred, in which the protagonist's self-loathing reaches such intensity that he becomes a neo-Nazi. In *L.I.E.*, a sympathetic pedophile antagonist—as sympathetic as *The Believer*'s self-hater is antipathetic—functions as a monster in the sense of pathos that the term can inspire. Like Dracula, a monster that could express both deep-seated fears and condescending pity for the immigrant Other, the pedophile can arouse sympathy only through his own self-sacrifice, as he subsumes his own pathology beneath the patriarchal order of the father. Once he has served his purpose, his life is expendable and the normalcy of the relation between father and son is complete. The pedophile is the child cipher who has grown into twisted adulthood, but who nonetheless supplicates his subjectivity for both the horror and the pleasure of his audience. That audience gazes upon a subjectivity whose motivation as monster is no more apparent than that of the cipher he seduces.

Both films manifest what John Fiske and John Hartley (1978) have dubbed the "clawback" feature of modern media, a process that works to insulate a preferred or dominant reading of a narrative from more so-called deviant interpretations. Popular texts—novels, television shows, films, and other forms of entertainment—walk a fine line between offering a completely new experience and maintaining enough consistency so that they will be recognizable to an audience. At first glance the potentially destabilizing aspects of these narratives, particularly in their emphasis upon fictional personas whose motivations appear to operate outside of conventional expectations and norms, might seem to defy the clawback process. Could these films succeed, for example, as Leonard Cohen does, in reversing the father's gaze upon the Jewish boy to one in which the Jewish boy stares back at the father? To some extent, both of these films fail to provide enough clawback for the respective standards of the MPAA and the Simon Wiesenthal Center.

Although it is a fictional account, *The Believer* takes as its inspiration an actual incident that took place in October 1965. Receiving reports that a local Ku Klux Klan leader and onetime head of the American Neo-Nazi Party was himself Jewish, the *New York Times* published a front-page interview exposing twenty-eight-year-old Daniel Burrous as a Jew. Upon reading the story, Burrous committed suicide. Editors A. M. Rosenthal and Arthur Gelb later recounted the incident in their 1967 book, *One More Victim*.

The Believer explores Burrous's motivation through the fictional conduit of Danny Balint, brilliantly played by Ryan Gosling. As a young boy, Danny challenges the interpretation of the story of Abraham and Isaac as proffered in his religious school classroom.

According to young Danny, God does not ask Abraham to sacrifice Isaac on Mount Moriah as a test of faith, but as a show of God's power. "God says, 'Do you know how powerful I am?'" Danny contends. "I can make you do anything I want, no matter how stupid. Even kill your own son. Because I'm everything and you're nothing." Appearing about thirty minutes into the film, this flashback prefigures a later scene in which a freelance journalist confronts Danny with information that proves he is indeed Jewish (and therefore a boy to whom the story of Abraham and Isaac can be expected to have some special importance). The scene also anchors the paradox of a Jewish neo-Nazi within the deeply religious allegory of a father-son relationship, or, to be more precise, the betrayal of this relationship. The film briefly presents Danny's own father as impotent, though it never explains why or how he is. The father simply sits by the television, waiting for the preparation of his meal and Danny's company. Without offering any explanation for such helplessness, the film places Danny's neo-Nazism within the context of a sexualized tension, one that offers anti-Semitic aggression as a reaction to apparent Jewish passivity. Like the story of Abraham and Isaac, the film here denies subjectivity to the one who lies upon a mountain even as it presents the story of a son.

The film returns to this metaphor when Danny and his neo-Nazi friends, unaware that Danny is Jewish, must attend a court-ordered sensitivity training session with Holocaust survivors after they instigate a fight at a Jewish delicatessen. Unmoved by the story of a female survivor who tells how a concentration camp commandant forced her to perform sexual favors, the group finally empathizes with the story of a male survivor who watched helplessly as a soldier impaled his young son upon a bayonet. The story signals a reawakening of Danny's faith, as the repeated black-and-white sequences depicting the slaughter signify his growing empathy for the father. Obsessed with the idea that a father could impotently bear witness to the murder of his own son and do nothing to stop it, Danny at first casts himself as the soldier. He finds himself returning to the Torah and to rituals such as wrapping tallith—the Jewish prayer shawl—underneath his clothes, and when a newspaper story finally exposes Danny's Jewish identity he imagines himself as the enraged father of the murdered boy. A final iteration of the black-and-white sequence, in which Danny imagines himself as both soldier and father, takes place right before he sacrifices his own life at the altar of a synagogue, where he and a fellow neo-Nazi have planted a time bomb.

Whether intentionally or not, the narrative of Cuesta's *L.I.E.* resonates with the story of Abraham and Isaac. While the film does not explicitly reference this story, as does *The Believer,* the thematic permutations of fatherly love, betrayal, and redemption imbue *L.I.E.*'s representation of dysfunctional relationships. In a performance more subdued though no less brilliant than Gosling's Danny Balint, Paul Franklin Dano plays Howie Blitzer, a semipubescent fifteen-year-old suburbanite who figuratively and at times literally finds himself precariously balanced between his sterile, upper-middle-class existence and suicidal oblivion. Grieving over the recent loss of his mother in an automobile accident on the Long Island Expressway, Howie grows increasingly estranged from his father Marty (Bruce Altman), a shady and sexually insatiable building contractor. Howie finds solace in two relationships: the first, a platonic though charged friendship with Gary (Billy Kay), a teenaged male prostitute; and the second, with Big John Harrigan (Brian Cox), a Vietnam veteran, pillar of the community, and pedophile. After Big John foils Howie and Gary's attempted robbery in the basement of his house, an uneasy friendship and mutual respect develops between Big John and the precocious Howie. When the FBI incarcerates Howie's father on fraud charges, Big John expels his current adolescent lover from his house and allows Howie to move in with him. To repay Big John, Howie initiates sexual advances with him. Rather than sexually exploit Howie, though, Big John finds a kind of redemption as Howie's surrogate father before the film ends with the pedophile's own sacrificial murder at the hands of his now distraught male lover.

While *L.I.E.*'s narrative does not make Jewish identity its central focus, a scene early in the film makes a surprising yet significant reference to Howie's Jewishness. After Howie, Gary, and two other boys rob a home, Gary discretely gives Howie some of the jewelry he's taken. Upon seeing the transaction, the two other boys joke about how the jewelry "is Jewry now." Although Gary angrily protests the remark, the film never returns to explore Howie's Jewish identity. Yet the scene cements the homoerotic link between Gary and Howie, for both share semisecret identities: Gary, a male hustler; and Howie, a Jew.

Howie represents the thoroughly assimilated suburban Jew whose roots remain dormant and thus at the periphery of both his and the viewer's consciousness. To understand how both of these divergent representations reactivate ancient assumptions regarding Jewish boyhood sexuality, one should first locate Danny Balint's and Howie Blitzer's characters as embodiments of an older literary and cinematic tradition that uses the bodies of young Jewish boys to explore the tenuous and at times hostile exchange between American assimilation and Jewish immigrant culture. This tradition extends at least from such naturalist-inflected novels as Michael Gold's *Jews without Money* (1930) and Henry Roth's *Call It Sleep* (1934), through the theatrical productions of Elmer Rice's *Street Scene* (1929) and Sidney Kingsley's *Dead End* (1935) to the subsequent cinematic adaptations of these phenomenally popular stage productions, through Budd Schulberg's assimilationist answer to *What Makes Sammy Run?* (1941), to such postassimilation novels as Philip Roth's *Goodbye, Columbus* (1959) and *Portnoy's Complaint* (1969) and eventually the films of Woody Allen. *Annie Hall* (1977) and *Manhattan* (1979) particularly solidified the one-time stand-up comedian as a Jewish American cinematic auteur, at least in part by overtly engaging in a semiautobiography of Allen's ethnic roots as an oversexed Jewish boy.

Thematically explicit and implicit emphases upon the ethnic identity of Jewish boys have long served as an indexical sign of larger tensions between assimilation and immigrant cultures occupying the consciousness of American middle-brow culture. As Mimi Ajzenstadt and Gabriel Cavaglion (2002) argue, this tension coursed throughout much of nineteenth- and twentieth-century discussions that attempted to establish a definitive explanation of masturbation among Jewish boys. Traditional Jewish beliefs cast masturbation as a moral sin worse than spilling blood, since it ostensibly interrupted the integrity and wholeness of the Jewish male body. Later, Zionist educators "symbolically linked the boy's body and the nation [of Israel] by defining masturbation as a national threat." Modern psychoanalysis finally established a socio-medical discourse that placed the stigma of masturbation at the cultural margins, but did so by assuring parents that masturbation and childhood sexuality more generally were themselves marginal concerns.

Both *L.I.E.* and *The Believer* demonstrate a unique shift as they seek to recover the sexuality of Jewish boys through distinctly visual strategies. *L.I.E* represents Howie's sexuality by looking away from the moments when he masturbates, eliding them with

The interplay of glances in
L.I.E.:counting money, from
Gary's point of view.

Gary eroticized in a reverse
shot before L.I.E. establishes
Howie's point of view.

a dream state and grainy, overexposed fantasies of Gary. *The Believer* establishes Danny as a hapless voyeur who discovers his lover Carla Moebius (Summer Phoenix) making love to her mother's boyfriend (Billy Zane). In both films, however, the depiction of these erotic bodies ultimately "claws back" the boy's sexuality, reenacting extremely traditional themes of patriarchy and heterosexism. In *Eros and the Jews*, David Biale (1997) locates a long-standing tension dating back to biblical times that wrestles between the polarities of sexual pleasure and procreation. *L.I.E.* and *The Believer* operate very much between these poles, acknowledging that the Jewish boy has both sexual potency and sexual appeal. Yet the films domesticate this desire—the boy's and the audience's—ultimately asserting normative depictions of heterosexual and familial roles. Howie's sexual advances are ultimately channeled into a "proper" father-son relationship. Danny's hypersexual rage ultimately transforms him into a "Jewish father."

L.I.E. explicitly establishes Howie's sexual desire through a set of subjective, shot/reaction shot sequences. The first of these occurs when Howie and the boys rob a typical suburban home. Part of a longer, rapidly edited sequence, a close-up from Gary's point of view shows him counting twenty-dollar bills. The next medium shot shows a shirtless Gary wearing a pearl necklace. The sequence cuts back to the close-up of the twenty-dollar bills, but this time the camera tilts up and rack focuses on the confused Howie as he literally stumbles into, and assumes, the subject position from which he and the audience have been gazing upon the stimulating Gary.

This moment in the film proves critical, for it establishes both Howie's sexual desire and the ambiguity of this desire. Without providing an initially identifiable subject position from which to gaze upon Gary, the sequence both justifies and obscures its eroticism. Once Howie enters, the point of view shifts from Gary's perspective to Howie's perspective. The film thus partly anchors the erotic image of pubescent Gary to Howie's desire. Having eroticized Gary before Howie enters, however, the film destabilizes the possibility that the palpable desire for Gary belongs centrally to Howie; it is a desire clearly present for us yet not originating with any identifiable character—until Howie is suddenly identified.

Even once the sequence does establish the subjectivity of Howie's eroticized gaze at Gary, the film still obscures Howie's desire through a series of shots in which Gary looks directly at the camera, but Howie glances offscreen. After the film establishes Howie's subject position, the film cuts back to the medium shot of a shirtless Gary, this time with him looking up and into the camera. A subsequent cut to an extreme close-up of Gary shows him putting his finger up to his lips and again looking directly into the camera, a gesture that implies not just secrecy but highly charged sensuality. The stark lighting contrast with minimal fill light on one side of Gary's face creates deep shadows, which reinforce the ambiguity of the shot. After the next cut, a medium close-up of

Howie watches Gary after literally stumbling into the shot. Note the slightly offscreen glance.

Howie looks away before he returns to looking at Gary, and then with his eyes cast slightly off camera.

Gary catches Howie, and us, with a direct glance.

A jumpcut to a close-up eroticizes Gary, but from whose point of view?

Whose gaze? An eroticized Gary furtively passes "Jewry" to Howie, after the preceding close-up of Gary.

Howie shows him looking toward Gary, but not directly into the camera. Howie briefly looks screen left, then returns to his off-screen glance. In a subsequent close-up, Gary once again looks directly at the camera and smiles. While *L.I.E.* leaves open the possibility for both Howie and the audience to desire Gary, the film does not allow for an expression of Howie's desire through an explicit definition of the gaze upon Gary as being Howie's gaze. It does not, then, fully permit Howie to express his own desire. One can look upon Gary looking directly at the camera because he is the object of desire, but while the film does not deny the possibility of that desire as coming from Howie, neither does the film depict this desire as explicitly belonging to him.

Of course, the homoerotic desire for Gary occurs within a range of sexualities depicted in *L.I.E.* The voiceover director's audio commentary on the DVD of the film reinforces the preferred ambiguity of a gaze that eroticizes Gary as an object of desire, while simultaneously obscuring the origins of that desire. After robbing the house, the still shirtless Gary wears a stolen fur as the four boys walk together. "It's not about hetero- or homosexuality," Michael Cuesta explains, regarding the presence of the fur coat. "It's about sensuality." For Cuesta, the coat has to do with the general sensuality of pop culture and Jim Morrison's appearance on an album cover, and not specifically with any gay sensibility. However, the scene has everything to do with heterosexuality, since it exoticizes not just Gary, but a way of looking—and not looking—at Gary. This looking and not looking persists throughout the film. The audience never sees Gary's parents, though he pointedly refers to his father as an asshole. One of the film's motifs involves another boy repeatedly having sex with his sister. Although deleted from the release print of the movie, a brief scene from the DVD shows both Gary and another boy watching through a window as brother and sister engage in sexual intercourse, though the audience—like the boy's parents—never sees what the voyeurs see. This range of aberrant sexual behavior hardly establishes an ambivalent attitude toward sexuality. There are not epic failures of heterosexuality, but rather, failures brought about by the absence of parents, especially fathers, who remain impotent to impose heterosexual order upon their households.

In asserting sensuality over sexuality, Cuesta enacts a striking parallel between the gay and Jewish subjectivities of this film. Both identities operate as structuring absences throughout the narrative, always partly emergent yet never fully apparent. Asserting sensuality, like using "jewelry" to address Jewishness, claws back upon these identities, subsuming them beneath the primacy of an assumed white and Protestant heterosexuality. Cuesta's comment suggests that there is a homoeroticism assimilated within popular culture just as there is an already assimilated Jewish identity requiring little if any explanation. One need not view Gary as gay, or Howie as Jewish. Rather, being gay or being Jewish simply function as labels devoid of any real subjectivity or personal experience. Howie is as gay as he is Jewish, which is to say that the film leaves open the possibility for either identity without making either of them explicit. The ambiguity of his identity makes him as inscrutable as Isaac appears on the mountain when his father is about to kill him.

At first glance, *The Believer* might appear to offer a clearer delineation of the sexuality of the Jewish boy, given its ultramacho image of the self-hating, neo-Nazi Jew in defiance of the impotent and passive Jewish father. Yet while *The Believer* deploys more conventional shot/reverse shot constructions to enact the subjectivity of its main character, its narrative ultimately renders the sexuality of Danny Balint ambiguous as well.

The Believer begins with Danny's savage beating of a religious, adolescent Jewish male. The beating portends the sadomasochism that defines both his female and his male encounters. As Danny kicks the supine "Yeshiva bucher," he begs his victim to "hit me, hit me, please." The scene renders the anonymous beating as a sexual encounter, complete with the foreplay of Danny stalking and terrorizing his hapless victim by crowding him and purposely step-ping on his shoes as the two ride on a commuter train. Before his heterosexual encounter with Carla Moebius, the daughter of a well-to-do fascist patron, she asks Danny to "hurt" her. The next shot shows him naked in her bed, and her with a large bruise on her mouth. When Danny and his friends go to a remote campground to meet other neo-Nazis, he fiercely beats one of the skinheads after getting sucker-punched. Unlike the beating of the "Yeshiva bucher," though, Danny uses his head to repeatedly ram his antag-onist's skull. The scene unfolds like a sexual encounter, with Danny thrusting his entire body into his victim's head until an orgasmic moment is achieved in which blood becomes smeared upon Danny's forehead.

The violence in this film bears out Danny's views toward Jewish sexuality, in which sex is not about pleasure but about penetration. Reflecting a parallel ambivalence that Biale (1997) has observed Jewish tradition holds toward sexuality, Danny uses violence to turn his entire body into a phallus that seeks only to penetrate. When Danny agrees to meet with a reporter to discuss his anti-Semitic views, he uses sexuality to elucidate why Judaism is a sickness:

> You ever fuck a Jewish girl? Jewish girls like to give head. And Jewish men love to get it. It's very pleasurable, but Jews are obsessed with it. You want to know why? Cause the Jews are essentially female. Real men, white Christian men, we fuck a woman. We make her come with our cocks. But the Jew doesn't like to penetrate, and thrust. He can't assert himself in that way, so he resorts to these perversions. All sex is technically a perversion, you know that, right? So that's why after a woman has been with a Jewish man, she's ruined. She never wants to be with a normal partner again. He gives pleasure; that's actually a weakness.

When the reporter finally confronts Danny, wondering "how you can believe all of this, when you're a Jew yourself?" Danny ulti-mately responds by thrusting a pistol into his mouth. However, rather than threaten to kill the reporter, Danny threatens to kill himself if the *New York Times* prints a story disclosing his true identity as a Jew.

While the representation of Danny in this monologue and elsewhere in the movie arguably establishes a superficial heterosex-uality, *The Believer* never fully resolves the tension or even offers an explanation regarding either Danny's sexuality or his religious identity. Yet the two seem inextricably intertwined. If Danny believes that all Jews are essentially female, then does Danny believe that he himself is essentially female? "Is this what makes him queer and self-loathing?" the film seems to ask. As the film depicts Danny's gradual reawakening to Jewishness, does the film suggest that he must ultimately come out as a Jew? While *The Believer* suggests less in terms of Danny's sexuality than *L.I.E.* suggests in terms of the range of possibilities for Howie's sexuality, both *The Believer* and *L.I.E.* share similar strategies in their ambiguous presentation of young Jewish male sexuality. Both films suggest a link between hidden Jewish identity, and hidden sexual identity. Yet neither film seems willing or able to explore this link. Rather, both films treat this link as a mysterious and shared secret, featuring shots that linger long enough upon the Jewish boy's body to suggest and titillate, but never long enough to sufficiently explore the boy's subjectivity in any depth. In both films, the camera averts its gaze long before this exploration can take place.

That these films offer no specific resolution of this ambiguity doesn't necessarily make them any more or less traditional than other representations of young Jewish male sexuality. In some ways, both films are unique from other texts in that they do not offer oversimplified resolutions to the sexual ambiguities of their respective representations. *The Believer* never attempts to resolve Danny's belief that all Jewish men are essentially feminine, and *L.I.E.* never explicitly establishes Howie as heterosexual, though the film clearly suggests that his confusion over love of the father and desire for the father stems from the absence of a real one. However, these films ultimately move away from the ambiguities of desire and self-loathing, and toward an assertion of patriarchal motifs that work to contain the possibilities of representing the sexuality of the desiring Jewish boy.

The Believer contains and delimits the possibility of Danny's sexuality through its explicit return to the leitmotif of the story of Abraham and Isaac. Danny perpetually encounters fathers and father figures throughout the film, from his own inexplicably impotent father to the boyfriend of Carla's mother, to the father-survivor who lost his young son to the Nazis. When Danny goes to climb in through Carla's bedroom window and finds her naked atop her mother's boyfriend as the two make love, the sight of this primal scene between lover and father renders him impotent. Through a series of shot/reaction shots, we see that Danny can no longer penetrate this scene using his body as a penis. Instead, he looks away. As Carla achieves orgasm, she closes her eyes, then looks out the window. Inconsequential as he is, Danny leaves as quickly as he came and there is no longer a diegetic subject position from which to view Carla. Like Howie watching Gary, Danny averts his gaze. And like the subjectivity of the sequence in *L.I.E.,* *The Believer* makes the position from which Carla appears erotic ambiguous once Danny disappears. The averted gaze in both these scenes suggests that the Jewish boy does not own an authentic perspective, or at least one worth respecting as distinct. Unlike the Leonard Cohen song, these boys do not stare back. They are simply the means through which one establishes a schema for reimposing a sexual order.

The Believer most powerfully invokes its modern-day story of Abraham and Isaac, however, with the account of the male Holocaust survivor. Untouched by the story of a female concentration camp survivor who was repeatedly raped, Danny and the other neo-Nazis show sympathy only for the father who lost his son. The story breaks the taboo narrowly averted in the near sacrifice of Isaac. While the father does not sacrifice his own son in the story of the survivor, God allows the soldier to take the life of the child. The interpretation of this narrative of violent sacrifice implicating the father is what leads Danny both away from his religion and back to it. Fighting his destiny as Isaac, Danny nonetheless ends up on an altar of his own making as one last challenge to the ultimate Father.

Similarly, while *L.I.E.* offers the possibility of Howie's desire, first for Gary and then for Big John, the movie averts its narrative from an explicit representation of homosexuality and instead offers a restoration of patriarchy. Rather than sacrifice Howie's virginity, the pedophile achieves redemption through assuming the role of Howie's absent father. In an intimate series of close-ups, Big John helps Howie shave for the first time. In the next scene, rather than take advantage of another boy Big John rebuffs Howie's sexual advances, eventually tucking him into his bed and making him breakfast the next morning. By depicting Big John as the surrogate father, *L.I.E.* claws back the possibility of Howie's homosexuality, containing his sexuality as a function of the lack of an adequate father.

Both *L.I.E.* and *The Believer* are remarkable in the ways they problematize fixed identities and even find commonalities between closeted or camouflaged ones. Both films offer the possibilities of homoeroticism and potential critiques of heterosexuality and identity politics. Yet both films also recall a much older, unresolved tension. Rather than directly address the possibility of young Jewish male desire, the films leave this desire inscrutable and unknown. Like the story of Abraham and Isaac, the potential for rape and for thrusts is stayed and, however temporarily, the law of the father restored. The sexual ambiguities and potential for violence that *L.I.E.* and *The Believer* recover for modern-day audiences make both of these films unique, if not comparatively radical in their insistence upon ambiguity. Yet neither film can emerge from the "clawback" of the emphasis upon the father, whose presence remains as persistent as his own tenuousness. And the sexuality of the Jewish boy, remaining unseen, unexamined, and unconfronted, can only, in the end, be imagined, dreamed, or invented—in a fantasy that grows ever more exploitative and unreal.

WORKS CITED

Ajzenstadt, Mimi, and Gabriel Cavaglion. 2002. "The Sexual Body of the Young Jew as an Arena of Ideological Struggle, 1821–1948. *Symbolic Interaction* 25, no. 1, 93–116.

Biale, David. 1997. *Eros and the Jews: From Biblical Israel to Contemporary America.* Berkeley: University of California Press.

Camhi, Leslie. 2002. "In a Skinhead's Tale, a Picture of Both Hate and Love." *New York Times,* March 17, 30. Online at LexisNexis. Accessed December 15, 2002.

Fiske, John, and John Hartley. 1978. *Reading Television.* London: Methuen.

18

THE FEMINIZATION AND VICTIMIZATION OF THE AFRICAN AMERICAN ATHLETE IN *BOYZ N THE HOOD, COOLEY HIGH,* AND *CORNBREAD, EARL AND ME*

Charlene Regester

Cinematic representations of black male camaraderie have occupied the center of discourse on black life over a period of nearly twenty years, in part because of mass appeal, in part because of the ability of these representations to generate crossover audiences, and in part because of their level of authenticity in revealing the fragility of black life. Three films that have most effectively presented the struggles of young black males are *Cooley High, Cornbread, Earl and Me* (both 1975) and *Boyz N the Hood* (1991). As representations of youthful black male camaraderie, these films collectively foreground the black male athlete and his tragic circumstances, exploring inner city life and its influences on the fate of the black male and displacing onto a young black male victim the larger sociopolitical dilemma of crime, poverty, and disenfranchisement.

In these three films, young black athletes systematically die, rendered passive victims somewhat in the manner of the femme fatale. This essay examines how these films feminize the black athletic boy and set his victimization at a moment just prior to his arriving at maturity. Death is used narratively as a signifier of the transcendence adolescent boys must achieve in their struggle to reach adulthood. Despite dissimilarities within the plots of these films, the same story is ultimately reconstructed in all three of them. Over a twenty-year time span, in three separate films, black male adolescents are shown as unavoidably unable to escape their tragic plight as they are targeted for victimization.

Black Athletes

The importance of depicting the black male as an athlete onscreen evolves out of the preeminence of sports in contemporary society and culture. Todd Boyd and Kenneth L. Shropshire suggest that because basketball symbolized dominance and superiority, it became a signifier of American culture more than did other sports (2000, 3). Boyd further argues that the sport of basketball becomes a microcosm for deconstructing the race and class politics that exist in contemporary culture (Baker and Boyd 1997, 133–34). Given the importance of sports, and basketball in particular, as cultural influences, the prominence of the black athlete in visual representation is certainly better understood.

But these mediated constructions of the black athlete have helped create complicit representations of the black male onscreen. Aaron Baker charges that many films that focus on basketball construct the NBA as a utopia and fabricate illusory constructions of blackness. It is in these mythical constructions that the image of the black male athlete is complicated by a conundrum of race and class politics. Specifically, Baker refers to the commodification of the image of Michael Jordan who presents the false ideal that success is achievable for blacks in America, when the reality is that most blacks will not find ready access to such success. According to Baker, the heroic image of Jordan is often juxtaposed to the "hypermasculine menace" image embodied by players such as Charles Barkley and others whose "'gangsta' personas" often intersect with those of rap artists (2000, 217). Ultimately, what evolves is a disturbing representation that proliferates in popular culture and plays into the public's imagination of blackness. John Hoberman charges that although integration has resulted in neutralizing racial differences, this progress is often directly opposed to the "merger of the athlete, the gangster rapper, and the criminal into a single black male persona that the sports industry, the music industry, and the advertising industry have made into the predominant image of black masculinity in the United States and around the world" (1997, xviii). Thus, a disturbing image of the black male athlete evolves, is popularized, and proliferates in contemporary culture, most vividly reified in films such as *Boyz N the Hood, Cooley High, and Cornbread, Earl and Me*—films that center the black male athlete in the narrative but that also manage to problematize his image.

Boyz N the Hood introduces three black males—Ricky (Morris Chestnut), Tre (Cuba Gooding Jr.), and Doughboy (Ice Cube)—who attempt to make the transition from adolescence into adulthood while growing up in the 'hood, South Central Los Angeles. Ricky is a rising football player who is recruited by the University of Southern California, while Doughboy, his brother, represents young black males who are displaced and disenfranchised as their paths lead to incarceration. Ricky develops a lifelong relationship with his best friend Tre, who is guided by a strong father figure, Furious (Laurence Fishburne). Unlike Tre, Ricky is guided by a single black mother who demonstrates favoritism for him over his drug-dealing brother, Doughboy. Ricky's life is suddenly snuffed out by gang rivals in Los Angeles, a moment that stunningly points to the ravages of black-on-black crime. *Boyz N the Hood* was well received by critics. To mention just two: the *New York Times* applauded the film not for what it conveyed but for "saying something familiar with new dramatic force" (Maslin 1991, C1). Thomas Doherty and Jacquie Jones elucidated the film's strengths and weaknesses noting that the film "illustrates clearly the crapshoot of being young, black, and male in America at this peculiar time in history" (1991, 17).

Cooley High focuses on a black inner city athletic high school senior, Cochise (Lawrence-Hilton Jacobs), who is murdered at the hands of former associates with whom he had experienced "a simple joy ride" in a stolen car. Cochise and his best friend Preach (Glynn Turman) evade charges of auto theft, while their less fortunate friends Stone (Sherman Smith) and Robert (Norman Gibson) face prosecution for their actions. Because their teacher, Mr. Mason (Garrett Morris), intervenes on behalf of Cochise and Preach, whom he sees as good kids with a future, they escape imprisonment. Cochise, however, is doomed. Stone and Robert, holding him and Preach responsible for their arrest, pummel Cochise to death in a street brawl. Cochise's death signals the loss of another black male to an act of violence perpetrated by black males. *Cooley High* was also well received by the *New York Times* despite the grimness of the film's plot. In fact, film critic Lawrence Van Gelder attempts to mitigate the tragic death at the film's end by asserting that "*Cooley High* pulsates with the careless exuberance of youth and captivates with characterizations and incidents presented not for the sake of nostalgia but out of the kind of understanding that cherishes and makes peace with the past" (1975b, 35). This review chooses to focus on the transition from adolescence into adulthood, rather than on the disturbing fact of another black male victim meeting a tragic death.

Cornbread, Earl and Me centers on a young black male athlete, Cornbread (former UCLA and NBA basketball player Keith Wilkes), who, in a case of mistaken identity, is accidentally shot by police in pursuit of a criminal in the inner city. As Cornbread's young friend, Wilford, Laurence Fishburne is seen in one of his first screen roles, displaying a wealth of talent hard to ignore (nearly twenty years later he plays the father figure in *Boyz N the Hood*). Here, the black community, aware that police brutality has taken the life of another innocent black male, is intimidated by police investigators who attempt to silence them and prevent them from testifying. Yet, in an act that allows him to make the transition from adolescence to adulthood, young Wilford steps forward to take the stand against these overzealous police. The officers are appropriately prosecuted. *Cornbread, Earl and Me* was also well received by critics. Although one reviewer begins, "While some of the issues presented in *Cornbread, Earl and Me* are as timely today as they were in 1975, several of the components feel rather dated." He concludes that the film is "well told" as it reconstructs a "sad story" (Metcalfe). The *New York Times* characterized the film as "part urban tragedy, part courtroom melodrama" and asserted that it "can appeal to youngsters on a wholesome ethical plane while telling a story that bears some resemblance to life, and death, on real city streets" (Van Gelder 1975a, 34). This critique takes note of the technical and plot devices by which these films reconstruct their narratives, at the same time commenting on the tragic circumstances that befall the black male victim onscreen.

That the black male athlete, of all possible types, became an embodiment of black masculinity can be traced back to the early screen appearances of world champion boxer Jack Johnson. Because Johnson's dominance over his white opponents was viewed as such a threat, it resulted in the banning of the interstate transportation of fight films. According to Dan Streible, since whites envisioned Johnson as a monster and because he personified the image of a disturber of the peace, "he knowingly fulfilled the role of the 'Bad Nigger'" (1996, 178). This image became ingrained in the public imagination as black masculinity became a symbol representing a dangerous, frightening menace that threatened society both racially and sexually. In academia, the laboratory study of the human being

advanced exponentially in the twentieth century, scientifically dis-
proving the prejudicial stigmas attached to "color," and seemingly
shattering the instant false images that associated black males'
strong muscles and athleticism with voracious, uncontrollable sexist predatory abusiveness. Nevertheless, the fear that accompanied
the image of the black male athlete onscreen was, and has continued to be, resistant to obliteration. Onscreen, this brutish image of
the black male athlete persists even in contemporary representations: Aaron Baker notes "the hypermasculine menace and intimidation represented by (some athletes) as their 'gangsta' personas
[overlap] to some degree with what certain rap performers have
been offering" (2000, 217).

In her examination of the action hero, Yvonne Tasker also
affirms the hypersexualization of the black male screen image.
Tasker surmises that the black male screen image "came from a
long visual history through which white western culture has
sought to project its fears and desires onto the black body" (1993,
37–38). She further notes that, "Within a representational system
that constructs black men as either hyper-sexualized or passive
castrated figures, the representation of the black action hero is
more than a little fraught" (40). Supporting Tasker's views and
expounding on her argument, Todd Boyd further explains the image
of the "bad Nigger" as an "exercise in the politics that define lower-
class Black masculinity. The meaningful explication to this phenomenon in contemporary society offers multiple and contradictory possibilities that can be articulated when using the linguistic
sign as a firm endorsement of empowerment and resistance" (Baker
and Boyd 1997, 127).

Yet because in *Boyz N the Hood, Cooley High,* and
Cornbread, Earl and Me the black male athlete who is victimized
is preeminent, and because he becomes a signifier of black maleness in general, the present essay argues that the black male athlete embodies both the aggressiveness that is inscribed in the black
male image, as critics have suggested, and the passivity associated
with subordination. Thus, in these films, the black male athlete
becomes a tragic figure. "Alongside Hollywood's construction of
the black male as a sexual threat," writes Tasker, "there exists an
established tradition of representation in which the black man is
suffused with a passive, Christian imagery" (1993, 40). The black
male athlete's becoming linked to the female is apparent in
Tasker's assumption that in many films women are utilized as

sidekicks to white male action heroes to represent the castrated figure, so as not to threaten the male action hero. Here, as the black male assumes the passive, victimized role, he represents a castrated figure who can no longer serve as a threat to white males. Given that this image of black males is grossly distorted in view of their preeminence in the popular culture, such representations are understandably disturbing and dangerous.

Black athletes dominate the black male image in popular culture at the expense of other representations of black maleness: the monolithic and one-dimensional black masculinity permeates the culture, indeed. Such powerfully threatening and damaging imagery invites a number of ongoing debates. According to John Hoberman, the ramifications of this essentialized image are wide-ranging, far reaching, and difficult to reverse. Hoberman contends that, "Confinement within the athletic syndrome is maintained by powerful peer-group pressures which ridicule academic achievement while stigmatizing blacks who do not beat 'whitey' at whichever game is at stake. In these and many other ways the sports fixation permeates the lives of countless people whose ideas about their own developmental possibilities are tightly bound to the world of physical self-expression" (1997, xvii). Thus Hoberman elucidates the dilemma that such a complicated image is likely to have for many black males who cannot escape the class and racial politics they confront.

The Class and Underclass of Black Masculinity

Kobena Mercer examines the intersection of racism and the politics of masculinity by suggesting that the black slave experience has resulted in a "subordinated masculinity" (1994, 143). Mercer contends that black masculinity has been inscribed with notions of criminality and sexuality. It is his position that masculinity is often defined by sexuality and that "the mythology of black [male] supersexuality" (150) is both one appropriated in cultural production and one to which black men lay claim. Similarly, Ed Guerrero argues that black masculinity is problematized in visual representations, black men being presented as either "celebrity spectacles" or "faceless black males" associated with violence and crime (1995, 396–97). Sharing Guerrero's position regarding the celebrity associated with the black male image, Herman Gray contends that black heterosexual masculinity is often personified by a black male image popularized by rappers, athletes, and gangsters (1995, 402). According to him, it is these aggressive representations that are circulated widely and that signify black masculinity in contemporary culture.

Black masculinity is also influenced by dynamics of class. Exploring colonialism in *Boyz N the Hood,* James Nadell argues for deconstructing the many factors that impact black life and force characters like those in the film to assume pathological lives that lead to untimely death: the pervasive black-on-black violence that proliferates in the 'hood; the crime that prevails there; and the lack of economic opportunities that creates the sociodynamics of the 'hood. Nadell concludes that despite the sins of the past, such as slavery and racism, ultimately those in the 'hood have to take responsibility for their own actions (1995, 451). This position is one that is affirmed by Kenneth Chan who argues that the 'hood promotes not only a distrust of the dominant political establishment but also what he terms "autodestruction" and racial self-hatred (1998, 38–43). Michael Eric Dyson suggests that in *Boyz N the Hood* the dilemma is presented as three-tiered: "at the immediate level, the brute problems of survival are refracted through the lens of black manhood; at the abstract level, the large social forces such as gentrification and the military's recruitment of black male talent undermines the black man's role in the community; at the intermediate level, police brutality contends with ongoing terror of gang violence" (1993, 99). It is Dyson's critique of the specific forces at work inhibiting one's ability to excel in the underclass that clearly explains the dilemma confronted by those confined to the 'hood.

Arguably, the problems afflicting the underclass cannot be viewed in isolation from how black males attempt to assert their humanity and masculinity while residing in the 'hood. These class issues are further complicated by adolescence. Dyson surmises that the overwhelming conditions of social neglect ranging from inadequate health care to joblessness in the 'hood "make the black male's passage into adulthood treacherous at best" (1993, 92). Despite the obstacles faced by black adolescent boys, they share in common with whites their innocence and youth as they personify males who are not men (202).

Steven Cohan examined white male figures onscreen in a postwar period in terms of the "trope of boyishness" (1997, 203) and attempted to investigate how gender and sexuality intersect at this particular point in the maturation process. His critique is useful to the extent that it provides a means of identifying characteristics of adolescence inscribed in visual representations and showing how these characteristics might transcend the black male screen image positioned in adolescence in any particular period. Cohan argues that manhood is distinguished from boyhood in that it is personified in action, not capital, and that masculinity is defined by male expertise (207). This assessment is affirmed by *Boyz N the Hood* when Furious teaches his son about manhood and the consequences of engaging in sex at an early age: Tre, failing to understand what it means to be a man by ignoring the responsibility of fatherhood and engaging in unprotected sex, is chastised by his father. Further, Furious delegates household chores to Tre, while he assumes the manlier task of serving as breadwinner. That Tre lacks knowledge and foresight and is dependent rather than independent (unlike Furious who represents the antithesis of these attributes) further distinguishes the roles assumed by mature and immature males. In Cohan's perspective, Furious becomes symbolic of manhood, while Tre invokes boyhood.

Space, Territory, Geography, and the Urban Landscape of the 'Hood

Scholars such as Murray Forman have examined space and territory as markers of the 'hood (2002). Discussing the intersection between race and the urban landscape associated with the 'hood, Laura Baker focuses on exhibition venues for *Boyz N the Hood* and the media frenzy that followed the film's release. Noting the violence that erupted in theaters after the film's initial exhibition, Baker argues that Hollywood's desire to screen out nonwhite audiences from mall multiplexes coupled with its desire to show race onscreen influenced much of what occurred in the aftermath of the film's premiere (1999, 5; see also Forman 1996, 46). Baker shows how the location and positioning of theaters allowed whites to vicariously experience racialized narratives without having to travel to see these productions in the 'hood itself—a strategic device that placated and alleviated the whites' fears by maintaining a safe distance from the subject matter that was titillating white audiences. Baker concludes that it is through the use of such strategies that the film industry succeeds in attracting white audiences for black films.

While Baker explores territory outside the narrative, Paula Massood examines territory within it, arguing that "'hood films indicate the split identifications, or 'two-ness,' which result from the mainstream practice of using fragments to produce a unified experience. [The result is that] the films expose African American identification as being at once inside the 'American' experience and, at the same time, outside that experience" (1996, 89). Massood views territory as much more a psychological space than a geographical one. Less concerned with the perimeters of space and more concerned with the power dynamics associated with space and territory, Chan notes that power structures such as dominance and subjugation are often established in the space of the 'hood. Moreover, he asserts that the stories of films such as *Boyz N the Hood* offer their characters only limited alternatives, thus implying that the only way out of the 'hood is to leave one's home behind or die. It is this implication that most disturbingly exposes the fragility of black life (1998, 46).

THE BLACK ATHLETE AS "FEMME FATALE"

Robyn Wiegman insightfully deconstructs the dilemma occupied by the young black male in *Boyz N the Hood* when she asserts:

> For in his relation of sameness to the masculine and in his threatening difference to the primacy of white racial supremacy, the African American male is stranded between competing—and at times overdetermining—logics of race and gender. Denied full admittance to the patriarchal province of the masculine through the social scripting of blackness as innate depravity, and occupying a position of enhanced status through masculine privilege in relation to black women, the African American male challenges our understanding of cultural identity and (dis)empowerment based on singular notions of inclusion and exclusion. (1992, 174)

While Wiegman employs a feminist critique in reading the black male, she is careful to avoid rewriting or reinscribing black masculinity. She declares, "The African American male is not a symbolic woman" (179). I would argue that the black male is in fact feminized in the films I am discussing, but feminized on a theoretical level, not as a practical matter for the purpose of participating in his subjugation in a white male patriarchy. Wiegman continues that it is in "the oscillation between feminization (buffoonish Uncle Tom) and hypermasculinization (well-endowed rapist) that the contradictory social positioning of the black male has been negotiated providing the means for disavowing his sameness to the masculine on one hand, while marking his masculinity as racially produced excess on the other" (180). Whereas Wiegman attempts to deconstruct this bipolarization of black male masculinity as depicted in *Boyz N the Hood,* what is important for me is the proposition that the black male is feminized in being a tragic figure. He falls victim to death, and because of the passivity he experiences and the fact that it leads to his demise, he is reminiscent of the femme fatale.

For example, in *Boyz N the Hood* Ricky meets his tragic fate when he is gunned down by gangsters while his friend Tre watches helplessly nearby. He is subordinate in death and subordinate, too (as females often are to males in American culture), in that his friend often serves as a surrogate father, protecting and caring for him. When the two take the SAT exam, Ricky becomes distracted but Tre coaxes him to complete it. Ricky's feminization is evident when he and Tre ride through the 'hood in Tre's Volkswagen, Tre driving, as always, while Ricky takes the passenger's position, a passive role. As a youngster, Ricky insists on taking his football (a gift from his never-seen father) into the 'hood, even after his brother insists that he should not. When the ball is ultimately taken away, Ricky has to be rescued by Doughboy. But when Doughboy and Ricky engage in a fight, Ricky is rescued by his mother.

Cooley High also focuses on a black athletic boy, Cochise, who is often protected by his best friend. The two are virtually inseparable even when their relationship is strained (as when Cochise has a sexual encounter with Preach's former girlfriend). Having formed strong ties with Preach, Cochise is rarely seen in the film without him, and it is through Preach that Cochise's identity is constructed. The two are often paired, which seems to convey Cochise's dependence rather than independence, thereby marking him relatively passive. In a fight at a house party, he has to be rescued by Preach; although Preach does little to intervene, he still proceeds to assist his friend. Cochise is allowed sexuality, hinting at the popularity that athletes enjoy because of their celebrity and signifying the hypersexuality inscribed in the figure of the black male athlete. Additionally, Cochise relies on Preach when it comes to classroom performance; Preach is the one whose

Preach finds his brutally battered friend Cochise under the tracks of the el.

intellect advances them in their escapades (e.g., acting on one of Preach's ideas, they pose as cops and extort money from prostitutes to garner enough cash to attend the theater). Later, Cochise rides in the back of a stolen car while Preach attempts to drive it, suggesting that Cochise is positioned as a weak figure rather than a dominant one. Cochise also assumes the position of the feminine Other as he meets his tragic fate through a violent death. When he is fatally wounded by Stone and Robert, Preach is unable to protect him, discovering and then cradling his body beneath the train track that hovers above.

Cornbread, Earl and Me focuses on a black athletic boy, Cornbread, who establishes a relationship with his younger friend Wilford, and becomes a tragic, victimized figure in dying violently at the hands of police. In one scene Cornbread is approached by dealers who have hidden drugs in a school locker. Because of his insistence on following the straight and narrow path, he disposes of the drugs. His action provokes the dealers to attack but Wilford comes to his rescue by informing the coach of Cornbread's unfortunate circumstances. In awe of Cornbread both for his athleticism and his desire to use his athletic talent to liberate himself from the chaos of impoverishment, Wilford rescues his best friend and serves as his protector. Later in the film, when he is the only member of the community who steps forward to testify against corrupt cops trying to disguise their murder of Cornbread, Wilford's action constitutes a continuing "defense" of Cornbread, even though the boy is dead. Cornbread is further feminized in the story because he rarely speaks, while Wilford assumes the voice of authority even though he is the much younger boy. The film also seems to privilege Wilford's gaze over Cornbread's, leaving Wilford to emerge as the central figure. The fact that Cornbread's athletic talent is constructed primarily through Wilford's gaze further demonstrates his dependence on Wilford for the construction of his identity.

In these three films, the black athletic boy is dependent rather than independent, helplessly takes on the role of victim, personifies consumption and passivity (both linked to femininity, while masculinity is associated with production and work [Modleski 1991, 28]), and repeatedly demonstrates weakness rather than strength. Because these three films tell the same story over a sixteen-year span—in *Boyz N the Hood* an athletic black boy is murdered by gangsters; in *Cooley High* an athletic black boy is murdered by associates seeking revenge for their incarceration; in *Cornbread, Earl and Me* an athletic black boy is accidentally shot by police in a case of mistaken identity—the perpetuity of the plight of the black male is candidly revealed in them. Although the method by which violence is inflicted may change, the lack of opportunity available to young black males, the inner city decay and decline, and the black-on-black crime and violence do not. The destructive conditions prevailing in the 'hood remain rooted in a sociological, cultural, and historical past from which young black males seem, at least onscreen, unable to escape.

DEATH AND ADULTHOOD

The death reconstructed in these films becomes a signifying moment to convey the transition from adolescence into adulthood. In examining the narrative placement of the deaths of Ricky, Cochise, and Cornbread, it is important to see that these boys of the 'hood leave adolescence only at the moment of death. Glen Masato Mimura argues that "The intimate relation between these themes—sex, violence, and death—has a long history in the patriarchal imagination" (1996, 48). Of *Boyz N the Hood* he adds that "from the initial scene onward, the immediate and random possibility of getting killed saturates the film: death's presence, its increasing proximity to the central characters through the story charts out the narrative development of suspense for the audience as it simultaneously signals important moments in the lives of Tre and his friends, internal to the diegesis itself" (49).

Ricky is feminized on another level as well: he is symbolically impregnated. He is constantly shown consuming food, for one thing, perhaps more significantly milk and ice cream (foods customarily associated with pregnancy). Then, as Ricky and Tre depart from a local store they walk into a blind alley to escape harassment by gang-bangers; the two young men decide to split up and head in different directions to distract their attackers, but before Ricky can make his getaway he first has to urinate. This act evokes an image from the film *Beloved* (1998), in which Sethe (Oprah Winfrey) urinates prior to Beloved's entrance into the film, representing the breaking of water prior to birth. It is conceivable that Ricky's urination similarly represents the breaking of water prior to giving birth—a birth that is figurative and not literal. All of this occurs at the same time that Ricky's friend Tre is attempting to come to terms with maleness and manhood as he pursues his first sexual conquest. Given the synchronicity of these two events (Ricky's "impregnation" and Tre's sexual conquest with Brandi), it is possible to view Ricky's death as representing a kind of birth. Indeed, as gunshots penetrate Ricky's body the camera depicts him falling to the ground in slow motion; and following Tre's infamous scream R-I-C-K-Y, the screen is silent. In this moment of silence, we hear a baby screaming in the background. Symbolically, in his death Ricky has given birth to another generation of young black males likely to be victimized by this same cycle of violence. Cradling the dead body, Tre assumes the motherly position in a Pietà. Doughboy arrives after the fact, evoking Linda Williams's view of the melodramatic narrative—that characters arrive either in the nick of time or moments too late (2001, 195–204).

Interestingly, Ricky's death occurs just prior to his receiving his SAT scores: he has met the standards to enter college on an athletic scholarship. The timing of his death thus coincides with the news that he stands only moments away from being liberated from the 'hood. Success was almost within his reach. It is at this point that the survivor, Tre, makes the transition from adolescence into adulthood. Facing the death of his friend, Tre is now forced to make an adult decision. Rather than join Doughboy who is set on avenging his brother's death, he draws upon the guidance he has received from his father and abandons the violence, making a mature decision. Doughboy, embittered, persists on hunting the killers until the perpetrators of the crime are gunned down.

In *Cooley High*, Preach arrives only moments after his friend's death, that death becoming a signifier that he has made the transition from adolescence to adulthood. As he stands by Cochise's graveside, he pays tribute to his friend by reading his poem that states, "We were friends a long time ago . . . rapping, chasing girls, obeying no laws but the law of caring." It is at this moment that we know that Preach is now an adult. He reflects on his adolescence while he leaves the cemetery, the Motown soundtrack gaining in intensity and signaling his voyage into the future.

In *Cornbread, Earl and Me*, Cornbread's death is linked to his ability to run—in this case homeward in a speed test for his friends' approval. The camera cuts back and forth from his flight and a police hunt for a criminal described only as "big and black." Rain is hindering both Cornbread's acceleration and the cops' pursuit (one cop is black, engaging in his own self-hatred [perhaps as a way to make the white cop appear less racist]) and signifies the ominousness of the death that is about to occur. As Cornbread crosses the street he is shot in the back and his orange soda flies into the air and splatters on the ground, representing the splattering of blood. Wilford, observing his death, runs to try to rescue him, screaming, "They killed Cornbread!" In the aftermath of this death, the blacks in the community attack the cops, aware that they have orchestrated another senseless killing of a young black male—incidentally, a black male who was not connected with crime. Once again, the timing of death is narratively significant. Cornbread's death occurs some two weeks prior to his departure to college. The airline ticket that his parents had already purchased is actually utilized for his defense in the aftermath of his death.

It is at Cornbread's death that Wilford makes the transition into adulthood. Called to testify during the trial proceedings against the two policemen, after other members of the community are afraid to testify, Wilford's maturity makes a mockery of the fear expressed by the so-called adults. He steps forward, urged on by his mother (Rosalind Cash) who tells him to "be a man and tell the truth, as you will be a man for the rest of your life."

In all three films the deaths of the young athletes occur in the public space of the inner city streets. Perhaps the street becomes a metaphor for both the birth and the death of young black males growing up in urban environs. All three films portray the young black male athlete inhabiting the inner city as feminized. All three films show him to be victimized by death. Most disturbing is the films' subtle implication that death is one means by which these young black males can escape inner city decay and destruction.

The parallel between these three films is unmistakable. In fact, the video release of *Cornbread, Earl and Me* advertised the film as the original *Boyz N the Hood*. The real-life horror of the shared similarities is that the plight of young black males has changed little in the last twenty years. In fact, it may have worsened. Women seem to have played a stronger role in the young black males' upbringing in the early 1970s. Earlier disputes may have been resolved through less violent means and the sense of community may have provided more support, rather than signifying moral decay and decline. Even in the earlier two movies—*Cooley* and *Cornbread*—women were endowed with more positive attributes: Preach's hard-working mother, confined to the underclass, assumes three jobs to provide for her family, while Cornbread's mother is strong, proud, dignified, and uncompromising.

As real or unreal as these three visual representations may be taken to be, one need not critique them for the details of their presentation. More profoundly important is that the young black male athletes centered in these narratives, instead of radiating with strength, dignity, grace, vitality, and talent, become objects of victimization, alas at the very moment of what would have been their transition into adulthood. All three films send a message: we must acknowledge the victimization of our young black males, and we must strive to eliminate the chaos of living in the 'hood.

Works Cited

Baker, Aaron. 2000. "Hoop Dreams in Black and White." In *Basketball Jones: America above the Rim*, ed. Todd Boyd and Kenneth L. Shropshire, 215–39. New York: New York University Press.

Baker, Aaron, and Todd Boyd, eds. 1997. *Out of Bounds: Sports, Media, and the Politics of Identity.* Bloomington: Indiana University Press.

Baker, Laura. 1999. "Screening Race: Responses to Theater Violence at *New Jack City* and *Boyz N the Hood.*" *Velvet Light Trap* 44, 4–19.

Boyd, Todd, and Kenneth L. Shropshire, eds. 2000. *Basketball Jones.* New York: New York University Press.

Chan, Kenneth. 1998. "The Construction of Black Male Identity in Black Action Films of the Nineties." *Cinema Journal* 37, no. 2, 35–48.

Cohan, Steven. 1997. *Masked Men: Masculinity and the Movies in the Fifties.* Bloomington: Indiana University Press.

Diawara, Manthia. 1993. "Black American Cinema: The New Realism." In *Black American Cinema,* 3–25. New York: Routledge.

Doane, Mary Ann. 1991. *Femmes Fatales: Feminism, Film Theory, Psychoanalysis.* New York: Routledge.

Doherty, Thomas, and Jacquie Jones. 1991. "Two Takes on *Boyz N the Hood.*" *Cineaste* 13, no. 4, 16–19.

Dyson, Michael Eric. 1993. *Reflecting Black: African American Cultural Criticism.* Minneapolis: University of Minnesota Press.

Forman, Murray. 2002. *The 'Hood Comes First: Race, Space, and Place in Rap and Hip-Hop.* Middletown, CT: Wesleyan University Press.

———. 1996. "The 'Hood Took Me Under: Urban Geographies of Danger in New Black Cinema." In *Pictures of a Generation on Hold: Selected Papers,* ed. Murray Pomerance and John Sakeris, 45–55. Toronto: Media Studies Working Group.

Gray, Herman. 1995. "Black Masculinity and Visual Culture." *Callaloo* 18, no. 2, 401–5.

Guerrero, Ed. 1995. "The Black Man on Our Screens and the Empty Space in Representation." *Callaloo* 18, no. 2, 395–400.

Hoberman, John. 1997. *Darwin's Athletes: How Sport Has Damaged Black America and Preserved the Myth of Race.* Boston: Houghton Mifflin.

Jones, Jacquie. 1991. "The New Ghetto Aesthetic." *Wide Angle* 13, no. 3/4, 32–43.

Jordan, Winthrop D. 1968. *White Over Black: American Attitudes Toward the Negro, 1550–1812.* Chapel Hill: University of North Carolina Press.

Maslin, Janet. 1991. "*Boyz N the Hood,*" *New York Times,* July 12, C1.

Massood, Paula. 1996. "Mapping the Hood: The Genealogy of City Space in *Boyz N the Hood* and *Menace II Society.*" *Cinema Journal* 35, no. 2, 85–97.

McKelly, James. 1998. "Raisin Caine in a Down Eden: *Menace II Society* and the Death of Signifyin(g)." *Screen* 39, no. 1, 36–52.

Mercer, Kobena. 1994. *Welcome to the Jungle: New Positions in Black Cultural Studies.* New York: Routledge.

Metcalfe, Nasser. "May '00: *Cornbread, Earl and Me*—Does Art Imitate Art?" Online at http://blackfilm.com/0205/reviews/vault/index.-shtml.

Mimura, Glen Masato. 1996. "On Fathers and Sons, Sex and Death: John Singleton's *Boyz N the Hood*." *Velvet Light Trap* 38, 14–27.

Modleski, Tania. 1991. *Feminism Without Women: Culture and Criticism in a "Postfeminist" Age*. New York: Routledge.

Morrison, Toni. 1987. *Beloved*. New York: Alfred A. Knopf.

Nadell, James. 1995. "*Boyz N the Hood*: A Colonial Analysis." *Journal of Black Studies* 25, no. 4, 447–64.

Streible, Dan. 1996. "Race and the Reception of Jack Johnson Fight Films." In *The Birth of Whiteness: Race and the Emergence of U.S. Cinema*, ed. Daniel Bernardi, 170–202. New Brunswick, NJ: Rutgers University Press.

Tasker, Yvonne. 1993. *Spectacular Bodies: Gender, Genre and the Action Cinema*. New York: Routledge.

Van Gelder, Lawrence. 1975a. "*Cornbread, Earl and Me*," *New York Times*, May 22, 34.

———. 1975b. "*Cooley High*," *New York Times*, June, 26, 35.

Wallace, Michele. 1992. "*Boyz N the Hood* and *Jungle Fever*." In *Black Popular Culture*, ed. Michele Wallace and Gina Dent, 123–31. Seattle: Bay Press.

Wiegman, Robyn. 1992. "Feminism, 'The Boyz,' and Other Matters Regarding the Male." In *Screening the Male: Exploring Masculinities in Hollywood Cinema*, ed. Steven Cohan and Ina Rae Hark, 173–93. New York: Routledge.

Williams, Linda. 2001. *Playing the Race Card: Melodramas of Black and White from Uncle Tom to O. J. Simpson*. Princeton: Princeton University Press.

Wilson, Stephen. 2000. *The Magical Universe: Everyday Ritual and Magic in Pre-Modern Europe*. London: Hambledon and London.

Wyatt, Justin. 2001. "Identity, Queerness, and Homosocial Bonding: The Case of *Swingers*." In *Masculinity: Bodies, Movies, Culture*, ed. Peter Lehman, 51–65. New York: Routledge.

19

BOMBAY BOYS
Dissolving the Male Child in Popular Hindi Cinema

Corey K. Creekmur

Although India's art and popular cinemas are conventionally opposed in terms of realism and fantasy, commercial films have not
shied away from depicting the poverty and suffering of Indian children, though they commonly treat childhood problems as familial
rather than social, in the manner of most commercial cinemas.
Except in rare films that focus entirely on the plight of children,
such as *Boot Polish* (1954) or *Dosti (Friendship)* (1964), childhood in
Hindi cinema is generally staged as a primal scene projecting the
adult protagonist's identity, actions, and fate.[1] Characters in Hindi
films are persistently wounded yet driven by their childhood pain,
drawing a direct causal—and conscious—chain between the suffering of youth and the acts of adulthood, a link regularly figured by
formal transitions that instantly transform boys into men.
Providing immediate maturation, such temporal leaps imply the
inconsequence or irrelevance of adolescent experience in shaping
both character and narrative.

In this essay I want to investigate the representation of boyhood in popular Hindi cinema by focusing upon a common formal
device for effecting a narrative ellipsis, a focus which also motivates
a historical inquiry revealing an unexpected continuity in Hindi cinema between independence and the early 1990s, when more significant but less obvious changes begin to alter the construction of masculinity in Indian popular culture. It can be demonstrated (though
also overstated) that the implicitly modern Hindi cinema maintains
a continuity with traditional Indian culture, relying, for instance, on
regular allusions to the ancient Sanskrit epics, the *Mahabarata* and
Ramayana, that are neither esoteric nor obscure for contemporary
and sometimes illiterate audiences. At the same time, perhaps especially in its treatment of the hero, popular Indian cinema is relentlessly topical and shamelessly trendy, and is recognized to have regularly reflected (and influenced) changing cultural and political

350

contexts. Most notably, film critics have commonly understood the mid-1970s redefinition of the Hindi film hero as an "angry young man" within the context of Prime Minister Indira Gandhi's "Emergency" (1975–77), her notorious clampdown on civil liberties following challenges to the legitimacy of her 1971 election. In what follows I will argue that this much-discussed revision of the film hero belies a deeper continuity, whereas more recent films, widely seen as drawing back the middle-class family audience displaced from cinema halls by two decades of violent action films, demonstrate a potentially more significant transformation in the popular performance of Indian masculinity.

DISSOLVING INDIAN BOYS INTO MEN

Since at least the 1940s, commercial Indian filmmakers have employed flashbacks, montage sequences, and frame-tales to creatively plot their typically long (three hours is the norm), sometimes convoluted, and frequently multigenerational narratives. Often spanning decades (if not centuries, sometimes via reincarnated characters), Hindi film plots necessarily employ formal ellipses that omit or condense large segments of story time. I will limit this analysis to a technique pervasive enough to constitute one of Hindi cinema's dominant tropes even though this device, familiar to all fans of Indian cinema, hasn't been explored in the growing body of Indian film criticism. What I will identify as the "maturation dissolve" suggests nothing less than a cultural perspective condensed into a narrative—and distinctively cinematic—technique.[2]

In numerous Hindi films, an opening segment—sometimes preceding a long-withheld credit sequence—introduces the main character as a boy before leaping forward in time, usually through a prominent formal transition, to depict him as a man, ensuring through various continuity devices that we recognize the adult onscreen (usually a familiar star) to be the grown embodiment of the same character whose childhood has already drawn our interest and sympathy. *Ganga Jumna* (1961) provides a typical example: after they are orphaned, young Ganga drives a bullock cart to support his younger brother Jumna's education. A shot of the boy atop his cart cuts to a close-up of the animals pulling it, and then to a shot of the revolving wheel of the cart: this image remains visible as rural fields are dissolved in, before they fade away to reveal the wheel alone again, reversing the pattern exactly through another cut to the animals and then back to Ganga singing as a young man, now played by the instantly recognizable star Dilip Kumar. Although the segment only needs to signify that "time passes," the image of the turning wheel and the backdrop of the seasonal cycles of agriculture load the transition with additional metaphorical weight.

Similar transitions of course appear in Hollywood cinema, and it's possible that Indian filmmakers adopted this technique from well-known examples like *The Public Enemy* (1931) or even *Citizen Kane* (1941) which swiftly age their protagonists while ensuring that no confusion derives from two (or more) actors of different ages playing the same character. Nevertheless, whatever its cinematic sources, the emphatic repetition of this device across decades of Hindi film compels closer examination, as does the apparently corollary effect that this cinema, in marked contrast to Hollywood, so rarely dramatizes adolescence, the transitional and—for the modern West, at least—crucial developmental stage so briskly elided by the "maturation dissolve."

In a well-known discussion, Christian Metz notes that the lap-dissolve functions as both condensation and displacement and recognizes that, "If a condensation begins to take shape, it does so en route towards its progressive extinction. As image 2 becomes clearer, as it 'arrives,' image 1 becomes less so, it 'goes away'—like two billiard balls which meet only to send each other off again, so that meeting and separation become the same thing" (1977, 277).

Although Metz characterizes the dissolve in any manifestation, his description is evocative of the heightened significance of its regular use in Hindi films. While representing key moments along the continuous path of a single life, and reinforcing the coherence of an individual character, the "maturation dissolve" never fully obscures the technique's reliance on two distinct, differently aged bodies, and on a visible rupture in time and space that must be imaginatively "mended" by the joining illusion of montage. Except as overlapping images, the younger and older actors who embody the same character cannot appear in the same frame, so their metamorphosis is the only place where and when they can "meet," as Metz says, during separation. Once the hero arrives onscreen to continue the child's life, the child (and the young actor) disappears: "he" will not appear again in the film, except perhaps through a flashback, usually marked as an adult's memory rather than the plot's return to the narrative past when the child still "exists."

But the common function of such moments in Hindi cinema is also to suggest that childhood, suddenly years past, remains painfully present insofar as its wounds still mark the hero. The conclusion of such transitions is usually the star's entrance, a privileged spectacle in commercial cinema: in a popular cinema largely driven by the audience's desire to view (or in the Hindu context, to "take *darshan* of") stars, one might say that this moment, often delayed to stir anticipation, is when the movie really begins, almost starts over.[3] No fan pays to see the child actor playing the hero; he is drawn to view the actor whose sudden appearance abruptly ends that child's "life." But the insistence upon nevertheless depicting the Hindi film hero's childhood serves a larger purpose that Hollywood, given its tacit promotion of the ideologies of self-development, individual choice, and personal growth, might find intolerable: these "meetings" of boy and man deny, or at least show no interest in promoting, "character development." The child's pain and loss direct the adult's search for love or quest for revenge; the boy's trauma in essence projects the overall film's plot. The rapid transition ensures that the hero's suffering of a decade ago in the story has been witnessed only moments earlier onscreen, and so cannot be easily forgotten or outgrown. In this regard A. K. Ramanujan's comments in "Repetition in the *Mahabharata*" offer a striking cultural precedent. Ramanujan finds that "the Western dramaturgic notions of acting issuing from character, character transformed by action in some direct way, do not fit here. Characters do not change here" (1999, 179). Instead, he emphasizes, "It's as if action is released from character. . . . It's as if there's a kind of autonomy of action. Once set into motion, the act chooses its personae, constitutes its agents" (178–79). In this sense, regular narratives of childhood trauma may have constituted many of the heroes of Hindi cinema.

Perhaps because it is so familiar from decades of repeated use, the "maturation dissolve" is often taken for granted by critics of Indian cinema, as a frequent descriptive error indicates: often summaries of Hindi films identify characters exclusively with their adult star, even when that character has been embodied, sometimes at length, by another (boy) actor. In a typical example, Vinay Lal summarizes the early flashback of *Deewar (The Wall)* (1975): "One day, Vijay, the elder brother (played by Amitabh Bachchan) is accosted by a group of . . . townspeople, and when he returns home that day, bruised and beaten, his arm is shown to have been tattooed with the words, 'Your [*sic*] father is a thief'" (1998, 238; my emphasis). However, for the first portion of the film (following an opening framing segment in which the character does not appear), Vijay is played *not* by Bachchan but by a boy selected for his resemblance to the then-thirty-three-year-old star. Since the star is so closely identified with the role, the film's actual construction of the character through two actors gets obscured.

I don't view such imprecision as critical carelessness so much as evidence that the technique is so familiar as to have become virtually unnoticed and literally unremarkable. But, again, the persistent recourse to this device alone argues for more careful consideration, as does the technique's function in some of Hindi cinema's most enduring classics. Gayatri Chatterjee has drawn brief attention to the fact that perhaps the most famous of all Hindi movies, *Mother India* (1957), propels its narrative forward when Radha (Nargis) is shown working in a muddy field alongside her sons Birju and Ramu, played by the usually unacknowledged "child artistes" Master Sajid and Master Surendra: "The younger actors are shown helping Radha; the camera is rewound and brought to the desired moment where the dissolve is to start; the older actors replace the younger ones, maintaining exactly the prior composition—the camera is run again" (2002, 59). As she also recognizes, "this hyphen-like section in the middle of the film" (59) motivates a transition between antithetical songs. When Birju and Ramu are played by the young actors, the accompanying song is a sorrowful plea; when Nargis rises up with the actors Sunil Dutt and Rajendra Kumar, now playing her sons, a new song of hope begins. As is common, the filmmaker takes advantage of the moment's prominent narrative advance to effect other kinds of transitions (musical, emotional, thematic) as well. In another classic, *Awaara (The Vagabond)* (1951), the principal characters are first introduced in court, where Raju (Raj Kapoor) is on trial before his father Judge Raghunath (Prithviraj Kapoor, the star's actual father), and being defended by Rita (Nargis), his former childhood sweetheart (and Raj Kapoor's rumored offscreen lover). The legal inquiry generates a lengthy flashback that introduces Rita and Raju as children. However, to introduce the adult Raju within the flashback, the narration leaps forward from the boy to his adult self. Chatterjee notes that "Showing the child protagonist growing up into an adult is a favourite theme with filmmakers . . . little Raj is given a roti, he looks at it silently for a while, and then bursts out laughing. The voice on the soundtrack is that of Raj Kapoor. The image cuts [sic] to the adult Raj in prison stripes laughing over a roti in hand. With the shift in time the mood of the film changes" (1992, 144–45). Chatterjee is unusual among critics in recognizing the significance of such moments, but also imprecise when she says the film "cuts" from the boy to the man, for it dissolves, more emphatically insuring that the transition is read as a temporal leap maintaining continuity of character. And her focus on a single text doesn't allow her to fully explore the "favourite theme" she identifies. Assuming that the device's frequency, gaining it the status of something like a "theme," indicates a greater function than simply advancing the plot, a historical survey of the "maturation dissolve" in Hindi cinema is in order.

I have casually employed "trauma" to describe the suffering of the boys in Hindi cinema, but recent work by Cathy Caruth reinforces the aptness of the term. As she emphasizes, "To be traumatized is precisely to be possessed by an image or event" (1995, 4–5), a description that readily applies to the films I am considering. Hindi films challenge psychoanalysis by insisting that trauma is not in a conventional sense pathological, or symbolic, but literal, and at least in a personal sense, historical. Trauma moreover describes a victim's inability to fully comprehend or endure a shock in its original, shocking moment: events, as Caruth says, "insofar as they are traumatic, assume their force precisely in their temporal delay" (9). Hindi films consistently provide just such a delay, at least in represented story time: the hero requires time to address his trauma, but the plot, leaping ahead without delay, does not allow spectators to forget the experience, viewed onscreen only minutes ago, though the narration indicates that years have passed. The heroes, as well as the narratives, are thus "possessed" by the painful events of childhood treated in the beginning sections of the film. Hindi films proceed, but often through reprised songs, repeated lines of dialogue, and significant objects that return to the foreground. Repeated elements not only hold together narratives that risk losing coherence, they also declare that early experiences still matter, that mementos retain the emotional value of their origins, and that repeated words and gestures gain rather than lose significance over time. Insofar as Hindi cinema is commonly "possessed" by structures of recurrence—rather than the Hollywood ideal of "development"—we might even identify it as a "traumatic" cinema, entirely appropriate for the repeated stories of childhood suffering it tells.

The Bombay boy Raju becomes a man (Raj Kapoor); the "maturation dissolve" from *Awaara* (1951).

The "maturation dissolve" might also be considered a popular figuration of the "common" trauma some psychoanalysts have identified with male childrearing in a Hindu context. In his 1958 study *The Twice-Born*, G. Morris Carstairs described this "desertion on the part of his mother" following years of indulgence as a "catastrophic reversal of an infant's early blissful situation" (1958, 159–60). Sudhir Kakar's 1978 *The Inner World*, though revising Carstairs's account, also represents what Kakar calls the male child's "second birth" as a psychic injury, claiming that "This second birth is as unpremeditated in the child as the first, and as traumatic" (1978, 130). More recently, Stanley N. Kurtz has persuasively challenged both Carstairs's and Kakar's accounts (by emphasizing the shared caretaking in joint families), but I am less concerned here with establishing the psycho-social accuracy of these claims than with providing possible explanations for the popular representation of Indian male maturation as instantaneous. If trauma identifies the narrativization of actual events, more conventional psychoanalytic approaches might understand "maturation dissolves" as cultural representations of "the narcissistic injury inherent in the abrupt dissolution of the mother-son bond" (Kakar 1978, 130). Taking advantage of narrative's temporal flexibility, such transitions may not represent *how* Indian boys mature, but may encapsulate how the unwilling projection into adulthood might *feel*.

Growing Up Too Fast in Hindi Cinema

The most prominent examples of the "maturation dissolve" in Hindi cinema in the decade following Indian independence depict male and female children who discover their true loves in childhood companions, are isolated from each other (often by class or caste prejudices) and then meet again as adults after a long separation, often following their (arranged) marriages to others. While these stories are usually found in the broad Hindi film genre of "socials," set in the newly constituted and secular nation, they often draw upon the models of Krishna and Radha.[4] Krishna is the most sensual and, as a child and young man, the naughtiest of the Hindu gods. His romance with Radha is idealized in Indian culture, and while available to represent a devotee's adoration of a god, has always maintained an explicit element of erotic passion. Significantly, their actual romance, though establishing an eternal love, is a youthful affair broken off before maturity. Sudhir Kakar has identified one of the major manifestations of the Hindi film hero with Krishna, emphasizing the figure's teasing, playful sexuality; for Kakar, "the Krishna-lover has the endearing narcissism of the boy on the eve of the Oedipus stage" (1989, 36–37). While embedded in its narrative, Krishna and Radha's story is confirmed as a source for Bimal Roy's 1955 version of *Devdas* with an early song about Radha's longing, performed for the young Paro by traveling Vaishnavite musicians.[5] Separated by their families, and later banned from marriage, Paro and the once-mischievous boy Devdas become passive social rebels by refusing to "outgrow" their childhood love. What Patricia Uberoi has called "the animating logic of South Asian romance," "the conflict between individual desire and social norms and expectations in respect of marriage choice" (1998, 306) structures classic films like *Awaara, Devdas, Deedar (Vision)* (1951), and *Anmol Ghadi (Precious Watch)* (1946), which all feature heroes, introduced as boys, who remain defiantly immature: their doomed romances gain our sympathy because they seem destined even if socially impossible. As men, these romantic heroes retain their boyish passions, avoiding the possible deflection of desire during (unseen) adolescence.

Although Kishore Valicha claims that *Andaz (Style)* (1949) first "immortalized the love triangle and focused attention on youth" (1988, 126), such claims force us to confront the instability of a cultural category like "youth," despite its apparent grounding in the "facts" of biology. The film's main characters (played by Raj Kapoor, Nargis, and Dilip Kumar) are post-university adults concerned with careers, marriage, and social obligations; the stars were all in their early to mid-twenties when the film was made. They represent youth in the way that Cary Grant, James Stewart, and Katherine Hepburn might be said to represent American youth in *The Philadelphia Story* (1940). But teenagers and the "youth culture" they inhabit as a distinct social category only appear in the decade between Hindi cinema's golden age and Mrs. Gandhi's Emergency. This period, neglected if not dismissed by critics, may be summarized by the career of Shammi Kapoor, whose phenomenal success between 1957 and 1969 is now recalled for introducing the Westernized teenager to Indian popular culture.[6] Frequently identified as the "Indian Elvis," Shammi Kapoor may indeed represent, in Sumita Chakravarty's words, "the first male star to break out of the mold of the fifties hero as champion and prototype of the underclass" (1993, 207). Through his "vigorous narcissistic male persona," Shammi Kapoor replaced "social markers of class and region" with "a more free-floating and individualized universe of rapid change and frantic movement" (208). More often than not this persona and its trappings (trendy clothing and "wild" physicality) were treated as Western exports: in his defining role in *Junglee (Savage)* (1961) the thirty-year-old Kapoor is introduced en route to India after up-to-date business training in England and America.

However, at least in retrospect, Shammi Kapoor's films suggest the sort of adult exploitation of a newly recognized youth market found in Hollywood's own desperate attempts to cater to, and cash in on, a changing audience by adopting superficial signs of hipness and rebellion. But whereas the United States provided film-makers with a rich discourse of adolescence, ranging from the antics of *Archie* comics to national fears of mass media–inspired juvenile delinquency, India does not appear to have offered Shammi Kapoor's films a similar discursive context. His films now seem less in touch with the "structure of feeling" linking Indian youth to Western teenagers than his older brother Raj's huge hit *Bobby* (1973), the legendary star's "comeback" as a director following his ambitious autobiographical disaster *Mera Naam Joker (My Name is Joker)* (1970). *Bobby* starred the director's son Rishi as the eighteen-year-old Raj and the newcomer Dimple Kapadia as sixteen-year-old Bobby, whose Christian character allowed her to appear in a famous bikini. Following, but simplifying, the structure of many of his earlier films, Raj Kapoor only depicts the character Raj as a boy in a brief opening sequence. he is sent off to boarding school and we next meet him at his graduation, just before his eighteenth birthday. As a child, Raj's poor little rich boy doesn't suffer the traumas of the director's earlier films or of films in the decade to come. Although Rachel Dwyer and Divia Patel acknowledge that *Bobby* "epitomized youth culture and 1960s fashions," they also tellingly note that its psychedelic poster "was not implying that this culture existed in India, rather it alluded to a period associated with youth culture, fun, romance, and rebellion" (2002, 169). This is a subtle distinction, but seems accurate insofar as it describes the depiction of an "international" youth culture that seems more borrowed or quoted than fully assimilated. As Raj Kapoor's brief depiction of his hero's childhood seems a half-hearted recourse to the old tech-nique, an incomplete survey of Shammi Kapoor's films during this period indicates that the "maturation dissolve" had apparently run its course: as in the West, Indian pop culture could finally locate trauma and the development of identity in "youth" rather than childhood. But traumatic childhood would return to Hindi cinema, literally with a vengeance.

THE BOYHOOD OF THE ANGRY YOUNG MAN

Critics now commonly locate a major transformation of the Hindi film hero in the early 1970s. In a sweeping claim, Vijay Mishra asserts that the figure of the "angry young man" embodied by Amitabh Bachchan "challenged the figure of the noble, transcendent Rama as the dharmik model of the hero" (2002, 128). In an especially perceptive analysis, Madhava Prasad has more convincingly positioned Bachchan's groundbreaking film *Deewar* within an arc starting in the 1940s, arguing that "the most striking feature, historically, of the development of the hero . . . paradoxically, is the regression from a state of adulthood which ends in the arrival at the state of infancy" (1987, 29). According to Prasad, the Hindi film hero of the 1940s and 1950s (characterized by Dev Anand) was an adult, "relatively free from the dominating presence of family authority," while the hero of the 1960s and early 1970s (Shammi Kapoor) "regressed to the adolescent stage and is a prized member of a happy family" (1987, 29). Even though he takes a wider view than other critics, Prasad also sees a crucial change in the mid-1970s: "Suddenly, with *Deewar* we go back, we begin, with childhood. And the hero, fixated in some traumatic movement of his childhood, never grows up" (1987, 30). While I find the terms of Prasad's analysis compelling, I can't agree with the "suddenness" he attributes to *Deewar*, nor with his surprising claim that in earlier decades "there is no reference to childhood as a significant element in the development of the hero's personality" (Prasad 1987, 30). But Prasad's recognition that Bachchan's 1970s films go back to the hero's childhood is accurate, with what was once a popular narrative option having become a virtual requirement.[7]

Recent critics have questioned the possible extent of the "angry young man's" rebellion (Fareeduddin Kazmi 1998), but few critics have denied that a major change in the representation of the hero takes place in the 1970s, especially motivated by the ten films written between 1973 and 1982 by Salim-Javed (Salim Khan and Javed Akhtar) starring Amitabh Bachchan. For more than a decade, the characters played by Bachchan as a man are traumatized as boys: in the film that inaugurated the cycle, *Zanjeer (The Chain)*

The boy Vijay stands up for his mother, an exploited laborer on the construction site of a high rise apartment building in *Deewar* (1975).

(1973), Vijay (Victory)—which becomes the most frequent name for Bachchan's screen characters—sees his parents murdered; in the career-defining *Deewar* his father is publicly disgraced and his own arm is tattooed; *Amar Akbar Anthony* (1977), although a more comic film, separates him suddenly from his parents and brothers; in *Muqaddar Ka Sikandar (Victor of Destiny)* (1979) he is an orphan taken in by a surrogate mother who dies after he has been labeled a thief and banished from his childhood sweetheart's home; *Trishul (Trident)* (1978) presents him as an illegitimate child who watches his mother slowly die, and in *Laawaris (Orphan)* (1981) he is again a bastard, taking the name of a pet dog who treats him better than his alcoholic guardian. In *Namak Halal (Loyal Servant)* (1982) he sees his father murdered, and is taken from his mother; in *Shakti (Power)* (1982) he is kidnapped and hears his policeman father (played by Dilip Kumar in a celebrated pairing) tell the villains to kill his own son rather than concede to their demands; in *Coolie* (1983) he sees his father killed and his mother abducted; and in a late example, *Mard (Man)* (1985) he is taken from his parents after his father carves the infant's name into his chest. The pain, shame, isolation, and physical abuse that the boys in these films endure provide the motives for the hero's identity and actions—seeking legitimacy, restoration, or revenge—that propel the narratives. Each film first depicts the hero as a boy, but only a preference for startling cuts rather than slow dissolves marks these films as "advances" upon the basic form, established in Hindi cinema's golden age, for advancing the protagonist's story.

I don't deny that Bachchan's persona introduced significant changes to popular Indian cinema (such as a distinctive new physicality), but the continuity his films maintain with earlier Hindi cinema is often overlooked as the changes are overemphasized. In an essay on P. C. Barua, the tormented director of the 1935 Hindi and Bengali versions of *Devdas*, Ashis Nandy concludes by noting the typical view that "it was by jettisoning Barua's model of the hero that a new generation of commercial Hindi films, from *Zanjeer* onward, supposedly made their presence felt in the mid-1970s. Amitabh Bachchan, actor-turned-politician-turned-actor, was to typify that genre for millions of Indians." "Yet," Nandy cautions, "despite much talk about a virile industrial man supplanting a chocolate-pie, effeminate hero, in this transition from the earlier romantic heroes on the Indian screen to the present breed of tough, modern killing machines, Barua . . . and *Devdas* have not been truly superseded" (2001, 157). Nandy's claim for the continuance of the Devdas-hero is especially intriguing for its invocation of Bachchan, whose screen image has so often been taken as a revolution in the presentation of the hero, yet Nandy's counterintuitive insight is partly convincing because heroes from both eras share and are defined by a traumatic childhood.

Like many star vehicles, Bachchan's films function virtually as a subgenre, accumulating a good deal of their meaning through repetition and variation rather than originality, but for convenience I'll rely upon a single example to emphasize points that could describe many of his films. Although clearly tailored to Bachchan's fully established persona, *Muqaddar Ka Sikandar* slyly remakes *Devdas* in its construction of a hero who takes to drink when torn between an unattainable woman, loved since childhood, and an adoring prostitute; it also reworks elements of *Awaara*, especially

The mistreated boy becomes an "angry young man" who laughs at death: Amitabh Bachchan as the adult Sikander in *Muqaddar Ka Sikandar* (1978).

in setting a poor boy's humiliation at a rich girl's birthday party, and these allusions alone might confirm my claim that Bachchan's films continue rather than break with the tradition of the romantic Hindi cinema associated with the 1950s. But among the star's defining films, *Muqaddar Ka Sikandar* most thoroughly demonstrates the hero's inability to escape his own childhood, despite its "rags to riches" story. The film introduces a poor, nameless orphan reluctantly taken in as a servant by a widower and his daughter Kamna; the boy becomes devoted to the girl, and after following her from Simla to Bombay, acquires a surrogate mother, sister, and name, Sikander (Alexander). After he is wrongly called a thief at Kamna's birthday party, his new mother dies and at her grave he encounters a *darvesh* (a Muslim holy man) who instructs the boy to laugh at sorrow. After a brief montage of Bombay locations, we meet the adult Sikander, still laughing at death fifteen years later as he rides a motorcycle through the city.

Sikander has grown and become a successful small businessman, but we immediately learn that all of his actions as an adult derive directly from childhood traumas: a flashback reveals that his success in business was motivated by a vow to defeat a smuggler who bullied him and his sister as children. He has also become successful in order to keep his promise to his surrogate mother to look after her daughter, whose marriage he has now arranged, and he keeps the darvesh as a kind of spiritual advisor; but he has also become wealthy in order to impress Kamna and her father, now down on their luck. As a boy, Sikander accidentally broke a doll in Kamna's home, which he is attempting to replace when he is banished from her home. Years later, he keeps the doll in a home shrine, still preparing to bestow it upon her and clear his name. In the film's most remarkable scene, Sikander finally explains his past actions to Kamna, weeping (with a loss of reserve unusual for Bachchan) as he reenacts the emotional scene just before he was banished from her life as a boy. He tells her that even alcohol cannot stop him from hearing her girlhood condemnation, and he declares his lifelong love for her. Kamna now understands everything, and apologizes for her previous actions: change is possible, and the couple now has a future. But this scene, dramatizing the hero's physical regression to an emotional stage he has never left, is suddenly revealed to be his fantasy. He will never in fact overcome his past in the manner of his daydream: the replacement-doll will also be broken rather than restored, and a series of decisions and misunderstandings prevents the fantasized declarations (that could clear the path toward a future) from actually being spoken or correctly heard.

Finally, *Muqaddar Ka Sikandar* employs song sequences to signal its hero's stunted development. As a boy he is transfixed by Kamna's performance of her late mother's favorite song "O Sathi Re" ("Oh Friend"); as an adult, he will perform the song at a charity benefit and recall moments from the early part of the film. Through flashbacks, the song's reprise thus serves his regression, recovering its original impact rather than acquiring any new meaning. A later sequence allows us to enter the imaginations of both Sikander and his friend (but unknown romantic rival) Vishal as both listen to Kamna sing: whereas Vishal dreams of an artificial, but maturely romantic, space (a heavenly nightclub decorated with a paper moon and manufactured clouds), Sikander returns to his and Kamna's childhood setting, in the snow of Simla, where the adult lovers frolic in the long-past world of virginal innocence. Like Devdas, this hero, incapable of overcoming his childhood feelings, cannot survive adulthood. The "angry young man" is, after all, a sad little boy.

The Happy Old Boy

Between 1985 and 1987 Amitabh Bachchan entered politics as a Member of Parliament, and from 1987 to 1990 he was investigated (and exonerated) for his possible role in a national bribery scandal; during the latter period he also made a series of unsuccessful "comeback" films. Although no single actor would secure Bachchan's near-exclusive dominance of the box office, among those whose careers began in the 1990s, Shah Rukh Khan, born in 1965, emerged as Bachchan's apparent successor when he appeared in a series of commercial blockbusters including *Dilwale Dulhania Le Jayenge (The Pure-Hearted Will Take the Bride)* (1995), *Dil To Pagal Hai (The Heart's Crazy)* (1997) and *Kuch Kuch Hota Hai (Things Happen)* (1998). Indeed, in both of the recent films that pair Shah Rukh Khan and Amitabh Bachchan, *Mohabbatein (Loves)* (2000) and *Kabhi Khushi Kabhie Gham (Sometimes Happiness, Sometimes Sorrow)* (2001), the latter plays the kind of stern patriarch that once made his "young man" so "angry." However, Shah Rukh Khan first emerged as a film star (after work in television) through a pair of successful but controversial films that brought an unprecedented twist to the Hindi cinema: the psychopathic hero. In *Darr (Fear)* (1994) and *Baazigar (Gambler)* (1993) Shah Rukh Khan gained the audience's sympathy even as his characters obsessively stalked his heroines or tossed them off tall buildings. While a traumatic offscreen event (his mother's death in a car accident) seems to motivate the demented Rahul of *Darr*, *Baazigar* more explicitly follows the established Bachchan formula by having its "hero" witness the humiliation of his parents while still a child, motivating his devious plan to infiltrate and destroy the family and business of the man who crushed his family.

At first glance, *Baazigar* thus resembles the model I've been tracing, but its images of the childhood past are brief and cryptic flashbacks interspersed within, rather than placed at the beginning of, the film: they reveal the past motivating the hero's vengeance only in fragments, instead of dramatizing the hero's trauma as a preface to the overall story. This structural distinction between a chronological and a slowly recovered presentation of the hero's childhood (reminiscent of Alfred Hitchcock's *Spellbound* [1945]) is most significant in terms of the control it maintains over the audience's knowledge. The typical structure of Hindi cinema offers preliminary access to the hero's childhood trauma so that the audience clearly understands its power over all his later actions: the flashbacks in *Baazigar* withhold full understanding from the viewer until well into the film. Despite its inclusion of the hero's childhood suffering, the film's organization (the familiar structure for Hollywood suspense) signals a shifting presentation and function of childhood in Hindi cinema. Indeed, in an illuminating essay, Ranjani Mazumdar offers "a dialectical juxtaposition of the 'angry man' of the Bachchan era and the psychotic persona of Shah Rukh Khan," arguing that "the emergence of Shah Rukh Khan's psychotic image seems to pose a radical discontinuity with the 'angry man' image" (2000, 239). In an especially acute observation, Mazumdar notes that "Shah Rukh's deployment was in many ways the negation of Bachchan's control—*excess* was re-invented to challenge the moral codes of the 1970s 'formula'" (241). While grounding a social distinction between the films of these stars in details of their performance styles is convincing, these early roles, though crucial in establishing Shah Rukh Khan's stardom, now appear eccentric and quite unlike the consistent persona of his later, bigger, hits and of his ongoing career. In fact, *Baazigar* now looks odd *not* because it features Shah Rukh in one of the antihero (*khalnayak*) roles that enjoyed a brief vogue in Hindi cinema, but because it presents him as a character burdened by his childhood past.

In his later blockbuster hits, and even his less successful films, Shah Rukh Khan typically plays a young man who, dramatically, requires—and so has—no narrated childhood. Mazumdar's contrasting Bachchan and Khan in terms of physical control and excess no longer seems to oppose, primarily, seething rage and violent psychosis, but maturity and youth. If Bachchan's characters were unhappy adults forced to grow up too soon, Shah Rukh Khan's characters, first encountered as young adults, threaten to never mature. Their childhood is unnecessary or irrelevant because as adults they are childish, happy old boys rather than angry young men. Nasreen Munni Kabir has observed that "Shammi Kapoor's character appears to have inspired the romantic modern Bollywood heroes as personified by Shah Rukh Khan, Salman Khan, Aamir Khan, and Hritik Roshan. The essential characteristics of this hero are that he is funny, irreverent, young and dances exceptionally well" (2001, 37). Kabir's claim is surprising and convincing, but most revealing for what it implies: this generation of actors has bypassed the influence of Hindi cinema's greatest superstar, whose persona dominated the era preceding their debuts. Bachchan's characters were depicted as boys or men, not teenagers. Shammi Kapoor indeed seems to have been ahead of his time: the teenager that he was too old to play has fully arrived in the Hindi cinema only through his heirs, who have managed to deflect Bachchan's more immediate impact and especially the longer cinematic inheritance of the traumatized boy that he so fully and frequently embodied. They have filled the previous generation gap of popular Hindi cinema.

Once his screen persona was codified in the record-breaking hit *Dilwale Dulhania Le Jayenge,* Shah Rukh Khan's nervous energy, comic vanity, and cocky self-confidence (in one film he sings "I'm the Best") functioned to render narrative excavations of the childhood of his characters unnecessary. If his characters suffer, their difficulties derive from immediate circumstances and the stern fathers of young women, not unresolved childhood pain or the class-conscious fathers of little girls. Patricia Uberoi, emphasizing that two of his major films depict Shah Rukh Khan as a Non-Resident Indian (NRI) in an unprecedented positive light, nicely describes the qualities as well as the social limits of his established screen image: "Clearly, boyish exuberance is a challenge to the deadly serious role of being an émigré Indian. It is also an index of a liminal stage in the male life cycle—the 'boys will be boys,' male bonding, 'I hate girls,' phase of flirtatious and teasing relations with the opposite sex, prior to acceptance of the responsibilities of adult heterosexuality" (1998, 317). Shah Rukh Khan and his peers (including Salman Khan and Aamir Khan, all unrelated) reduce the rituals of romance to "eve-teasing," the Indian-English term that can describe behavior ranging from mild flirtation to sexual harassment. Apparently immune to the childhood infatuations that begin 1950s films, these young men (paired with often tomboyish heroines) participate in the imported rites of adolescent dating, often masking attraction under the veneer of irritation: Shah Rukh specializes in playing the young lover as a persistent pest, annoying his heroines into submission even as, as Uberoi notes, his true Indian manners and chivalry (forbidding premarital sex) surface. In this way, Shah Rukh and his recent Bombay brothers more fully exemplify the Krishna-hero posited by Kakar than do earlier film stars. In fact, by the time of his being cast in *Dil Se . . . (From the Heart)* (1998) Shah Rukh's screen persona was so clearly established as a self-confident narcissist that it could serve a critical function (in a film by a controversial Tamil director) to emphasize the political blindness of his character, arrogantly attempting to represent the nation for All India Radio during the country's fiftieth anniversary: in love with a female terrorist whose personal feelings cannot displace her childhood trauma and political history, he simply cannot understand her; his emotional immaturity and her political maturity doom them. His life, lived only in the present, cannot free her from a life that constantly recalls the past.

Other recent films, more unselfconscious about the meaning of their young male stars, have attracted complaints from Indian critics for the qualities I'm describing. For instance, Rustom Bharucha condemns *Hum Aapke Hain Koun . . . ! (Who Am I To You?)* (1994), in which, "counterpointing the formalities of marriage, the younger couple [played by Salman Khan and Madhuri Dixit] tease and flirt with each other throughout the film" (1995, 802). Bharucha accuses the film's director Sooraj Barjatya of "tuning very ingeniously into the infantalisation of desire that seems to be pervading our society through a craze for novelties and commodities" (804). This "infantalisation," defined by consumer desire, in fact resembles what American critics understand as the "youth market," driven by the tastes and increased purchasing power of post–World War II teenagers. The soft drinks, designer clothing, hi-tech electronic gadgets, and brand logo sports equipment on ostentatious display in so many recent Hindi films are the most obvious sign of the transformation of the young Indian into a global teenage consumer. Rachel Dwyer (2000) attributes this conspicuous consumption to the rise of a middle class in Bombay, but she perhaps underemphasizes the extent to which this transformation has allowed the development of a youth culture, too mainstream to constitute a subculture, within or alongside that class. In any case, the reinscription of Indian masculinity is not just visible on the shop-window screens of contemporary Hindi cinema, but is embedded in these films' revised structures as well.

Again, the new young heroes generally exist in and are only defined by their present circumstances, so when recent films such as *Kuch Kuch Hota Hai* or *Kabhi Khushi Kabhie Gham* do include flashbacks, these revert only a few years, so that the young actors can easily play their slightly younger selves: in the latter, Shah Rukh Khan's character is briefly seen as a child in shots without dialogue, but in the long flashback that occupies the film's first half he plays his younger self opposite the chubby boy who will transform into actor Hritik Roshan. In these films, which ostensibly provide more mature roles for Shah Rukh Khan (playing a father), there's little difference between his performance or physical appearance (other than costume changes) as a college student and as a widowed businessman: he plays silly games with his girlfriends in the same way that he cavorts with his children. In other films, the effort to avoid representing his characters as boys is striking: a hit film featuring the then-rising male stars Shah Rukh Khan and Salman Khan, *Karan Arjun* (1995) echoes classic mother-and-two-sons melodramas, but whereas earlier films all transport their heroes from childhood to adulthood, the boyish brothers Karan and Arjun are introduced as young men competing for their mother's affection; when they are killed by a ruthless villain, their mother prays to the goddess Kali and her sons are reborn but raised by different families. While both boys are briefly depicted growing up haunted by semiconscious visions of their previous life, their entire (second) childhood is traversed during the film's delayed credit sequence, and we quickly meet them again embodied by the young stars viewed earlier. To Western viewers, the way in which the film treats reincarnation may be its most curious element, but in the tradition I'm analyzing, *Karan Arjun* is most telling for shifting the focus away from childhood as the location for establishing character traits and traumas that will direct adult life. The visions that appear as flashes of consciousness to the young boys whose mother's faith has recovered them reflect their previous lives as young men, not their childhoods.

Notably, the recent, ornate remake of *Devdas* (2002) starring Shah Rukh Khan does not follow the well-known previous version starring Dilip Kumar (or the suggestion of its source novel) in depicting Devdas as a boy, even though the story and dialogue emphasize the importance of events that originate in his childhood. (A single brief flashback of young Devdas being punished by his father, filmed from above so the child's face isn't visible, is the sole depiction of an

Shah Rukh Khan as
Rahul, the "happy
old boy" in *Dil To
Pagal Hai* (1997).

earlier portion of the character's life.) Because Devdas's mischievous
behavior during his childhood is only described, Shah Rukh Khan's
familiar teasing of his mother and Paro when he first returns from
college offers the only explanation of why this particular Devdas
doesn't need to have his childhood represented: here he is embodied
by a star who is perpetually childish, whatever his actual age. We
needn't see him as a child so long as he continues to act like one.

Finally, it's revealing that recent Hindi film stars have appeared
in films that mine key films of 1950s American youth culture for
their plots and images, the heroes often evoking the iconic figures of
James Dean and Marlon Brando as rebellious teens. *Josh (Frenzy)*
(2000), with Shah Rukh Khan, remakes *West Side Story* (1961),
while *Ghulam (Slave)* (1998), with Aamir Khan, explicitly invokes
both *Rebel Without a Cause* (1955) and *On the Waterfront* (1954).
Although Shammi Kapoor was often compared to Elvis Presley in
the early 1960s, Shah Rukh Khan actually impersonates the King
(albeit in 1970s-era sideburns, sneer, and jumpsuit) in *Phir Bhi Dil
Hai Hindustani (But the Heart's Still Indian)* (2000). College dances
in Aamir Khan's debut *Qayamat Se Qayamat Tak (Doomsday to
Doomsday)* (1988) and *Kuch Kuch Hota Hai* evoke the sock-hop
world of *Grease* (1978), itself already a later era's fantasy of the
American 1950s most popular among viewers who were born
decades later. Other recent and popular Hindi movies, such as the
semi-art film *Bombay Boys* (2000) and *Dil Chahta Hai (The Heart
Yearns)* (2001) affirm the successful construction of the Indian male-

centered coming-of-age film, which wastes no screen time on its protagonists' childhoods. Both films feature a trio of young men whose status as NRIs or as rich kids literally affords them the opportunity to spend their early adulthood "finding themselves" in fairly aimless adventures. While these characters encounter difficulties, these surmountable problems provide valuable "life lessons" in the manner of melodramatic Hollywood films, and hardly resemble the devastating crises that stunt children in earlier Hindi films. Adorned in the latest Western fashions, hanging out in high-tech discos, cell phones at the ready, and often working in India's recently expanded mass media industries (the hero and heroine of *Phir Bhi Dil Hai Hindustani* are competing cable television personalities), these Bombay teens proclaim the true arrival of youth culture in popular Hindi film, with boys and men relegated to an increasingly distant cinematic past.

NOTES

Bahut shukriya to Priya Joshi, Nasreen Munni Kabir, Priya Kumar, Philip Lutgendorf, Neepa Majumdar, Jyotika Virdi, and Vinu Warrier for suggestions and encouragement. Thanks too to my writing group, Kathleen Diffley, Matt Brown, and Tom Lutz, for additional suggestions, and to Murray and Frances for support and patience. Special thanks to Teresa Mangum for helping me grow up.

1. This essay does not just restrict itself to the representation of boyhood for the sake of this volume. While women in Hindi cinema offer rich material for analysis, which some critics have undertaken, girls remain a virtually unexplored topic by filmmakers as well as critics. As Sudhir Kakar added in *The Inner World,* his pioneering 1978 study of childhood in India, "large parts of the Indian tradition of childhood are solely concerned with boys and ignore, if not dispossess, girls of their childhood." (1978: 191) However, Kakar can himself be criticized for perpetuating the bias he bemoans, and the evident male bias in Hindi cinema could be countered by examples of young female participation and visibility in other realms of Indian popular culture.

2. I must emphasize that the transitions I am identifying may or may not actually employ the cinematic device of the dissolve; match cuts or rhymed sequences of shots are also common in the films I discuss, though dissolves mark most "classic" examples. Nevertheless, I prefer to draw upon the rich connotations of the term "dissolve," following the work of Christian Metz and Rick Altman, the latter in his analysis of the Hollywood musical. Altman also does not restrict his terms to the literal presence of the device: I am not, however, draw-

ing upon his emphasis on "dissolves" between elements (such as reality and dream, talking and singing, or walking and dancing) especially distinctive to the musical genre.

3. A number of critics have suggested that the central Hindu religious practice of *darshan* (or *darshana*), in which worshipers and (images of) gods gaze upon one another, operates within Indian films and in the relation between Indian spectators and cinema, especially in their attraction to stars. The challenge this concept poses to concepts of the gaze in Western film theory is significant. See Eck 1998 for a now-classic discussion of darshan, and Vasudevan 2000, 139–47 for a suggestive application to Hindi cinema.

4. The scholarly treatment of Krishna is extensive; for discussions emphasizing Radha that can be helpful in understanding the ongoing popularity of her romance with Krishna for Hindi cinema, see Kakar and Ross 1986, 74–103; Kinsley 1986; and Wulff 1996. Krishna, while a very popular god "himself," is the eighth avatar or incarnation of Vishnu, the second god in the great trinity that also includes Brahma and Shiva; Radha is sometimes understood to be an incarnation of Vishnu's consort the goddess Lakshmi.

5. *Devdas* has accumulated a rich critical commentary. On *Devdas* in its various incarnations see: Nandy 2001, Nazir 2002, and Valicha 1988, 43–60. Chatterji's original Bengali novella is available in an unfortunately abridged English translation. The novella does introduce the main characters as children, but handles the passage of time as Devdas and Parvati (Paro) grow up with regular abruptness, noting simply, for instance, "A year passed" (1996, 39), "Two months passed" (40), or that "Four years passed" (41). Maturation is described efficiently: "Parvati, still in her teens, was fast growing into a woman" (41–42). Although best known in its two earlier Hindi versions (P. C. Barua, 1936, starring K. L. Saigal) (Bimal Roy, 1955, starring Dilip Kumar) and now in its elaborate third Hindi incarnation (Sanjay Leela Bhansali, 2002, starring Shah Rukh Khan), discussed below, the story was also produced in a silent version (Naresh Chandra Mitra, 1928), and a (recently rediscovered) Bengali version filmed simultaneously with the first Hindi sound version and starring its director (P. C. Barua, 1936). *Devdas* also exists in a Tamil (P. V. Rao, 1936), Malayalam (Ownbelt Mani, 1989), and two (1953 and 1974) Telegu versions, as well as a Bengali remake (Dilip Roy, 1979). As writers like Nandy and Valicha make clear, *Devdas* has also been the inspiration for various "unofficial" versions of the story, including Guru Dutt's self-reflexive *Kaagaz Ke Phool (Paper Flowers)* (1959), about a failing filmmaker (played by Dutt) attempting to remake *Devdas*.

6. I am only aware of two scholarly attempts to assess the significance

of Shammi Kapoor's career, by Chakravarty 1993, 207–10 and Rai 1994.

7. Although Amitabh Bachchan remains virtually unknown for most Western film fans and critics, he is arguably the world's most famous film star, known to approximately a billion worldwide fans. Because his career has received a fair amount of critical attention (though, again, this work remains marginal within mainstream film studies), I won't provide much information that is available elsewhere. For treatments of the "angry young man" cycle and the career of Amitabh Bachchan, see: Chandrasekhar 1988; Dwyer 2002, 71–105; Fareeduddin Kazmi 1996; Nikhat Kazmi 1996, 29–53; Lal 1998, 238–44; Mazumdar 2000, 238–50; Mishra et al. 1989; Mishra 2002, 125–56; Prasad 1987; Prasad 1998, 138–59; and Vachani 1999. Somaaya's biography (1999) of Bachchan is useful as a career overview. For specific discussions of *Deewar* (sometimes contained within texts already cited) see Dwyer 2002, 76–82; Lal 1998, 238–42; Mazumdar 2000, 243–50; Prasad 1998, 144–53; and Virdi 1993. At least one Bachchan film, *Namak Halal,* seems to humorously acknowledge that the "maturation dissolves" in so many of his films challenge character development. After the hero, as a small boy, is put to sleep by his grandfather playing a lullaby on the gramophone, the film cuts to the grandfather, visibly older, waking a full-grown man while the same song continues to play. When Bachchan wakes up, he is still infantilized, telling his grandfather that he has been dreaming about him. The grandfather admonishes the young man for being twenty-five years old yet still such a baby, telling him that he should be dreaming about women by this point in his life. The young man clearly disapproves of such unsavory thoughts.

Works Cited

Altman, Rick. 1987. *The American Film Musical.* Bloomington: Indiana University Press.

Bharucha, Rustom. 1995. "Utopia in Bollywood: *Hum Aapke Hain Koun . . . !" Economic and Political Weekly,* April 15, 801–4.

Carstairs, G. Morris. 1958. *The Twice-Born: A Study of a Community of High-Caste Hindus.* Bloomington: Indiana University Press.

Caruth, Cathy, ed. 1995. *Trauma: Explorations in Memory.* Baltimore: Johns Hopkins University Press.

Chakravarty, Sumita S. 1993. *National Identity in Indian Popular Cinema, 1947–1987.* Austin: University of Texas Press.

Chandrasekhar, K. 1988. "The Amitabh Persona: An Interpretation." *Deep Focus* 1, no. 3, 52–57.

Chatterjee, Gayatri. 1992. *Awaara.* New Delhi: Wiley Eastern.

————. 2002. *Mother India.* London: BFI.

Chatterji, Sarat Chandra. 1996. "Devdas." In *Devdas and Other Stories,* ed, and trans. V. S. Naravane, 31–78. New Delhi: Roli.

Dwyer, Rachel. 2000. *All You Want Is Money, All You Need Is Love: Sex and Romance in Modern India.* London: Cassell.

————. 2002. *Yash Chopra.* London: BFI.

Dwyer, Rachel, and Divia Patel. 2002. *Cinema India: The Visual Culture of Hindi Film.* London: Reaktion.

Eck, Diana L. 1998. *Darsan: Seeing the Divine Image in India.* 3rd ed. New York: Columbia University Press.

Kabir, Nasreen Munni. 2001. *Bollywood: The Indian Cinema Story.* London: Channel 4.

Kakar, Sudhir. 1979. *Indian Childhood: Cultural Ideals and Social Reality.* Delhi: Oxford University Press.

————. 1978 [rpt. 1981]. *The Inner World: A Psycho-Analytic Study of Childhood and Society in India.* Oxford: Oxford University Press.

————. 1989. "Lovers in the Dark." In *Intimate Relations: Exploring Indian Sexuality,* 25–41. Chicago: University of Chicago Press.

Kakar, Sudhir, and John M. Ross. 1986. *Tales of Love, Sex, and Danger.* Oxford: Oxford University Press.

Kazmi, Fareed. 1999. *The Politics of India's Conventional Cinema: Imaging a Universe, Subverting a Multiverse.* New Delhi: Sage.

Kazmi, Fareeduddin. 1998. "How Angry Is the Angry Young Man? 'Rebellion' in Conventional Hindi Films." In *The Secret Politics of Our Desires: Innocence, Culpability and Indian Popular Cinema,* ed. Ashis Nandy, 134–56. London: Zed.

Kazmi, Nikhat. 1996. *Ire in the Soul: Bollywood's Angry Years.* New Delhi: HarperCollins.

Kinsley, David R. 1986 [rpt. 1997]. *Hindu Goddesses: Visions of the Divine Feminine in the Hindu Religious Tradition.* Berkeley: University of California Press.

Kurtz, Stanley N. 1992. *All the Mothers Are One: Hindu India and the Cultural Reshaping of Psychoanalysis.* New York: Columbia University Press.

Lal, Vinay. 1998. "The Impossibility of the Outsider in the Modern Hindi Film." In *The Secret Politics of Our Desires: Innocence, Culpability and Indian Popular Cinema,* ed. Ashis Nandy, 228–59. London: Zed.

Mazumdar, Ranjani. 2000. "From Subjectification to Schizophrenia: The 'Angry Man' and the 'Psychotic' Hero of Bombay Cinema." In *Making Meaning in Indian Cinema,* ed. Ravi S. Vasudevan, 238–64. New Delhi: Oxford University Press.

Metz, Christian. 1977. *The Imaginary Signifier: Psychoanalysis and the Cinema.* Trans. Celia Britton, Annwyl Williams, Ben Brewster and Alfred Guzzetti. Bloomington: Indiana University Press.

Mishra, Vijay. 2002. "The Actor as Parallel Text: Amitabh Bachchan." In *Bollywood Cinema: Temples of Desire,* 125–56. New York:

Routledge.

Mishra, Vijay, Peter Jeffrey, and Brian Shoesmith. 1989. "The Actor as Parallel Text in Bombay Cinema." *Quarterly Review of Film and Video* 2, 49–67.

Nandy, Ashis. 2001. "Invitation to an Antique Death: The Journey of Pramathesh Barua as the Origin of the Terribly Effeminate, Maudlin, Self-Destructive Heroes of Indian Cinema." In *Pleasure and the Nation: The History, Politics and Consumption of Public Culture in India*, ed. Rachel Dwyer and Christopher Pinney, 139–60. New Delhi: Oxford University Press.

Narayan, R. K. 1977. *The Ramayana.* London: Penguin.

Nazir, Asjad. 2002. "The Changing Faces of *Devdas,*" *Eastern Eye*, London, July 5, Emag 8–9.

Prasad, M. Madhava. 1987. "Escape from Childhood: The Development of Hero in Popular Cinema." *Deep Focus* 1, no. 1, 28–32.

———. 1998. *Ideology of the Hindi Film: A Historical Construction.* Delhi: Oxford University Press.

Rai, Amit. 1994. "An American Raj in Filmistan: Images of Elvis in Indian Films." *Screen* 35, no. 1, 51–77.

Ramanujan, A. K. 1999. "Repetition in the *Mahabharata.*" In *The Collected Essays of A. K. Ramanujan*, ed. Vinay Dharwadker, 161–83. Oxford: Oxford University Press.

Ray, Satyajit. 1998. *Childhood Days: A Memoir.* Trans. Bijoya Ray. New Delhi: Penguin.

Sharma, Ashwani. 1993. "Blood, Sweat and Tears: Amitabh Bachchan, Urban Demi-God." In *You Tarzan: Masculinity, Movies, and Men*, ed. Pat Kirkham and Janet Thumim, 167–80. London: Lawrence and Wishart.

Somaaya, Bhawana. 1999. *Amitabh Bachchan: The Legend.* Delhi: Macmillan.

Uberoi, Patricia. 1998. "The Diaspora Comes Home: Disciplining Desire in *DDLJ,*" *Contributions to Indian Sociology*, n.s., 32, no. 2, 305–36.

Vachani, Lalit. 1999. "Bachchan-Alias: The Many Faces of a Film Icon." In *Image Journeys: Audio-Visual Media and Cultural Change in India*, ed. Christiane Brosius and Melissa Butcher, 199–230. New Delhi: Sage.

Valicha, Kishore. 1988. *The Moving Image: A Study of Indian Cinema.* Hyderabad: Orient Longman.

Vasudevan, Ravi, 1989. "The Melodramatic Mode and the Commercial Hindi Cinema: Notes on Film History, Narrative, and Performance in the 1950s." *Screen* 30, no. 3, 29–50.

———. 2000. "The Politics of Cultural Address in a 'Transitional' Cinema: A Case Study of Indian Popular Cinema." In *Reinventing Film Studies*, ed. Christine Gledhill and Linda Williams, 130–64. London: Arnold.

Virdi, Jyotika. 1993. "The 'Fiction' of Film and 'Fact' of Politics in

Deewar." *Jump Cut* 38, 26–32.

Wulff, Donna M. 1996. "Radha: Consort and Conqueror of Krishna." In *Devi: Goddesses of India,* ed. John Stratton Hawley and Donna Marie Wulff, 109–34. Berkeley: University of California Press.

20

JERKUS INTERRUPTUS
The Terrible Trials of Masturbating Boys
in Recent Hollywood Cinema

Steven Jay Schneider

> I tear off my pants, furiously I grab that battering ram to free-
> dom, my adolescent cock, even as my mother begins to call from
> the other side of the bathroom door. "Now this time don't flush.
> Do you hear me, Alex? I have to see what's in that bowl!" [. . .]
> Oh my secrets, my shame, my palpitations, my flushes, my
> sweats! The way I respond to the simple vicissitudes of human
> life! Doctor, I can't stand any more being frightened like this
> over nothing! Bless me with manhood! Make me brave! Make
> me strong! Make me *whole*!
>
>   Philip Roth, *Portnoy's Complaint*

WOMEN *DO* DO IT BETTER

That teenage boys masturbate is of course a truism, albeit one that
remains—in real life as well as in popular Hollywood film—a
source of great embarrassment, even shame, for those young men
who (all too) frequently partake of its all-too-fleeting pleasures.
With the embarrassment and shame bequeathed by a generally
homophobic culture that somehow equates the desire for self-stimulation to a preference for same-sex union comes the potential for
humiliation, the masturbating male subject capable of being transformed the instant his secret activity is revealed into an object of
disgust, horror, and, above all, humor. Literally caught with his
pants down, the would-be whacker must face the unpleasant facts
that he is at the mercy of his raging hormones, that he is horny,
wretched, and utterly incapable of finding a partner willing to
assist him in satisfying his sexual urges. What is worse, humiliation is mixed with frustration whenever the desperate, pent-up
masturbator gets stymied in his humble though frenetic attempt to
seek momentary relief from the assorted angst and awkwardness of
adolescence. For only a real loser—a mere child, in mind if not in

body (like Philip Roth's infamous/ignominious Portnoy)—is incapable of finding himself a suitable safe haven in which he can comfortably bring himself to climax. We laugh at these mostly lovable losers when we hear their tales of woe; even better, when we watch them suffer the prying eyes, ears, and slew of assorted interruptions while trying to get off on the big screen. After all, we've all been there ourselves: now it's time to enjoy someone *else* getting busted simply for being a masturbator!

This essay treats as case studies in pop cinematic sadism five of the most memorable adolescent male masturbation scenes (with a couple of apparent exceptions that really aren't exceptions at all; see below) to appear in American movies over the past twenty years: Amy Heckerling's coming-of-age classic *Fast Times at Ridgemont High* (1982), David O. Russell's award-winning indie *Spanking the Monkey* (1994), Chris and Paul Weitz's raunchy summer sleeper *American Pie* (1999), Joel Gallen's underrated high school spoof *Not Another Teen Movie* (2001), and Sam Raimi's comic-book spectacular *Spider-Man* (2002). In all five of these films, the masturbatory acts in question are rudely interrupted before self-consummation can occur, leading to momentary mortification followed by exasperation and exclamations on the part of the teen protagonist, and often unrestrained (not to mention cruel) laugher on the part of the viewer.

It would be worth constructing a contrast between this theme-and-variations and the manner in which attractive adolescent females are voyeuristically admired by the moviegoing masses when they endeavor to "learn about their bodies" and/or "pleasure themselves" all by themselves. In one scene in *American Pie,* luscious and apparently unrepressed (because foreign?) exchange student Nadia (Shannon Elizabeth) gratifies herself on Jim's (Jason Biggs) bed to the porno mags the sex-obsessed boy's well-meaning but dorky dad (Eugene Levy) purchased on his behalf some days earlier. Unbeknownst to Nadia—not that she would care, clearly—her masturbation session is being broadcast across the Internet via a hidden camera attached to Jim's computer. The camera cuts back and forth between "live" shots of the impossibly gorgeous (and impossibly teenaged), topless (no way she's bottomless, this film is only rated R after all) Nadia with her hand down her panties, moaning quietly as she leisurely flips the pages of the girlie mags—her inherent bisexuality taken as given—and reaction shots of what looks like the entire male student body of her All-American Pie high school thanking God for their good fortune and thoroughly enjoying the virtual peep show.

Unlike the treatment accorded her male counterpart by filmmakers in the scenes discussed below, no attempt is made by the directors of *American Pie*, the Weitz brothers, to provide any insight into Nadia's subjectivity; there is no sense of haste, resignation, or compulsiveness associated with her onanistic behavior, just spontaneity and vitality (she looks as though she could go on all day, pausing for the occasional orgasm and starting right up again); and when she gets caught in the act by a scheming Jim, she immediately turns the tables on her onlooker, making the young man feel ashamed for having spoiled her good time. In short, there seems to be a gendered double standard at play in teen movies when it comes to teens busted for playing with themselves: whereas the guys who try unsuccessfully to get off on their own are depicted as spiritual children—mamma's boys with father issues who can't even find solace in fantasy—the gals are seen (often by diegetic male audiences) as full-figured, fully bloomed, hot-blooded *women*, for whom masturbation is a pleasant prelude to, rather than a cheap substitute for, sex, and for whom the act is erotic rather than aggressive, a turn-on rather than a turn-off. Even on that all-too-rare occasion when the guy actually does get to ejaculate, for example, Ted Stroehmann (Ben Stiller) in the Farrelly Brothers' *There's Something About Mary* (1998)—a movie about a man stalking the former high school sweetheart of his dreams and stuck in perpetual pubescent agony while he waits for her to say yes years down the line—he *still* has to pay for his sin with the horrifying knowledge that his jism is now being used as extra-hold hair gel by his beloved. At least *she* seems oblivious to the hair solution's "special" properties; but perhaps she's just pretending to seem nice.

BEATING OFF: A BRIEF HISTORY

And "sin" is indeed the operative word here. As a sexual act that both waylays reproduction and qualifies in an admittedly thin sense as homosexual—the latter insofar as it implies sex with a person of the same sex, namely oneself—masturbation has incurred the wrath of oft-hypocritical priests and Puritans alike for centuries. The Bible refers to the deed as the sin of Onan. In Genesis 38:4, we read that the Lord slew Onan's brother for wickedness. His father Judah told Onan to marry his brother's wife "and raise up seed to thy brother"

(Genesis 38:8). But Onan didn't want to have children by his sister-in-law: "And Onan knew that the seed should not be his; and it came to pass, when he went in unto his brother's wife, that he spilled it on the ground, lest that he should give seed to his brother" (Genesis 38:9). This misdeed displeased the Lord; "wherefore he slew him also" (Genesis 38:9–10). Clearly Onan was punished for pulling out, not for playing with himself, but because both activities imply a form of sexual conduct that eschews the possibility of reproduction as a result, masturbation has forever been aligned with withdrawal as one of the seedy sins of onanism. And although Onan at least got to get off before being killed by an angry and nosy God, he nevertheless serves as a biblical precursor for our busted teenage boys in that a meddlesome parent figure became aware of his illicit act even while he was performing it. Nowadays, repentant masturbators are advised to appeal to God's lighter side: self-proclaimed "experts" such as Lambert Dolphin write that the sinful act "is best dealt with by reassurance of God's grace and forgiveness and by focusing on spiritual growth to the end that the individual moves on to spiritual and emotional maturity, leaving masturbation behind as a symptom of spiritual immaturity" (1991).

The religious (Judeo-Christian) injunction against onanism found psychoanalytic support in the theories of Sigmund Freud, who warned of the potential perversity inherent in the narcissistic youth's masturbatory fixation. In a 1914 essay, Freud explained that "the word 'narcissism' is taken from clinical terminology to denote the attitude of a person who treats his own body in the same way as otherwise the body of a sexual object is treated":

> that is to say, he experiences sexual pleasure in gazing at, caressing and fondling his body, till complete gratification ensues upon these activities. Developed to this degree, narcissism has the significance of a perversion, which has absorbed the whole sexual life of the subject; consequently, in dealing with it we may expect to meet with phenomena similar to those for which we look in the study of all perversions. ([1914] 1953–1974, 73–102)

Presumably the underlying problem here is that, in becoming overly invested in the promises of self-pleasure, the teenage narcissist will forever fail to mature into a productive, not to say reproductive, member of society.

The outcry against onanism reached nearly hysterical (certainly hyperbolic) proportions in both Britain and America during the nineteenth and early twentieth centuries. In 1868, the editors of the *New Orleans Journal of Medical Surgery* declared that "neither plague, nor war, nor smallpox, nor a crowd of similar evils, have resulted more disastrously for humanity than the habit of masturbation: it is the destroying element of civilized humanity" (Down and Langden 1867, 359–60). As early as 1834, in fact, Dr. John Harway Kellogg and Sylvester Graham were publishing antimasturbation medical papers in the United States. Alan Hunt, who has traced the history of antimasturbation campaigns during this period, connects such "medical"—more like moral—treatises to the social purity movement as well as to the early feminist movement in Great Britain, while arguing nevertheless that "the content of British and American texts is virtually indistinguishable; indeed, many of the texts were published on both sides of the Atlantic" (1998, 580). For present purposes, it is sufficient to point out that the primary target of the social purity movement's campaign against playing with oneself was adolescent males.

Where does this background on masturbation leave us when it comes to our horny but sexually stymied Hollywood boys? By way of answering this question, I would like to highlight a dilemma of adolescent development in American society that I shall here dub the "Paradox of Masturbation," one that receives exaggerated expression in the five films I treat here. On the one hand, the ability and desire to successfully masturbate signifies the teenage boy's entrance into the pangs and pleasures of pubescence (i.e., physical manhood); while on the other hand, to *actually engage* in masturbatory activity is widely perceived as a symptom of spiritual and social *immaturity,* a sign that one has not agreed—has in fact refused—to take on the normative adult responsibilities that come with being a reproductive heterosexual. It is an open question, one that must be determined on a case-by-case basis, whether or not *Fast Times at Ridgemont High, Spanking the Monkey, American Pie, Not Another Teen Movie,* and *Spider-Man* are ideologically conservative films, whether or not they reinforce through cinematic narrative discourse the ostensibly shameful and shame-filled ramifications of the paradox of masturbation. At the very least, however, we can state in advance that all five films serve to *reflect* the conservatism of the country in which they were made, an ideologically enforced homophobia that is largely responsible for the structures of avoidance and disavowal attached by mainstream America to masturbatory activity. As such, the films in question deliberately milk the anxieties of onanism as these are experienced by young male teens.

BIG BROTHER IS WATCHING: *FAST TIMES AT RIDGEMONT HIGH*

In bringing Brad Hamilton (Judge Reinhold) to his knees, or at least to the bathroom, where he furtively spies on his younger sister's best friend while pleasuring himself before being busted, *Fast Times* methodically deconstructs the teenage boy's grand illusions of a being a "single, successful" high school senior who is ready to put outgrown relationships, menial labor, and masturbatory fantasies behind him as he approaches the threshold of male adulthood. Vividly portraying Brad's mounting frustration as the narrative proceeds, as well as his father issues, his subjective experience during the act of masturbation, and his depressing inability to get himself off, the scene in question (along with the film in which it appears) provides a paradigm of sorts for future Hollywood jerk-off efforts.

We first catch site of a beaming Brad in a framed photograph hanging on the wall of the "All-American Burger" joint where he works as shift manager, the caption underneath the photo reading "Employee of the Month." Behind the counter, an annoyingly self-assured Brad informs the losers under his supervision that "Daddy's home, boys," then orders a few stoner dudes who are sitting topless at one of the tables to put their shirts back on; pointing to a nearby sign with the house credo written on it, he instructs them to "Learn it, know it, live it." When we next see him, he is bopping to a hackneyed 1980s rock tune ("Raised on the radio / Just an all-American boy / I got my favorite toy . . .") while fetishistically (and somewhat anachronistically) wiping down the "beautiful" blue Ford sedan for which he just finished making payments. This time he orders around his freshman sister Stacy (Jennifer Jason Leigh) without a second thought. And in a final introductory scene, we locate Brad standing around chatting with some buddies on the gym floor during orientation day. "I love Lisa and all," he tells them; "I mean, she's great in bed. But I'm a single, successful guy. This is my last year in school—could be the best year of my life. I just need my freedom, y'know?"

The first indication that Brad is not nearly as on top of his game as he would have himself (and everyone else) believe comes when we see him washing from a mirror at work graffiti that reads "Big Hairy Pussy." Although he doesn't contemplate for a second the applicability of these effeminizing words to his own status and personality, they provide an ironic, undercutting backdrop to his bloated practice speech in the mirror for when he breaks up with Lisa: "I think I need my freedom . . . Oh, don't do that . . . Please . . ." From this point, things quickly begin to fall apart. First, a middle-aged male customer berates Brad about a bad breakfast and talks to him as though he is a child: "Put your little hand in the register and give me my $2.75 . . . *Braad.*" When the store manager Dennis (Tom Nolan), Brad's immediate supervisor and institutional father figure—comes out from the back room to mediate, he immediately takes the customer's side and fires his employee/"son" on the spot. Put in his place and made shockingly aware of his vulnerability, Brad decides against trying to end things with Lisa. To his great surprise and chagrin, however, she turns the tables and tells him during a school basketball game, "I just want to be friends."

The humiliation continues as Brad takes a new job at a pirate-themed fast food restaurant, where he is forced to wear a cheesy costume and deliver crappy food in his prized blue Ford while wearing it. Fed up with the way events have been conspiring against him, he abruptly quits the pirate job and heads home to find Stacy, her nubile girlfriend Linda (Phoebe Cates), and a couple of freshman boys hanging around the pool. Still playing the part of an adult working man, acting as if his ridiculous buccaneer uniform were a three-piece suit, Brad tells his sister and her friends to "keep it down. I have some work to do inside." The work in question is Brad's attempt to get himself off in the bathroom. Opening the window slightly, he focuses on Linda, whom we see via a point of view shot standing on the diving board. We then cut to a sopping wet Linda coming out of the water like a James Bond sex siren in slo-mo, followed by the start of a prototypical masturbation fantasy sequence. As the nondiegetic guitar rock swells on the soundtrack, she walks slowly toward the camera, removing her bikini top to expose her breasts while telling Brad, "You know how cute I always thought you were." For a moment we can't be certain that what we are watching isn't really happening (our full enjoyment of Brad's fantasy thereby being ensured), but our perspective quickly changes as we cut to Brad feverishly masturbating while sitting on the toilet bowl. We then cut back to a swirling shot of the half-naked Linda approaching a fully dressed Brad—now wearing an Armani—wrapping her arms around him, and kissing him fully on the lips.

Nearing his climax, Brad is suddenly interrupted by the real Linda, who, unbeknownst to him (since at this point he is only seeing the Linda in his head), has left the pool and entered the house in search of a Q-tip. Opening the door to an over-the-shoulder view of Brad doing his business on the toilet, Linda gasps, the look of shock and disgust on her face contrasted for a split second with the look of pleasurable intensity on his own. Linda quickly scuttles out of the bathroom, and since he has no chance of hiding his crime, Brad screams one of the film's most familiar lines, an Alexander Portnoyish "Doesn't anybody fucking knock anymore?!"

After failing in his attempt to pass himself off as a man amongst boys in his real life at work and at school, Brad is depicted as "regressing" to a more childish stage of development, one in which he can achieve satisfaction only through fantasy and self-stimulation. His dreams of dominating others through a paternalistic laying down of the law having been shot to shreds by the father figures in his life (notably his bosses at the two fast food restaurants), he makes himself lord and master at least in his own mind. The fact that he is unsuccessful in his efforts even here—and because of the very same young woman who serves as desirable and desiring partner in his masturbatory fantasy[1]—only reinforces the extent to which Brad must mature as a person before he can qualify as a true grown-up. Heckerling, in full command of Cameron Crowe's screenplay, actually makes Brad's moment of *jerkus interruptus* a turning point in the movie: seemingly a light-hearted comedy early on, *Fast Times* progressively takes on elements of a teen melodrama, with Brad eventually making good by coming to his sister's aid (and promising not to tell Mom and Dad) when she goes to have an abortion near the end.

DADDY DOESN'T KNOW SHIT: *SPANKING THE MONKEY*

David Russell's film contains a similar transition from comedy to drama, though the audience is never quite sure until the final scenes whether laughing at the masturbation troubles and incest episodes engaged in by home-from-school med student Raymond Aibelli (Jeremy Davies) is truly inappropriate. A gifted MIT undergrad with a chance at a lucrative summer internship, Ray is bullied by his traveling salesman father into staying at home during break and caring for his temporarily (and conveniently) laid-up mother. Mrs. Aibelli (Alberta Watson)—a younger, hotter Mrs. Robinson from *The Graduate* (1969)—is suffering from more than just a broken leg; she seems clinically depressed and extremely miserable in her marriage to a philandering husband for whom she gave up her own dreams of being a doctor years ago. Ray hates the idea of putting his future (with all the success and recognition that implies) on hold to go back home and serve as errand-boy, nurse, and housemaid for his mom. The only good thing about his return is the interest shown in him by a local high school cutie, Toni (Carla Gallo), who considers loner Ray a sort of stud because he attends such a prestigious university. But even this potentially pleasant relationship turns sour as Ray's attempts at scoring with Toni like a true college man result in mixed messages and the extreme awkwardness of an inexperienced schoolboy fumbling around trying to get past second base.

Increasingly annoyed by his mother's lame requests and all-around shitty attitude, like Brad in *Fast Times* Ray finally seeks relief in his bathroom. In the scene in question, we watch Ray from behind as he walks into the room, shuts the door, pulls down his pants, sits down on the toilet, and begins jerking off. All of this is done methodically and without even the slightest hint of eagerness or spontaneity; the boy just needs to cum, and quickly, before he hurts somebody (or himself, as it turns out). Ray's eyes are shut tight as he concentrates on his presumably erect penis like a good student working on a difficult lab experiment at school. We then cut to a shot of his father's beloved German shepherd sniffing around the bathroom door, excited by the strange, rhythmic noises coming from inside. Although they do not produce humiliation of the kind Brad experienced, the dog's unbridled curiosity and cries to be allowed entrance constitute a significant interruption for Ray nevertheless, and after shouting, "Go away!" to no avail, he finally gives up on his pipe dream of getting off on his own. Shortly thereafter, a drunk and horny Ray gives in to his oedipal urges and has sex with his mom, a sin far greater than masturbation in the eyes of the Church (not to mention the State) and one that eventually leads to the boy's meltdown during the latter third of the picture.

As we saw earlier, in *Fast Times at Ridgemont High*, Brad's surrender to the temptations of masturbation is used in the film to signify his giving up on the pretence of being a "man"—a socially constructed identity that allows him to give orders and make difficult decisions, both personally and professionally—in exchange for being what he still actually is: a teenage boy who is subject to the whims of more powerful males, and who can find ecstasy only through fantasy. The fact that Brad can't even achieve this latter aim simply supports the notion that he is not yet in control of his environment, much less his hormones. By way of both comparison and contrast, in *Spanking the Monkey*, Ray, too, is depicted as a boy who confuses physical manhood with emotional and psychological maturity. The extent of his confusion/delusion is shown when he returns home from med school, as he submits to prioritizing first his father's and then his mother's unfair orders over his own, quite reasonable desires. As opposed to the situation with Brad, however, the manner in which events in *Spanking the Monkey* unfold leads one to speculate that for Ray, an inability to successfully get himself off does not reinforce his immaturity so much as it encourages an even more desperate, more destructive attempt at playing the part of man about town—as well as man of the house.

Ray's mounting frustration at not having the space or the freedom to jerk off in peace plays an important role in weakening his indoctrinated defenses against coming on to his mother. Getting back at his priggish dad by taking the latter's role in the bedroom, Ray gives up his role as narcissistic teen while giving his self-centered mother the husband she has been longing for for so long. But the new arrangement does not (and cannot) last. Mrs. Aibelli treats the sex with her son like a pleasant enough one-night stand—an event not to be repeated and, more importantly, never to be mentioned. When Ray, unable to play "normal," fails to convince his father that what happened really happened, he starts to snap and eventually tries (and fails) to hang himself in the same bathroom in which he formerly tried (and failed) to masturbate. In the case of his attempted suicide, Ray's mother plays the part of Dad's dog in the earlier scene, banging on the door and eventually spoiling Ray's chances of success. Echoing Brad after Linda's unanticipated bathroom entrance in *Fast Times*, a flustered and red-faced Ray screams out, "Can't I do anything around here?" As in Heckerling's film, the ending of *Spanking the Monkey* shows Ray finally getting a clue as to what it really takes to be a man, as he defies his dad's wishes and heads off with neither a goodbye to mom nor a clue as to where he'll eventually end up. It's not clear if and when he will get the

urge to masturbate again, but at least we know he won't be interrupted trying to do it in *this* unhealthy home.

PILING ON THE PUNISHMENT: *AMERICAN PIE* AND *NOT ANOTHER TEEN MOVIE*

Unlike Brad, *American Pie*'s Jim Levinstein has no pretensions
regarding his supposedly privileged status as a high school senior.
He may be single, but he is anything but successful when it comes
to the ladies; in fact, his entire raison d'être during the course of the
movie (like that of his three best male friends) is to have sex for the
very first time before prom night comes to an end. Thus, the decision to beat off does not hold anything near the same significance
for Jim as it does for Brad in *Fast Times:* since he never claims to be
a macho man, acting like a horny boy represents less a coming
down to reality than a living up to stereotype. Moreover, as opposed
to Ray in *Spanking the Monkey,* for whom just one uninterrupted
masturbation session might well have stifled the ultra-taboo urge
to commit incest, Jim's failure to ejaculate under his own power
only seems to strengthen his resolve to gain sexual satisfaction
through proper/normal channels—namely, a hot female foreign
exchange student. Once that attempt fails due to not one but two
premature ejaculations (broadcast live over the Internet, no less), he
succeeds with a super ditzy but surprisingly willing Band Camp
girl. (Perhaps this is why *American Pie* qualifies as an unabashed
teen comedy à la *Porky's* [1981], while *Spanking the Monkey* offers
only black humor at its brightest; to its great credit, *Fast Times*
manages to cross effortlessly back and forth between both worlds.)

It is precisely because jerking off is *already* par for the course
for poor Jim that *American Pie* opens with a frustrated masturbation scene (a second, even more over-the-top, "into-the-pie" scene
occurs midway through the picture). With diegetic porn music
coming from somewhere offscreen left, the camera tracks slowly
across a bedroom floor, locating various articles of clothing—
including undergarments—scattered on the ground. First we hear a
female voice moaning, then a muffled male response, and were this
not the sort of movie we know it is we would have every reason to
believe we were about to see some hot sex taking place. As the
camera finally comes to rest on an isolated Jim sitting on the edge
of his bed watching scrambled pay-TV pornography and playing
with himself, he does his best Ron Jeremy impression and groans

out loud, "I am the best, baby. I am *soooo* big." This start to the scene is reminiscent of the one in *Fast Times* discussed above, in that the audience is momentarily misled into thinking that what they are watching is the "real" thing rather than mere fantasy. In *Fast Times* we are intended to be fooled by Brad's subjective vision of Linda; however, in *American Pie* the mistaken impression results from an objective trick played on us for fun by the director.

Suddenly, Mom walks into the room, talking some nonsense and only getting a clue as to what is going on when Jim fails in his frenzied effort to quickly change the channel with the TV remote. Things go from awful to unbearable when Jim's dad decides to pay a visit as well. Without intending to humiliate his beloved son any more than he already is, Mr. Levinstein accomplishes precisely that by lifting the pillow Jim is holding over his crotch, revealing a hard-on with a sock on it underneath. Clearly what we have here is one more example of a teenage boy's inability to beat off in tranquility, signifying both the extent of his sexual frustration and, at a less literal but more significant level, his still-subjugated status at home; no longer a child, but not yet a man, Jim must pursue his pleasure where he can get it, that is, until he can really get it. But *American Pie* is a more committed comedy than *Fast Times at Ridgemont High*. In *Fast Times,* Brad got busted near the end of the film, and thus had very little diegetic recuperation time to find his manhood again. In *Pie,* Jim at least gets to be busted at the beginning of the picture, thus enabling him to cut a straight (if rocky) path to his ultimate goal of getting laid. That there is a second interrupted masturbation scene in this film, the eponymous pie-humping scene, hardly presents an objection, since the latter is nothing but a caricature of exactly the kind of masturbation scene we saw earlier and with more effect.

It is worth comparing *American Pie*'s opening sequence with its mirror image spoof in *Not Another Teen Movie*. Taking the place of Jim in the latter production is Janey Briggs (Chyler Leigh), a beautiful brunette who is dressed down (in this parody of various teen film classics) to look unconvincingly like an ugly ducking high school loser. *NATM*'s opening is a virtual shot-for-shot rewrite of its source material, down to the tracking shot over strewn-about underwear on the floor. Instead of porn music, however, we hear something sappy and romantic; and instead of the predictable moans and groans, we hear a snippet of dialogue: "I hope it doesn't cause any permanent damage." Turns out that Janey isn't touching herself to the *Playboy* channel; rather, she is weeping while watch-

Jim (Jason Biggs) gets some unwanted advice from Dad (Eugene Levy) on how to best get off in Chris and Paul Weitz's *American Pie* (1999).

ing one of Freddie Prinze Jr.'s substandard soaps (the fact that this movie of the week is scrambled like Jim's porno counts as one of the film's funniest moments). Now Janey changes modes, reaching over and grabbing a sock that we soon find out serves to cover up a hi-tech dildo. The porn music finally kicks in—better late than never—and as Janey puts the vibrating toy to work under the covers, she gets a grotesque look on her face and begins convulsing with pleasure. Instead of playing the part of a nubile Nadia turning on her male admirers while also turning herself on, Janey mocks Jim's ungainly mannerisms during masturbation, as well as those of Brad, Ray, and most likely the entire audience of adolescent males watching her do her thing.[2]

Following the script to its inevitable conclusion, Janey quickly gets caught by her own doofy dad . . . then her little brother . . . her grandparents . . . the local priest . . . and the collection of little kids who have all chosen to congregate in her room. Such inane excess is the only resort of a film that seeks to parody that which *already* is a parody. In the case of *American Pie,* though, the object of parody is not so much previous fictional entries in the genre of teenage boys whose attempts at masturbation are met with nothing but frustration and humiliation—from *Portnoy's Complaint* through *Fast Times* and *Spanking the Monkey*—as all those real-life cases of *jerkus interruptus* experienced by the young men who flock to see their memories of being busted brought vividly to life on the big screen.

Sublimating Masturbating

I have been seeking to show that there is more to the ideological pressures informing the representation of frustrated masturbating boys in recent Hollywood film than mere prudishness on the part of the MPAA—or at least that this prudishness itself calls for further (and deeper) explanation in terms of a larger-scale sociocultural dilemma here dubbed the "paradox of masturbation." Peter Lehman has written eloquently of the late-twentieth-century artistic and journalistic obsession with breaking down the taboo surrounding depictions of the penis in cinema and other forms of popular culture. With reference to such 1990s American films as *The Crying Game* (1992), *Cobb* (1994), *Angels and Insects* (1995), and *Boogie Nights* (1997), Lehman identifies a "third category" of male genitalia imagery—the so-called melodramatic penis—which he claims succeeds in problematizing the traditional, oversimplistic dichotomy of the penis visualized as a large, awesome (typically erect) phallic spectacle versus the penis understood as a pathetic, collapsed (typically flaccid) source of humor. In his own words, "the melodrama surrounding the representation of the penis" in the films in question "paradoxically cries out to reaffirm the spectacular importance of the penis even as the very assault on the taboo seeks to dislodge that importance" (2001, 39).

Without wishing to dispute the validity of Lehman's latest addition to his taxonomy of penis portrayals, I would nevertheless argue for the recent coming-into-being of yet another (fourth) category that serves a similar complicating function: call it the "up-and-down penis." For in each of the male teen masturbation movies we have been examining here, the focus is on a penis that goes from flaccid to erect and back to flaccid again in almost no time flat—a penis that is constructed as both awesome (potentially pornographic) and comical (making its handler the butt end of jokes). Here, as in the melodramatic penis pictures discussed by Lehman, the supposedly "spectacular importance" of the male member is paradoxically affirmed and denied at one and the same time. And this paradoxical affirmation and denial is almost exclusively attached to the penises of characters who are not merely males, but boys.

There has been one theme underlying this brief investigation into onscreen onanism. Even though—or perhaps precisely because—masturbation remains widely regarded in American culture as a shameful activity, for religious (reproductive) and social (stereotypical) reasons alike, it is a topic that is only talked about awkwardly—when it is talked about at all. Even if everyone has at least *tried* it at one time or another, admitting it in public and describing it in detail still proves a very sticky subject indeed. What makes the films examined here of such interest is the fact that they each operate so as to reinforce the negative feelings surrounding sexual self-satisfaction while nevertheless responding to our collective need (especially on the part of those adolescent males just getting used to the act) to bring jerking off out of the closet.

Even where masturbation (interrupted or otherwise) is not given explicit expression in popular movies about teenage boys, it can still receive sublimated treatment. A recent and dramatic example of the latter occurs in *Spider-Man*, where director Sam Raimi evidently enjoyed bringing out the beat-off subplot inherent in the original Stan Lee/Steve Ditko comic. On the surface level of the text we have here the story of a high school loser who suddenly gains super powers, vanquishes the equally super bad guy—not to mention the school bully—and finally gets the girl of his dreams, only to let her walk away for reasons that can be made clear only in a sequel. But if you strip away the science fiction and cartoon characters, you find the story of a weak and timid boy who, upon going through puberty (admittedly one with a seriously rapid onset), suddenly finds himself a man. Thus Peter Parker's (Tobey Maguire) delightful mirror scene a quarter of the way through the picture.

Having been bitten by a radioactive spider on a school trip, Peter awakens from a rough night's sleep to a slew of self-discoveries. First he puts his nerdy eyeglasses on, only to find the world much blurrier than when he takes them off again. He then catches sight of himself in a conveniently placed full-length mirror in his bedroom. His chest and arms are seriously buff, quite a contrast to the ninety-eight pound weakling we saw in an earlier scene. His annoyingly ubiquitous Aunt May (Rosemary Harris) then asks Peter from the hallway if he's all right: "Any change from last night?" As he pulls open his briefs and takes a look at what we can only assume is now a super-sized schlong, an impish grin creeps across his face. "Yeah . . . Big change," Peter replies, and at this point Aunt May is the only one of us who doesn't know what he means.

A little later, after discovering his apparently unique ability to shoot a sticky, white, weblike substance from his wrists—more like the messy after-effects of a successful jerk-off session than any superglue any fantasist ever dreamed up—Peter starts spraying the stuff around his room. Since Peter is making way too much noise *not* to be busted, Aunt May knocks on his door and pokes her head in. "What's going on in there," she asks too innocently. "I'm exercising," is the lame but oh-so-familiar reply. "I'm not dressed, Aunt May." She replies a little less innocently this time: "You're acting so strangely, Peter." "Oh . . . Thanks," he tells her, and promptly shuts the door in her face. Perhaps it's only because he has super powers, but unlike our other interrupted masturbating boys Peter at least will get the chance to go back to what he started.

But in the extremely allusive *Spider-Man*, Peter's peter, and Peter's delight, are in the end all code, and that's why audiences can stand to let him finish. He isn't really finishing, and he isn't really jerking off. In Hollywood films where boys' masturbation is shown point-blank, by contrast, they just can't get no satisfaction. And neither, because the MPAA is so uptight (like the culture from which it has grown), can we. For a wholly unrepressed alternative, one need only consider Alfonso Cuarón's recent Mexican sensation *Y tu mamá también (And Your Mother Too)* (2001), a coming-of-age road movie in which, as Peter Bradshaw observes, "masturbation is treated with an unapologetic frankness rarely found in our genteel anglophone cinema" (2002). Not only does *Y tu mamá* grant the two teenage boys who whack off in tandem some momentary relief from their sexual frustration. By sharing the names of their fantasy females with one another (including Salma Hayek, a hot cousin, and a girlfriend's mom), the pair manage to achieve an ostensibly heterosexual yet homoerotic form of simultaneous orgasm, finally emptying their loads from the twin diving boards on which they lay into the shimmering pool below. Beat that, Spidey!

NOTES

1. It is worth noting that Linda herself suffers from delusions of emotional maturity. Much of her dialogue concerns an older, mostly out-of-the-picture boyfriend to whom she gives far more credit for being a "real man" than it turns out he deserves.
2. Whereas Nadia in *American Pie* is given the same sort of eroticized treatment found in porn made primarily for hetero men viewers, *Not Another Teen Movie*'s equally attractive Janey—insofar as she serves as a comic (because female) counterpart for *American Pie*'s Jim—is at great pains to look as ridiculous and distinctly *un*erotic while pleasuring herself as he does.

WORKS CITED

Bradshaw, Peter. 2002. *"Y tu mamá también"* (review), *The Guardian*, London, April 12. Online at http://film.guardian.co.uk/News_Story/-Critic_Review/Guardian_film_of_the_week/0,4267,682544,00.html.

Dolphin, Lambert. 1991. "Masturbation and the Bible." Online at http://www.ldolphin.org/Mast.shtml.

Freud, Sigmund. 1953–1974. "On Narcissism: An Introduction (1914)." In *The Standard Edition of the Complete Psychological Works of Sigmund Freud*, ed. James Strachey, 73–102. London: Hogarth.

Down, J., and H. Langden. 1867. "Influence of Sewing Machine on Female Health." *New Orleans Journal of Medical Surgery* 20, 359–60.

Hunt, Alan. 1998. "The Great Masturbation Panic and the Discourses of Moral Regulation in Nineteenth- and Early Twentieth-Century Britain," *Journal of the History of Sexuality* 8, no. 4, 575–615.

Lehman, Peter. 2001. "Crying over the Melodramatic Penis: Melodrama and Male Nudity in Films of the 90s." In *Masculinity: Bodies, Movies, Culture*, 25–41. New York: Routledge.

Contributors

CHRISTOPHER AMES is a Ph.D. student in ethnology at the University of Michigan, specializing in urban anthropology, film, East Asian youth culture, and Japanese tourism. He is the author of *Okinawa: An Introduction.* His dissertation is on urban community revitalization amid the postcolonial contradictions of U.S. military base reduction in a hybrid residential-entertainment community comprised of Okinawan residents, U.S. military sojourners, and Japanese tourists in Okinawa, Japan.

DIANNE BROOKS has been teaching at the University of Massachusetts, Amherst, for twelve years. She was trained as a lawyer at Harvard, practiced family law, and since her time as an academic has been exploring through teaching and writing the ways in which law in the largest sense constructs and is constructed by culture with particular interest in film and the arts.

STEVEN ALAN CARR is an Associate Professor of Communication at Indiana University–Purdue University Fort Wayne and a 2002–3 Center for Advanced Holocaust Studies Postdoctoral Fellow at the United States Holocaust Memorial Museum in Washington, D.C. He is the author of *Hollywood and Anti-Semitism: A Cultural History up to World War II,* and is currently exploring the response of the American film industry to the growing public awareness of the Holocaust.

PETER CLANDFIELD teaches English and Film at Royal Military College of Canada in Kingston, Ontario. His research interests and publications fall into three main areas: questions of place and space in contemporary novels and films (particularly British and Canadian); questions of race and cultural hybridity in contemporary literature, film, and TV; and theories and practices of censorship. With Christian Lloyd, he has recently published an article on class and urban redevelopment in Mike Hodges's film *Get Carter* and Jeff Torrington's novel *Swing Hammer Swing.*

COREY K. CREEKMUR is an Associate Professor in the Departments of English, and Cinema and Comparative Literature at the University of Iowa, where he also directs the Institute for Cinema and Culture. He is the author of forthcoming studies of the film western and the musical, and his essays on outlaw couple films, Oscar Micheaux, the western biopic, and the contemporary film soundtrack have appeared in recent collections. His current work focuses on the function of songs and stars in Hindi cinema.

FRANCES GATEWARD is an Assistant Professor in the Unit for Cinema Studies at the University of Illinois, Urbana-Champaign. Her work has been published in numerous journals and anthologies including *Multiple Modernities: Cinema and Popular Media in Transcultural East Asia* and *Still Lifting Still Climbing: Contemporary African American Women's Activism.* She is the editor of *Zhang Yimou: Interviews* and coeditor of *Sugar, Spice, and Everything Nice: Cinemas of Girlhood.*

NICOLE MARIE KEATING is Assistant Professor of Communication at the University of the Arts in Philadelphia. She has also worked for a number of years in the documentary production industry. After studying philosophy at McGill University, she did her graduate work in communication at the University of Pennsylvania (specializing in documentary theory and historiography). She has published on a variety of media studies topics and is particularly interested in issues concerning gender and media. She became the mother of a baby boy in May 2001 and a baby girl in June 2003.

CHRISTIAN LLOYD teaches English and Interdisciplinary Studies at the Queen's International Study Centre, Herstmonceux, England. His current research interests include the prehistory of Mod culture in England, and questions of onomastics in contemporary Irish literature. With Peter Clandfield, he has recently published an article on class and urban redevelopment in Mike Hodges's film *Get Carter* and Jeff Torrington's novel *Swing Hammer Swing.*

SUDHIR MAHADEVAN is a doctoral candidate in Cinema Studies at New York University. His interests include histories of technology, including visual technologies, and religion and film.

GINA MARCHETTI is an Associate Professor in the Department of Cinema and Photography at Ithaca College. In 1995, her book, *Romance and the "Yellow Peril": Race, Sex and Discursive Strategies in Hollywood Fiction* won the award for best book in the area of cultural studies from the Association of Asian American Studies. She has essays in several anthologies, including *At Full Speed: Hong Kong Cinema in a Borderless World, Ladies and Gentlemen, Boys and Girls,* and *Unspeakable Images: Ethnicity and the American Cinema.* Her book, *From Tian'anmen to Times Square: China on Global Screens,* is forthcoming.

CHANI MARCHISELLI is currently a Ph.D. student in the Department of Communications at the University of Minnesota. She teaches courses on film and video and is currently writing her dissertation on technology and feminine writing.

JERRY MOSHER teaches film studies at California State University-Long Beach and is a doctoral candidate in the Department of Film, Television and Digital Media at UCLA. His dissertation examines how the American film industry has represented the fat body. He has published essays on fat and culture in the anthologies *Bodies Out of Bounds: Fatness and Transgression* and *The End of Cinema as We Know It: American Film in the Nineties.*

MARY B. O'SHEA is a doctoral candidate at Indiana University, where she works as an academic advisor. Her dissertation examines images of youth identity and the form and functions of the contemporary American coming-of-age film.

MURRAY POMERANCE is Chair of the Department of Sociology at Ryerson University and the author of *An Eye for Hitchcock.* He is coeditor, with Frances Gateward, of *Sugar, Spice, and Everything Nice: Cinemas of Girlhood,* and has also edited numerous volumes including *Enfant Terrible! Jerry Lewis in American Film,* and *BAD: Infamy, Darkness, Evil, and Slime on Screen.* His *Johnny Depp*

Starts Here is forthcoming. With Lester D. Friedman he is coeditor of the *Screen Decades: American Cinema/American Culture* series from Rutgers University Press and he is editor of the Horizons of Cinema series from State University of New York Press.

CORDULA QUINT is currently Assistant Professor at Mount Allison University, Sackville, New Brunswick, Canada. Her doctoral dissertation focuses on the stage works of American director Robert Wilson and reads his innovative aesthetics in the context of postmodern and poststructural theory. Her articles have appeared in *Closely Watched Brains, Space and the Postmodern Stage,* and *Müller in America.*

CHARLENE REGESTER is Adjunct Assistant Professor in the Department of African and Afro-American Studies at the University of North Carolina, Chapel Hill. She has published essays on early black film stars and filmmakers in *Film Literature Quarterly, Popular Culture Review, Western Journal of Black Studies, Studies in American Culture, Film History, and Journal of Film and Video* and coedits the *Oscar Micheaux Society Newsletter.* She is a member of the editorial board of *Journal of Film and Video.*

STEVEN JAY SCHNEIDER is a Ph.D. candidate in philosophy at Harvard University and in Cinema Studies at New York University's Tisch School of the Arts. He is co-editor of *Underground U.S.A.: Filmmaking Beyond the Hollywood Canon, Horror International, Traditions in World Cinema,* and *Dark Thoughts: Philosophic Reflections on Cinematic Horror;* editor of *Horror Film and Psychoanalysis: Freud's Worst Nightmares, New Hollywood Violence, Fear Without Frontiers: Horror Cinema Across the Globe,* and *1001 Movies You Must See Before You Die;* and author of *Designing Fear: An Aesthetics of Cinematic Horror.*

TIMOTHY SHARY is the author of *Generation Multiplex: The Image of Youth in Contemporary American Cinema.* He has written extensively on the representation of teenagers for various publications such as *The Journal of Popular Film and Television, Post Script, Film Quarterly,* and *The Journal of Film and Video* and has appeared in *Pictures of a Generation on Hold: Selected Papers* and *Sugar, Spice, and Everything Nice: Cinemas of Girlhood.* He is a Professor of Screen Studies at Clark University.

TARSHIA L. STANLEY is an Assistant Professor in the English Department at Spelman College where she is developing courses in Film Studies. Her research interests include African American, African, and Caribbean Cinema. Her current project is developing a comprehensive text on film actress Whoopi Goldberg and her place in African American Film Studies.

MATTHEW TINKCOM is the author of *Working like A Homosexual: Camp, Capital, Cinema* and coeditor of *Keyframes: Popular Cinema and Cultural Studies.* He is an Associate Professor in the Department of English and the Graduate Program in Communication, Culture and Technology at Georgetown University.

JOHN TROYER is currently a Ph.D. student in the Department of Cultural Studies and Comparative Literature at the University of Minnesota. He teaches a course on the Reading and Writing of History and is pursuing the invention of the modern corpse via late-nineteenth- and early-twentieth-century funeral embalming as a dissertation project.

PATRICK E. WHITE is Vice President and Dean of Faculty at Saint Mary's College and was founding Director of the Center for Academic Innovation there. He is a Professor of English teaching courses in women in film, linguistics, and twentieth-century literature. White has written two prize-winning plays and has published widely on the visual arts, nostalgia in film, and the representation of leadership in the movies.

Index

Page numbers in italics refer to photographs